OUTREACH
SPANISH

William C. Harvey, M.S.

BARRON'S

A note from the author

It seems that most Spanish guidebooks on the market today either target the needs of folks who travel to Spanish-speaking countries or those in the workforce who need to speak Spanish while on the job.

However, many people want to learn Spanish simply because they would like to communicate with a Latino friend, neighbor, or foreigner *in need.*

This guidebook is designed for anyone who intends to befriend, assist, or minister to those who speak only Spanish. We hope that, by removing the language and cultural barriers between our English- and Spanish-speaking communities, many people will be able to reach out and connect for the very first time.

All inquiries should be addressed to:
Barron's Educational Series, Inc.
250 Wireless Boulevard
Hauppauge, NY 11788
http://www.barronseduc.com

International Standard Book No. 0-7641-1324-0

Library of Congress Catalog Card No. 00-131725

Printed in the United States of America

9   8   7   6   5   4

Contents

How to use this guidebook

Outreach Spanish provides readers with the Spanish vocabulary and phrases needed to communicate with Spanish-speakers of all ages. Skills are taught gradually and are systematically reinforced through practice and review.

One basic feature of this guidebook is its name: guidebook. It is neither a grammar-intensive textbook nor a general phrasebook plus dictionary. Instead, it is a *guide* for people busy at helping people who understand no other language but Spanish.

Grammar and exercises are kept to a minimum. Your immediate task will be to go through each page of this guide with a bright yellow marker, and highlight the areas that are vital to you. Your secondary job will be to go with a red pen through all the highlighted areas and underline in red the most important vocabulary and sentences. Once this is done, the rest will be up to you: if you wish to learn fluent Spanish, then buy a small Spanish grammar book and use it along with this guide as you memorize and practice. If you don't have the time and patience, then make the most of your highlighted and underlined text, become familiar with the most basic expressions, and let this guide be a first-aid Spanish communication tool.

Aside from the convenient specialized glossaries in the back, you may try focusing on the icons provided below. They can be helpful when you are working on a specific skill or topic of interest.

 ¡MÁS AYUDA! *(mahs ah-'yoo-dah)* (**More Help!**)
Information, tips, and suggestions on how to learn Spanish

 ¡LA CULTURA! *(lah kool-'too-rah)* (**Culture!**)
Insights into Hispanic culture

 ¡LAS ÓRDENES! *(lahs 'ohr-deh-nehs)* (**Commands!**)
Spanish command words

 ¡ACCIÓN! *(ahk-see-'ohn)* (**Action!**)
Shortcuts to the use of verb tenses in Spanish

 ¡NECESITA PRACTICAR! *(neh-seh-'see-tah prahk-tee-'kahr)*
(**You Need to Practice!**) Review practice exercises

Pronunciation Every Spanish word in this book is followed by its pronunciation. The accent (') indicates the stress.

Important news It's normal to be a little fearful about learning any language, so here's some exciting news:

• Grammar and pronunciation don't have to be perfect in order to be understood.
• Thousands of words are similar in both Spanish and English, which makes it easier for you to remember new vocabulary.
• Messages in Spanish can be communicated with only a few simple expressions.

Read through these facts about learning Spanish one more time. Believe me, by following the proven suggestions mentioned in this guidebook, you can pick up *mucho español* in no time at all!

Chapter One

(kah-'pee-too-loh 'oo-noh)

Basic Skills
Las Habilidades Básicas

(lahs ah-bee-lee-'dah-dehs 'bah-see-kahs)

The sounds of Spanish
Los sonidos del lenguaje español

(lohs soh-'nee-dohs dehl lehn-'gwah-heh ehs-pahn-'yohl)

As a beginner in the language, your first step is to learn what Spanish sounds like. Fortunately, you don't have to pronounce everything correctly in order to be understood. Not only are people generally forgiving, but in reality there aren't that many differences between the two sound systems. In fact, you'll need to remember **only five sounds** in order to speak well enough to be understood. These are the vowels, and unlike their English equivalents, each one is pronounced the way it is written. Go ahead—read each letter aloud, and follow the corresponding pronunciation guide:

> **a** *(ah)* as in yacht
> **e** *(eh)* as in met
> **i** *(ee)* as in keep
> **o** *(oh)* as in open
> **u** *(oo)* as in tool

• Very important: every Spanish word that you will read in this book is accompanied by its approximate pronunciation, e.g., **amigo** *(ah-'mee-goh)*. Note also the (') symbol, which indicates stress.

Now, let's learn how to pronounce all the other letters. And, remember—each letter has its own unique sound:

SPANISH LETTER	ENGLISH SOUND
c (before an e or i)	s as in sit (**cigarro** *[see-'gah-rroh]*)
g (before an e or i)	h as in hop (**general** *[heh-neh-'rahl]*)
h	silent, like **k** in **knives** (**hombre** *['ohm-breh]*)
j	h as in **hat** (**julio** *['hoo-lee-oh]*)
ll	y as in **yes** (**pollo** *['poh-yoh]*)
ñ	ny as in **canyon** (**señor** *[sehn-'yohr]*)
qu	k as in **kit** (**tequila** *[teh-'kee-lah]*)
rr	the rolled **r** sound (**burro** *['boo-rroh]*)
z	s as in **son** (**zapato** *[sah 'pah-toh]*)

Although some dialects may vary slightly, the rest of the letters in Spanish are similar to their equivalents in English.

b	**bueno** *('bweh-noh)*	p	**pronto** *('prohn-toh)*
d	**dinero** *(dee-'neh-roh)*	r	**tres** *(trehs)*
f	**flan** *(flahn)*	s	**sí** *(see)*
l	**límite** *('lee-mee-teh)*	t	**taco** *('tah-koh)*
m	**mucho** *('moo-choh)*	x	**máximo** *('maks-ee-moh)*
n	**nada** *('nah-dah)*		

Now, read the following words aloud, and then guess at their meanings.

amigo *(ah-'mee-goh)*	**excelente** *(ehk-seh-'lehn-teh)*
burro *('boo-rroh)*	**Feliz Navidad** *(feh-'lees nah-vee-'dahd)*
Cinco de Mayo	**problema** *(proh-'bleh-mah)*
('seen-koh deh 'mah-yoh)	
escuela *(ehs-kweh-lah)*	**televisión** *(teh-leh-vee-see-'ohn)*
español *(ehs-pahn-'yohl)*	**tortilla** *(tohr-'tee-yah)*

¡*M á s   A y u d a !*

- Any part of a word with an accent mark (´) needs to be pronounced LOUDER and with more emphasis (i.e., María). If there's no accent mark, say the last part of the word louder and with more emphasis (i.e., Bea**triz**). For words ending in a vowel, or in **n** or **s**, the next to the last part of the word is stressed (i.e., Fer**nan**do).

- In some cases, the letter **u** doesn't make the *oo* sound (i.e., **guitarra** *[gee-'tah-rrah]* or **guerra** *['geh-rrah]*).

- It will be wise to find out how to pronounce all the letters in the Spanish alphabet. Write them down on a piece of paper. Whenever you need to spell something, it's always good to have a "cheat-sheet" like that around.

¡*N e c e s i t a   P r a c t i c a r !*

If you're having problems with the sounds of Spanish, try listening to the language for a few minutes each day. Spanish radio and TV stations, CD ROM, DVD, or audio and video cassettes are fun yet effective ways to become familiar with your new pronunciation patterns.

Key expressions
Las expresiones claves
(lahs ehks-preh-see-'oh-nehs 'klah-vehs)

The best way to get started in Spanish is to try out your new sounds in everyday conversations. Regardless of your situation, these basic expressions are a must for every Spanish speaker.

Excuse me!	**¡Con permiso!** *(kohn pehr-'mee-soh)*
Go ahead!	**¡Pase!** *('pah-seh)*
I'm sorry!	**¡Lo siento!** *(loh see-'ehn-toh)*
Thanks a lot!	**¡Muchas gracias!** *('moo-chahs 'grah-see-ahs)*

Please!	**¡Por favor!** *(pohr fah-'vohr)*
Yes!	**¡Sí!** *(see)*
You're welcome!	**¡De nada!** *(deh 'nah-dah)*
Hi!	**¡Hola!** *('oh-lah)*
Good morning!	**¡Buenos días!** *('bweh-nohs 'dee-ahs)*
Good afternoon!	**¡Buenas tardes!** *('bweh-nahs 'tahr-dehs)*
Good evening!/ Good night!	**¡Buenas noches!** *('bweh-nahs 'noh-chehs)*
Good-bye!	**¡Adiós!** *(ah-dee-'ohs)*
See you later!	**¡Hasta luego!** *('ahs-tah 'lweh-goh)*
How are you!	**¿Cómo está usted?** *('koh-moh ehs-'tah oos-'tehd)*
What's happening?	**¿Qué pasa?** *(koh 'pah-sah)*
How's it going?	**¿Qué tal?** *(keh tahl)*
Nice to meet you!	**¡Mucho gusto!** *('moo-choh 'goos-toh)*
Fine, thanks!	**¡Bien, gracias!** *(bee-'ehn 'grah-see-ahs)*
And you?	**¿Y usted?** *(ee oos-'tehd)*
Very good!	**¡Muy bien!** *('moo-ee bee-'ehn)*
Nothing much!	**¡Sin novedad!** *(seen noh-veh-'dahd)*
Same to you!	**¡Igualmente!** *(ee-gwahl-'mehn-teh)*

¡ M Á S   A Y U D A !

• Several words in English are spelled the same in Spanish, and they usually have the same meaning. But, watch out! They are NOT pronounced the same!

> **chocolate** *(choh-koh-'lah-teh)*
> **color** *(koh-'lohr)*
> **final** *(fee-'nahl)*
> **idea** *(ee-'deh-ah)*
> **natural** *(nah-too-'rahl)*
> **terror** *(teh-'rrohr)*

• The upside-down exclamation point (¡) and question mark (¿) are found at the beginning of sentences, and must be used when you write in Spanish.

• Scan these other "excuse me" phrases:

"Excuse me" (if you cough or sneeze): **¡Perdón!** *(pehr-'dohn)*
"Excuse me" (if you need someone's attention): **¡Disculpe!** *(dees-'kool-peh)*

• Look! Some words change meanings if you drop the accent mark:

yes	**sí** *(see)*	if	**si** *(see)*
how	**cómo** *('koh-moh)*	I eat	**como** *('koh-moh)*
give	**dé** *(deh)*	from	**de** *(deh)*

¡ L A   C U L T U R A !

Friendly greetings in Spanish are used all day long. Being courteous is the key to establishing trust with your new friends and their families. Throughout the Spanish-speaking world, a smile and a pleasant word can lead to respect and complete cooperation.

¡ N E C E S I T A   P R A C T I C A R !

Practice this dialogue with a friend:

Hola. *('oh-lah)*
¿Qué pasa? *(keh 'pah-sah)*
¿Cómo está?
   ('koh-moh ehs-'tah)
Muy bien. Hasta luego.
   ('moo-ee bee-'ehn 'ahs-tah 'lweh-goh)

Buenas tardes. *('bweh-nahs 'tahr-dehs)*
Sin novedad. *(seen noh-veh-'dahd)*
Bien, gracias. ¿Y usted?
   (bee-'ehn 'grah-see-ahs ee oos-'tehd)
Adiós. *(ah-dee-'ohs)*

More essential phrases
Más frases esenciales
(mahs 'frah-sehs eh-sehn-see-'ah-lehs)

Spanish is full of common expressions that are used regularly in normal conversation. A lot can be communicated simply by saying a few short phrases. Interject one of these whenever it is appropriate:

Don't worry.	**No se preocupe.** *(noh seh preh-oh-'koo-peh)*
Good idea.	**Buena idea.** *('bweh-nah ee-'deh-ah)*
I see.	**Ya veo.** *(yah 'veh-oh)*
I think so.	**Creo que sí.** *('kreh-oh keh see)*
Maybe.	**Quizás.** *(kee-'sahs)*
More or less.	**Más o menos.** *(mahs oh 'meh-nohs)*
Not yet.	**Todavía no.** *(toh-dah-'vee-ah noh)*
Ready?	**¿Listo?** *('lees-toh)*
Sure.	**Claro.** *('klah-roh)*
That depends.	**Depende.** *(deh-'pehn-deh)*

Put a little more emotion into these!

Bless you!	**¡Salud!** (sah-'lood)
Congratulations!	**¡Felicitaciones!** *(feh-lee-see-tah-see-'oh-nehs)*
Good luck!	**¡Buena suerte!** *('bweh-nah 'swehr-teh)*
Happy Birthday!	**¡Feliz cumpleaños!** *(feh-'lees koom-pleh-'ahn-yohs)*
Welcome!	**¡Bienvenidos!** *(bee-ehn-veh-'nee-dohs)*
Wow!	**¡Caramba!** *(kah-'rahm-bah)*
For heaven's sake!	**¡Dios mío!** *(dee-'ohs 'mee-oh)*

Bear in mind that most idiomatic expressions cannot be translated word for word. Therefore, try to memorize each phrase as one long string of individual sounds.

¡ *M Á S   A Y U D A* !

• The word **Qué** *(keh)* is often part of an emotional comment:

What a shame!	**¡Qué lástima!** *(keh 'lahs-tee-mah)*
That's great!	**¡Qué bueno!** *(keh 'bweh-noh)*
How funny!	**¡Qué chistoso!** *(keh chees-'toh-soh)*

• And don't forget these holidays:

Merry Christmas!	**¡Feliz Navidad!** *(feh-'lees nah-vee-'dahd)*
Happy New Year!	**¡Feliz Año Nuevo!** *(feh-'lees 'ahn-yoh 'nweh-voh)*
Happy Easter!	**¡Felices Pascuas!** *(feh-'lee-sehs 'pahs-kwahs)*

• There are several ways to say good-bye in Spanish, so continue to wave and shout:

Have a nice day!	**¡Que le vaya bien!** *(keh leh 'vah-yah bee-'ehn)*
We'll see you!	**¡Nos vemos!** *(nohs 'veh-mohs)*

¡ *N E C E S I T A   P R A C T I C A R* !

Connect each phrase with its appropriate response:

Mucho gusto.	**Nos vemos.**
¿Cómo está?	**Salud.**
Gracias.	**De nada.**
¡Ah-choo!	**Bien. ¿Y usted?**
Hasta luego.	**Igualmente.**

Do you speak Spanish?
¿Habla usted español?
('ah-blah oos-'tehd ehs-pahn-'yohl)

Once you finish with the greetings and common courtesies, you will face the inevitable problem of not being able to understand one another. To make things easier, try saying a few of these one-liners. They send the message that you are doing the best you can!

Again.	**Otra vez** *('oh-trah vehs)*
Do you understand?	**¿Entiende?** *(ehn-tee-'ehn-deh)*
How do you say it?	**¿Cómo se dice?** *('koh-moh seh 'dee-seh)*
How do you spell it?	**¿Cómo se deletrea?**
	('koh-moh seh deh-leh-'treh-ah)
I don't understand!	**¡No entiendo!** *(noh ehn-tee-'ehn-doh)*
I'm learning Spanish.	**Estoy aprendiendo el español.**
	(ehs-'toh-ee ah-prehn-dee-'ehn-doh ehl
	ehs-pahn-'yohl)
I speak a little Spanish.	**Hablo poquito español.**
	('ah-bloh poh-'kee-toh ehs-pahn-'yohl)
More slowly!	**¡Más despacio!** *(mahs dehs-'pah-see-oh)*
Thanks for your patience.	**Gracias por su paciencia.**
	('grah-see-ahs pohr soo pah-see-'ehn-
	see-ah)
What does it mean?	**¿Qué significa?** *(keh seeg-nee-'fee-kah)*
Word by word!	**¡Palabra por palabra!**
	(pah-'lah-brah pohr pah-'lah-brah)
Please repeat.	**Repita, por favor.**
	(reh-'pee-tah pohr fah-'vohr)

Necessary vocabulary
El vocabulario necesario
(ehl voh-kah-boo-'lah-ree-oh neh-seh-'sah-ree-oh)

It's impossible to carry on intelligent conversations in Spanish without the basic vocabulary words. To learn them quickly, let's list the terms by category, beginning with everyday things.

bed	**la cama** *(lah 'kah-mah)*
book	**el libro** *(ehl 'lee-broh)*
car	**el carro** *(ehl 'kah-rroh)*

chair	**la silla** *(lah 'see-yah)*
desk	**el escritorio** *(ehl ehs-kree-'toh-ree-oh)*
door	**la puerta** *(lah 'pwehr-tah)*
floor	**el piso** *(ehl 'pee-soh)*
food	**la comida** *(lah koh-'mee-dah)*
house	**la casa** *(lah 'kah-sah)*
light	**la luz** *(lah loos)*
office	**la oficina** *(lah oh-fee-'see-nah)*
paper	**el papel** *(ehl pah-'pehl)*
pen	**el lapicero** *(ehl lah-pee-'seh-roh)*
pencil	**el lápiz** *(ehl 'lah-pees)*
restroom	**el servicio** *(ehl sehr-'vee-see-oh)*
room	**el cuarto** *(ehl 'kwahr-toh)*
table	**la mesa** *(lah 'meh-sah)*
telephone	**el teléfono** *(ehl teh-'leh-foh-noh)*
trash	**la basura** *(lah bah-'soo-rah)*
water	**el agua** *(ehl 'ah-gwah)*
window	**la ventana** *(lah vehn-'tah-nah)*
work	**el trabajo** *(ehl trah-'bah-hoh)*

People

La gente *(lah 'hehn-teh)*

baby	**el bebé** *(ehl beh-'beh)*
boy	**el niño** *(ehl 'nee-nyoh)*
brother	**el hermano** *(ehl ehr-'mah-noh)*
daughter	**la hija** *(lah 'ee-hah)*
father	**el padre** *(ehl 'pah-dreh)*
girl	**la niña** *(lah 'nee-nyah)*
man	**el hombre** *(ehl 'ohm-breh)*
mother	**la madre** *(lah 'mah-dreh)*
person	**la persona** *(lah pehr-'soh-nah)*
sister	**la hermana** *(lah ehr-'mah-nah)*
son	**el hijo** *(ehl 'ee-hoh)*

teenager (female)	**la muchacha** *(lah moo-'chah-chah)*
teenager (male)	**el muchacho** *(ehl moo-'chah-choh)*
woman	**la mujer** *(lah moo-'hehr)*

The colors
Los colores *(lohs koh-'loh-rehs)*

black	**negro** *('neh-groh)*
blue	**azul** *(ah-'sool)*
brown	**café** *(kah-'feh)*
green	**verde** *('vehr-deh)*
orange	**anaranjado** *(ah-nah-rahn-'hah-doh)*
purple	**morado** *(moh-'rah-doh)*
red	**rojo** *('roh-hoh)*
white	**blanco** *('blahn-koh)*
yellow	**amarillo** *(ah-mah-'ree-yoh)*

More important words
Más palabras importantes
(mahs pah-'lah-brahs eem-pohr-'tahn-tehs)

all	**todo** *('toh-doh)*
bad	**malo** *('mah-loh)*
big	**grande** *('grahn-deh)*
a few	**pocos** *('poh-kohs)*
good	**bueno** *('bweh-noh)*
less	**menos** *('meh-nohs)*
a little	**poco** *('poh-koh)*
many	**muchos** *('moo-chohs)*
more	**más** *(mahs)*
much	**mucho** *('moo-choh)*
small	**pequeño** *(peh-'kehn-yoh)*

¡ *M* Á *S*   *A* Y U D A !

• Notice that the names for people, places, and things are either masculine or feminine, and so have either **el** *(ehl)* or **la** *(lah)* in front. **El** and **la** mean "the." Generally, if the word ends in the letter **o,** there's an **el** in front (i.e., **el cuarto** *[ehl 'kwahr-toh],* **el niño** *[ehl 'neen-yoh]*). Conversely, if the word ends in an **a,** there's a **la** in front (i.e., **la mesa** *[lah 'meh-sah],* **la persona** *[lah pehr-'soh-nah]*). Some Spanish words are exceptions: i.e., **el agua** *(ehl 'ah-gwah),* **el sofá** *(ehl soh-'fah).*

• Words not ending in either an **o** or **a** need to be memorized (i.e., **el amor** *[ehl ah-'mohr]* **la luz** *[lah loos]*). In the case of single objects, use **el** and **la** much like the word "the" in English: The house is big. **La casa es grande** *(lah 'kah-sah ehs 'grahn-deh).*

• Remember too, that **el** and **la** are used in Spanish to indicate a person's sex. **El doctor** *(ehl dohk-'tohr)* is a male doctor, while **la doctora** *(lah dohk-'toh-rah)* is a female doctor.

• One effective method to remember the names for things is to write their names on removable stickers and then place them on the objects you are trying to remember.

¡ *N* E C E S I T A   *P* R A C T I C A R !

Fill in the blank with an English translation:

el lápiz	_____
el libro	_____
la mesa	_____
el trabajo	_____
el agua	_____

Now match the opposites:

padre	**menos**
pequeño	**mujer**
hombre	**negro**
blanco	**grande**
más	**madre**

Numbers

Los números *(lohs 'noo-meh-rohs)*

No one can survive in Spanish without the numbers, so repeat each of these words as much as it takes:

0	**cero** *('seh-roh)*		14	**catorce** *(kah-'tohr-seh)*
1	**uno** *('oo-noh)*		15	**quince** *('keen-seh)*
2	**dos** *(dohs)*		16	**dieciséis** *(dee-ehs-ee-'seh-ees)*
3	**tres** *(trehs)*		17	**diecisiete** *(dee-ehs-ee-see-'eh-teh)*
4	**cuatro** *('kwa-troh)*		18	**dieciocho** *(dee-ehs-ee-'oh-choh)*
5	**cinco** *('seen-koh)*		19	**diecinueve** *(dee-ehs-ee-'nweh-veh)*
6	**seis** *('seh-ees)*		20	**veinte** *('veh-een-teh)*
7	**siete** *(see-'eh-teh)*		30	**treinta** *('treh-een-tah)*
8	**ocho** *('oh-choh)*		40	**cuarenta** *(kwah-'rehn-tah)*
9	**nueve** *('nweh-veh)*		50	**cincuenta** *(seen-'kwehn-tah)*
10	**diez** *(dee-'ehs)*		60	**sesenta** *(seh-'sehn-tah)*
11	**once** *('ohn-seh)*		70	**setenta** *(seh-'tehn-tah)*
12	**doce** *('doh-seh)*		80	**ochenta** *(oh-'chehn-tah)*
13	**trece** *('treh-seh)*		90	**noventa** *(noh-'vehn-tah)*

For all the numbers in-between, just add **y** *(ee)*, which means "and":

21   **veinte y uno** *('veh-een-teh ee 'oo-noh)*
22   **veinte y dos** *('veh-een-teh ee dohs)*
21   **veinte y tres** *('veh-een-teh ee trehs)*

Sooner or later, you'll also need to know how to say the larger numbers in Spanish. They aren't that difficult, so practice aloud:

100	**cien** *(see-'ehn)*
200	**doscientos** *(dohs-see-'ehn-tohs)*
300	**trescientos** *(trehs-see-'ehn-tohs)*
400	**cuatrocientos** *(kwah-troh-see-'ehn-tohs)*
500	**quinientos** *(kee-nee-'ehn-tohs)*
600	**seiscientos** *(seh-ees-see-'en-tohs)*
700	**setecientos** *(seh-teh-see-'ehn-tohs)*
800	**ochocientos** *(oh-choh-see-'ehn-tohs)*
900	**novecientos** *(noh-veh-see-'ehn-tohs)*
1000	**mil** *(meel)*

¡MÁS AYUDA!

• The cardinal numbers are valuable, too! Practice:

first	**primero** *(pree-'meh-roh)*
second	**segundo** *(seh-'goon-doh)*
third	**tercero** *(tehr-'seh-roh)*
fourth	**cuarto** *('kwahr-toh)*
fifth	**quinto** *('keen-toh)*
sixth	**sexto** *('sehks-toh)*
seventh	**séptimo** *('sehp-tee-moh)*
eighth	**octavo** *(ohk-'tah-voh)*
ninth	**noveno** *(noh-'veh-noh)*
tenth	**décimo** *('deh-see-moh)*

• By the way, "first" and "third" lose a letter when they go before a masculine noun:

first car	**primer carro** *(pree-'mehr 'kah-rroh)*
second house	**segunda casa** *(seh-'goon-dah 'kah-sah)*
third floor	**tercer piso** *(tehr-'sehr 'pee-soh)*

Are you ready to form a few phrases? You'll need the following:

for	**para** *('pah-rah)*	**para la casa** *('pah-rah lah 'kah-sah)*
in, on, at	**en** *(ehn)*	**en el cuarto** *(ehn ehl 'kwahr-toh)*
of, from	**de** *(deh)*	**de la persona** *(deh lah pehr-'soh-nah)*
to	**a** *(ah)*	**a la oficina** *(ah lah oh-fee-'see-nah)*
with	**con** *(kohn)*	**con el agua** *(kohn ehl 'ah-gwah)*
without	**sin** *(seen)*	**sin el carro** *(seen ehl 'kah-rroh)*

• There are only two contractions in Spanish:

| to the | **al** *(ahl)* | **al hombre** *(ahl 'ohm-breh)* |
| of the, from the | **del** *(dehl)* | **del trabajo** *(dehl trah-'bah-hoh)* |

• Use these words to link everything together·

and = **y** *(ee)*   or = **o** *(oh)*   but = **pero** *('peh-roh)*

Thank you and good-bye!
¡Gracias y adiós! *('grah-see-ahs ee ah-dee-'ohs)*

¡ *L A   C U L T U R A !*

If you get stuck in the middle of a sentence, don't be afraid to send messages using hand gestures or facial expressions. Body signals are used frequently in conversations throughout the Spanish-speaking world. And remember, there's nothing wrong with repeating your message several times until you're understood!

Follow the rules!
¡Siga las reglas! *('see-gah lahs 'reh-glahs)*

Regardless of the language, certain grammatical rules must be followed if you want to be clearly understood. In Spanish, these two should always be taken seriously:

1. THE REVERSE ORDER RULE:

As you begin to link your Spanish words together, you will find that often words are positioned in reverse order. This Reverse Order Rule is applied when you give a description: The descriptive word (adjective) goes after the word being described (noun). Study these examples.

The big house.	**La casa grande.** *(lah 'kah-sah 'grahn-deh)*
The green chair.	**La silla verde.** *(lah 'see-yah 'vehr-deh)*
The important paper.	**El papel importante.**
	(ehl pah-'pehl eem pohr-'tahn-teh)

2. THE AGREEMENT RULE:

This rule must be followed when you are referring to more than one item in Spanish. First, the words **el** and **la** ("he" and "she") become **los** and **las**, respectively.

el bebé (the baby)	**los bebés** (the babies)
la mesa (the table)	**las mesas** (the tables)
el servicio (the restroom)	**los servicios** (the restrooms)

Second, not only do all the nouns and adjectives need to end in **s** or **es** to make the sentence plural, but when they are used together, the genders (the **o**'s and **a**'s) must match as well.

Two white doors.	**Dos puertas blancas.**
	(dohs 'pwehr-tahs 'blahn-kahs)
Many red cars.	**Muchos carros rojos.**
	('moo-chohs 'kah-rrohs 'roh-hohs)
Six little children.	**Seis niños pequeños.**
	('seh-ees 'neen-yohs peh-'kehn-yohs)

By the way, to say "a" or "an" in Spanish, use **un** or **una**:

A man.	**Un hombre.**	**Un hombre americano.**
		(oon 'ohm-breh ah-meh-ree-'kah-noh)
A window.	**Una ventana.**	**Una ventana blanca.**
		('oo-nah vehn-'tah-nah 'blahn-kah)

And to say "some" or "a few," use **unos** or **unas**, depending on the gender:

Some men.	**Unos hombres. Unos hombres americanos.**
	('oo-nohs 'ohm-brehs ah-meh-ree-'kah-nohs)
A few windows.	**Unas ventanas. Unas ventanas blancas.**
	('oo-nahs vehn-'tah-nahs 'blahn-kahs)

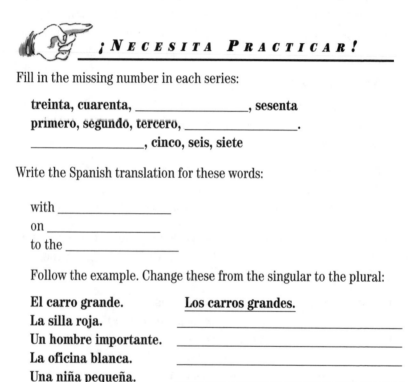

¡*N E C E S I T A   P R A C T I C A R !*

Fill in the missing number in each series:

treinta, cuarenta, _____, sesenta

primero, segundo, tercero, _____.

_____, cinco, seis, siete

Write the Spanish translation for these words:

with _____

on _____

to the _____

Follow the example. Change these from the singular to the plural:

El carro grande.	**Los carros grandes.**
La silla roja.	_____
Un hombre importante.	_____
La oficina blanca.	_____
Una niña pequeña.	_____

The question words
Las preguntas *(lahs preh-'goon-tahs)*

The following set of Spanish interrogation words should be memorized right away. See if you can recognize any of these from the expressions we learned earlier:

How?	**¿Cómo?** *('koh-moh)*
How many?	**¿Cuántos?** *('kwahn-tohs)*
How much?	**¿Cuánto?** *('kwahn-toh)*
What?	**¿Qué?** *(keh)*
When?	**¿Cuándo?** *('kwahn-doh)*
Where?	**¿Dónde?** *('dohn-deh)*
Which?	**¿Cuál?** *(kwahl)*
Who?	**¿Quién?** *(kee-'ehn)*
Whose?	**¿De quién?** *(deh kee-'ehn)*
Why?	**¿Por qué?** *(pohr keh)*

Now, cover up the right column and try to translate without looking. How many can you remember?

¡ M á s   A y u d a !

• A few questions are actually common one-liners used regularly in simple conversations. Notice how they are not literal translations.

How's it going?	**¿Qué tal?** *(keh tahl)*
What's your name?	**¿Cómo se llama?** *('koh-moh seh 'yah-mah)*
How old are you?	**¿Cuántos años tiene?**
	('kwahn-tohs 'ahn-yohs tee-'eh-neh)

Powerful pronouns!
Los pronombres poderosos
(lohs proh-'nohm-brehs poh-deh-'roh-sohs)

Your new Spanish-speaking friends will probably ask who everyone is. This is the quickest way to respond:

I	**Yo** *(yoh)*
We	**Nosotros** *(noh-'soh-trohs)*
You	**Usted** *(oos-'tehd)*
You (plural)	**Ustedes** *(oos-'teh-dehs)*

She	**Ella** *('eh-yah)*
He	**Él** *(ehl)*
They (feminine)	**Ellas** *('eh-yahs)*
They (masculine)	**Ellos** *('eh-yohs)*

Practice:

She's from Mexico.	**Ella es de México.** *('eh-yah ehs deh 'meh-hee-koh)*
How are you?	**¿Cómo está usted?** *('koh-moh ehs-'tah oos-'tehd)*
I speak Spanish!	**¡Yo hablo español!** *(yoh 'ah-bloh ehs-pahn-'yol)*

¡ *M Á S   A Y U D A !*

• **Nosotras** *(noh-'soh-trahs)* is "we" in the feminine:

¿Ustedes? *(oos-'teh-dehs)*   **¡Sí, nosotras!** *(see noh-'soh-trahs)*

• Would any of the following words be helpful? Think of ways these can be used to answer outreach-related questions:

anyone	**cualquiera** *(kwahl-kee-'eh-rah)*
anything	**cualquier cosa** *(kwahl-kee-'ehr 'koh-sah)*
anywhere	**en cualquier parte** *(ehn kwahl-kee-'ehr 'pahr-teh)*
everyone	**todos** *('toh-dohs)*
everything	**todo** *('toh-doh)*
everywhere	**por todas partes** *(pohr 'toh-dahs 'pahr-tehs)*
no one	**nadie** *('nah-dee-eh)*
nothing	**nada** *('nah-dah)*
nowhere	**por ninguna parte** *(pohr neen-'goo-nah 'pahr-teh)*
someone	**alguien** *('ahl-ghee-ehn)*
	¿Quién? *(kee-'ehn)* **Alguien** *('ahl-ghee-ehn)*
something	**algo** *('ahl-goh)*
	¿Qué? *(keh)* **Algo** *('ahl-goh)*
somewhere	**por alguna parte** *(pohr ahl-'goo-nah 'pahr-teh)*
	¿Dónde? *('dohn-deh)* **Por alguna parte** *(pohr ahl-'goo-nah 'pahr-teh)*

Whose is it?

¿De quién es? *(deh kee-'ehn ehs)*

A similar group of Spanish words is used to indicate possession. They tell us "whose" is it:

It's <u>my</u> desk.	**Es <u>mi</u> escritorio.**
	(ehs mee ehs-kree-'toh-ree-oh)
It's <u>your, his, her</u> or <u>their</u> desk.	**Es <u>su</u> escritorio.**
	(ehs soo ehs-kree-'toh-ree-oh)
It's <u>our</u> desk.	**Es <u>nuestro</u> escritorio.**
	(ehs noo-'ehs-troh ehs-kree-'toh-ree-oh)

Notice what happens to pronouns when you talk about more than one:

mi escritorio	<u>**mis**</u> **escritorios** *(mees ehs-kree-'toh-ree-ohs)*
su escritorio	<u>**sus**</u> **escritorios** *(soos ehs-kree-'toh-ree-ohs)*
nuestro escritorio	<u>**nuestros**</u> **escritorios**
	(noo-'ehs-trohs ehs-kree-'toh-ree-ohs)

Now try these other possessive words. Are you able to translate the sentences?

mine	**mío** or **mía** *('mee-oh, 'mee-ah)*
	Es mío. *(ehs 'mee-oh)*
yours, his, hers, theirs	**suyo** or **suya** *('soo-yoh, 'soo-yah)*
	Es suya. *(ehs 'soo-yah)*

By the way, if something "belongs to" someone else, use **de** *(deh)* to indicate possession:

It's Mary's.	**Es de María.** *(ehs deh mah-'ree-ah)*
It's the baby's.	**Es del bebé.** *(ehs dehl beh-'beh)*
It's his.	**Es de él.** *(ehs deh ehl)*

¡LA CULTURA!

When referring to others by name, it really helps if you are able to pronounce people's names correctly, as it makes them much more at ease. Always remember that Spanish is pronounced the way it is written. Also, it is not uncommon for someone in Spain or Latin America to have two last names. Don't get confused. Here's the order:

First name	Father's last name	Mother's last name
primer nombre	**apellido paterno**	**apellido materno**
(pree-'mehr 'nohm-breh)	*(ah-peh-'yee-doh pah-'tehr-noh)*	*(ah-peh-'yee-doh mah-'tehr-noh)*
Juan Carlos	**Espinoza**	**García**
(wahn 'kahr-lohs)	*(eh-spee-'noh-sah)*	*(gahr-'see-ah)*

¡MÁS AYUDA!

• Don't be afraid to answer simple questions with brief, effective responses. Notice these examples:

¿Cuántos? *('kwahn-tohs)*	**Muchos.** *('moo-chohs)*
¿Quién? *(kee-'ehn)*	**Ella.** *('eh-yah)*
¿Dónde? *('dohn-deh)*	**Los Angeles.** *(lohs 'ahn-heh-lehs)*

¡NECESITA PRACTICAR!

Connect the names with the corresponding pronouns:

Laura	**ustedes**
Francisco	**nosotros**
Carolina y yo	**ellos**
Raul y Paula	**él**
Samuel y usted	**ella**

What to say about está and es?
¿Qué decir sobre **está** y **es**?
(keh deh-'seer 'soh-breh ehs-'tah ee ehs)

Now that you can form short phrases on your own, it's time to join all of your words together. To accomplish this, you'll need to understand the difference between **está** *(ehs-'tah)* and **es** *(ehs)*. Both words mean "is," but they are used differently.

The word **está** *(ehs-'tah)* expresses a temporary state, condition, or location:

The girl is fine.	**La niña está bien.**
	(lah 'nee-nyah ehs-'tah bee-'ehn)
The girl is in the room.	**La niña está en el cuarto.**
	(lah 'nee-nyah ehs-'tah ehn ehl 'kwahr-toh)

The word **es** *(ehs)* expresses an inherent characteristic or quality, including origin and ownership.

The girl is small.	**La niña es pequeña.**
	(lah 'nee-nyah ehs peh-'keh-nyah)
The girl is Maria.	**La niña es María.**
	(lah 'nee-nyah ehs mah-'ree-ah)
The girl is American.	**La niña es americana.**
	(lah 'nee-nyah ehs ah-meh-ree-'kah-nah)
The girl is my friend.	**La niña es mi amiga.**
	(lah 'nee-nyah ehs mee ah-'mee-gah)

Can you see how helpful these two words can be? Countless comments can be made with only a minimum of vocabulary. You'll also need to talk about more than one person, place, or thing. To do so, replace **está** with **están**, and **es** with **son**. And don't forget that words must agree when you change to plurals.

The book is on the table.	**El libro está en la mesa.**
	(ehl 'lee-broh ehs-'tah ehn lah 'meh-sah)
The books are on the table.	**Los libros están en la mesa.**
	(lohs 'lee-brohs ehs-'tahn ehn lah 'meh-sah)

The book is important. **El libro es importante.**
(ehl 'lee-broh ehs eem-pohr-'tahn-teh)

The books are important. **Los libros son importantes.**
(lohs 'lee-brohs sohn eem-pohr-'tahn-tehs)

Check out these other examples. Read them aloud as you focus on their structure and meaning:

The chairs are black. **Las sillas son negras.**
(lahs 'see-yahs sohn 'neh-grahs)

The papers are at my house. **Los papeles están en mi casa.**
(lohs pah-'peh-lehs ehs-'tahn ehn mee 'kah-sah)

They are not friends. **No son amigos.**
(noh sohn ah-'mee-gohs)

Are they good? **¿Están buenos?**
(ehs-'tahn 'bweh-nohs)

The best way to learn how to use these words correctly is to listen to Spanish speakers in real-life conversations. They constantly use **es**, **está**, **son**, and **están** to communicate everyday messages.

¡MÁS AYUDA!

• A lot more can be said when you learn these vocabulary terms. Remember that they change according to gender:

that **ese** *('eh-seh)* or **esa** *('eh-sah)*
Ese muchacho está aquí.
('eh-seh moo-'chah-choh ehs-'tah ah-'kee)

these **estos** *('ehs-tohs)* or **estas** *('ehs-tahs)*
Estos tacos están malos.
('ehs-tohs 'tah-kohs ehs-'tahn 'mah-lohs)

this **este** *('ehs-teh)* or **esta** *('ehs-tah)*
Este es mi carro amarillo.
('ehs-teh ehs mee 'kah-rroh ah-mah-'ree-yoh)

those	**esos** *('eh-sohs)* or **esas** *('eh-sahs)*
	Esos son hombres grandes.
	('eh-sohs sohn 'ohm-brehs 'grahn-dehs)

I am and we are
Yo soy y nosotros somos
(yoh 'soh-ee ee noh-'soh-trohs 'soh-mohs)

To say "I am" and "we are" in Spanish, you must also acquire their different forms. As with **está** and **están**, the words **estoy** and **estamos** refer to the location or condition of a person, place, or thing. And just like **es** and **son**, the words **soy** and **somos** are used with everything else.

I am fine.	**Estoy bien.** *(ehs-'toh-ee 'bee-ehn)*
We are in the house.	**Estamos en la casa.**
	(ehs-'tah-mohs ehn lah 'kah-sah)
I am Lupe.	**Soy Lupe.** *('soh-ee 'loo-peh)*
We are Cuban.	**Somos cubanos.** *('soh-mohs koo-'bah-nohs)*

Now let's group all of these forms together. Look over these present tense forms of the verbs **estar** and **ser**:

To Be	**Estar** *(ehs-'tahr)*	**Ser** *(sehr)*
I am	**estoy** *(ehs-'toh-ee)*	**soy** *('soh-ee)*
You are, he is, she is	**está** *(ehs-'tah)*	**es** *(ehs)*
You are (pl.), they are	**están** *(ehs-'tahn)*	**son** *(sohn)*
We are	**estamos** *(ehs-'tah-mohs)*	**somos** *('soh-mohs)*

¡ A c c i ó n !

• You don't have to use the subject pronouns in every sentence. It's usually understood who's involved:

Nosotros somos *(noh-'soh-trohs 'soh-mohs)* and **Somos** *('soh-mohs)* both mean "We are."

• Two other words, **estás** *(ehs-'tahs)* and **eres** *('eh-rehs)*, may also be used to mean "you are" among family, friends, and small children. We'll learn more about their uses very soon.

¡ N E C E S I T A   P R A C T I C A R !

Translate quickly:

¿Quién? _____
¿Cuántos? _____
¿Dónde? _____

Fill in each blank with the appropriate verb form:

está, son, hay, estoy, somos

Estos _____ muy buenos.
Pedro _____ en la oficina.
Ella y yo _____ amigas.
No _____ problema.
Yo _____ bien.

To have
Tener *(teh-'nehr)*

Tener (to have) is another common linking word in Spanish, and its forms will become more necessary as you begin to create Spanish sentences on your own. Here are the basics to get you started:

To Have	Tener
I have	**tengo** *('tehn-goh)*
You have, He has, She has	**tiene** *(tee-'eh-neh)*
You have (pl.), They have	**tienen** *(tee-'eh-nehn)*
We have	**tenemos** *(teh-'neh-mohs)*

Study these examples:

I have a pen.	**Tengo un lapicero.**
	('tehn-goh oon lah-pee-'seh-roh)
She has a white car.	**Tiene un carro blanco.**
	(tee-'eh-neh oon 'kah-rroh 'blahn-koh)
They have seven children.	**Tienen siete niños.**
	(tee-'eh-nen see-'eh-teh 'neen-yohs)
We have a big house.	**Tenemos una casa grande.**
	(teh-'neh-mohs 'oo-nah 'kah-sah 'grahn-deh)

¡A C C I Ó N !

• Even though **tener** literally means "to have," sometimes it is used instead of the verb **estar** to express a temporary condition. Review these expressions often:

(I am) afraid	**(tengo) miedo** *(mee-'eh-doh)*
(we are) at fault	**(tenemos) la culpa** *(lah 'kool-pah)*
(they are) cold	**(tienen) frío** *('free-oh)*
(she is) 15 years old	**(tiene) quince años** *('keen-seh 'ahn-yohs)*
(I am) hot	**(tengo) calor** *(kah-'lohr)*
(they are) hungry	**(tienen) hambre** *('ahm-breh)*
(he is) sleep	**(tiene) sueño** *('swehn-yoh)*
(we are) thirsty	**(tenemos) sed** *(sehd)*

• To say "not" in Spanish, interject the word **no** *(noh)* in front of the verb:

He is not my father.	**Él no es mi padre.**
	(ehl noh ehs mee 'pah-dreh)
I do not have the paper.	**No tengo el papel.**
	(noh 'tehn-goh ehl pah-'pehl)
There are no more chairs.	**No hay más sillas.**
	(noh 'ah-ee mahs 'see-yahs)

- **Tienes** is the informal way to say "you have":

My friend, do you have a car? ¿**Amigo, tienes un carro?**

(ah-'mee-goh tee-'eh-nehs oon 'kah-rroh)

Spanish verbs
Los verbos en español
(lohs 'vehr-bohs ehn ehs-pahn-'yohl)

Putting a few words together in a new language is a thrilling experience, but real communication begins once you start using verbs or "action words." Although **estar**, **ser**, and **tener** are extremely useful, they do not express action. Learning how to use Spanish verbs will allow us to talk about what's going on in the world around us. Spend a few moments memorizing this brief list of helpful beginning verbs. Notice that all Spanish action words end in the letters **ar**, **er**, or **ir**:

to come	**venir** *(veh-'neer)*
to drink	**beber** *(beh-'behr)*
to drive	**manejar** *(mah-neh-'hahr)*
to eat	**comer** *(koh-'mehr)*
to follow	**seguir** *(seh-'geer)*
to go	**ir** *(eer)*
to help	**ayudar** *(ah-'yoo-dahr)*
to learn	**aprender** *(ah-prehn-'dehr)*
to leave	**salir** *(sah-'leer)*
to listen	**escuchar** *(ehs-koo-'chahr)*
to look	**mirar** *(mee-'rahr)*
to play	**jugar** *(hoo-'gahr)*
to read	**leer** *(leh-'ehr)*
to run	**correr** *(koh-'rrehr)*
to sleep	**dormir** *(dohr-'meer)*
to speak	**hablar** *(ah-'blahr)*
to study	**estudiar** *(ehs-too-dee-'ahr)*
to understand	**entender** *(ehn-tehn-'dehr)*

to wait	**esperar** *(ehs-peh-'rahr)*
to walk	**caminar** *(kah-mee-'nahr)*
to work	**trabajar** *(trah-bah-'hahr)*
to write	**escribir** *(ehs-kree-'beer)*

¡ A C C I Ó N !

• You can never learn enough action words in Spanish. Over one hundred verbs are listed in the English–Spanish Verb List at the end of this book, so use it as a reference tool. When you come across a verb as you study and practice, look it up in Spanish or English to learn its base form and meaning.

• Many Spanish verb infinitives that relate to outreach are similar to English. Look at these examples:

to communicate	**comunicar** *(koh-moo-nee-'kahr)*
to consult	**consultar** *(kohn-sool-'tahr)*
to converse	**conversar** *(kohn-vehr-'sahr)*
to organize	**organizar** *(ohr-gah-nee-'sahr)*
to plan	**planear** *(plah-neh-'ahr)*
to practice	**practicar** *(prahk-tee-'kahr)*

The shortcuts
Los atajos *(lohs ah-'tah-hohs)*

One of the most effective ways to use your verbs is to combine them with simple phrases and create complete sentences. For example, look what happens when you add these verb infinitives to **Favor de . . .** *(fah-'vohr deh)*, which implies, "Would you please . . .":

Please . . .	**Favor de . . .** *(fah-'vohr deh)*
write everything	**escribir todo** *(ehs-kree-'beer 'toh-doh)*
read the paper	**leer el papel** *(leh-'ehr ehl pah-'pehl)*
speak in English	**hablar en inglés** *(ah-'blahr ehn een-'glehs)*

Here are some other shortcuts. By adding these phrases to verb infinitives or vocabulary you can make statements, ask questions, or give commands. First read the phrase, and then try out the sample sentence:

Don't	**No** *(noh)*
Don't leave.	**No salir.** *(noh sah-'leer)*
You have to	**Tiene que** *(tee-'eh-neh keh)*
You have to work.	**Tiene que trabajar.**
	(tee-'eh-neh keh trah-bah-'hahr)
You should	**Debe** *('deh-beh)*
You should read.	**Debe leer.** *('deh-beh leh-'ehr)*

A word of caution with "should." In English, we politely soften our commands by using "should" instead of the intended "must." In Spanish this softening is seldom used, and **debe** means "must."

I'm going to	**Voy a** *('voh-ee ah)*
I'm going to eat.	**Voy a comer.** *('voh-ee ah koh-'mehr)*
You need	**Necesita** *(neh-seh-'see-tah)*
You need to learn.	**Necesita aprender.**
	(neh-seh-'see-tah ah-prehn-'dehr)

You're doing fine. This time, work on a few question phrases:

Do you want	**Quiere** *(kee-'eh-reh)*
Do you want to come?	**¿Quiere venir?** *(kee-'eh-reh veh-'neer)*
Can you	**Puede** *('pweh-deh)*
Can you wait?	**¿Puede esperar?**
	('pweh-deh ehs-peh-'rahr)
Do you like	**Le gusta** *(leh 'goos-tah)*
Do you like to play?	**¿Le gusta jugar?** *(leh 'goos-tah hoo-'gahr)*

¡MÁS AYUDA!

• "There is" and "There are" are very easy in Spanish. In both cases you use the little word **hay** (pronounced " *'ah-ee'*").

There's one floor.	**Hay un piso.** *('ah-ee oon 'pee-soh)*
There are two floors.	**Hay dos pisos.** *('ah-ee dohs 'pee-sohs)*

• Check out these other one-liners. Add them to the verbs you have learned:

One must	**Hay que** *('ah-ee keh)*
Do you prefer	**Prefiere** *(preh-fee-'eh-reh)*
I would like	**Quisiera** *(kee-see-'eh-rah)*
Let's	**Vamos a** *('vah-mohs ah)*
Could you	**Podría** *(poh-'dree-ah)*

¡NECESITA PRACTICAR!

Use forms of **tener** to translate the following:

They are cold.	_____
I don't have the money.	_____
We are hungry.	_____

Insert the verb infinitive that best fits each sentence:

comer, hablar, escribir, leer, escuchar

Favor de _____ **en el papel.**
Tiene que _____ **el libro.**
Necesita _____ **inglés.**
¿Quiere _____ **en el restaurante?**
Voy a _____ **la radio.**

Let's see one of the easiest verb forms. It's the Present Progressive tense, and it refers to actions that are taking place at this moment. It is similar to our "ing" form in English. Simply change the verb's ending slightly, and then combine the new form with the four forms of the verb **estar** *(ehs-'tahr)*. The **ar**-ending verbs will end in -**ando** *('ahn-doh),* and the **er**- and **ir**-ending verbs will end in -**iendo** *(ee-'ehn-doh).* Study these examples closely:

To Work	**Trabajar** *(trah-bah-'hahr)*
working	**trabajando** *(trah-bah-'hahn-doh)*
We're working.	**Estamos trabajando.**
	(ehs-'tah-mohs trah-bah-'hahn-doh)

To Eat	**Comer** *(koh-'mehr)*
eating	**comiendo** *(koh-mee-'ehn-doh)*
He is eating.	**Está comiendo.** *(ehs-'tah koh-mee-'ehn-doh)*

To Write	**Escribir** *(ehs-kree-'beer)*
writing	**escribiendo** *(ehs-kree-bee-'ehn-doh)*
I'm writing.	**Estoy escribiendo.**
	(ehs-'toh-ee ehs-kree-bee-'ehn-doh)

• Some verbs change in spelling and pronunciation when you add the -**ndo** ending. Look at these examples:

to sleep	**dormir** *(dohr-'meer)*
sleeping	**durmiendo** *(door-mee-'ehn-doh)*
to read	**leer** *(leh-'ehr)*
reading	**leyendo** *(leh-'yehn-doh)*

¡*L A S   O R D E N E S !*

As long as we're talking about working with Spanish speakers in need, review the following command or request words. They are unique forms of verbs that can be used all by themselves. Try using them in work-related situations—and always say **por favor** *(pohr fah-'vohr):*

Please . . .	**Por favor . . .** *(pohr fah-'vohr)*
come	**venga** *('vehn-gah)*
follow	**siga** *('see-gah)*
go	**vaya** *('vah-yah)*
listen	**escuche** *(ehs-'koo-cheh)*
read	**lea** *('leh-ah)*
wait	**espere** *(ehs-'peh-reh)*
watch	**mire** *('mee-reh)*
write	**escriba** *(ehs-'kree-bah)*

¡*M Á S   A Y U D A !*

• Any vocabulary item can be learned quickly if it's practiced in conjunction with a command word. For example, to pick up the names for furniture, have a native Spanish speaker command you to touch or point to things throughout the home. This exercise really works, and more importantly, it can be lots of fun:

Touch . . .	**Toque . . .**	. . . the table	. . . **la mesa**
	('toh-keh)		*(lah 'meh-sah)*
Point to . . .	**Señale . . .**	. . . the chair	. . . **la silla**
	(seh-'nyah-leh)		*(lah 'see-yah)*

• Several important command words have the suffix -**se** at the end. Notice the pattern:

Hurry up!	**¡Apúrese!** *(ah-'poo-reh-seh)*
Sit down!	**¡Siéntese!** *(see-'ehn-teh-seh)*

Stand up!	**¡Levántese!** *(leh-'vahn-teh-seh)*
Stop!	**¡Párese!** *('pah-reh-seh)*
Stay!	**¡Quédese!** *('keh-deh-seh)*

¡ *L A   C U L T U R A !*

Commands are practical and easy to use, but you may quickly become overbearing. Try to give your orders sparingly and *always* add **por favor** *(pohr fah-'vohr)*.

¡ *N E C E S I T A   P R A C T I C A R !*

Follow the pattern as you practice:

trabajar	trabajando	Estoy trabajando.
hablar	_____	_____
comer	_____	_____
escribir	_____	_____
aprender	_____	_____
dormir	_____	_____

Connect the opposites:

Siéntese	**Vaya**
Venga	**Lea**
Escriba	**Levántese**

Chapter Two

Capítulo Dos
(kah-'pee-too-loh dohs)

In the Neighborhood
En el vecindario
(ehn ehl veh-seen-'dah-ree-oh)

The first conversation
La primera conversación
(lah pree-'meh-rah kohn-vehr-sah-see-'ohn)

Make contact with your Spanish neighbors or acquaintances by exchanging a greeting in Spanish, and then following it up with a familiar expression or two.

¡Hola, buenos días!
('oh-lah 'bweh-ahs)

¿Cómo está?
('koh-moh ehs-'tah)

Muy bien.
('moo-ee bee-'ehn)

¡Buenos días!
('bweh-nohs nohs 'dee-'dee-ahs)

Bien, gracias, ¿Y usted?
(bee-'ehn 'grah-see-ahs ee oos-'tehd)

Now, keep the conversation going by adding a phrase about the weather:

What weather we're having! **¡Qué tiempo hace!**
(keh tee-'ehm-poh 'ah-seh)

Do you like the climate? **¿Le gusta el clima?**
(leh 'goos-tah ehl 'klee-mah)

This is my favorite season.

Esta es mi estación favorita.
('ehs-tah ehs mee ehs-tah-see-'ohn fah-voh-'ree-tah)

I like . . .	**Me gusta . . .** *(meh 'goos-tah)*
spring	**la primavera** *(lah pree-mah-'veh-rah)*
summer	**el verano** *(ehl veh-'rah-noh)*
fall	**el otoño** *(ehl oh-'toh-nyoh)*
winter	**el invierno** *(ehl een-vee-'ehr-noh)*

It's . . .	**Hace . . .** *('ah-seh)*
cold	**frío** *('free-oh)*
hot	**calor** *(kah-'lohr)*
nice weather	**buen tiempo** *(bwehn tee-'ehm-poh)*
sunny	**sol** *(sohl)*
windy	**viento** *(vee-'ehn-toh)*

It's . . .	**Está . . .** *(ehs-'tah)*
clear	**despejado** *(dehs-peh-'hah-doh)*
cloudy	**nublado** *(noo-'blah-doh)*
cool	**fresco** *('frehs-koh)*
drizzling	**lloviznando** *(yoh-vees-'nahn-doh)*
freezing	**helado** *(eh-'lah-doh)*
raining	**lloviendo** *(yoh-vee-'ehn-doh)*
snowing	**nevando** *(neh-'vahn-doh)*
stormy	**tempestuoso** *(tehm-pehs-too-'oh-soh)*

I don't like . . .	**No me gusta . . .** *(noh meh 'goos-tah)*
clouds	**las nubes** *(lahs 'noo-behs)*
frost	**la escarcha** *(lah ehs-'kahr-chah)*
hail	**el granizo** *(ehl grah-'nee-soh)*
ice	**el hielo** *(ehl ee-'eh-loh)*
lightning	**el relámpago** *(ehl reh-'lahm-pah-goh)*
rain	**la lluvia** *(lah 'yoo-vee-ah)*
snow	**la nieve** *(lah nee-'eh-veh)*
thunder	**el trueno** *(ehl troo-'eh-noh)*

¡N E C E S I T A   P R A C T I C A R!

Answer these questions:

¿Dónde vive?

_____

¿Cuándo hace calor allí?

_____

¿Cómo está el tiempo hoy?

_____

How's it going?
¡Qué tal! *(keh tahl)*

Once you break the ice, find out how everyone is feeling. Act out these emotions as you practice. For females, change the final letter **o** to an **a**:

Are you . . . ?	**¿Está . . . ?** *(ehs-'tah)*
I am . . .	**Estoy . . .** *(ehs-'toh-ee)*
anxious	**ansioso** *(ahn-see-'oh-soh)*
bored	**aburrido** *(ah-boo-'rree-doh)*
calm	**calmado** *(kahl-'mah-doh)*
comfortable	**cómodo** *('koh-moh-doh)*
confused	**confundido** *(kohn-foon-'dee-doh)*
excited	**emocionado** *(eh-moh-see-oh-'nah-doh)*
happy	**feliz** *(feh-'lees)*
interested	**interesado** *(een-teh-reh-'sah-doh)*
nervous	**nervioso** *(nehr-vee-'oh-soh)*
not bad	**así-así** *(ah-'see ah-'see)*
OK	**regular** *(reh-goo-'lahr)*
relaxed	**relajado** *(reh-lah-'hah-doh)*
sad	**triste** *('trees-teh)*
scared	**espantado** *(ehs-pahn-'tah-doh)*

sick	**enfermo** *(ehn-'fehr-moh)*
surprised	**sorprendido** *(sohr-prehn-'dee-doh)*
tired	**cansado** *(kahn-'sah-doh)*
upset	**enojado** *(eh-noh-'hah-doh)*
worried	**preocupado** *(pre-oh-koo-'pah-doh)*

¡*MÁS AYUDA!*

• When necessary, use one of these common words:

I'm . . .	**Estoy . . .** *(ehs-'toh-ee)*
available	**disponible** *(dees-poh-'nee-bleh)*
busy	**ocupado** *(oh-koo-'pah-doh)*
hurt	**herido** *(eh-'ree-doh)*
lost	**perdido** *(pehr-'dee-doh)*
ready	**listo** *('lees-toh)*

• Now, add one of these questions as you offer to help, and then focus on any key words that may sound familiar:

How can I help you?	**¿En que puedo servirle?**
	(ehn keh 'pweh-doh sehr-'veer-leh)
What do you need?	**¿Qué necesita usted?**
	(keh neh-seh-'see-tah oos-'tehd)
What is the problem?	**¿Cuál es el problema?**
	(kwahl ehs ehl proh-'bleh-mah)

¡*NECESITA PRACTICAR!*

Connect the opposites:

muy bien	**triste**
feliz	**emocionado**
calmado	**enfermo**

The visit

La visita *(lah vee-'see-tah)*

Beyond the everyday greetings and salutations lies the actual visit:

My name is _____	**Me llamo** _____
	(meh 'yah-moh)
Nice to meet you.	**Mucho gusto.**
	('moo-choh 'goos-toh)
Do you speak English?	**¿Habla usted inglés?**
	('ah-blah oos-'tehd een-'glehs)

As you meet Spanish speakers for the first time, you may select useful terms from the following list. Note that "a" or "an" can be **un** (for masculine nouns) or **una** (for feminine nouns):

I'm a/an ...	**Soy un/una ...** *('soh-ee oon, 'oo-nah)*
acquaintance	**compañero(a)** *(kohm-pahn-'yeh-roh, rah)*
associate	**asociado(a)** *(ah-soh-see-'ah-doh, dah)*
contributor	**contribuyente** *(kohn-tree-boo-'yehn-teh)*
donor	**donante** *(doh-'nahn-teh)*
friend	**amigo(a)** *(ah-'mee-goh, gah)*
helper	**ayudante** *(ah-yoo-'dahn-teh)*
member	**miembro** *(mee-'ehm-broh)*
neighbor	**vecino(a)** *(veh-'see-noh, nah)*
official	**funcionario(a)** *(foon-see-oh-'nah-ree-oh, ah)*
partner	**socio(a)** *('soh-see-oh, ah)*
relative	**pariente** *(pah-ree-'ehn-teh)*
renter	**inquilino(a)** *(een-kee-'lee-noh, nah)*
resident	**residente** *(reh-see-'dehn-teh)*
roommate	**compañero(a) de cuarto**
	(kohm-pahn-'yeh-roh, rah deh 'kwahr-toh)
sponsor	**patrocinador(a)**
	(pah-troh-see-nah-'dohr, 'doh-rah)
supporter	**partidario(a)** *(pahr-tee-'dah-ree-oh, ah)*
visitor	**visitante** *(vee-see-'tahn-teh)*
volunteer	**voluntario(a)** *(voh-loon-'tah-ree-oh, ah)*

Do you understand? It can be **un vecino** or **una vecina, un compañero** or **una compañera**. And sometimes there are instances when the noun does not change, so you have **un contribuyente** and **una contribuyente, un donante** and **una donante**.

If you're visiting on behalf of a business or an organization, don't forget to mention your title. Both sexes are mentioned; see if you can spot a pattern.

I'm (the) . . .	**Soy . . .** *('soh-ee)*
assistant	**el asistente, la asistente**
	(ehl, lah ah-sees-'tehn-teh)
boss	**el patrón, la patrona**
	(ehl pah-'trohn, lah pah-'troh-nah)
clerk	**el dependiente, la dependiente**
	(ehl, lah deh-pehn-dee-'ehn-teh)
employee	**el empleado, la empleada**
	(ehl ehm-ple-'ah-doh, lah ehm-pleh-'ah-dah)
employer	**el empresario, la empresaria**
	(ehl ehm-preh-'sah-ree-oh, lah ehm-preh-'sah-ree-ah)
leader	**el líder, la líder** *(ehl, lah 'lee-dehr)*
manager	**el gerente, la gerente** *(ehl, lah heh-'rehn-teh)*
owner	**el dueño, la dueña**
	(ehl 'dwehn-yoh, lah 'dwehn-yah)
representative	**el representante, la representante**
	(ehl, lah reh-preh-sehn-'tahn-teh)
secretary	**el secretario, la secretaria**
	(ehl seh-kreh-'tah-ree-oh, lah seh-kreh-'tah-ree-ah)
worker	**el trabajador, la trabajadora**
	(ehl trah-bah-hah-'dohr, lah trah-bah-hah-'doh-rah)

As you can see again, most of the time the noun changes according to gender: **el patrón** and **la patrona**, although sometimes it remains the same: **el asistente** and **la asistente**.

It is, however, beyond the scope of this book to offer the masculine and feminine possibilities with every noun, and so in most cases we will present the masculine aspect only.

These professionals need to make visits all the time:

It's (the) . . .	**Es . . .** *(ehs)*
consultant	**el consultor** *(ehl kohn-sool-'tohr)*
counselor	**el consejero** *(ehl kohn-seh-'heh-roh)*
doctor	**el doctor** *(ehl dohk-'tohr)*
educator	**el educador** *(ehl eh-doo-kah-'dohr)*
facilitator	**el facilitador** *(ehl fah-see-lee-tah-'dohr)*
interpreter	**el intérprete** *(ehl een-'tehr-preh-teh)*
lawyer	**el abogado** *(ehl ah-boh-'gah-doh)*
midwife	**la comadrona** *(lah koh-mah-'droh-nah)*
minister	**el pastor** *(ehl pahs-tohr)*
missionary	**el misionario** *(ehl mee-see-oh-'nah-ree-oh)*
nun	**la monja** *(lah 'mohn-hah)*
nurse	**la enfermera** *(lah ehn-fehr-'meh-rah)*
police officer	**el policía** *(ehl poh-lee-'see-ah)*
priest	**el sacerdote** *(ehl sah-sehr-'doh-teh)*
psychologist	**el psicólogo** *(ehl see-'koh-loh-goh)*
social worker	**el trabajador social**
	(ehl trah-bah-hah-'dohr soh-see-'ahl)
sociologist	**el sociólogo** *(ehl soh-see-'oh-loh-goh)*
specialist	**el especialista** *(ehl ehs-peh-see-ah-'lees-tah)*
teacher	**el maestro** *(ehl mah-'ehs-troh)*
technician	**el técnico** *(ehl 'tehk-nee-koh)*
therapist	**el terapista** *(ehl teh-rah-'pees-tah)*
trainer	**el entrenador** *(ehl ehn-treh-nah-'dohr)*
translator	**el traductor** *(ehl trah-dook-'tohr)*

¡MÁS AYUDA!

• Some titles are longer than others:

case worker	**el asistente social** *(ehl ah-sees-'tehn-teh soh-see-'ahl)*
parole officer	**el agente de libertad condicional** *(ehl ah-'hehn-teh deh lee-behr-'tahd kohn-dee- see-oh-'nahl)*
youth worker	**el consejero juvenil** *(ehl kohn-seh-'heh-roh hoo-veh-'neel)*

• These will be easy.

> **el tutor** *(ehl too-'tohr)*
> **el mentor** *(ehl mehn-'tohr)*
> **el supervisor** *(ehl soo-pehr-vee-'sohr)*

• Acquire any term that defines who everyone is:

adolescent	**el adolescente** *(ehl ah-doh-leh-'sehn-teh)*
adult	**el adulto** *(ehl ah-'dool-toh)*
child	**el niño** *(ehl 'neen-yoh)*
senior citizen	**la persona de la tercera edad** *(lah pehr-'soh-nah deh lah tehr-'seh-rah eh-'dahd)*
youth	**el joven** *(ehl 'hoh-vehn)*

¡LA CULTURA!

• It's common for native Hispanics to use nicknames when referring to others, once a friendly relationship has been established. It is meant to show intimacy, and not disrespect.

¡NECESITA PRACTICAR!

Connect the words that belong together:

dueño	**maestro**
enfermero	**trabajador**
estudiante	**monja**
patrón	**inquilino**
sacerdote	**doctor**

The administration

La administración *(lah ahd-mee-nees-trah-see-'on)*

Are you an administrator? As you introduce yourself to a Spanish speaker, one of the following may come in handy:

I'm (the) . . .	**Soy . . .** *('soh-ee)*
administrator	**el administrador** *(ehl ahd-mee-nees-trah-'dohr)*
chief	**el jefe** *(ehl 'heh-feh)*
coordinator	**el coordinador** *(ehl koh-ohr-dee-nah-'dohr)*
director	**el director** *(ehl dee-rehk-'tohr)*
executive	**el ejecutivo** *(ehl eh-heh-koo-'tee-voh)*
president	**el presidente** *(ehl preh-see-'dehn-teh)*
superintendent	**el superintendente** *(ehl soo-pehr-een-tehn-'dehn-teh)*
vice president	**el vicepresidente** *(ehl vee-seh-preh-see-'dehn-teh)*

Fill in the blanks with words of your choice:

I'm the director of _____.	**Soy el director de _____.** *('soh-ee ehl dee-rehk-'tohr deh)*
finance	**las finanzas** *(lahs fee-'nahn-sahs)*
personnel	**el personal** *(ehl pehr-soh-'nahl)*
special services	**los servicios especiales** *(lohs sehr-'vee-see-ohs ehs-peh-see-'ah-lehs)*

What's your occupation?
¿Cuál es su ocupación?
(kwahl ehs soo oh-koo-pah-see-'ohn)

While you're on the subject of job titles, take a moment to find out what your new friend does for a living:

Are you (the) . . . ?	¿**Es usted . . . ?** *(ehs oos-'tehd)*
artist	el **artista** *(ehl ahr-'tees-tah)*
bartender	el **cantinero** *(ehl kahn-tee-'neh-roh)*
bellhop	el **botones** *(ehl boh-'toh-nehs)*
busboy	el **ayudante de camarero** *(ehl ah-yoo-'dahn-teh deh kah-mah-'reh-roh)*
carpenter	el **carpintero** *(ehl kahr-peen-'toh-roh)*
cashier	el **cajero** *(ehl kah-'heh-roh)*
contractor	el **contratista** *(ehl kohn-trah-'tees-tah)*
cook	el **cocinero** *(ehl koh-see-'neh-roh)*
data processor	el **procesador de datos** *(ehl proh-seh-sah-'dohr deh 'dah-tohs)*
dishwasher	el **lavaplatos** *(ehl lah-vah-'plah-tohs)*
farmer	el **campesino** *(ehl kahm-peh-'see-noh)*
gardener	el **jardinero** *(ehl hahr-dee-'neh-roh)*
janitor	el **conserje** *(ehl kohn-'sehr-heh)*
laborer	el **obrero** *(ehl oh-'breh-roh)*
mechanic	el **mecánico** *(ehl meh-'kah-nee-koh)*
office worker	el **oficinista** *(ehl oh-fee-see-'nees-tah)*
painter	el **pintor** *(ehl peen-'tohr)*
plumber	el **plomero** *(ehl ploh-'meh-roh)*
programmer	el **programador** *(ehl proh-grah-mah-'dohr)*
recepcionist	el **recepcionista** *(ehl reh-sehp-see-oh-'nees-tah)*
servant	el **criado** *(ehl kree-'ah-doh)*
truck driver	el **camionero** *(ehl kah-mee-oh-'neh-roh)*
typist	el **mecanógrafo** *(ehl meh-kah-'noh-grah-foh)*
waiter	el **mesero** *(ehl meh-'seh-roh)*

Here are some more standard professions. Make changes if they're female:

architect	**el arquitecto** *(ehl ahr-kee-'tehk-toh)*
dentist	**el dentista** *(ehl dehn-'tees-tah)*
engineer	**el ingeniero** *(ehl een-heh-nee-'eh-roh)*
firefighter	**el bombero** *(ehl bohm-'beh-roh)*
foreman	**el capataz** *(ehl kah-pah-'tahs)*
lawyer	**el abogado** *(ehl ah-boh-'gah-doh)*
librarian	**el bibliotecario** *(ehl beeb-lee-oh-teh-'kah-ree-oh)*
mail carrier	**el cartero** *(ehl kahr-'teh-roh)*
musician	**el músico** *(ehl 'moo-see-koh)*
operator	**el operario** *(ehl oh-peh-'rah-ree-oh)*
pilot	**el piloto** *(ehl pee-'loh-toh)*
police officer	**el policía** *(ehl poh-lee-'see-ah)*
salesperson	**el vendedor** *(ehl vehn-deh-'dohr)*
soldier	**el soldado** *(ehl sohl-'dah-doh)*
student	**el estudiante** *(ehl ehs-too-dee-'ahn-teh)*
surgeon	**el cirujano** *(ehl see-roo-'hah-noh)*
tailor	**el sastre** *(ehl 'sahs-treh)*
teacher	**el maestro** *(ehl mah-'ehs-troh)*

And what's their legal status?

Are you a . . . ?	**¿Es usted un . . . ?** *(ehs oos-'tehd oon)*
citizen	**ciudadano** *(see-oo-dah-'dah-noh)*
foreigner	**extranjero** *(ehks-trahn-'heh-roh)*
immigrant	**inmigrante** *(een-meeg-'rahn-teh)*
prisoner	**prisionero** *(pree-see-oh-'neh-roh)*
refugee	**refugiado** *(reh-foo-ghee-'ah-doh)*

¡*Necesita Practicar!*

Fill in any occupation that fits:

El _____ está en el hospital.
El _____ está en el restaurante.
El _____ está en la oficina.

The family
La familia *(lah fah-'mee-lee-ah)*

Speaking of titles, see below to clarify everyone's relationship:

Are you (the) . . . ?	¿**Es usted . . . ?** *(ehs oos-'tehd)*
aunt	**la tía** *(lah 'tee-ah)*
brother	**el hermano** *(ehl ehr-'mah-noh)*
cousin	**el primo** *(ehl 'preeh-moh)*
daughter	**la hija** *(la 'ee-hah)*
father	**el padre** *(ehl 'pah-dreh)*
granddaughter	**la nieta** *(lah nee-'eh-tah)*
grandfather	**el abuelo** *(ehl ah-'bweh-loh)*
grandmother	**la abuela** *(lah ah-bweh-lah)*
grandson	**el nieto** *(ehl nee-'eh-toh)*
husband	**el esposo** *(ehl ehs-'poh-soh)*
mother	**la madre** *(lah 'mah-dreh)*
nephew	**el sobrino** *(ehl soh-'breeh-noh)*
niece	**la sobrina** *(lah soh-'bree-nah)*
sister	**la hermana** *(lah ehr-'mah-nah)*
son	**el hijo** *(ehl 'ee-hoh)*
uncle	**el tío** *(ehl 'tee-oh)*
wife	**la esposa** *(lah ehs-'poh-sah)*

¡MÁS AYUDA!

• Add these words if you need to:

It's our _____ child.	**Es nuestro niño _____.**
	(ehs noo-'ehs-troh 'neen-yoh)
adopted	**adoptado** *(ah-dohp-'tah-doh)*
foster	**acogido** *(ah-koh-'hee-doh)*
sponsored	**apadrinado** *(ah-pah-dree-'nah-doh)*

¡LA CULTURA!

Because the traditional Hispanic family includes many members, you may want to learn the names of each one of them:

boyfriend	**el novio** *(ehl 'noh-vee-oh)*
girlfriend	**la novia** *(lah 'noh-vee-ah)*
goddaughter	**la ahijada** *(lah ah-ee-'hah-dah)*
godson	**el ahijado** *(ehl ah-ee-'hah-doh)*
godfather	**el compadre** *(ehl kohm-'pah-dreh)*
godmother	**la comadre** *(lah koh-'mah-dreh)*
godparents	**los padrinos** *(lohs pah-'dree-nohs)*
legal guardian	**el tutor legal** *(ehl too-'tohr leh-'gahl)*
stepfather	**el padrastro** *(ehl pah-'drahs-troh)*
stepmother	**la madrastra** *(lah mah-'drahs-trah)*
stepson	**el hijastro** *(ehl ee-'has-troh)*
stepdaughter	**la hijastra** *(lah ee-'has-trah)*

¡NECESITA PRACTICAR!

Answer these questions about yourself:

¿Cuántos hermanos tiene usted?
¿Dónde viven sus primos?
¿Tiene un esposo o una esposa?

What kind of a person?
¿Qué tipo de persona?
(keh 'tee-poh deh pehr-'soh-nah)

Care to know more about the person you're talking to? Use the words below, and remember that most descriptive word endings change from an **o** to an **a** when they refer to females:

Jose is . . . ?	**José es** . . . *(hoh-'seh ehs)*
ambitious	**ambicioso** *(ahm-bee-see-'oh-soh)*
brave	**valiente** *(vah-lee-'ehn-teh)*
bright	**despierto** *(dehs-pee-'ehr-toh)*
cruel	**cruel** *(kroo-'ehl)*
famous	**famoso** *(fah-'moh-soh)*
fast	**rápido** *('rah-pee-doh)*
fat	**gordo** *('gohr-doh)*
funny	**chistoso** *(chees-'toh-soh)*
good-looking	**guapo** *('gwah-poh)*
healthy	**saludable** *(sah-loo-'dah-bleh)*
immature	**inmaduro** *(een-mah-'doo-roh)*
industrious	**trabajador** *(trah-bah-hah-'dohr)*
intelligent	**inteligente** *(een-teh-lee-'hehn-teh)*
lazy	**perezoso** *(peh-reh-'soh-soh)*
mature	**maduro** *(mah-'doo-roh)*
nice	**simpático** *(seem-'pah-tee-koh)*
old	**viejo** *(vee-'eh-hoh)*
older	**mayor** *(mah-'yohr)*
pleasant	**agradable** *ah-grah-'dah-bleh)*
patient	**paciente** *(pah-see-'ehn-teh)*
polite	**cortés** *(kohr-'tehs)*
poor	**pobre** *('poh-breh)*
quiet	**quieto** *(kee-'eh-toh)*
rich	**rico** *('ree-koh)*
short (in height)	**bajo** *('bah-hoh)*
sick	**enfermo** *(ehn-'fehr-moh)*

slow	**lento** *('lehn-toh)*
strange	**raro** *('rah-roh)*
strong	**fuerte** *('fwehr-teh)*
sure	**seguro** *(seh-'goo-roh)*
tall	**alto** *('ahl-toh)*
thin	**delgado** *(dehl-'gah-doh)*
unpleasant	**desagradable** *(deh-sah-grah-'dah-bleh)*

¡ M á s   A y u d a !

• Description words that begin with **no**, **in**, or **des** often refer to an opposite.

qualified	**calificado** *(kah-lee-fee-'kah-doh)*
unqualified	**no calificado** *(noh kah-lee-fee-'kah-doh)*
correct	**correcto** *(koh-'rrehk-toh)*
incorrect	**incorrecto** *(een-koh-'rrehk-toh)*
employed	**empleado** *(ehm-pleh-'ah-doh)*
unemployed	**desempleado** *(deh-sehm-pleh-'ah-doh)*

• Use these little words to compare things:

a little big	**un poco grande** *(oon 'poh-koh 'grahn-deh)*
as big as	**tan grande como** *(tahn 'grahn-deh 'koh-moh)*
bigger than	**más grande que** *(mahs 'grahn-deh keh)*
biggest	**el (or la) más grande** *(ehl, lah mahs 'grahn-deh)*
so big	**tan grande** *(tahn 'grahn-deh)*
too big	**demasiado grande** *(deh-mah-see-'ah-doh 'grahn-deh)*
very big	**muy grande** *('moo-ee 'grahn-deh)*

Carlos es más grande que Manuel.

('kahr-lohs ehs mahs 'grahn-deh keh mahn-'well)

Samuel es tan grande como una casa.

(sahm-'well ehs tahn 'grahn-deh 'koh-moh 'oo-nah 'kah-sah)

Felipe es el más grande.

(fel-'lee-peh ehs ehl mahs 'grahn-deh)

• Physical differences? Again, females would end in **a**:

black	**negro** (*'neh-groh*)
blonde	**rubio** (*'roo-bee-oh*)
brunette	**moreno** (*moh-'reh-noh*)
disabled	**incapacitado** (*een-kah-pah-see-'tah-doh*)
female	**femenino** (*feh-meh-'nee-noh*)
handicapped	**minusválido** (*mee-noos-'vah-lee-doh*)
left-handed	**zurdo** (*'soor-doh*)
male	**masculino** (*mahs-koo-'lee-noh*)
red-haired	**pelirrojo** (*peh-lee-'rroh-hoh*)
right-handed	**diestro** (*dee-'ehs-troh*)
twin	**gemelo** (*heh-'meh-loh*)
white	**blanco** (*'blahn-koh*)

Describe things

Describa las cosas *(dehs-'kree-bah lahs 'koh-sahs)*

Expand your descriptive vocabulary by reading the list of opposites below:

It's . . .	**Es** or **está** . . . *(ehs, ehs-'tah)*
cheap	**barato** (*bah-'rah-toh*)
expensive	**caro** (*'kah-roh*)
clean	**limpio** (*'leem-pee-oh*)
dirty	**sucio** (*'soo-see-oh*)
deep	**profundo** (*proh-'foon-doh*)
shallow	**bajo** (*'bah-hoh*)
difficult	**difícil** (*dee-'fee-seel*)
easy	**fácil** (*'fah-seel*)
hard	**duro** (*'doo-roh*)
soft	**blando** (*'blahn-doh*)

narrow	**estrecho** *(ehs-'treh-choh)*
wide	**ancho** *('ahn-choh)*
pretty	**bonito** *(boh-'nee-toh)*
ugly	**feo** *('feh-oh)*
rough	**áspero** *('ahs-peh-roh)*
smooth	**liso** *('lee-soh)*
dry	**seco** *('seh-koh)*
wet	**mojado** *(moh-'hah-doh)*
thin	**delgado** *(dehl-'gah-doh)*
thick	**grueso** *(groo-'eh-soh)*

• Keep in mind that the Spanish adjective (the word used to describe anything) usually goes after the noun. Here are some more vocabulary words:

It's an _____ job.	**Es un trabajo _____.**
excellent	**excelente** *(ehk-seh-'lehn-teh)*
important	**importante** *(eem-pohr-'tahn-teh)*
interesting	**interesante** *(een-teh-reh-'sahn teh)*

¡NECESITA PRACTICAR!

Look up each word and fill in its opposite:

mojado _____

liso _____

delgado _____

limpio _____

pequeño _____

duro _____

caro _____

The purpose

El propósito *(ehl proh-'poh-see-toh)*

Before you say anything else, follow up your introduction with a brief explanation for the visit. After you give your name and title, tell them where you're from:

I'm from (the) . . .	**Soy de . . .** *('soh-ee deh)*
agency	**la agencia** *(lah ah-'hehn-see-ah)*
association	**la asociación** *(lah ah-soh-see-ah-see-'ohn)*
center	**el centro** *(ehl 'sehn-troh)*
city	**la ciudad** *(lah see-oo-'dahd)*
class	**la clase** *(lah 'klah-seh)*
clinic	**la clínica** *(lah 'klee-nee-kah)*
club	**el club** *(ehl kloob)*
committee	**el comité** *(ehl koh-mee-'teh)*
convalescent home	**la clínica de reposo**
	(lah 'klee-nee-kah deh reh-'poh-soh)
council	**el consejo** *(ehl kohn-'seh-hoh)*
crew	**la tripulación** *(lah tree-poo-lah-see-'ohn)*
foundation	**la fundación** *(lah foon-dah-see-'ohn)*
group	**el grupo** *(ehl 'groo-poh)*
hospital	**el hospital** *(ehl ohs-pee-'tahl)*
institution	**la institución** *(lah eens-tee-too-see-'ohn)*
league	**la liga** *(lah 'lee-gah)*
local church	**la iglesia local** *(lah eeg-'leh-see-ah loh-'kahl)*
neighborhood	**el vecindario** *(ehl veh-seen-'dah-ree-oh)*
orphanage	**el orfanato** *(ehl ohr-fah-'nah-toh)*
shelter	**el refugio** *(ehl reh-'foo-hee-oh)*
team	**el equipo** *(ehl eh-'kee-poh)*

And here is another easy pattern:

We go to (the) . . .	**Vamos a . . .** *('vah-mohs ah)*
cathedral	**la catedral** *(lah kah-teh-'drahl)*
chapel	**la capilla** *(lah kah-'pee-yah)*
church	**la iglesia** *(lah eeg-'leh-see-ah)*

convent	**el convento** *(ehl kohn-'vehn-toh)*
mission	**la misión** *(lah mee-see-'ohn)*
mosque	**la mesquita** *(lah mehs-'kee-tah)*
parish	**la parroquia** *(lah pah-'rroh-kee-ah)*
school	**la escuela** *(lah ehs-'kweh-lah)*
seminary	**el seminario** *(ehl seh-mee-'nah-ree-oh)*
synagogue	**la sinagoga** *(lah see-nah-'goh-gah)*
temple	**el templo** *(ehl 'tehm-ploh)*

Most of the time it's okay to use English when you name your club or association:

It's called (the) . . .   **Se llama** . . . *(seh 'yah-mah)*

Alcoholics Anonymous	Kiwanis Club
American Legion	Lions Club
Amnesty International	Make-a-Wish Foundation
Big Brothers	Meals on Wheels
Big Sisters	Moose Lodge
Boy Scouts	Operation Hope
Boys Club	Peace Corps
Chamber of Commerce	Planned Parenthood
Easter Seals	Red Cross
Elks Lodge	Ronald MacDonald House
Girl Scouts	Rotary Club
Girls Club	Salvation Army
Habitat for Humanity	Toastmasters
Headstart	United Way

Describe the organization
Describa la organización
(dehs-'kree-bah lah ohr-gah-nee-sah-see-'ohn)

It's . . .   **Es** . . . *(ehs)*

charitable	**benéfico** *(beh-'neh-fee-koh)*
crosscultural	**intercultural** *(een-tehr-kool-too-'rahl)*

humanitarian	**humanitario** *(oo-mah-nee-'tah-ree-oh)*
international	**internacional** *(een-tehr-nah-see-oh-'nahl)*
nonprofit	**sin fines lucrativos**
	(seen 'fee-nehs loo-krah-'tee-vohs)
private	**privado** *(pree-'vah-doh)*
public	**público** *('poob-lee-koh)*
tax-deductible	**desgravable** *(dehs-grah-'vah-bleh)*

It's (the) . . .	**Es . . .** *(ehs)*
Bible study group	**el grupo de estudio bíblico**
	(ehl 'groo-poh deh ehs-'too-dee-oh 'beeb-lee-koh)
Christian organization	**la organización cristiana**
	(lah ohr-gah-nee-sah-see-'ohn krees-tee-'ah-nah)

It's a . . .	**Es una . . .** *(ehs 'oo-nah)*
brotherhood	**cofradía** *(koh-frah-'dee-ah)*
coalition	**coalición** *(koh-ah-lee-see-'ohn)*
fraternity	**congregación** *(kohn-greh-gah-see-'ohn)*
guild	**corporación** *(kohr-poh-rah-see-'ohn)*
network	**cadena** *(kah-'deh-nah)*
partnership	**sociedad** *(soh-see-eh-'dahd)*

¡MÁS AYUDA!

• Acronyms are confusing and require more of an explanatory translation than a literal one. These are too complicated for pronunciation; just point with the finger.

NAACP	**Asociación Nacional para el Progreso de Gente de Color**
UNICEF	**Fondo Nacional de Emergencia de las Naciones Unidas para los Niños**
USO	**Unión de Organizaciones de las Fuerzas Armadas**
4H Club	**Organización de Fomento Agrícola para Jóvenes**

YMCA	**Asociación de Jóvenes Cristianos**
YWCA	**Asociación de Jóvenes Cristianas**
HUD	**Desarrollo Urbano y de Vivienda**

• Several federally funded groups participate in outreach, too:

National Safety Council	**Consejo de Seguridad Nacional**
National Urban League	**Liga Urbana Nacional**
National Endowment for the Arts	**Dotación Gubernamental para las Artes**

• Learn these words if you belong to an educational institution:

We have (the) . . .	**Tenemos . . .** *(teh-'neh-mohs)*
academy	**la academia** *(lah ah-kah-'deh-mee-ah)*
college or university	**la universidad** *(lah oo-nee-vehr-see-'dahd)*
district	**el distrito** *(ehl dees-'tree-toh)*
institute	**el instituto** *(ehl eens-tee-'too-toh)*
nursery school	**el parvulario** *(ehl pahr-voo-'lah-ree-oh)*
primary school	**la escuela primaria** *(lah ehs-'kweh-lah pree-'mah-ree-ah)*
secondary school	**la escuela secundaria** *(lah ehs-'kweh-lah seh-koon-'dah-ree-ah)*

• Practice pronunciation with the various institutions below, and try to make sentences with them.

I work with the . . .	**Trabajo con . . .** *(trah-'bah-hoh kohn)*
benevolent society	**la sociedad caritativa** *(lah soh-see-eh-'dahd kah-ree-tah-'tee-vah)*
charitable institution	**la institución benéfica** *(lah eens-tee-too-see-'ohn beh-'neh-fee-kah)*
civil service club	**el club de servicio civil** *(ehl kloob deh sehr-'vee-see-oh see-'veel)*
fraternal order	**la orden fraternal** *(lah 'ohr-dehn frah-tehr-'nahl)*
halfway house	**el hogar de transición** *(ehl oh-'gahr deh trahn-see-see-'ohn)*

local welcoming committee	**el comité local de bienvenida** *(ehl koh-mee-'teh loh-'kahl deh bee-ehn-veh-'nee-dah)*
neighborhood outreach group	**el grupo comunitario de ayuda** *(ehl 'groo-poh koh-moo-nee-'tah-ree-oh deh ah-'yoo-dah)*
religious affiliation	**la afiliación religiosa** *(lah ah-fee-lee-ah-see-'ohn reh-lee-hee-'oh-sah)*
social action organization	**la organización de acción social** *(lah ohr-gah-nee-sah-see-'ohn deh ahk-see-'ohn soh-see-'ahl)*
treatment center	**el centro de tratamiento** *(ehl 'sehn-troh deh trah-tah-mee-'ehn-toh)*

¡*N E C E S I T A   P R A C T I C A R* !

Name three religious facilities in Spanish.
Name three educational facilities in Spanish.
Name three benevolent organizations in Spanish.

How can I help you?
¿En qué puedo servirle?
(ehn keh 'pweh-doh sehr-'veer-leh)

Now use the patterns below to explain the reason for your visit.

I'd like to . . .	**Quisiera . . .** *(kee-see-'eh-rah)*
speak with _____	**hablar con** _____ *(ah-'blahr kohn)*
know what happened	**saber qué pasó** *(sah-'behr keh pah-'soh)*
practice Spanish	**practicar español** *(prahk-tee-'kahr ehs-pahn-'yohl)*
explain	**explicar** *(ehks-plee-'kahr)*
recommend	**recomendar** *(reh-koh-mehn-'dahr)*

check	**averiguar** *(ah-veh-ree-'gwahr)*
see if you're available	**ver si usted está disponible**
	(vehr see oos-'tehd ehs-'tah dees-poh-'nee-bleh)
discuss this	**tratar esto** *(trah-'tahr 'ehs-toh)*
have some information	**tener alguna información**
	(teh-'nehr ahl-'goo-nah een-fohr-mah-see-'ohn)

Notice how this selection of verbs uses **le** to express "you":

I want to . . .	**Quiero . . .** *(kee-'eh-roh)*
say hello to you	**saludarle** *(sah-loo-'dahr-leh)*
invite you	**invitarle** *(een-vee-'tahr-leh)*
get to know you better	**conocerle mejor**
	(koh-noh-'sehr-leh meh-'hohr)
tell you something	**decirle algo** *(deh-'seer-leh 'ahl-goh)*
give you this	**darle esto** *(dahr-leh 'ehs-toh)*
ask you a question	**preguntarle** *(preh-goon-'tahr-leh)*
introduce _____ to you	**presentarle a** _____
	(pre-sehn-'tahr-leh ah)
ask your permission	**pedirle permiso**
	(peh-'deer-leh pehr-'mee-soh)
send you	**enviarle** *(ehn-vee-'ahr-leh)*
offer you	**ofrecerle** *(oh-freh-'sehr-leh)*
call you later	**llamarle más tarde**
	(yah-'mahr-leh mahs 'tahr-deh)
return this to you	**devolverle esto**
	(deh-vohl-'vehr-leh 'ehs-toh)
leave this with you	**dejarle esto** *(deh-'hahr-leh 'ehs-toh)*
You're invited to (the) . . .	**Le invitamos a . . .**
	(leh een-vee-'tah-mohs ah)
Please come to (the) . . .	**Por favor, venga a . . .**
	(pohr fah-'vohr 'vehn-gah ah)
assembly	**la asamblea** *(lah ah-sahm-'bleh-ah)*

celebration	**la celebración** *(lah seh-leh-brah-see-'ohn)*
ceremony	**la ceremonia** *(lah seh-reh-'moh-nee-ah)*
conference	**la conferencia** *(lah kohn-feh-'rehn-see-ah)*
course	**el curso** *(ehl 'koor-soh)*
dance	**el baile** *(ehl 'bah-ee-leh)*
event	**el evento** *(ehl eh-'vehn-toh)*
gathering	**la junta** *(la 'hoon-tah)*
meeting	**la reunión** *(lah reh-oo-nee-'ohn)*
party	**la fiesta** *(lah fee-'ehs-tah)*
program	**el programa** *(ehl proh-'grah-mah)*
seminar	**el seminario** *(ehl seh-mee-'nah-ree-oh)*
session	**la sesión** *(lah seh-see-'ohn)*
tribute	**el tributo** *(ehl tree-'boo-toh)*

It's about . . .	**Tiene que ver con . . .** *(tee-'ehn-neh keh vehr kohn)*
child care	**el cuidado del niño**
	(ehl kwee-'dah-doh dehl neen-'yoh)
family	**la familia** *(lah fah-'mee-lee-ah)*
guidance	**la orientación** *(lah oh-ree-ehn-tah-see-'ohn)*
marriage	**el matrimonio** *(ehl mah-tree-'moh-nee-oh)*
parenting skills	**el entrenamiento paternal**
	(ehl ehn-treh-nah-mee-'ehn-toh pah-tehr-'nahl)
psychotherapy	**la psicoterapia** *(lah see-koh-teh-'rah-pee-ah)*
public education	**la educación pública**
	(lah eh-doo-kah-see-'ohn 'poob-lee-kah)
safety	**la seguridad** *(lah seh-goo-ree-'dahd)*

Local social activities
Las actividades sociales locales
(lahs ahk-tee-vee-'dah-dehs soh-see-'ah-lehs loh-'kah-lehs)

Can you attend (the) . . . ?	**¿Puede asistir a . . . ?**
	(pweh-deh ah-sees-'teer ah)
auction	**la subasta** *(lah soo-'bahs-tah)*
banquet	**el banquete** *(ehl bahn-'keh-teh)*

fair	**la feria** *(la 'feh-ree-ah)*
festival	**el festival** *(ehl fehs-tee-'vahl)*
game	**el juego** *(ehl 'hweh-goh)*
parade	**el desfile** *(ehl dehs-'fee-leh)*
performance	**la función** *(lah foon-see-'ohn)*
picnic	**la merienda campestre**
	(lah meh-ree-'ehn-dah kahm-'pehs-treh)
raffle	**el sorteo** *(ehl sohr-'teh-oh)*
show	**el espectáculo**
	(ehl ehs-pehk-'tah-koo-loh)
summer camp	**el campamento del verano**
	(ehl kahm-pah-'mehn-toh deh veh-'rah-noh)
Can you . . . ?	**¿Puede . . . ?** *(pweh-deh)*
attend	**asistir** *(ah-sees-'teer)*
deliver	**entregar** *(ehn-treh-gahr)*
enroll	**matricular** *(mah-tree-koo-'lahr)*
go	**ir** *(eer)*
park	**estacionar** *(ehs-tah-see-oh-'nahr)*
sign	**firmar** *(feer-'mahr)*
try	**tratar** *(trah-'tahr)*
visit	**visitar** *(vee-see-'tahr)*
Do you want (the) . . . ?	**¿Quiere . . . ?** *(kee-'eh-reh)*
application	**la solicitud** *(lah soh-lee-see-'tood)*
directions	**las instrucciones**
	(lahs eens-trook-see-'oh-nehs)
form	**el formulario** *(ehl fohr-moo-'lah-ree-oh)*
information	**la información** *(lah een-fohr-mah-see-'ohn)*
list	**la lista** *(lah 'lees-tah)*
map	**el mapa** *(ehl 'mah-pah)*
schedule	**el horario** *(ehl oh-'rah-ree-oh)*
Here's (the) . . .	**Aquí tiene . . .** *(ah-'kee tee-'eh-neh)*
date	**la fecha** *(lah 'feh-chah)*
name	**el nombre** *(ehl 'nohm-breh)*

number	**el número** *(ehl 'noo-meh-roh)*
place	**el lugar** *(ehl loo-'gahr)*
time	**la hora** *(lah 'oh-rah)*

It is . . .	**Es . . .** *(ehs)*
free	**gratis** *('grah-tees)*
fun	**divertido** *(dee-vehr-'tee-doh)*
important	**importante** *(eem-pohr-'tahn-teh)*
necessary	**necesario** *(neh-seh-'sah-ree-oh)*
serious	**serio** *('seh-ree-oh)*
urgent	**urgente** *(oor-'hehn-teh)*
worthwhile	**valioso** *(vah-lee-'oh-soh)*

These are the hours. **Estas son las horas.**
('ehs-tahs sohn lahs 'oh-rahs)

You have to arrive early. **Tiene que llegar temprano.**
(tee-'eh-neh keh yeh-'gahr tehm-'prah-noh)

Don't be late. **No llegue tarde.** *(noh 'yeh-geh 'tahr-deh)*

¡ M Á S   A Y U D A !

• While looking for contributions, use this phrase to explain yourself:

We need money for (the) . . . **Necesitamos el dinero para . . .**
(neh-seh-see-'tah-mohs ehl dee-'neh-roh 'pah-rah)

charity	**la caridad** *(lah kah-ree-'dahd)*
clothing	**la ropa** *(lah 'roh-pah)*
donations	**las donaciones**
	(lahs doh-nah-see-'oh-nehs)
gifts	**los regalos** *(lohs reh-'gah-lohs)*
lodging	**la habitación** *(lah ah-bee-tah-see-'ohn)*
meals	**las comidas** *(lahs koh-'mee-dahs)*
relief	**la ayuda** *(lah ah-'yoo-dah)*
research	**la investigación**
	(lah een-vehs-tee-gah-see-'ohn)

Continue to practice:

It's for (the) . . .	**Es para . . .** *(ehs 'pah-rah)*
abused	**los abusados** *(lohs ah-boo-'sah-dohs)*
blind	**los ciegos** *(lohs see-'eh-gohs)*
deaf	**los sordos** *(lohs 'sohr-dohs)*
disadvantaged	**los desfavorecidos**
	(lohs dehs-fah-voh-reh-'see-dohs)
elderly	**los ancianos** *(lohs ahn-see-'ah-nohs)*
helpless	**los indefensos** *(lohs een-deh-'fehn-sohs)*
homeless	**los desamparados** *(lohs deh-sahm-pah-'rah-dohs)*
hungry	**los hambrientos** *(lohs ahm-bree-'ehn-tohs)*
orphans	**los huérfanos** *(lohs oo-'ehr-fah-nohs)*
poor	**los pobres** *(lohs 'poh-brehs)*
sick	**los enfermos** *(lohs ehn-'fehr-mohs)*
survivors	**los sobrevivientes** *(lohs soh-breh-vee-vee-'ehn-tehs)*
victims	**las víctimas** *(lahs 'veek-tee-mahs)*

• If you work out of an office, and wish to attend to all who happen to drop by:

With whom would you like to speak?
¿Con quién quiere hablar? *(kohn kee-'ehn kee-'eh-reh ah-'blahr)*

Someone will help you in a few minutes.
Alguien le atenderá en algunos minutos.
('ahl-gee-ehn leh ah-tehn-deh-'rah ehn ahl-'goo-nohs mee-'noo-tohs)

Please have a seat.
Por favor, tome asiento. *(pohr fah-'vohr 'toh-meh ah-see-'ehn-toh)*

• Check out the word order:

fire department	**el cuartel de bomberos**
	(ehl kwahr-'tehl deh bohm-'beh-rohs)
health department	**el departamento de salud**
	(ehl deh-pahr-tah-'mehn-toh deh sah-'lood)
housing department	**el departamento de viviendas**
	(ehl deh-pahr-tah-'mehn-toh deh vee-vee-'ehn-dahs)

¡NECESITA PRACTICAR!

Translate these sentences into Spanish:

I'd like to discuss this program.

_____

I want to leave this with you.

_____

It's about family and marriage.

_____

We need money for the homeless.

_____

Can you go to the meeting?

_____

Personal information
La información personal
(lah een-fohr-mah-see-'ohn pehr-soh-'nahl)

The following vocabulary will help you gather personal information.

What is your . . . ?	**¿Cuál es su . . . ?** *(kwahl ehs soo)*
address	**dirección** *(dee-rehk-see-'ohn)*
telephone	**teléfono** *(teh-'leh-foh-noh)*
age	**edad** *(eh-'dahd)*
date of birth	**fecha de nacimiento**
	('feh-chah deh nah-see-mee-'ehn-toh)
first language	**lengua materna** *('lehn-gwah mah-'tehr-nah)*
first name	**primer nombre** *(pree-'mehr 'nohm-breh)*
last name	**apellido** *(ah-peh-'yee-doh)*
maiden name	**nombre de soltera**
	('nohm-breh deh sohl-'teh-rah)
middle initial	**segunda inicial** *(seh-'goon-dah ee-nee-see-'ahl)*

nationality	**nacionalidad** *(nah-see-oh-nah-lee-'dahd)*
nickname	**apodo** *(ah-'poh-doh)*
place of birth	**lugar de nacimiento**
	(loo-'gahr deh nah-see-mee-'ehn-toh)
race	**raza** *('rah-sah)*
relationship	**relación** *(reh-lah-see-'ohn)*
zip code	**zona postal** *('soh-nah pohs-'tahl)*

Here's another helpful pattern:

What's your _____ number?	¿**Cuál es su número de** _____?
	(kwahl ehs soo 'noo-meh-roh deh)
apartment	**apartamento**
	(ah-pahr-tah-'mehn-toh)
code	**código** *('koh-dee-goh)*
I .D.	**identificación**
	(ee-dehn-tee-fee-kah-see-'ohn)
license	**licencia** *(lee-'sehn-see-ah)*
social security	**seguro social**
	(seh-'goo-roh soh-see-'ahl)
telephone	**teléfono** *(teh-'leh-foh-noh)*

Tell me about yourself
Hábleme de usted mismo
('ah-bleh-meh deh oos-'tehd 'mees-moh)

Seldom will you be able to provide help without first doing an interview. Although we've covered a few personal questions already, this next selection will go into greater detail. Notice the **(a)** ending for females:

Are you . . . ?	¿**Es usted . . . ?** *(ehs oos-'tehd)*
divorced	**divorciado(a)** *(dee-vohr-see-'ah-doh, dah)*
married	**casado(a)** *(kah-'sah-doh, dah)*
separated	**separado(a)** *(seh-pah-'rah-doh, dah)*
single	**soltero(a)** *(sohl-'teh-roh, rah)*

widowed	**viudo(a)** *(vee-'oo-doh, dah)*
Cuban	**cubano(a)** *(koo-'bah-noh, nah)*
Guatemalan	**guatemalteco(a)**
	(gwah-teh-mahl-'teh-koh, kah)
Mexican	**mexicano(a)** *(meh-hee-'kah-noh, nah)*
Puerto Rican	**puertorriqueño(a)**
	(pwehr-toh-rree-'kehn-yoh, yah)
Spanish	**español(a)** *(ehs-pahn-'yohl, 'yoh-lah)*

Pronounce this list of religions, and change the ending to **a** to address females.

Are you . . . ?	¿**Es usted . . . ?** *(ehs oos-'tehd)*	
Baptist	**bautista** *(bah-oo-'tees-tah)*	**bautista**
Buddhist	**budista** *(boo-'dees-tah)*	_____
Catholic	**católico** *(kah-'toh-lee-koh)*	_____
Christian	**cristiano** *(krees-tee-'ah-noh)*	_____
Jewish	**judío** *(hoo-'dee-oh)*	_____
Lutheran	**luterano** *(loo-teh-'rah-noh)*	**luterana**
Methodist	**metodista** *(meh-toh-'dees-tah)*	_____
Mormon	**mormón** *(mohr-'mohn)*	_____
Moslem	**musulmán** *(moo-sool-'mahn)*	_____
Orthodox	**ortodoxo** *(ohr-toh-'dohk-soh)*	_____
Presbyterian	**presbiteriano**	_____
	(prehs-bee-teh ree-'ah-noh)	_____
Protestant	**protestante** *(proh-tehs-'tahn-teh)*	_____

And don't forget to use the verb **tener** ("to have"):

Do you have (the) . . . ?	¿**Tiene . . . ?** *(tee-'eh-neh)*
appointment	**la cita** *(lah 'see-tah)*
employment	**el empleo** *(ehl ehm-'pleh-oh)*
form	**el formulario** *(ehl fohr-moo-'lah-ree-oh)*
insurance	**el seguro** *(ehl seh-'goo-roh)*
money	**el dinero** *(ehl dee-'neh-roh)*
transportation	**el transporte** *(ehl trahns-'pohr-teh)*

¡MÁS AYUDA!

• Practice these delicate questions:

Let's talk about (the) . . .	**Vamos a hablar de . . .**
	('vah-mohs ah ah-'blahr deh)
financial problems	**los problemas financieros**
	(lohs proh-'bleh-mahs fee-nahn-see-'eh-rohs)
personal problems	**los problemas personales**
	(lohs proh-'bleh-mahs pehr-soh-'nah-lehs)
medical problems	**los problemas médicos**
	(lohs pro-'bleh-mahs 'meh-dee-kohs)

• Be careful with your pronunciation as you try out the pattern below:

Have you . . . ?	**¿Ha . . . ?** *(ah)*
been arrested	**sido arrestado** *('see-doh ah-rrehs-'tah-doh)*
studied English	**estudiado inglés**
	('ehs-too-dee-'ah-doh een-'glehs)
received help	**recibido ayuda** *(reh-see-'bee-doh ah-'yoo-dah)*

¡NECESITA PRACTICAR!

Complete the personal questionnaire:

Nombre completo _____

Número de seguro social _____

Lugar de nacimiento _____

Words that tell where
Palabras que indican dónde
(pah-'lah-brahs keh een-'dee-kahn 'dohn-deh)

As you move through the room, be sure to know where everything is located.

It's . . .	**Está . . .** *(ehs-'tah)*
above	**encima** *(ehn-'see-mah)*
at the bottom	**al fondo** *(ahl 'fohn-doh)*
behind	**detrás** *(deh-'trahs)*
down	**abajo** *(ah-'bah-hoh)*
far	**lejos** *('leh-hohs)*
here	**aquí** *(ah 'koo)*
in front of	**enfrente de** *(ehn-'frehn-teh deh)*
inside	**dentro de** *('dehn-troh deh)*
next to	**al lado de** *(ahl 'lah-doh deh)*
outside	**afuera** *(ah-'fweh-rah)*
over there	**allá** *(ah-'yah)*
straight ahead	**adelante** *(ah-deh-'lahn-teh)*
there	**allí** *(ah-'yee)*
to the left	**a la izquierda** *(ah la ees-kee-'ehr-dah)*
near	**cerca** *('sehr-kah)*
to the right	**a la derecha** *(ah lah deh-'reh-chah)*
up	**arriba** *(ah-'rree-bah)*

If a geographical location is required, then say "it's in the . . ." **está al . . .** *(ehs-'tah ahl)*

east	**este** *('ehs-teh)*
north	**norte** *('nohr-teh)*
south	**sur** *(soor)*
west	**oeste** *(oh-'ehs-teh)*

¡ M á s   A y u d a !

- Check out these popular variations of the word **dónde** *('dohn-deh)*:

Where are you from?	**¿De dónde es?** *(deh 'dohn-deh ehs)*
Where did you go?	**¿Adónde fue?** *(ah-'dohn-deh fweh)*

- You'll need these for larger dwellings and buildings:

first floor	**primer piso** *(pree-'mehr 'pee-soh)*
second floor	**segundo piso** *(seh-'goon-doh 'pee-soh)*
third floor	**tercer piso** *(tehr-'sehr 'pee-soh)*

- By the way, **en** *(ehn)*, meaning "in," "on," and "at," is one of the most commonly used words in Spanish. Watch:

She's in her apartment,	**Está <u>en</u> su apartmento,**
	(ehs-'tah ehn soo ah-pahr-tah-'mehn-toh)
on the second floor,	**<u>en</u> el segundo piso,**
	(ehn ehl seh-'goon-doh 'pee-soh)
at her table.	**<u>en</u> su mesa.** *(ehn soo 'meh-sah)*

- And always use **estar** instead of **ser** when you deal with location:

The man is here.	**El hombre está aquí.**
	(ehl 'ohm-breh ehs-'tah a-'kee)

- Be familiar with as many location words as you can:

It's . . .	**Está . . .** *(ehs-'tah)*
face down	**boca abajo** *('boh-kah ah-'bah-hoh)*
face up	**boca arriba** *('boh-kah ah-'rree-bah)*
on its way	**en camino** *(ehn kah-'mee-noh)*
backwards, inside out or upside down	**al revés** *(ahl reh-'vehs)*
in back	**atrás** *(ah-'trahs)*
in front	**al frente** *(ahl 'frehn-teh)*
in the middle	**al medio** *(ahl 'meh-dee-oh)*

at the corner	**en la esquina** *(ehn lah ehs-'kee-nah)*
on the side	**al lado** *(ahl 'lah-doh)*
along	**a lo largo** *(ah loh 'lahr-goh)*
around	**alrededor** *(ahl-reh-deh-'dohr)*
between	**entre** *('ehn-treh)*
over	**sobre** *('soh-breh)*
toward	**hacia** *('ah-see-ah)*

¡NECESITA PRACTICAR!

This group of opposites should be simple. Just draw a line to connect each pair:

adentro	**derecha**
abajo	**arriba**
izquierda	**norte**
sur	**cerca**
lejos	**afuera**
detrás	**al frente**

¡LA CULTURA!

Trust is very important in the Hispanic culture. Throughout the visit, feel free to open up about yourself, your family, your work, and your home. If they are visiting you, consider showing your new friends pictures of your family. Don't be shy, always be honest, and make them feel at home.

Words that tell *when*

Palabras que expresan *cuándo*

(pah-'lah-brahs keh ehks-'preh-sahn 'kwahn-doh)

One of the most frequently asked questions in the field of outreach is "when?" Be prepared. Begin by learning the most popular responses:

afterward	**después** *(dehs-'pwehs)*
always	**siempre** *(see-'ehm-preh)*
before	**antes** *('ahn-tehs)*
early	**temprano** *(tehm-'prah-noh)*
late	**tarde** *('tahr-deh)*
later	**más tarde** *(mahs 'tahr-deh)*
never	**nunca** *('noon-kah)*
now	**ahora** *(ah-'oh-rah)*
often	**a menudo** *(ah meh-'noo-doh)*
once	**una vez** *('oo-nah vehs)*
sometimes	**a veces** *(ah 'veh-sehs)*
soon	**pronto** *('prohn-toh)*
then	**entonces** *(ehn-'tohn-sehs)*
today	**hoy** *('oh-ee)*
tomorrow	**mañana** *(mahn-'yah-nah)*
tonight	**esta noche** *('ehs-tah 'noh-cheh)*
yesterday	**ayer** *(ah-'yehr)*

¡MÁS AYUDA!

• All sorts of time expressions will be needed. A good way to learn is to group your related phrases into sets of three:

last month	**el mes pasado** *(ehl mehs pah-'sah-doh)*
last night	**anoche** *(ah-'noh-cheh)*
last week	**la semana pasada**
	(lah seh-'mah-nah pah-'sah-dah)
next month	**el próximo mes** *(ehl 'prohk-see-moh mehs)*

next week	**la próxima semana**
	(lah 'prohk-see-mah seh-'mah-nah)
next year	**el próximo año**
tomorrow morning	**mañana por la mañana**
	(mahn-'yah-nah pohr lah mahn-'yah-nah)
the day before yesterday	**anteayer** *(ahn-teh-ah-'yehr)*
the day after tomorrow	**pasado mañana**
	(pah-'sah-doh mahn-'yah-nah)
in a moment	**en un momento** *(ehn oon moh-'mehn-toh)*
in a while	**en un rato** *(ehn oon 'rah-toh)*
in a minute	**en un minuto** *(ehn oon mee-'noo-toh)*
at dawn	**a la madrugada**
	(ah lah mah-droo-'gah-dah)
at dusk	**al anochecer** *(ahl ah-noh-cheh-'sehr)*
at sunset	**a la puesta del sol**
	(ah lah 'pwehs-tah dehl sohl)
each day	**cada día** *('kah-dah 'dee-ah)*
every day	**todos los días** *('toh-dohs lohs 'dee-ahs)*
daily	**a diario** *(ah dee-'ah-ree-oh)*
yet	**todavía** *(toh-dah-'vee-ah)*
just	**apenas** *(ah-'peh-nahs)*
already	**ya** *(yah)*

• The best way to learn how to use question words is to focus on the first word of each sentence and then try to get a general feel for what the person might be asking. Attempting to translate every word will only lead to frustration.

• "Time" in general is **el tiempo** *(ehl tee-'ehm-poh)*. The specific time is **la hora** *(lah 'oh-rah)*. "Time" in reference to an ocurrence is **la vez** *(lah vehs)*.

Telling time

Decir la hora *(deh-'seer lah 'oh-rah)*

You can't discuss your outreach activities without mentioning the clock. To read the clock in Spanish, simply give the hour, followed by the word **y** ("and"), and the minutes. For example, 8:15 is **ocho y quince** *('oh-choh ee 'keen-seh)*. Read through these other questions and answers:

What time is it?	**¿Qué hora es?** *(keh 'oh-rah ehs)*
At what time?	**¿A qué hora?** *(ah keh 'oh-rah)*
On time	**a tiempo** *(ah tee-'ehm-poh)*
A.M.	**de la mañana** *(deh lah mahn-'yah-nah)*
P.M.	**de la tarde** *(deh lah 'tahr-deh)*
It's . . .	**Son las . . .** *(sohn lahs)*
At . . .	**A las . . .** *(ah lahs)*
10:40	**diez y cuarenta** *(dee-'ehs ee kwah-'rehn-tah)*
3:25	**tres y veinte y cinco**
	(trehs ee 'veh-een-teh ee 'seen-koh)
12:05 A.M.	**doce y cinco de la mañana** *('doh-seh ee 'seen-*
koh	*deh lah mahn-'yah-nah)*
4:00 P.M.	**cuatro de la tarde**
	('kwah-troh deh lah 'tahr-deh)
9:30 P.M.	**nueve y treinta de la noche**
	('nweh-veh ee 'treh-een-tah deh lah 'noh-cheh)

¡ *M Á S   A Y U D A !*

• For 1:00–1:59, use **Es la . . .** *(ehs lah)* instead of **Son las . . .** *(sohn lahs).* For example:

It's one o'clock.	**Es la una.** *(ehs lah 'oo-nah)*
It's one-thirty.	**Es la una y treinta.**
	(ehs lah 'oo-nah ee 'treh-een-tah)

What day?

¿Qué día? *(keh 'dee-ah)*

Spend a few minutes learning the days of the week. They'll allow you to say things about the calendar and to make schedules.

THE DAYS OF THE WEEK	LOS DÍAS DE LA SEMANA
	(lohs 'dee-ahs deh lah se-'mah-nah)
Monday	**lunes** *('loo-nehs)*
Tuesday	**martes** *('mahr-tehs)*
Wednesday	**miércoles** *(mee-'ehr-koh-lehs)*
Thursday	**jueves** *('hweh-vehs)*
Friday	**viernes** *(vee-'ehr-nehs)*
Saturday	**sábado** *('sah-bah-doh)*
Sunday	**domingo** *(doh-'meen-goh)*

Now read these questions and answers. See how **los días** *(lohs 'dee-ahs)* function as one-word responses to "when" questions:

When do they have meetings?	**¿Cuándo tienen las reuniones?**
	('kwahn-doh tee-'eh-nen lahs reh-oo-nee-'oh-nehs)
Tuesday and Thursday	**El martes y el jueves**
	(ehl 'mahr-tehs ee ehl 'hweh-vehs)
When is the service?	**¿Cuándo es el servicio?**
	('kwahn-doh ehs ehl sehr-'vee-see-oh)
Sunday	**El domingo** *(ehl doh-'meen-goh)*
When are we going there?	**¿Cuándo vamos allá?**
	('kwahn-doh 'vah-mohs ah-'yah)
Friday	**El viernes** *(ehl vee-'ehr-nehs)*

Did you notice that the Spanish days of the week are lowercased?

¡MÁS AYUDA!

• Most students of Spanish get confused when using the words **por** *(pohr)* and **para** *('pah-rah)* because they are similar in meaning. The differences between the two are not easy to explain, so it may be best to listen to Spanish speakers as they use them, and try them out in short, practical phrases.

by Friday	**para el viernes**
	('pah-rah ehl vee-'ehr-nehs)
for two days	**por dos días** *(pohr dohs 'dee-ahs)*
in order to go	**para ir** *('pah-rah eer)*
throughout the afternoon	**por la tarde** *(pohr lah 'tahr-deh)*

• "On Friday" is **el viernes** *(ehl vee-'ehr-nehs)* but "on Fridays" is **los viernes** *(lohs vee-'ehr-nehs)*.

• Use **¿Hace cuánto?** *('ah-seh 'kwahn-toh)* for "How long ago?"

How long ago?	**¿Hace cuánto?** *('ah-seh 'kwahn-toh)*
Two weeks ago.	**Hace dos semanas.**
	('ah-seh dohs seh-'mah-nahs)

What month?
¿Qué mes? *(keh mehs)*

As far as the months are concerned, most are similar in both Spanish and English.

THE MONTHS OF THE YEAR	LOS MESES DEL AÑO
	(lohs 'meh-sehs dehl 'ahn-yoh)
January	**enero** *(eh-'neh-roh)*
February	**febrero** *(feh-'breh-roh)*
March	**marzo** *('mahr-soh)*
April	**abril** *(ah-'breel)*

May	**mayo** *('mah-yoh)*
June	**junio** *('hoo-nee-oh)*
July	**julio** *('hoo-lee-oh)*
August	**agosto** *(ah-'gohs-toh)*
September	**septiembre** *(seh-tee-'ehm-breh)*
October	**octubre** *(ohk-'too-breh)*
November	**noviembre** *(noh-vee-'ehm-breh)*
December	**diciembre** *(dee-see-'ehm-breh)*

What's the date?

¿Cuál es la fecha? *('kwahl ehs lah 'feh-chah)*

To give the date, reverse the order of your words. For example, February 2nd is **el dos de febrero** *(ehl dohs deh feh-'breh-roh)*.

And how do you say "the first" in Spanish? **El primero** *(ehl pree-'meh-roh)*.

January 1st	**el primero de enero**
	(ehl pree-'meh-roh deh eh-'neh-roh)

We have already seen the numbers, so years should be no problem.

2005	**dos mil cinco** *(dohs meel 'seen-koh)*
1998	**mil novecientos noventa y ocho**
	(meel no-veh-see-'ehn-tohs noh-'vehn-tah ee 'oh-choh)

Can you give today's date in Spanish? Use a calendar to practice your new vocabulary!

¡Más Ayuda!

• When working in any outreach situation, make the person feel comfortable about the conversation itself:

Let's . . .	**Vamos a . . .** *('vah-mohs ah)*
be alone	**estar solos** *(ehs-'tahr 'soh-lohs)*
chat	**platicar** *(plah-tee-'kahr)*
discuss it	**conversarlo** *(kohn-vehr-'sahr-loh)*
go out	**salir** *(sah-'leer)*
take a walk	**dar un paseo** *(dahr oon pah-'seh-oh)*

¡La Cultura!

Not all folks panic when it comes to the time—some cultures put less emphasis on "beating the clock" than others. Be direct, and explain the importance of punctuality in serious matters, but be sensitive to those who believe that personal health, family, and friends are valid reasons for being a little late.

¡Necesita Practicar!

Choose the best word to complete each series:

mes	ayer	a veces

siempre, nunca, _____

hoy, mañana, _____

día, semana, _____

Complete these lists, without any help:

lunes, martes, miércoles,

_____

enero, febrero, marzo,

_____

¡ A C C I Ó N !

We have learned that Spanish verbs change when we talk about current action (see the Present Progressive toward the end of Chapter 1).

To Speak   **Hablar** *(ah-'blahr)*
I'm speaking   **Estoy hablando.** *(ehs-'toh-ee ah-'blahn-doh)*

To Eat   **Comer** *(koh-'mehr)*
We're eating   **Estamos comiendo.** *(ehs-'tah-mohs koh-mee-'ehn-doh)*

To Write   **Escribir** *(ehs-kree-'beer)*
He's writing   **Está escribiendo.** *(ehs-'tah ehs-kree-bee-'ehn-doh)*

Now, the time has come to conjugate a few very important verbs. Have courage! Soon you will be creating fairly complex sentences!

To Speak   **Hablar** *(ah-'blahr)*
I speak   **hablo** *('ah-bloh)*
Hablo poco español. *('ah-bloh 'poh-koh ehs-pahn-'yohl)*

You speak; he, she speaks   **habla** *('ah-blah)*
Habla mucho inglés. *('ah-blah 'moo-choh een-'glehs)*

You (plural), they speak   **hablan** *('ah-blah)*
Hablan siempre. *('ah-blan see-'ehm-preh)*

We speak   **hablamos** *(ah-'blah-mohs)*
Hablamos hoy. *(ah-'blah-mohs 'oh-ee)*

To Eat   **Comer** *(koh-'mehr)*
I eat   **como** *('koh-moh)*
Como en mi casa. *('koh-moh ehn mee 'kah-sah)*

You eat; he, she eats   **come** *('koh-meh)*
¿Dónde come ella? *('dohn-deh 'koh-meh 'eh-yah)*

You (plural), they eat   **comen** *('koh-mehn)*
Ellos comen allá. *('eh-yohs 'koh-men ah-'yah)*

We eat   **comemos** *(koh-'meh-mohs)*
¿Comemos aquí? *(koh-'meh-mohs ah-'kee)*

To Write   **Escribir** *(ehs-kree-'beer)*
I write   **escribo** *(ehs-'kree-boh)*
Escribo en inglés. *(ehs-'kree-boh ehn een-'glehs)*

You write; he, she writes   **escribe** *(ehs-'kree-beh)*
El escribe y come. *(ehl ehs-'kree-beh ee 'koh-meh)*

You (plural), they write   **escriben** *(ehs-'kree-ben)*
Ustedes escriben y hablan. *(oos-'teh-dehs ehs-'kree-behn ee 'ah-blahn)*

We write   **escribimos** *(ehs-kree-'bee-mohs)*
Escribimos a veces. *(ehs-kree-'bee-mohs ah 'veh-sehs)*

¡ M Á S   A Y U D A !

• To describe an action word, try one of these:

completely	**completamente**	*(kohm-pleh-tah-'mehn-teh)*
quickly	**rápidamente**	*('rah-pee-dah-mehn-teh)*
slowly	**lentamente**	*(lehn-tah-'mehn-teh)*

• Serving people involves finding out their needs. To do so in Spanish, use the following expression of courtesy.

Would you like . . . ?   **¿Quisiera . . . ?** *(kee-see-'eh-rah)*

   to contribute something   **contribuir algo**
         (kohn-tree-boo-'eer 'ahl-goh)

   to fill out the form   **llenar el formulario**
         (yeh-'nahr ehl fohr-moo-'lah-ree-oh)

   to work with us   **trabajar con nosotros**
         (trah-bah-'hahr kohn noh-'soh-trohs)

   to see the pamphlet   **ver el folleto** *(vehr ehl foh-'yeh-toh)*

to speak with the director	**hablar con el director**
	(ah-'blahr kohn ehl dee-rehk-'tohr)
to have more information	**tener más información**
	(teh-'nehr mahs een-fohr-mah-see-'ohn)

¡ *L A S   O R D E N E S !*

A simple approach to forming a command in Spanish requires knowledge of the three different action word (verb) endings. As we stated before, the endings are:

ar *(ahr)* as in **hablar** *(ah-blahr)*
or *(ohr)* as in **comer** *(koh 'mohr)*
ir *(eer)* as in **escribir** *(ehs-kree-'beer)*

To make a command, drop the last two letters of the infinitive form and replace them as follows:

ar *(ahr)*	**e** *(eh)*
hablar *(ah-'blahr)*: to speak	**hable** *('ah-bleh)*: speak
er *(ehr)*	**a** *(ah)*
comer *(koh-'mehr)*: to eat	**coma** *('koh-mah)*: eat
ir *(eer)*	**a** *(ah)*
escribir *(ehs-kree-'beer)*: to write	**escriba** *(ehs-'kree-bah)*: write

But beware. Some verbs are irregular and simply have to be memorized.

To go: **ir** *(eer)*	Go (command): **vaya** *('vah-yah)*
To come: **venir** *(veh-'neer)*	Come (command): **venga** *('vehn-gah)*
To say: **decir** *(deh-'seer)*	Say (command): **diga** *('dee-gah)*

Chapter Three

Capítulo Tres
(kah-'pee-too-loh trehs)

Within the Community
Dentro de la comunidad
('dehn-troh deh lah koh-moo-nee-'dahd)

City Spanish
El español urbano
(ehl ehs-pahn-'yohl oor-'bah-noh)

Countless outreach programs take place in urban areas, so you must learn the appropriate vocabulary. Start off with some words that describe the general vicinity:

They live in (the) . . .	**Viven en . . .** *('vee-vehn ehn)*
area	**el área** *(ehl 'ah-reh-ah)*
border	**la frontera** *(lah frohn-'teh-rah)*
city	**la ciudad** *(lah see-oo-'dahd)*
community	**la comunidad** *(lah koh-moo-nee-'dahd)*
county	**el condado** *(ehl kohn-'dah-doh)*
district	**el distrito** *(ehl dees-'tree-toh)*
downtown	**el centro** *(ehl 'sehn-troh)*
neighborhood	**el vecindario** *(ehl veh-seen-'dah-ree-oh)*
outskirts	**las afueras** *(lahs ah-'fweh-rahs)*
site	**el sitio** *(ehl 'see-tee-oh)*
state	**el estado** *(ehl ehs-'tah-doh)*
town	**el pueblo** *(ehl 'pweh-bloh)*
village	**la villa** *(lah 'vee-yah)*
zone	**la zona** *(lah 'soh-nah)*

It's next to (the) . . .	**Está al lado de . . .**
	(ehs-'tah ahl 'lah-doh deh)
airport	**el aeropuerto** *(ehl ah-eh-roh-'pwehr-toh)*
bank	**el banco** *(ehl 'bahn-koh)*
beauty salon	**el salón de belleza**
	(ehl sah-'lohn deh beh-'yeh-sah)
bookstore	**la librería** *(lah lee-breh-'ree-ah)*
bus station	**la estación de autobús**
	(lah ehs-tah-see-'ohn deh ow-toh-'boos)
church	**la iglesia** *(lah eeg-'leh-see-ah)*
courthouse	**la corte** *(lah 'kohr-teh)*
factory	**la fábrica** *(lah 'fah-bree-kah)*
fire department	**el cuartel de bomberos**
	(ehl kwahr-'tehl deh bohm-'beh-rohs)
gas station	**la gasolinera** *(lah gah-soh-lee-'neh-rah)*
hospital	**el hospital** *(ehl ohs-pee-'tahl)*
library	**la biblioteca** *(lah beeb-lee-oh-'teh-kah)*
market	**el mercado** *(ehl mehr-'kah-doh)*
movie theater	**el cine** *(ehl 'see-neh)*
museum	**el museo** *(ehl moo-'seh-oh)*
office	**la oficina** *(lah oh-fee-'see-nah)*
park	**el parque** *(ehl 'pahr-keh)*
pharmacy	**la farmacia** *(lah fahr-'mah-see-ah)*
police station	**la estación de policía**
	(lah ehs-tah-see-'ohn deh poh-lee-'see-ah)
post office	**el correo** *(ehl koh-'rreh-oh)*
school	**la escuela** *(lah ehs-'kweh-lah)*
store	**la tienda** *(lah tee-'ehn-dah)*
We meet at (the) . . .	**Nos reunimos en . . .**
	(nohs reh-oo-'nee-mohs ehn)
auditorium	**el auditorio** *(ehl ow-dee-'toh-ree-oh)*
cafeteria	**la cafetería** *(lah kah-feh-teh-'ree-ah)*
gym	**el gimnasio** *(ehl heem-'nah-see-oh)*
stadium	**el estadio** *(ehl ehs-'tah-dee-oh)*

Familiarize yourself with everything around you. Call out their names as you pass by!

Look at (the) . . .	**Mire** . . . *('mee-reh)*
building	**el edificio** *(ehl eh-dee-'fee-see-oh)*
city block	**la cuadra** *(lah 'kwah-drah)*
parking lot	**el estacionamiento**
	(ehl ehs-tah-see-oh-nah-mee-'ehn-toh)
sidewalk	**la acera** *(lah ah-'seh-rah)*
street	**la calle** *(lah 'kah-yeh)*
traffic light	**el semáforo** *(ehl seh-'mah-foh-roh)*
I see (the) . . .	**Yo veo** . . . *(yoh 'veh-oh)*
billboard	**el letrero** *(ehl leh-'treh-roh)*
bridge	**el puent**e *(ehl 'pwehn-teh)*
bus stop	**la parada de autobús**
	(lah pah-'rah-dah deh ow-toh-'boos)
courtyard	**el patio** *(ehl 'pah-tee-oh)*
crosswalk	**el cruce de peatones**
	(ehl 'kroo-seh deh peh-ah-'toh-nehs)
fence	**la cerca** *(lah 'sehr-kah)*
fountain	**la fuente** *(lah 'fwehn-teh)*
parking meter	**el parquímetro** *(ehl pahr-'kee-meh-troh)*
railroad track	**la vía del ferrocarril**
	(lah 'vee-ah dehl feh-rroh-kah-'rreel)
sign	**la señal** *(lah sehn-'yahl)*
skyscraper	**el rascacielos** *(ehl rahs-kah-see-'eh-lohs)*
station	**la estación** *(lah ehs-tah-see-'ohn)*
stop sign	**la señal de parada**
	(lah sehn-'yalh deh pah-'rah-dah)
telephone pole	**el poste de teléfono**
	(ehl 'pohs-teh deh teh-'leh-foh-noh)
toll booth	**la caseta de peaje**
	(lah kah-'seh-tah deh peh-'ah-heh)
tower	**la torre** *(lah 'toh-rreh)*
tunnel	**el túnel** *(ehl 'too-nehl)*
wall	**la pared** *(lah pah-'rehd)*

¡ MÁS AYUDA !

• Here's some more urban Spanish:

I'm going to park on (the) . . .	**Voy a estacionar en . . .**
	('voh-ee ah ehs-tah-see-oh-'nahr ehn)
alley	**el callejón** *(ehl kah-yeh-'hohn)*
avenue	**la avenida** *(lah ah-veh-'nee-dah)*
boulevard	**el bulevar** *(ehl boo-leh-'vahr)*
highway	**la carretera** *(lah kah-rreh-'teh-rah)*
path	**el sendero** *(ehl sehn-'deh-roh)*
road	**el camino** *(ehl kah-'mee-noh)*
route	**la ruta** *(lah 'roo-tah)*

• The **-ería** *(eh-'ree-ah)* ending informs us that it's a shop or factory:

bakery	**la panadería** *(lah pah-nah-deh-'ree-ah)*
barber shop	**la peluquería** *(lah peh-loo-keh-'ree-ah)*
florist	**la floristería** *(lah floh-rees-teh-'ree-ah)*
furniture store	**la mueblería** *(lah mweh-bleh-'ree-ah)*
jewelry store	**la joyería** *(lah hoh-yeh-'ree-ah)*
laundromat	**la lavandería** *(lah lah-vahn-deh-'ree-ah)*
meat market	**la carnicería** *(lah kahr-nee-seh-'ree-ah)*
shoe store	**la zapatería** *(lah sah-pah-teh-'ree-ah)*

• You may also need to learn these particular places:

bar	**el bar** *(ehl bahr)*
campgrounds	**el campamento** *(ehl kahm-pah-'mehn-toh)*
cemetery	**el cementerio** *(ehl seh-mehn-'teh-ree-oh)*
city hall	**el municipio** *(ehl moo-nee-'see-pee-oh)*
jail	**la cárcel** *(lah 'kahr-sehl)*
pier	**el muelle** *(ehl 'mweh-yeh)*
warehouse	**el almacén** *(ehl ahl-mah-'sehn)*
The . . . station	**La estación de . . .** *(lah ehs-tah-see-'ohn deh)*
bus	**autobús** *(ow-toh-'boos)*

| train | **tren** *(trehn)* |
| subway | **metro** *('meh-troh)* |

The . . . center	**El centro de . . .** *(ehl 'sehn-troh)*
commerce	**comercio** *(koh-'mehr-see-oh)*
recreation	**recreo** *(reh-'kreh-oh)*
visitors	**visitantes** *(vee-see-'tahn-tehs)*

• And where do people live?

They're in the . . .	**Están en . . .** *(ehs-'tahn ehn)*
apartment	**el apartamento** *(ehl ah-pahr-tah-'mehn-toh)*
condominium	**el condominio** *(kohn-doh-'mee-nee-oh)*
home	**el hogar** *(ehl oh-'gahr)*
hut	**la choza** *(lah 'choh-sah)*
shed	**la cabaña** *(lah kah-'bahn-yah)*

 ¡ N E C E S I T A   P R A C T I C A R !

Take a few city-related vocabulary items, and plug them into the sentence patterns below. Then read each one aloud:

I'm working at (the)	**Estoy trabajando en . . .**
	(ehs-'toh-ee trah-bah-'hahn-doh ehn)
She works at (the) . . .	**Ella trabaja en . . .**
	('eh-yah trah-'bah-hah ehn)
We're going to work at (the) . . .	**Vamos a trabajar en . . .**
	('vah-mohs ah trah-bah-'hahr ehn)

Translate these sentences, without peeking:

La iglesia está allí, a la derecha de la fuente.

_____

La parada de autobús está cerca del patio.

_____

El edificio no está muy lejos de la torre.

_____

Follow the example given:

El piloto <u>trabaja</u> en el aeropuerto.

El profesor   trabaja en _____.

El pastor   _____.

El mecánico   _____.

El abogado   _____.

Read the sign!

¡Lea el letrero! *('leh-hah ehl leh-'treh-roh)*

Use your English skills to help others in the community. Translate for your Spanish-speaking clients, friends, and families the following English words.

Curve	**Curva** *('koor-vah)*
Detour	**Desviación** *(dehs-vee-ah-see-'ohn)*
Do Not Cross	**No Cruzar** *(noh kroo-'sahr)*
Do Not Litter	**No Tirar Basura** *(noh tee-'rahr bah-'soo-rah)*
Emergency	**Emergencia** *(eh-mehr-'hehn-see-ah)*
Entrance	**Entrada** *(ehn-'trah-dah)*
Exit	**Salida** *(sah-'lee-dah)*
Handicapped	**Minusválidos** *(mee-noos-'vah-lee-dohs)*
Narrow Road	**Camino Estrecho** *(kah-'mee-noh ehs-'treh-choh)*
No Entrance	**Paso Prohibido** *('pah-soh proh-ee-'bee-doh)*
No Passing	**No Pasar** *(noh pah-'sahr)*
No U Turn	**Prohibida la Vuelta en U** *(proh-ee-'bee-dah lah voo-'ehl-tah en oo)*
One Way	**Circulación** *(seer-koo-lah-see-'ohn)*
Parking	**Estacionamiento** *(ehs-tah-see-oh-nah-mee-'ehn-toh)*
Pedestrian Crossing	**Paso de Peatones** *('pah-soh deh peh-ah-'toh-nehs)*
Railroad Crossing	**Cruce de Ferrocarril** *('kroo-seh deh feh-rroh-kah-'rreel)*

Slow	**Despacio** *(dehs-'pah-see-oh)*
Speed Limit	**Límite de Velocidad**
	('lee-mee-teh deh veh-loh-see-'dahd)
Stop	**Alto** *('ahl-toh)*
Tow Away Zone	**Se Usará Grúa** *(seh oo-sah-'rah 'groo-ah)*
Traffic Circle	**Glorieta** *(glo-ree-'eh-tah)*
Wait	**Espere** *(ehs-'peh-reh)*
Walk	**Camine** *(kah-'mee-neh)*
Wrong Way	**Vía Equivocada**
	('vee-ah eh-kee-voh-'kah-dah)
Yield	**Ceda el Paso** *('seh-dah ehl 'pah-soh)*

Speaking of written signs, what about those around your place of employment? Learn and teach:

Closed	**Cerrado** *(seh-'rrah-doh)*
Danger	**Peligro** *(peh-'lee-groh)*
For Rent	**Se Alquila** *(seh ahl-'kee-lah)*
For Sale	**Se Vende** *(seh 'vehn-deh)*
No Smoking	**No Fumar** *(noh foo-'mahr)*
Open	**Abierto** *(ah-bee-'ehr-toh)*
Out of Order	**Descompuesto** *(dehs-kohm-'pwehs-toh)*
Pull	**Jale** *('hah-leh)*
Push	**Empuje** *(ehm-'poo-heh)*
Red Cross	**Cruz Roja** *(kroos 'roh-hah)*
Restrooms	**Servicios** *(sehr-'vee-see-ohs)*

Keep going:

Authorized Personnel Only	**Sólo para Personal Autorizado**
	('soh-loh 'pah-rah pehr-soh-'nahl ow-
	toh-ree-'sah-doh)
Change Machine	**Máquina de Cambio**
	('mah-kee-nah deh 'kahm-bee-oh)
Do Not Block Entrance	**No Obstruir la Entrada**
	(noh ohbs-troo-'eer lah ehn-'trah-dah)

Emergency Exit   **Salida de Emergencia**
(sah-'lee-dah deh eh-mehr-'hehn-see-ah)

Employee Parking   **Estacionamiento para Empleados**
(ehs-tah-see-oh-nah-mee-'ehn-toh 'pah-rah ehm-pleh-'ah-dohs)

Next Window Please   **Pase a la Siguiente Ventanilla**
('pah-seh ah lah see-gee-'ehn-teh vehn-tah-'nee-yah)

¡ *L A* C *U L T U R A !*

Do not translate names of businesses, brands, streets. All over the world, most formal titles in English remain the same.

Parking
El estacionamiento
(ehl ehs-tah-see-oh-nah-mee-'ehn-toh)

When the local community comes calling, make sure everyone understands the parking situation:

You need (the) . . .   **Necesita** . . . *(neh-seh-'see-tah)*
  permit   **el permiso** *(ehl pehr-'mee-soh)*
  sticker   **la etiqueta** *(lah eh-tee-'keh-tah)*
  ticket   **el boleto** *(ehl boh-'leh-toh)*

This is . . .   **Este está** . . . *('ehs-teh ehs-'tah)*
  reserved   **reservado** *(reh-sehr-'vah-doh)*
  parked poorly   **mal estacionado**
(mahl ehs-tah-see-'oh-nah-doh)
  double parked   **estacionado en doble hilera**
(ehs-tah-see-oh-'nah-doh ehn 'doh-bleh ee-'leh-rah)

Use (the) . . .	**Use** . . . *('oo-seh)*
handicapped parking	**el estacionamiento para incapacitados** *(ehl ehs-tah-see-oh-nah-mee-'ehn-toh 'pah-rah een-kah-pah-see-'tah-dohs*
parking lot	**el lote de estacionamiento** *(ehl 'loh-teh deh ehs-tah-see-oh-nah-mee-'ehn-toh)*
parking structure	**el edificio de estacionamiento** *(ehl eh-dee-'fee-see-oh deh ehs-tah-see-oh-nah-mee-'ehn-toh)*
Look at (the) . . .	**Mire** . . . *('mee-reh)*
arrow	**la flecha** *(lah 'fleh-chah)*
cone	**el cono** *(ehl 'koh-noh)*
hydrant	**la llave de incendios** *(lah 'yah-veh deh een-'sehn-dee-ohs)*
line	**la línea** *(lah 'lee-neh-ah)*
meter	**el parquímetro** *(ehl pahr-'kee-meh-troh)*
sign	**la señal** *(lah sehn-'yahl)*
space	**el espacio** *(ehl ehs-'pah-see-oh)*
zone	**la zona** *(lah 'soh-nah)*

¡ *M Á S   A Y U D A !*

• How about some other ways of travel? Folks often get around town by means of one of these:

I come by . . .	**Vengo en** . . . *('vehn-goh ehn)*
bicycle	**la bicicleta** *(lah bee-see-'kleh-tah)*
bus	**el autobús** *(ehl ow-toh-'boos)*
moped	**la bicicleta motorizada** *(lah bee-see-'kleh-tah moh-toh-ree-'sah-dah)*
motorcycle	**la motocicleta** *(lah moh-toh-see-'kleh-tah)*
school bus	**el autobús escolar** *(ehl ow-toh-'boos ehs-koh-'lahr)*

streetcar	**el tranvía** *(ehl trahn-'vee-ah)*
subway	**el metro** *(ehl 'meh-troh)*
train	**el tren** *(ehl trehn)*
truck	**el camión** *(ehl kah-mee-'ohn)*

At work
En el trabajo *(ehn ehl trah-'bah-hoh)*

In many parts of the country, staff members at major outreach organizations are required to speak Spanish on a regular basis. Therefore, words that describe the workplace are a must. Begin by helping Spanish speakers who are unfamiliar with your location:

We work at (the) . . .	**Trabajamos en . . .** *(trah-bah-'hah-mohs ehn)*
agency	**la agencia** *(lah ah-'hehn-see-ah)*
area	**el área** *(ehl 'ah-reh-ah)*
branch	**la sucursal** *(lah soo-koor-'sahl)*
building	**el edificio** *(ehl eh-dee-'fee-see-oh)*
business	**el negocio** *(ehl neh-'goh-see-oh)*
company	**la compañía** *(lah kohm-pah-'nee-ah)*
department	**el departamento** *(ehl deh-pahr-tah-'mehn-toh)*
division	**la división** *(lah dee-vee-see-'ohn)*
facility	**la instalación** *(lah eens-tah-lah-see-'ohn)*
factory	**la fábrica** *(lah 'fah-bree-kah)*
firm	**la empresa** *(ehm-'preh-sah)*
franchise	**la concesión** *(lah kohn-seh-see-'ohn)*
institution	**la institución** *(lah eens-tee-too-see-'ohn)*
organization	**la organización** *(lah ohr-gah-nee-sah-see-'ohn)*
plant	**la planta** *(lah 'plahn-tah)*
property	**la propiedad** *(lah proh-pee-eh-'dahd)*
shop	**el taller** *(ehl tah-'yehr)*
station	**la estación** *(lah ehs-tah-see-'ohn)*
store	**la tienda** *(lah tee-'ehn-dah)*
warehouse	**el almacén** *(ehl ahl-mah-'sehn)*

Now, be a little more specific:

There is a _____ room.	**Hay un cuarto de _____.**
	('ah-ee oon 'kwahr-toh deh)
conference	**conferencias** *(kohn-feh-'rehn-see-ahs)*
copying	**copias** *('koh-pee-ahs)*
mail	**correo** *(koh-'rreh-oh)*
storage	**depósito** *(deh-'poh-see-toh)*
training	**entrenamiento**
	(ehn-treh-nah-mee-'ehn-toh)
waiting	**espera** *(ehs-'peh-rah)*
It's in the _____ department.	**Está en el departamento de _____.** *(ehs-'tah ehn ehl deh-pahr-tah-'mehn-toh deh)*
administration	**administración**
	(ahd-mee-nees-trah-see-'ohn)
billing	**contabilidad** *(kohn-tah-bee-lee-'dahd)*
customer service	**servicio para clientes**
	(sehr-'vee-see-oh 'pah-rah klee-'ehn-tehs)
finance	**finanzas** *(fee-'nahn-sahs)*
human resources	**personal** *(pehr-soh-'nahl)*
marketing	**mercadeo** *(mehr-kah-'deh-oh)*
sales	**ventas** *('vehn-tahs)*

Outreach organizations vary, so pull useful words from this group if they apply:

I'm working with . . .	**Estoy trabajando con . . .**
	(ehs-'toh-ee trah-bah-'hahn-doh kohn)
advertising	**la publicidad** *(lah poob-lee-see-'dahd)*
assembly	**el montaje** *(ehl mohn-'tah-heh)*
communications	**las comunicaciones**
	(lahs koh-moo-nee-kah-see-'oh-nehs
credit	**crédito** *(ehl 'kreh-dee-toh)*
custodial	**la limpieza** *(lah leem-pee-'eh-sah)*

inspection	**la inspección** *(lah eens-pehk-see-'ohn)*
laboratory	**el laboratorio** *(ehl lah-boh-rah-'toh-ree-oh)*
maintenance	**el mantenimiento** *(ehl mahn-teh-nee-mee-'ehn-toh)*
manufacturing	**la fabricación** *(lah fah-bree-kah-see-'ohn)*
operations	**las operaciones** *(lahs oh-peh-rah-see-'oh-nehs)*
packaging	**el embalaje** *(ehl ehm-bah-'lah-heh)*
production	**la producción** *(lah proh-dook-see-'ohn)*
quality control	**el control de calidad** *(ehl kohn-'trohl deh kah-lee-'dahd)*
receiving	**la recepción** *(lah reh-sehp-see-'ohn)*
research	**la investigación** *(lah een-vehs-tee-gah-see-'ohn)*
security	**la seguridad** *(lah seh-goo-ree-'dahd)*
shipping	**el envío** *(ehl ehn-'vee-oh)*

¡*NECESITA PRACTICAR!*

Translate these useful terms:

warehouse	_____
factory	_____
storage room	_____
advertising	_____
sales department	_____

¡*MÁS AYUDA!*

• Never stop learning Spanish words that describe your job in outreach. Same as in English, there are sentences in Spanish that do not require the use of articles. That is what happens with the following sentences. You don't say "I need more <u>the</u> awareness," and you don't say **Necesita más** la **conciencia.** Articles are given in parentheses just to indicate the gender.

I have . . .	**Tengo . . .** *('tehn-goh)*
I need more . . .	**Necesito más . . .** *(neh-seh-'see-toh mahs)*
awareness	**(la) conciencia** *(kohn-see-'ehn-see-ah)*
care	**(el) cuidado** *(kwee-'dah-doh)*
commitment	**(el) compromiso** *(kohm-proh-'mee-soh)*
compassion	**(la) compasión** *(kohm-pah-see-'ohn)*
dedication	**(la) dedicación** *(deh-dee-kah-see-'ohn)*
desire	**(el) deseo** *(deh-'seh-oh)*
determination	**(la) determinación** *(deh-tehr-mee-nah-see-'ohn)*
development	**(el) desarrollo** *(deh-sah-'rroh-yoh)*
dignity	**(la) dignidad** *(deeg-nee-'dahd)*
direction	**(la) dirección** *(dee-rehk-see-'ohn)*
effort	**(el) esfuerzo** *(ehs-'fwehr-soh)*
empathy	**(la) empatía** *(ehm-pah-'tee-ah)*
energy	**(la) energía** *(eh-nehr-'hee-ah)*
faith	**(la) fe** *(feh)*
friendship	**(la) amistad** *(ah-mees-'tahd)*
generosity	**(la) generosidad** *(heh-neh-roh-see-'dahd)*
gratitude	**(la) gratitud** *(grah-tee-'tood)*
growth	**(el) crecimiento** *(kre-see-mee-'ehn-toh)*
happiness	**(la) felicidad** *(feh-lee-see-'dahd)*
honor	**(el) honor** *(oh-'nohr)*
hope	**(la) esperanza** *(ehs-peh-'rahn-sah)*
inspiration	**(la) inspiración** *(eens-pee-rah-see-'ohn)*
kindness	**(la) bondad** *(bohn-'dahd)*
love	**(el) amor** *(ah-'mohr)*
loyalty	**(la) lealtad** *(leh-ahl-tahd)*
motivation	**(la) motivación** *(moh-tee-vah-see-'ohn)*
passion	**(la) pasión** *(pah-see-'ohn)*

patience	**(la) paciencia** *(pah-see-'ehn-see-ah)*
peace	**(la) paz** *(pahs)*
pride	**(el) orgullo** *(ohr-'goo-yoh)*
respect	**(el) respeto** *(rehs-'peh-toh)*
sacrifice	**(el) sacrificio** *(sah-kree-'fee-see-oh)*
service	**(el) servicio** *(sehr-'vee-see-oh)*
smile	**(la) sonrisa** *(sohn-'ree-sah)*
spirit	**(el) espíritu** *(ehs-'pee-ree-too)*
strength	**(la) fuerza** *('fwehr-sah)*
support	**(el) apoyo** *(ah-'poh-yoh)*
trust	**(la) confianza** *(kohn-fee-'ahn-sah)*
will	**(la) voluntad** *(voh-loon-'tahd)*
wisdom	**(la) sabiduría** *(sah-bee-doo-'ree-ah)*

• Can you use a few more volunteers? If they speak Spanish, describe
what you're looking for:

You must . . .	**Tiene que . . .** *(tee-'eh-neh keh)*
be certified	**estar certificado**
	(ehs-'tahr sehr-tee-fee-'kah-doh)
be confident	**estar convencido**
	(ehs-'tahr kohn-vehn-'see-doh)
be cooperative	**ser cooperativo** *(sehr koh-oh-peh-rah-'tee-voh)*
be dedicated	**ser dedicado** *(sehr deh-dee-'kah-doh)*
be emotional	**ser emotivo** *(sehr eh-moh-'tee-voh)*
be independent	**ser independiente**
	(sehr een-deh-pehn-dee-'ehn-teh)
be mature	**ser maduro** *(sehr mah-'doo-roh)*
be objective	**ser objetivo** *(sehr ohb-heh-'tee-voh)*
be responsible	**ser responsable** *(sehr rehs-pohn-'sah-bleh)*
be sensitive	**ser sensible** *(sehr sehn-'see-bleh)*
be trained	**ser entrenado** *(sehr ehn-treh-nah-doh)*
	(you ought to be trained)
	estar entrenado *(ehs-'tahr ehn-treh-'nah-doh)*
	(you must have been trained)

• And which project are you currently working on?

It's (the) . . .   **Es** . . . *(ehs)*
  adoption   **la adopción** *(lah ah-dohp-see-'ohn)*
  affordable housing   **la vivienda asequible**
                                  (lah vee-vee-'ehn-dah ah-seh-'kee-bleh)
  child protection   **la protección infantil**
                                  (lah proh-tehk-see-'ohn een-fahn-'teel)
  crime prevention   **la prevención del crimen**
                                  (lah preh-vehn-see-'ohn dehl 'kree-mehn)
  family planning   **la planificación familiar**
                                  (lah plah-nee-fee-kah-see-'ohn fah-mee-lee-'ahr)
  hospice care   **la atención de hospicio**
                                  (lah ah-tehn-see-'ohn deh ohs-'pee-see-oh)
  mental health   **la salud mental**
                                  (lah sah-'lood mehn-'tahl)
  personal development   **el desarrollo personal**
                                  (ehl deh-sah-'rroh-yoh pehr-soh-'nahl)
  project assistance   **la ayuda para proyectos**
                                  (lah ah-'yoo-dah 'pah-rah pro-'yehk-tohs)
  residential treatment   **el tratamiento residencial**
                                  (ehl trah-tah-mee-'ehn-toh reh-see-dehn-see-'ahl)
  youth development   **el desarrollo de los jóvenes**
                                  (ehl deh-sah-'rroh-yoh deh lohs 'hoh-veh-nehs)

It's the 24-hour . . .   **Es** . . . **de veinte y cuatro horas**
                                  (ehs deh veh-een-teh ee 'kwah-troh 'oh-rahs)
  crisis hotline   **el número telefónico en caso de**
                                  emergencia *(ehl 'noo-meh-roh teh-leh-'foh-nee-koh ehn 'kah-soh deh eh-mehr-'hehn-see-ah)*
  emergency service   **el servicio de emergencia**
                                  (ehl sehr-'vee-see-oh deh eh-mehr-'hehn-see-ah)

group care	**el cuidado de grupo**
	(ehl 'kwee-dah-doh deh 'groo-poh)
ministry	**la asistencia religiosa**
	(lah ah-sees-'tehn-see-ah reh-lee-hee-'oh-sah)
shelter	**el refugio** *(ehl reh-'foo-hee-oh)*

• Simply insert the word you need:

The program is _____.	**El programa es _____.**
	(ehl proh-'grah-mah ehs)
long-term	**a largo plazo** *(ah 'lahr-goh 'plah-soh)*
permanent	**permanente** *(pehr-mah-'nehn-teh)*
short-term	**a corto plazo** *(ah 'kohr-toh 'plah-soh)*
temporary	**temporal** *(tehm-poh-'rahl)*
year-round	**para todo el año**
	('pah-rah 'toh-doh ehl 'ahn-yoh)

They are _____ services.	**Son servicios _____.**
	(sohn sehr-'vee-see-ohs)
consulting	**de consulta** *(deh kohn-'sool-tah)*
employment	**de empleo** *(deh ehm-'pleh-oh)*
funeral	**funerarios** *(foo-neh-'rah-ree-ohs)*
housing	**de la vivienda**
	(deh lah vee-vee-'ehn-dah)
legal	**legales** *(leh-'gah-lehs)*
nutrition	**de nutrición** *(deh noo-tree-see-'ohn)*
religious	**religiosos** *(reh-lee-hee-'oh-sohs)*
sanitation	**de sanidad** *(deh sah-nee-'dahd)*
social	**sociales** *(soh-see-'ah-lehs)*
transportation	**de transporte** *(deh trahns-'pohr-teh)*

• Notice these useful phrases:

We have _____ service.	**Tenemos servicio de _____**
	(teh-'neh-mohs sehr-'vee-see-oh deh)
community assistance	**ayuda para la comunidad**
	(ah-'yoo-dah 'pah-rah lah koh-moo-nee-'dahd)

home contact	**contacto con el hogar**
	(kohn-'tahk-toh kohn ehl oh-'gahr)
home delivery	**entregas a domicilio**
	(ehn-'treh-gahs ah doh-mee-'see-lee-oh)
home visit	**visitas al hogar**
	(vee-'see-tahs ahl oh-'gahr)
manpower	**mano de obra**
	('mah-noh deh 'oh-brah)

In the building
En el edificio *(ehn ehl eh-dee-'fee-see-oh)*

Repeat the parts of the office building as you give a tour of the outreach facility:

It's next to (the) . . .	**Está al lado de . . .** *(ehs-'tah ahl 'lah-doh deh)*
aisle	**el pasillo** *(ehl pah-'see-yoh)*
basement	**el sótano** *(ehl 'soh-tah-noh)*
cafeteria	**la cafetería** *(lah kah-feh-teh-'ree-ah)*
elevator	**el ascensor** *(ehl ah-sehn-'sohr)*
entrance	**la entrada** *(lah ehn-'trah-dah)*
escalator	**la escalera mecánica**
	(lah ehs-kah-'leh-rah meh-'kah-nee-kah)
exit	**la salida** *(lah sah-'lee-dah)*
garage	**el garaje** *(ehl gah-'rah-heh)*
hallway	**el corredor** *(ehl koh-rreh-'dohr)*
lobby	**el vestíbulo** *(ehl vehs-'tee-boo-loh)*
office	**la oficina** *(lah oh-fee-'see-nah)*
reception desk	**la recepción** *(lah reh-sehp-see-'ohn)*
restroom	**el baño** *(ehl 'bahn-yoh)*
room	**el cuarto** *(ehl 'kwahr-toh)*
stairs	**la escalera** *(lah ehs-kah-'leh-rah)*
steps	**los escalones** *(lohs ehs-kah-'loh-nehs)*

It's near the . . .	Está cerca de . . . *(ehs-'tah 'sehr-kah deh)*
ATM machine	el cajero automático
	(ehl kah-'heh-roh ow-toh-'mah-tee-koh)
cash register	la registradora *(lah reh-hees-trah-'doh-rah)*
clerk's window	la ventanilla *(lah vehn-tah-'nee-yah)*
front counter	el mostrador principal
	(ehl mohs-trah-'dohr preen-see-'pahl)
front desk	la mesa de recepción
	(lah 'meh-sah deh reh-sehp-see-'ohn)
mailbox	el buzón *(ehl boo-'sohn)*
public telephone	el teléfono público
	(ehl teh-'leh-foh-noh 'poob-lee-koh)
trash can	el bote de basura
	(ehl 'boh-teh deh bah-'soo-rah)
vending machine	la máquina vendedora
	(lah 'mah-kee-nah vehn-deh-'doh-rah)
water fountain	el surtidor de agua
	(ehl soor-tee-'dohr deh 'ah-gwah)

¡MÁS AYUDA!

• To describe the building in detail, you'll need to identify the structures on the property:

It has the big _____.	Tiene _____ grande.
	(tee-'eh-neh ehl)
ceiling	el cielo raso *(ehl see-'eh-loh 'rah-soh)*
door	la puerta *(lah 'pwehr-tah)*
floor	el piso *(ehl 'pee-soh)*
roof	el techo *(ehl 'teh-choh)*
wall	la pared *(lah pah-'rehd)*
window	la ventana *(lah vehn-'tah-nah)*

¡*LA CULTURA!*

In every language, people use slang to talk about routine activities. If you're having trouble understanding certain words or expressions, use the phrase, **¿Qué significa eso?** *(keh seeg-nee-'fee-kah 'eh-soh)* , which translates as "What does that mean?" Chances are they'll come up with Spanish words that are more familiar to you.

¡*NECESITA PRACTICAR!*

Put an X through the word that doesn't belong:

la escalera, las escalones, la escuela
el cielo raso, el techo, el empleo
la lluvia, la entrada, la salida

The furniture

Los muebles *(lohs 'mweh-blehs)*

Your everyday vocabulary has to include the names for furniture and decor. To keep these words fresh in our mind, apply removable labels so that you can read the Spanish as you walk by. Don't laugh, it works!

It's behind (the) . . .	**Está detrás de . . .** *(ehs-'tah deh-'trahs deh)*
armchair	**el sillón** *(ehl see-'yohn)*
bench	**el banco** *(ehl 'bahn-koh)*
bookshelf	**el librero** *(ehl lee-'breh-roh)*
chair	**la silla** *(lah 'see-yah)*
chest	**el baúl** *(ehl bah-'ool)*
desk	**el escritorio** *(ehl ehs-kree-'toh-ree-oh)*
file cabinet	**el archivo** *(ehl ahr-'chee-voh)*
lamp	**la lámpara** *(lah 'lahm-pah-rah)*
sofa	**el sofá** *(ehl soh-'fah)*

stool	**el banquillo** *(ehl bahn-'kee-yoh)*
table	**la mesa** *(lah 'meh-sah)*
trash basket	**el cesto de basura** *(ehl 'sehs-toh deh bah-'soo-rah)*

Some things inside your building appear more often in the plural form. Take what you need from the list below:

Do you like (the) . . . ?	**¿Le gustan . . . ?** *(leh 'goos-tahn)*
blinds	**las persianas** *(las pehr-see-'ah-nahs)*
cabinets	**los gabinetes** *(lohs gah-bee-'neh-tehs)*
carpeting	**las alfombras** *(lahs ahl-'fohm-brahs)*
curtains	**las cortinas** *(lahs kohr-'tee-nahs)*
drawers	**los cajones** *(lohs kah-'hoh-nohs)*
faucets	**los grifos** *(lohs 'gree-fohs)*
shelves	**las repisas** *(lahs reh-'pee-sahs)*

¡ M Á S   A Y U D A !

• Sit down at your desk and start naming the supplies that fill your office. Sooner or later all these items will be required in the field:

Bring (the) . . .	**Traiga . . .** *('trah-ee-gah)*
binder	**el encuadernador** *(ehl ehn-kwah-dehr-nah-'dohr)*
calendar	**el calendario** *(ehl kah-lehn-'dah-ree-oh)*
card	**la tarjeta** *(lah tahr-'heh-tah)*
eraser	**el borrador** *(ehl boh-rrah-'dohr)*
folders	**las carpetas** *(lahs kahr-'peh-tahs)*
ink	**la tinta** *(lah 'teen-tah)*
label	**la etiqueta** *(lah eh-tee-'keh-tah)*
marker	**el marcador** *(ehl mahr-kah-'dohr)*
paper	**el papel** *(ehl pah-'pehl)*
paper clips	**los clips** *(lohs kleeps)*
pen	**el lapicero** *(ehl lah-pee-'seh-roh)*

pencil	**el lápiz** *(ehl 'lah-pees)*
scissors	**las tijeras** *(lahs tee-'heh-rahs)*
stapler	**la engrapadora** *(lah ehn-grah-pah-'doh-rah)*
stationery	**los objetos de escritorio**
	(lohs ohb-'heh-tohs deh ehs-kree-'toh-ree-oh)
tacks	**las tachuelas** *(lahs tah-'chweh-lahs)*
tape	**la cinta engomada**
	(lah 'seen-tah ehn-goh-'mah-dah)

¡NECESITA PRACTICAR!

Fill in the word that completes each series:

mesa, repisa, lápiz

escritorio, silla, _____

borrador, lapicero, _____

gabinete, cajón, _____

Do you need clothing?

¿Necesita ropa? *(neh-seh-'see-tah 'roh-pah)*

It's time to leave the office and head out into the community. One of the most common activities in community outreach is the distribution of clothing or food. Let's start with a list of items that you can practice daily. And whenever you get dressed, always name each article of clothing in Spanish.

Here's (the) . . .	**Aquí tiene** . . . *(ah-'kee tee-'eh-neh)*
Do you need (the) . . .	**¿Necesita** . . . **?** *(neh-seh-'see-tah)*
We're going to give you (the) . . .	**Vamos a darle** . . .
	('vah-mohs ah 'dahr-leh)
bathing suit	**el traje de baño**
	(ehl 'trah-heh deh 'bahn-yoh)
belt	**el cinturón** *(ehl seen-too-'rohn)*

blouse	**la blusa** *(lah 'bloo-sah)*
boots	**las botas** *(lahs 'boh-tahs)*
bra	**el sostén** *(ehl sohs-'tehn)*
cap	**la gorra** *(lah 'goh-rrah)*
dress	**el vestido** *(ehl vehs-'tee-doh)*
girdle	**la faja** *(lah 'fah-hah)*
gloves	**los guantes** *(lohs 'gwahn-tehs)*
jacket	**la chaqueta** *(lah chah-'keh-tah)*
mittens	**los mitones** *(lohs mee-'toh-nehs)*
overcoat	**el abrigo** *(ehl ah-'bree-goh)*
pajamas	**el pijama** *(ehl pee-'yah-mah)*
panties	**las bragas** *(lahs 'brah-gahs)*
pants	**los pantalones**
	(lohs pahn-tah-'loh-nehs)
raincoat	**el impermeable**
	(ehl eem-pehr-meh-'ah-bleh)

Now use the new vocabulary with these expressions:

She's putting on (the) . . .	**Se viste con . . .** *(seh 'vees-teh kohn)*
He's taking off (the) . . .	**Se saca . . .** *(seh 'sah-kah)*
She's wearing (the) . . .	**Lleva . . .** *('yeh-vah)*
sandals	**las sandalias** *(lahs sahn-'dah-lee-ahs)*
scarf	**la bufanda** *(lah boo-'fahn-dah)*
shirt	**la camisa** *(lah kah-'mee-sah)*
shoes	**los zapatos** *(lohs sah-'pah-tohs)*
shorts	**los calzoncillos**
	(lohs kahl-sohn-'see-yohs)
skirt	**la falda** *(lah 'fahl-dah)*
slip	**la combinación**
	(lah kohm-bee-nah-see-'ohn)
sneakers	**las zapatillas** *(lahs sah-pah-'tee-yahs)*
socks	**los calcetines**
	(lohs kahl-seh-'tee-nehs)
sportcoat	**el saco** *(ehl 'sah-koh)*

stockings	**las medias** *(lahs 'meh-dee-ahs)*
suit	**el traje** *(ehl 'trah-heh)*
sweater	**el suéter** *(ehl 'sweh-tehr)*
T-shirt	**la camiseta** *(lah kah-mee-'seh-tah)*
tie	**la corbata** *(lah kohr-'bah-tah)*
underwear	**la ropa interior**
	(lah 'roh-pah een-teh-ree-'ohr)

• These one-liners related to clothing distribution may come in handy:

We're collecting clothing for the poor.
Estamos colectando ropa para los pobres.
(ehs-'tah-mohs koh-lehk-'tahn-doh 'roh-pah 'pah-rah lohs 'poh-brehs)

Our truck will pick it up tomorrow.
Nuestro camión la recogerá mañana.
('nwehs-troh ka-mee-'ohn lah reh-koh-heh-'rah mahn-'yah-nah)

Take it, it's free.
Llévela, es gratis. *('yeh-veh-lah ehs 'grah-tees)*

I hope it fits.
Espero que le quede bien. *(ehs-'peh-roh keh leh 'keh-deh bee-'ehn)*

Try it on.
Pruébela. *(proo-'eh-beh-lah)*

Personal items
Las cosas personales
(lahs 'koh-sas pehr-soh-'nah-lehs)

Bring (the) . . .	**Traiga . . .** *('trah-ee-gah)*
Do you want (the) . . . ?	**¿Quiere . . . ?** *(kee-'eh-reh)*
comb	**el peine** *(ehl 'peh-ee-neh)*
conditioner	**el acondicionador**
	(ehl ah-kohn-dee-see-oh-nah-'dohr)

cosmetics	**los cosméticos** *(los kohs-'meh-tee-kohs)*
cotton	**el algodón** *(ehl ahl-goh-'dohn)*
cream	**la crema** *(lah 'kre-mah)*
deodorant	**el desodorante** *(ehl deh-soh-doh-'rahn-teh)*
feminine napkins	**los paños femeninos** *(lohs 'pahn-yohs feh-meh-'nee-nohs)*
hairbrush	**el cepillo de pelo** *(ehl seh-'pee-yoh deh 'peh-loh)*
hairpin	**la horquilla** *(lah ohr-'kee-yah)*
hairspray	**la laca** *(lah 'lah-kah)*
makeup	**el maquillaje** *(ehl mah-kee-'yah-heh)*
nail file	**la lima de uñas** *(lah 'lee-mah deh 'oon-yahs)*
nail polish	**la pintura de uñas** *(lah peen-'too-rah deh 'oon-yahs)*
perfume	**el perfume** *(ehl pehr-'foo-meh)*
razor blade	**la hoja de afeitar** *(lah 'oh-hah deh ah-feh-ee-'tahr)*
scissors	**las tijeras** *(lahs tee-'heh-rahs)*
shampoo	**el champú** *(ehl chahm-'poo)*
shaver	**la afeitadora** *(lah ah-feh-ee-tah-'doh-rah)*
suntan lotion	**el bronceador** *(ehl brohn-seh-ah-'dohr)*
toilet paper	**el papel higiénico** *(ehl pah-'pehl ee-hee-'eh-nee-koh)*
toothbrush	**el cepillo de dientes** *(ehl seh-'pee-yoh deh dee-'ehn-tehs)*
toothpaste	**la pasta de dientes** *(lah 'pahs-tah deh dee-'ehn-tehs)*
tweezers	**las pinzas** *(lahs 'peen-sahs)*

More important things
Más cosas importantes
(mahs 'koh-sahs eem-pohr-'tahn-tehs)

Here are some miscellaneous but necessary items that often come up in conversation.

They need (the) . . .	Necesitan . . . *(neh-seh-'see-tahn)*
batteries	**las pilas** *(lahs 'pee-lahs)*
diapers	**los pañales** *(lohs pahn-'yah-lehs)*
envelopes	**los sobres** *(lohs 'soh-brehs)*
light bulbs	**los focos** *(lohs 'foh-kohs)*
lock	**el candado** *(ehl kahn-'dah-doh)*
luggage	**el equipaje** *(ehl eh-kee-'pah-heh)*
magazines	**las revistas** *(lahs reh-'vees-tahs)*
matches	**los fósforos** *(lohs 'fohs-foh-rohs)*
medicine	**la medicina** *(lah meh-dee-'see-nah)*
needle	**la aguja** *(lah ah-'goo-hah)*
newspapers	**los periódicos** *(los peh-ree-'oh-dee-kohs)*
notebook	**el cuaderno** *(ehl kwah-'dehr-noh)*
pin	**el alfiler** *(ehl ahl-fee-'lehr)*
postcard	**la tarjeta postal** *(lah tahr-'heh-tah pohs-'tahl)*
roll of film	**el rollo de fotos** *(ehl 'roh-yoh deh 'foh-tohs)*
stamps	**las estampillas** *(lahs ehs-tahm-'pee-yahs)*
sunglasses	**los lentes de sol** *(lohs 'lehn-tehs deh sohl)*
tape	**la cinta** *(lah 'seen-tah)*
thread	**el hilo** *(ehl 'ee-loh)*
tools	**las herramientas** *(lahs eh-rrah-mee-'ehn-tahs)*
umbrella	**el paraguas** *(ehl pah-'rah-gwahs)*

¡M Á S   A Y U D A !

• Notice other things that may need to be distributed:

Pick up (the) . . .	**Recoja** . . . *(reh-'koh-hah)*
Let's give away (the) . . .	**Vamos a donar** . . .
	('vah-mohs ah doh-'nahr)
blanket	**la frazada** *(lah frah-'sah-dah)*
mattress	**el colchón** *(ehl kohl-'chohn)*
pillow	**la almohada** *(lah ahl-moh-'ah-dah)*
sheets	**las sábanas** *(lahs 'sah-bah-nahs)*
towel	**la toalla** *(lah toh-'ah-yah)*

¡N E C E S I T A   P R A C T I C A R !

In Spanish, name (write if you can):

Three articles of clothing.   _____
Three bedding items.   _____
Three toiletry items.   _____

Translate:

needle and thread   _____
envelopes and stamps   _____
newspapers and magazines   _____

Food distribution
La distribución de alimentos
(lah dees-tree-boo-see-'ohn deh ah-lee-'mehn-tohs)

Hunger is a concern in many communities. Practice this list of food words, and you will be better prepared for food distribution.

Take (the) . . .   **Tome** . . . *('toh-meh)*

We're serving (the) . . .	**Estamos sirviendo . . .**
	(ehs-'tah-mohs seer-vee-'ehn-doh)
bread	**el pan** *(ehl pahn)*
butter	**la mantequilla** *(lah mahn-teh-'kee-yah)*
cheese	**el queso** *(ehl 'keh-soh)*
chicken	**el pollo** *(ehl 'poh-yoh)*
eggs	**los huevos** *(lohs 'hweh-vohs)*
fish	**el pescado** *(ehl pehs-'kah-doh)*
ham	**el jamón** *(ehl hah-'mohn)*
meat	**la carne** *(lah 'kahr-neh)*
noodles	**los fideos** *(lohs fee-'deh-ohs)*
pork	**el cerdo** *(ehl 'sehr-doh)*
rice	**el arroz** *(ehl ah-'rros)*
roast beef	**el rosbif** *(ehl ros-'beef)*
roll	**el panecillo** *(ehl pah-neh-'see-yoh)*
salad	**la ensalada** *(lah ehn-sah-'lah-dah)*
seafood	**el marisco** *(ehl mah-'rees-koh)*
soup	**la sopa** *(lah 'soh-pah)*
steak	**el bistec** *(ehl bees-'tehk)*
turkey	**el pavo** *(ehl 'pah-voh)*

Vegetables
Los vegetales *(lohs veh-heh-'tah-lehs)*

Let's toss in these additional lists dealing with food. Combine the useful verbs below with the new vocabulary to create key command phrases:

Eat (the) . . .	**Coma . . .** *('koh-mah)*
Distribute (the) . . .	**Distribuya . . .** *(dees-tree-'boo-yah)*
Try (the) . . .	**Pruebe . . .** *(proo-'eh-beh)*
artichoke	**la alcachofa** *(lah ahl-kah-'choh-fah)*
asparagus	**el espárrago** *(ehl ehs-'pah-rrah-goh)*
beans	**los frijoles** *(lohs free-'hoh-lehs)*
beet	**la remolacha** *(lah reh-moh-'lah-chah)*

broccoli	**el brécol** *(ehl 'breh-kohl)*
cabbage	**el repollo** *(ehl reh-'poh-yoh)*
carrot	**la zanahoria** *(lah sah-nah-'oh-ree-ah)*
cauliflower	**el coliflor** *(ehl koh-lee-'flohr)*
celery	**el apio** *(ehl 'ah-pee-oh)*
corn	**el maíz** *(ehl mah-'ees)*
cucumber	**el pepino** *(ehl peh-'pee-noh)*
eggplant	**la berenjena** *(lah beh-rehn-'heh-nah)*
green beans	**la judía verde**
	(lah hoo-'dee-ah 'vehr-deh)
green onion	**la cebolleta** *(lah seh-boh-'yeh-tah)*
lettuce	**la lechuga** *(lah leh-'choo-gah)*
mushroom	**el champiñón** *(ehl chahm-poon-'yohn)*
onion	**la cebolla** *(lah seh-'boh-yah)*
peas	**las arvejitas** *(lahs ahr-veh-'hee-tahs)*
potato	**la papa** *(lah 'pah-pah)*
pumpkin	**la calabaza** *(lah kah-lah-'bah-sah)*
radish	**el rábano** *(ehl 'rah-bah-noh)*
spinach	**la espinaca** *(lah ehs-pee-'nah-kah)*
sweet potato	**el camote** *(ehl kah-'moh-teh)*
tomato	**el tomate** *(ehl toh-'mah-teh)*
turnip	**el nabo** *(ehl 'nah-boh)*
watercress	**el berro** *(ehl 'beh-rroh)*
zucchini	**el calabacín** *(ehl kah-lah-bah-'seen)*

Fruit
La fruta *(lah 'froo-tah)*

Take (the) . . .	**Tome** . . . *('toh-meh)*
Pick up (the) . . .	**Recoja** . . . *(reh-'koh-hah)*
Give (the) . . .	**Dé** . . . *(deh)*
apple	**la manzana** *(lah mahn-'sah-nah)*
apricot	**el albaricoque** *(ehl ahl-bah-ree-'koh-keh)*
banana	**el plátano** *(ehl 'plah-tah-noh)*

blackberrry	**la mora** *(lah 'moh-rah)*
blueberry	**el arándano** *(ehl ah-'rahn-dah-noh)*
cantaloupe	**el melón** *(ehl meh-'lohn)*
cherry	**la cereza** *(lah seh-'reh-sah)*
coconut	**el coco** *(ehl 'koh-koh)*
fig	**el higo** *(ehl 'ee-goh)*
grape	**la uva** *(lah 'oo-vah)*
grapefruit	**la toronja** *(lah toh-'rohn-hah)*
lemon	**el limón** *(ehl lee-'mohn)*
orange	**la naranja** *(lah nah-'rahn-hah)*
peach	**el melocotón** *(ehl meh-loh-koh-'tohn)*
pear	**la pera** *(lah 'peh-rah)*
pineapple	**la piña** *(lah 'peen-yah)*
plum	**la ciruela** *(lah see-'rweh-lah)*
prune	**la ciruela pasa** *(lah see-'rweh-lah 'pah-sah)*
raisin	**la pasa** *(lah 'pah-sah)*
strawberry	**la fresa** *(lah 'freh-sah)*

The desserts
Los postres *(lohs 'pohs-trehs)*

You can't forget the sweets. These items seem to bring smiles to every-one you're trying to reach:

We also have (the) . . .	**También tenemos . . .**
	(tahm-bee-'ehn teh-'neh-mohs)
cake	**la torta** *(lah 'tohr-tah)*
candy	**el dulce** *(ehl 'dool-seh)*
cookie	**la galleta** *(lah gah-'yeh-tah)*
ice cream	**el helado** *(ehl eh-'lah-doh)*
gelatin	**la gelatina** *(lah heh-lah-'tee-nah)*
pie	**el pastel** *(ehl pahs-'tehl)*

¡*MÁS AYUDA!*

- Don't skip your meals:

Let's serve . . .	**Vamos a servir . . .**
breakfast	**el desayuno** *(ehl deh-sah-'yoo-noh)*
lunch	**el almuerzo** *(ehl ahl-'mwehr-soh)*
dinner	**la cena** *(lah 'seh-nah)*
snack	**la merienda** *(lah meh-ree-'ehn-dah)*

- Now, speak about all the different kinds of meats:

They want (the) . . .	**Quieren . . .** *(kee-'eh-rehn)*
bacon	**el tocino** *(ohl toh 'ooo noh)*
clams	**las almejas** *(lahs ahl-'meh-hahs)*
crab	**el cangrejo** *(ehl kahn-'greh-hoh)*
ground beef	**la carne molida** *(lah 'kahr-neh moh-'lee-dah)*
hamburger	**la hamburguesa** *(lah ahm-boor-'geh-sah)*
hot dog	**el perro caliente** *(ehl 'peh-rroh kah-lee-'ehn-teh)*
lamb	**el cordero** *(ehl kohr-'deh-roh)*
lobster	**la langosta** *(lah lahn-'gohs-tah)*
meatball	**la albóndiga** *(lah ahl-'bohn-dee-gah)*
sausage	**la salchicha** *(lah sahl-'chee-chah)*
shrimp	**el camarón** *(ehl kah-mah-'rohn)*
tuna	**el atún** *(ehl ah-'toon)*
veal	**la ternera** *(lah tehr-'neh-rah)*

You're in big trouble if you can't figure out what these mean, but watch out for some of the stresses:

el Nutrasweet *(ehl noo-trah-'sweet)*
el pyrex *(ehl 'pah-ee-reks)*
el sandwich *(ehl 'sahn-veech)*
el yogurt *(ehl yoh-'goor)*

el **cereal** *(ehl seh-reh-'ahl)*
la **pizza** *(lah 'pee-sah)*
el **ketchup** *(ehl 'keht-chahp)*
el **chocolate** *(ehl choh-koh-'lah-teh)*

Have a drink
Tome una bebida
('toh-meh 'oo-nah beh-'bee-dah)

Make sure everyone has the appropriate beverage. While giving instructions, use either "to take" (**tomar**, *toh-'mahr*) or "to drink" (**beber**, *beh-'behr*). Develop comments using all the verb tenses.

Is she drinking tea?	**¿Está bebiendo té?**
	(ehs-'tah beh-bee-'ehn-doh teh)
No, she takes coffee.	**No, toma café.**
	(noh 'toh-mah kah-'feh)
Do you want to drink soft drinks?	**¿Quieren beber refrescos?**
	(kee-'eh-rehn beh-'behr reh-'frehs-kohs)
Yes, we're taking diet soda.	**Sí, estamos tomando soda dietética.** *(see ehs-'tah-mohs toh-'mahn-doh 'soh-dah dee-eh-'teh-tee-kah)*

beer	**la cerveza** *(lah sehr-'veh-sah)*
coffee	**el café** *(ehl kah-'feh)*
decaffeinated coffee	**el café descafeinado**
	(ehl kah-'feh dehs-kah-feh-ee-'nah-doh)
diet soda	**la soda dietética**
	(lah 'soh-dah dee-eh-'teh-tee-kah)
hot chocolate	**el chocolate caliente**
	(ehl choh-koh-'lah-teh kah-lee-'ehn-teh)
iced tea	**el té helado** *(ehl teh eh-'lah-doh)*
juice	**el jugo** *(ehl 'hoo-goh)*

lemonade	**la limonada** *(lah lee-moh-'nah-dah)*
milk	**la leche** *(lah 'leh-cheh)*
shake	**el batido** *(ehl bah-'tee-doh)*
soft drink	**el refresco** *(ehl reh-'frehs-koh)*
tea	**el té** *(ehl teh)*
water	**el agua** *(ehl 'ah-gwah)*
wine	**el vino** *(ehl 'vee-noh)*

¡*Necesita Practicar*!

Fill out this chart. Take as much time as you need:

las carnes	**los vegetales**	**las frutas**	**las bebidas**

Use logic to finish these phrases:

bread and _____	**pan y** _____
soup and _____	**sopa y** _____
salt and _____	**sal y** _____
oil and _____	**aceite y** _____

¡*Más Ayuda*!

• Ponder these new tips on how to use verb infinitives. Just stick one of these expressions in front.

Además de cocinar,	Besides cooking,
Después de tomar,	After drinking,
Sin comer,	Without eating,

The soup kitchen
El comedor de beneficencia
(ehl koh-meh-'dohr deh beh-neh-fee-'sehn-see-ah)

If you get involved in serving meals, be sure you know what to say in Spanish when everyone is hungry.

Welcome!	**¡Bienvenido!** *(bee-ehn-veh-'nee-doh)*
Please get in line.	**Póngase en fila.** *('pohn-gah-seh ehn 'fee-lah)*
Sit over there.	**Siéntese allí.** *(see-'ehn-teh-seh ah-'ee)*
Wait for your turn.	**Espere su turno.** *(ehs-'peh-reh soo 'toor-noh)*
Give me your ticket.	**Déme su boleto.** *('deh-meh soo boh-'leh-toh)*
Go to (the) . . .	**Vaya a . . .** *('vah-yah ah)*
benches	**las bancas** *(lahs 'bahn-kahs)*
cafeteria	**la cafetería** *(lah kah-feh-teh-'ree-ah)*
kitchen	**la cocina** *(lah koh-'see-nah)*
lunch room	**el comedor** *(ehl koh-meh-'dohr)*
tables	**las mesas** *(lahs 'meh-sahs)*
Use (the) . . .	**Use . . .** *('oo-seh)*
glass	**el vaso** *(ehl 'vah-soh)*
machine	**la máquina** *(lah 'mah-kee-nah)*
napkin	**la servilleta** *(lah sehr-vee-'yeh-tah)*
plate	**el plato** *(ehl 'plah-toh)*
silverware	**los cubiertos** *(lohs koo-bee-'ehr-tohs)*
trash can	**el bote de basura** *(ehl 'boh-teh deh bah-'soo-rah)*
tray	**la bandeja** *(lah bahn-'deh-hah)*

¡MÁS AYUDA!

• How many one-liners can you come up with for use during the meal service?

You may sit where you want.
Puede sentarse dónde quiera.
('pweh-deh sehn-'tahr-seh 'dohn-deh kee-'eh-rah)

These are the hours of service.
Estas son las horas de servicio.
 ('ehs-tahs sohn lahs 'oh-rahs deh sehr-'vee-see-oh)

The food is very good.
La comida es muy buena.
 (lah koh-'mee-dah ehs 'moo-ee 'bweh-nah)

You don't have to pay.
No tiene que pagar. *(noh tee-'eh-neh keh pah-'gahr)*

You may eat all you want.
Puede comer todo lo que quiera. *('pweh-deh koh-'mehr 'toh-doh loh keh 'keh-rah)*

• Several foods are linguistically related, but watch out for some of the stresses:

macaroni	**los macarrones** *(lohs mah-kah-'rroh-nehs)*
pancake	**el panqueque** *(ehl pahn-'keh-keh)*
pizza	**la pizza** *(lah 'pee-sah)*
pudding	**el budín** *(ehl boo-'deen)*
sardines	**las sardinas** *(lahs sahr-'dee-nahs)*
spaghetti	**el espagueti** *(ehl ehs-pah-'geh-tee)*

Ingredients, spices, and condiments
Los ingredientes, las especias y los condimentos
(los een-gre-dee-'ehn-tehs lahs ehs-'peh-see-ahs ee lohs kohn-dee-'mehn-tohs)

If you enjoy the kitchen, flavor your Spanish with these words. Don't forget to continue using verbs and forming full sentences.

We add (the) . . .	**Añadimos . . .** *(ahn-yah-'dee-mohs)*
It needs (the) . . .	**Necesita . . .** *(neh-seh-'see-tah)*
broth	**el caldo** *(ehl 'kahl-doh)*
cinnamon	**la canela** *(lah kah-'neh-lah)*

cornstarch	**el almidón de maíz**
	(ehl ahl-mee-'dohn deh mah-'ees)
flour	**la harina** *(lah ah-'ree-nah)*
garlic	**el ajo** *(ehl 'ah-hoh)*
honey	**la miel** *(lah mee-'ehl)*
hot pepper	**el ají** *(ehl ah-'hee)*
marmalade	**la mermelada** *(lah mehr-meh-'lah-dah)*
mayonnaise	**la mayonesa** *(lah mah-yoh-'neh-sah)*
mustard	**la mostaza** *(lah mohs-'tah-sah)*
nuts	**las nueces** *(lahs 'nweh-sehs)*
oil	**el aceite** *(ehl ah-'seh-ee-teh)*
olive	**las aceitunas** *(lahs ah-seh-ee-'too-nahs)*
parsley	**el perejil** *(ehl peh-reh-'heel)*
peanut butter	**la crema de maní**
	(lah 'kreh-mah deh mah-'nee)
pepper	**la pimienta** *(lah pee-mee-'ehn-tah)*
pickle	**el encurtido** *(ehl ehn-koor-'tee-doh)*
salad dressing	**el aliño de ensalada**
	(ehl ah-'leen-yoh deh ehn-sah-'lah-dah)
salt	**la sal** *(lah sahl)*
sauce	**la salsa** *(lah 'sahl-sah)*
sugar	**el azúcar** *(ehl ah-'soo-kahr)*
tomato sauce	**la salsa de tomate**
	(lah 'sahl-sah deh toh-'mah-teh)
vanilla	**la vainilla** *(lah vah-ee-'nee-yah)*
vinegar	**el vinagre** *(ehl vee-'nah-greh)*

Kitchen employees
Los empleados de la cocina
(lohs ehm-pleh-'ah-dohs deh lah koh-'see-nah)

As a volunteer who works with Spanish speakers, practice at home by labeling your kitchen objects with removable stickers. Once you begin serving food, you'll know what everyone is talking about:

Bring (the) . . .	**Traiga** . . . *('trah-ee-gah)*
apron	**el delantal** *(ehl deh-lahn-tahl)*
bowl	**el plato hondo** *(ehl 'plah-toh 'ohn-doh)*
butter dish	**la mantequillera**
	(lah mahn-teh-kee-'yeh-rah)
coffeepot	**la cafetera** *(lah kah-feh-'teh-rah)*
creamer	**la cremera** *(lah kreh-'meh-rah)*
cup	**la taza** *(lah 'tah-sah)*
fork	**el tenedor** *(ehl teh-neh-'dohr)*
grill	**la parrilla** *(lah pah-'rree-yah)*
knife	**el cuchillo** *(ehl koo-'chee-yoh)*
matches	**los fósforos** *(los 'fohs-foh-rohs)*
napkin	**la servilleta** *(lah sehr-vee-'yeh-tah)*
pan	**la sartén** *(lah sahr-'tehn)*
pepper shaker	**el pimentero** *(ehl pee-mehn-'teh-roh)*
pitcher	**el cántaro** *(ehl 'kahn-tah-roh)*
platter	**la fuente** *(lah 'fwehn-teh)*
pot	**la olla** *(lah 'oh-yah)*
rack	**el estilador** *(ehl ehs-tee-lah-'dohr)*
salad bowl	**la ensaladera** *(lah ehn-sah-lah-'deh-rah)*
salt shaker	**el salero** *(ehl sah-'leh-roh)*
saucepan	**la cacerola** *(lah kah-seh-'roh-lah)*
saucer	**el platillo** *(ehl plah-'tee-yoh)*
spoon	**la cuchara** *(lah koo-'chah-rah)*
sugar bowl	**el azucarero** *(ehl ah-soo-kah-'reh-roh)*
tablecoth	**el mantel** *(ehl mahn-'tehl)*
thermos	**el termo** *(ehl 'tehr-moh)*
towel	**la toalla** *(lah toh-'ah-yah)*

How can you just eat and say nothing about your meal? Make sentences with this new vocabulary:

This is . . .	**Esto está** . . . *('ehs-toh ehs-'tah)*
bitter	**amargo** *(ah-'mahr-goh)*
burned	**quemado** *(keh-'mah-doh)*

cold	**frío** *('free-oh)*
cooked	**cocinado** *(koh-see-'nah-doh)*
delicious	**delicioso** *(deh-lee-see-'oh-soh)*
dry	**seco** *('seh-koh)*
fresh	**fresco** *('frehs-koh)*
fried	**frito** *('free-toh)*
frozen	**congelado** *(kohn-heh-'lah-doh)*
hard	**duro** *('doo-roh)*
hot	**caliente** *(kah-lee-'ehn-teh)*
lukewarm	**tibio** *('tee-bee-oh)*
moist	**húmedo** *('oo-meh-doh)*
raw	**crudo** *('kroo-doh)*
rotten	**podrido** *(poh-'dree-doh)*
salty	**salado** *(sah-'lah-doh)*
sour	**agrio** *('ah-gree-oh)*
spicy	**picante** *(pee-'kahn-teh)*
sweet	**dulce** *('dool-seh)*
tasty	**sabroso** *(sah-'broh-soh)*

Needy people may still have special needs:

It's a _____ dish.	**Es un plato _____.**
	(ehs oon 'plah-toh)
diet	**dietético** *(dee-eh-'teh-tee-koh)*
fat-free	**desengrasado** *(dehs-ehn-grah-'sah-doh)*
kosher	**preparado según ley judía** *(preh-pah-'rah-doh seh-'goon 'leh-ee hoo-'dee-ah)*
organic	**orgánico** *(ohr-'gah-nee-koh)*
salt-free	**sin sal** *(seen sahl)*
sugar-free	**sin azúcar** *(seen ah-'soo-kahr)*
vegetarian	**vegetariano** *(veh-heh-tah-ree-'ah-noh)*

¡*N E C E S I T A   P R A C T I C A R !*

Practice this dialogue:

¡Bienvenido! Póngase en fila, por favor.

        Gracias. Tengo mucha hambre. ¿Cuánto cuesta?

Es gratis. No tiene que pagar.

        ¡Qué bueno! ¿Dónde están las mesas?

Están allí. Puede sentarse dónde quiera.

 ¡*A C C I Ó N !*

The last time we looked at Spanish infinitive verb forms, we learned that the endings of action words must change according to the tense and the person, and that most forms follow a familiar pattern:

AR verbs

To WORK	**TRABAJAR** *(trah-bah-'hahr)*
I work	**Trabajo** *(trah-'bah-hoh)*
You work; he, she works	**Trabaja** *(trah-'bah-hah)*
You (pl.), they work	**Trabajan** *(trah-'bah-hahn)*
We work	**Trabajamos** *(trah-bah-'hah-mohs)*

However, some verbs have irregular changes. Notice that the four forms below each infinitive refer to the same persons as the translated forms above. And remember that this is only a brief selection of irregular patterns. To learn more, buy a Spanish grammar textbook.

To COUNT	To CLOSE
Contar *(kohn-'tahr)*	**Cerrar** *(seh-'rrahr)*
cuento *('kwehn-toh)*	**cierro** *(see-'eh-rroh)*
cuenta *('kwehn-tah)*	**cierra** *(see-'eh-rrah)*
cuentan *('kwehn-tahn)*	**cierran** *(see-'eh-rran)*
contamos *(kohn-'tah-mohs)*	**cerramos** *(seh-'rrah-mohs)*

To Go

Ir *(eer)*

voy *('voh-ee)*
va *(vah)*
van *(vahn)*
vamos *('vah-mohs)*

To Hear

Oír *(oh-'eer)*

oigo *('oh-ee-goh)*
oye *('oh-yeh)*
oyen *('oh-yehn)*
oímos *(oh-'ee-mohs)*

To Laugh

Reír *(reh-'eer)*

río *(reh-'eer)*
ríe *('ree-eh)*
ríen *('ree-ehn)*
reímos *(reh-'ee-mohs)*

To Do

Hacer *(ah-'sehr)*

hago *('ah-goh)*
hace *('ah-seh)*
hacen *(ah-sehn)*
hacemos *(ah-'seh-mohs)*

Watch:

They do the job.	**Hacen el trabajo.** *('ah-sehn ehl trah-'bah-hoh)*
I count the children.	**Cuento los niños.** *('kwehn-toh lohs 'neen-yohs)*
We go to this church.	**Vamos a esta iglesia.** *('vah-mohs ah 'ehs-tah eeg-'leh-see-ah)*

¡ *M Á S   A Y U D A !*

• Try out this new pattern with the irregular verbs **querer** *(keh-'rehr)*, "to want," and **preferir** *(preh-feh-'reer)*, "to prefer." Can you translate each sample sentence all by yourself?

To want

I Want
Quiero ayudar a la familia.
(kee-'eh-roh ah-yoo-'dahr ah lah fah-'mee-lee-ah)

Querer *(keh-'rehr)*

Quiero *(kee-'eh-roh)*

You want; he/she wants   **Quiere** *(kee-'eh-reh)*
Quiere recibir su dinero.
  (kee-'eh-reh reh-see-'beer soo dee-'neh-roh)

You (pl.) want; they want   **Quieren** *(kee-'eh-rehn)*
Quieren usar el carro. *(kee-'eh-rehn oo-'sahr ehl 'kah-rroh)*

We want   **Queremos** *(keh-'reh-mohs)*
Queremos comprar más ropa.
  (keh-'reh-mohs kohm-'prahr mahs 'roh-pah)

To Prefer   **Preferir** *(preh-feh-'reer)*

I prefer   **Prefiero** *(preh-fee-'eh-roh)*
Prefiero hablar español. *(preh-fee-'eh-roh ah-'blahr ehs-pahn-'yohl)*

You prefer; he/she prefers   **Prefiere** *(preh-fee-'eh-reh)*
Prefiere comer la fruta. *(preh-fee-'eh-reh koh-mehr lah 'froo-tah)*

You (pl.) prefer; they prefer   **Prefieren** *(preh-fee-'eh-rehn)*
Prefieren salir hoy. *(preh-fee-'eh-rehn sah-'leer 'oh-ee)*

We prefer   **Preferimos** *(preh-feh-'ree-mohs)*
Preferimos trabajar en la ciudad.
  (preh-feh-'ree-mohs trah-bah-'hahr ehn lah see-oo-'dahd)

 ¡ L A S   O R D E N E S !

This group of key command words will be needed as you discuss outreach procedures. Care to fill in your own examples?

add	**añada** *(ahn-'yah-dah)*	<u>Añada los números</u>.
take away	**quite** *('kee-teh)*	<u>Quite los papeles.</u>
use	**use** *('oo-seh)*	<u>Use el lápiz.</u>
change	**cambie** *('kahm-bee-eh)*	_____
close	**cierre** *(see-'eh-rreh)*	_____
count	**cuente** *('kwehn-teh)*	_____
enter	**entre** *('ehn-treh)*	_____

get	**consiga** *(kohn-'see-gah)*	_____
hear	**oiga** *('oh-ee-gah)*	_____
open	**abra** *('ah-brah)*	_____
pay	**pague** *('pah-geh)*	_____
put	**ponga** *('pohn-gah)*	_____
put in	**meta** *('meh-tah)*	_____
remove	**saque** *('sah-keh)*	_____

¡ M á s   A y u d a !

• While working in the soup kitchen, use the following cooking commands. Say each phrase aloud as you translate.

bake   **hornee** *(ohr-'neh-eh)*
Hornee el pastel. *(ohr-'neh-eh ehl pahs-'tehl)*

barbecue   **ase** *('ah-seh)*
Ase la carne en las brasas. *('ah-seh lah 'kahr-neh ehn lahs 'brah-sahs)*

beat   **bata** *('bah-tah)*
Bata los huevos. *('bah-tah lohs 'hweh-vohs)*

boil   **hierva** *(ee-'ehr-vah)*
Hierva el agua. *(ee-'ehr-vah ehl 'ah-gwah)*

broil, brown   **dore** *('doh-reh)*
Dore el pescado. *('doh-reh ehl pehs-'kah-doh)*

cook   **cocine** *(koh-'see-neh)*
Cocine por dos horas. *(koh-'see-neh pohr dohs 'oh-rahs)*

cover   **cubra** *('koo-brah)*
Cubra la sartén. *('koo-brah lah sahr-'tehn)*

cut   **corte** *('kohr-teh)*
Corte la lechuga. *('kohr-teh lah leh-'choo-gah)*

defrost   **descongele** *(dehs-kohn-'heh-leh)*
Descongele la hamburguesa. *(dehs-kohn-'heh-leh lah ahm-boor-'geh-sah)*

fry   **fría** *('free-ah)*
Fría las papas. *('free-ah lahs 'pah-pahs)*

heat   **caliente** *(kah-lee-'ehn-teh)*
Caliente el pan. *(kah-lee-'ehn-teh ehl pahn)*

measure   **mida** *('mee-dah)*
Mida el agua. *('mee-dah ehl 'ah-gwah)*

mix   **mezcle** *('mehs-kleh)*
Mezcle con aceite. *('mehs-kleh kohn ah-'seh-ee-teh)*

peel   **pele** *('peh-leh)*
Pele las papas. *('peh-leh lahs 'pah-pahs)*

prepare   **prepare** *(proh 'pah roh)*
Prepare el desayuno. *(preh-'pah-reh ehl deh-sah-'yoo-noh)*

remove   **quite** *('kee-teh)*
Quite la carne. *('kee-teh lah 'kahr-neh)*

roast   **ase** *('ah-seh)*
Ase el pavo. *('ah-seh ehl 'pah-voh)*

serve   **sirva** *('seer-vah)*
Sirva con arroz. *('seer-vah kohn ah-'rrohs)*

stir   **revuelva** *(reh-voo-'ehl-vah)*
Revuelva rápidamente. *(reh-voo-'ehl-vah 'rah-pee-dah-mehn-teh)*

 **¡ *La Cultura!* **

Ask a Spanish friend to prepare a traditional home-cooked meal, and get ready for a culinary treat! Contrary to popular belief, not all Latin Americans eat spicy foods, many dishes resemble our traditional meals, and many more will be welcome additions to your kitchen.

Chapter Four

Capítulo Cuatro
(kah-'pee-too-loh 'kwah-troh)

All Across the Country
A través de todo el país
(ah trah-'vehs deh 'toh-doh ehl pah-'ees)

National projects
Los proyectos nacionales
(lohs proh-'yehk-tohs nah-see-oh-'nah-lehs)

Outreach programs at the national level will require several new vocabulary and grammar skills. Start off by collecting information with more question phrases. You should know a lot of this terminology already. Carefully pronounce each sentence and memorize all critical vocabulary:

What's your . . . ?	**¿Cuál es su . . . ?** *(kwahl ehs soo)*
address	**dirección** *(dee-rehk-see-'ohn)*
business	**negocio** *(neh-'goh-see-oh)*
concern	**problema** *(proh-'bleh-mah)*
name	**nombre** *('nohm-breh)*
organization	**organización** *(ohr-gah-nee-sah-see-'ohn)*
phone number	**número de teléfono**
	('noo-meh-roh deh teh-'leh-foh-noh)
program	**programa** *(proh-'grah-mah)*
state	**estado** *(ehs-'tah-doh)*
title	**título** *('tee-too-loh)*

Who's (the) . . . ?   **¿Quién es . . . ?** *(kee-'ehn ehs)*

  client   **el cliente** *(ehl klee-'ehn-teh)*

  contact person   **la persona de contacto**
       (lah pehr-'soh-nah deh kohn-'tahk-toh)

  governor   **el gobernador** *(ehl goh-behr-nah-'dohr)*

  leader   **el líder** *(ehl 'lee-der)*

  program director   **el director del programa**
       (ehl dee-rehk-'tohr dehl proh-'grah-mah)

  representative   **el diputado** *(ehl dee-poo-'tah-doh)*

  secretary   **el secretario** *(ehl seh-kreh-'tah-ree-oh)*

  senator   **el senador** *(ehl seh-nah-'dohr)*

  supervisor   **el supervisor** *(ehl soo-pehr-vee-'sohr)*

Where . . . ?   **¿Dónde . . . ?** *('dohn-deh)*

  do you live   **vive** *('vee-veh)*

  do you work   **trabaja** *(trah-'bah-hah)*

  do you meet   **se reúnen** *(seh reh-'oo-nehn)*

  is it located   **está ubicado** *(ehs-'tah oo-bee-'kah-doh)*

  do you need help   **necesita ayuda** *(neh-seh-'see-tah ah-'yoo-dah)*

Do you have (the) . . . ?   **¿Tiene . . . ?** *(tee-'eh-neh)*

  appointment date   **la fecha de la cita**
       (lah 'feh-chah deh lah 'see-tah)

  business card   **la tarjeta comercial**
       (lah tahr-'heh-tah koh-mehr-see-'ahl)

  business brochure   **el folleto de negocios**
       (ehl foh-'yeh-toh deh neh-'goh-see-ohs)

  office location   **la ubicación de la oficina**
       (lah oo-bee-kah-see-'ohn deh lah oh-fee-'see-nah)

  room number   **el número del cuarto**
       (ehl 'noo-meh-roh dehl 'kwahr-toh)

Is there a . . . ?   **¿Hay un . . . ?** *('ah-ee oon)*

  plan   **plan** *(plahn)*

  procedure   **procedimiento** *(proh-seh-dee-mee-'ehn-toh)*

  process   **proceso** *(proh-'seh-soh)*

Do you need (the) . . . ?	**¿Necesita . . . ?** *(neh-seh-'see-tah)*
approval	**la aprobación**
	(lah ah-proh-bah-see-'ohn)
copy	**la copia** *(lah 'koh-pee-ah)*
document	**el documento** *(ehl doh-koo-'mehn-toh)*
endorsement	**el endoso** *(ehl ehn-'doh-soh)*
explanation	**la explicación**
	(lah ehks-plee-kah-see-'ohn)
form	**el formulario** *(ehl fohr-moo-'lah-ree-oh)*
request	**la petición** *(lah peh-tee-see-'ohn)*
resource	**el recurso** *(ehl reh-'koor-soh)*
signature	**la firma** *(lah 'feer-mah)*

And use this pattern with the verb **saber,** "to know," to find out what they already know:

Do you know how to speak English?
¿Sabe hablar inglés? *('sah-beh ah-'blahr een-'glehs)*
Do you know how to read and write?
¿Sabe leer y escribir? *('sah-beh leh-'ehr ee ehs-kree-'beer)*
Do you know how to do it?
¿Sabe hacerlo? *('sah-beh ah-'sehr-loh)*

¡ M Á S   A Y U D A !

• In Spanish, there are two ways to say "to know." "To know something" requires the verb **saber,** while "to know someone" requires the verb **conocer.** Instead of working on all the conjugated forms of these new verbs, why not put them to practical use:

I don't know.	**No sé.** *(noh seh)*
I don't know him.	**No le conozco.** *(noh leh koh-'nohs-koh)*
Do you know English?	**¿Sabe usted inglés?**
	('sah-beh oos-'tehd een-'glehs)
Do you know her?	**¿La conoce?** *(lah koh-'noh-seh)*

| I didn't know it. | **No lo sabía.** *(noh loh sah-'bee-ah)* |
| I didn't know him. | **No le conocía.** *(noh leh koh-noh-'see-ah)* |

• Here's more work-related vocabulary. Can you create any useful one-liners without any help?

responsibility	**la responsabilidad**	**Es nuestra responsabilidad.**
experience	**la experiencia**	**Tengo mucha experiencia.**
interview	**la entrevista**	_____
reference	**la referencia**	_____
agreement	**el contrato**	_____
training	**el entrenamiento**	_____
machine	**la máquina**	_____

¡NECESITA PRACTICAR!

Translate into English:

¿Dónde está localizado el problema?
¿Necesita usted una copia del formulario?
María, ¿sabe leer el contrato en inglés?

The business
El negocio *(ehl neh-'goh-see-oh)*

Large-scale projects involve conversations related to business and finances. Familiarize yourself with all the basics:

I need (the) . . .	**Necesito . . .** *(neh-seh-'see-toh)*
claim	**la reclamación** *(lah reh-klah-mah-see'ohn)*
invoice	**la factura** *(lah fahk-'too-rah)*
order	**el pedido** *(ehl peh-'dee-doh)*
receipt	**el recibo** *(ehl reh-'see-boh)*
ticket	**el boleto** *(ehl boh-'leh-toh)*
bill	**la cuenta** *(lah 'kwehn-tah)*

Move (the) . . .	**Mueva** . . . *('mweh-vah)*
cargo	**la carga** *(lah 'kahr-gah)*
delivery	**el reparto** *(ehl reh-pahr-toh)*
inventory	**el inventario** *(ehl een-vehn-'tah-ree-oh)*
merchandise	**la mercancía** *(lah mehr-kahn-'see-ah)*
product	**el producto** *(ehl proh-'dook-toh)*
sample	**la muestra** *(lah 'mwehs-trah)*
shipment	**el envío** *(ehl ehn-'vee-oh)*
supply	**la existencia** *(lah ehk-sees-'tehn-see-ah)*

You know your environment. Take a big yellow marker and highlight the vocabulary you need. Then concentrate on it.

Who is (the) . . . ?	**¿Quién es . . . ?** *(kee-'ehn ehs)*
boss	**el jefe** *(ehl 'heh-feh)*
buyer	**el jefe de compras**
	(ehl 'heh-feh deh 'kohm-prahs)
carrier	**el transportador** *(ehl trahns-pohr-tah-'dohr)*
cashier	**el cajero** *(ehl kah-'heh-roh)*
clerk	**el oficinista** *(ehl oh-fee-see-'nees-tah)*
consultant	**el consultor** *(ehl kohn-sool-'tohr)*
customer	**el cliente** *(ehl klee-'ehn-teh)*
dealer	**el concesionario**
	(ehl kohn-seh-see-oh-'nah-ree-oh)
manager	**el gerente** *(ehl heh-'rehn-teh)*
manufacturer	**el fabricante** *(ehl fah-bree-'kahn-teh)*
partner	**el socio** *(ehl 'soh-see-oh)*
salesperson	**el vendedor** *(ehl vehn-deh-'dohr)*
shipper	**el fletador** *(ehl fleh-tah-'dohr)*
trustee	**el fideicomisario**
	(ehl fee-deh-ee-koh-mee-'sah-ree-oh)
Which is (the) . . . ?	**¿Cuál es . . . ?** *(kwahl ehs)*
bargain	**la ganga** *(lah 'gahn-gah)*
discount	**el descuento** *(ehl dehs-'kwehn-toh)*
down payment	**el pago inicial** *(ehl 'pah-goh ee-nee-see-'ahl)*

installment	**el plazo** *(ehl 'plah-soh)*
loss	**la pérdida** *(lah 'pehr-dee-dah)*
offer	**la oferta** *(lah oh-'fehr-tah)*
payment	**el pago** *(ehl 'pah-goh)*
purchase order	**la orden de compra**
	(lah 'ohr-dehn deh 'kohm-prah)
refund	**el reembolso** *(ehl reh-ehm-'bohl-soh)*
return	**la devolución** *(lah deh-voh-loo-see-'ohn)*
sale	**la venta** *(lah 'vehn-tah)*
tax	**el impuesto** *(ehl eem-'pwehs-toh)*
Where is (the) . . . ?	**¿Dónde está . . . ?** *('dohn-deh ehs-'tah)*
amount	**la cantidad** *(lah kahn-tee-'dahd)*
content	**el contenido** *(ehl kohn-teh-'nee-doh)*
percentage	**el porcentaje** *(ehl pohr-sehn-'tah-heh)*
price	**el precio** *(ehl 'preh-see-oh)*
profit	**la ganancia** *(lah gah-'nahn-see-ah)*
quality	**la calidad** *(lah kah-lee-'dahd)*
quantity	**la cantidad** *(lah kahn-tee-'dahd)*
rate	**la tarifa** *(lah tah-'ree-fah)*
reduction	**la reducción** *(lah reh-dook-see-'ohn)*
subtotal	**el subtotal** *(ehl soob-toh-'tahl)*
sum	**la suma** *(lah 'soo-mah)*
total	**el total** *(ehl toh-'tahl)*
weight	**el peso** *(ehl 'peh-soh)*
Does it have (the) . . . ?	**¿Tiene . . . ?** *(tee-'eh-neh)*
brand	**la marca** *(lah 'mahr-kah)*
label	**la etiqueta** *(lah eh-tee-'keh-tah)*
logo	**el logotipo** *(ehl loh-goh-'tee-poh)*
patent	**la patente** *(lah pah-'tehn-teh)*
stamp	**el sello** *(ehl 'seh-yoh)*
trademark	**marca registrada**
	(lah 'mahr-kah reh-gees-'trah-dah)

¡ M á s   A y u d a !

• Ask about money, using various verbs in the present tense:

How much . . . ?	¿Cuánto . . . ? *('kwahn-toh)*
does it cost	**cuesta** *('kwehs-tah)*
is it worth	**vale** *('vah-leh)*
do you want to order	**quiere pedir** *(kee-'eh-reh peh-'deer)*
can you pay	**puede pagar** *('pweh-deh pah-'gahr)*
are you buying	**está comprando** *(ehs-'tah kohm-'prahn-doh)*

• Now describe the product or price:

It's . . .	Está . . . *(ehs-'tah)* or Es . . . *(ehs)*
damaged	**Está dañado** *(ehs-'tah dahn-'yah-doh)*
delayed	**Está retrasado** *(ehs-'tah reh-trah-'sah-doh)*
free	**Es gratis** *(ehs 'grah-tees)*
imported	**Es importado** *(ehs eem-pohr-'tah-doh)*
included	**Está incluído** *(ehs-'tah een-kloo-'ee-doh)*
paid	**Está pagado** *(ehs-'tah pah-'gah-doh)*
retail	**Es al por menor** *(ehs ahl pohr meh-'nohr)*
used	**Está usado** *(ehs-'tah oo-'sah-doh)*
wholesale	**Es al por mayor** *(ehs ahl pohr mah-'yohr)*

¡ N e c e s i t a   P r a c t i c a r !

Connect the related words:

descuento	**jefe**
reparto	**usado**
factura	**envío**
dañado	**cuenta**
gerente	**ganga**

Talk to the customer

Hable con el cliente *('ah-bleh kohn ehl klee-'ehn-teh)*

Thrift stores, religious gift shops, and nonprofit organizations may sell directly to the public. Before serving any Spanish-speaking customers, practice these one-liners with your sales staff:

Which one do you like?	**¿Cuál le gusta?** *(kwahl leh 'goos-tah)*
Which one do you want?	**¿Cuál quiere?** *(kwahl kee-'eh-reh)*
Which one do you prefer?	**¿Cuál prefiere?**
	(kwahl preh-fee-'eh-reh)

Continue to learn sentences in smaller sets:

We are here to serve you.	**Estamos aquí para servirle.** *(ehs-'tah-mohs ah-'kee 'pah-rah sehr-'veer-leh)*
How may I assist you?	**¿Cómo puedo servirle?** *('koh-moh 'pweh-doh sehr-'veer-leh)*
How many would you like?	**¿Cuántos quisiera?** *('kwahn-tohs kee-see-'eh-rah)*
We can order more.	**Podemos pedir más.** *(poh-'deh-mohs peh-'deer mahs)*
Here's another one.	**Aquí hay otro.** *(ah-'kee 'ah-ee 'oh-troh)*
Do you like it?	**¿Le gusta?** *(leh 'goos-tah)*
Is that all?	**¿Es todo?** *(ehs 'toh-doh)*
Something else?	**¿Algo más?** *('ahl-goh mahs)*

We accept . . .	**Aceptamos . . .** *(ah-sehp-'tah-mohs)*
bills	**los billetes** *(lohs bee-'yeh-tehs)*
cash	**el efectivo** *(ehl eh-fehk-'tee-voh)*
cashier's checks	**los cheques bancarios** *(lohs 'cheh-kehs bahn-'kah-ree-ohs)*
change	**el cambio** *(ehl 'kahm-bee-oh)*
checks	**los cheques** *(lohs 'cheh-kehs)*
coins	**las monedas** *(lahs moh-'neh-dahs)*
coupons	**los cupones** *(lohs koo-'poh-nehs)*

credit cards	**las tarjetas de crédito**
	(lahs tahr-'heh-tahs deh 'kreh-dee-toh)
money orders	**los giros** *(lohs 'hee-rohs)*

¡ M Á S   A Y U D A !

• Learn how to share the bad news:

I'm sorry.	**Lo siento.** *(loh see-'ehn-toh)*
We don't have any more.	**No tenemos más.**
	(noh teh-'neh-mohs mahs)
We no longer sell them.	**Ya no los vendemos.**
	(yah noh lohs vehn-'deh-mohs)

• Take extra time to practice the terms below:

Do you have (the) . . . ?	**¿Tiene . . . ?** *(tee-'eh-neh)*
billfold	**la billetera** *(lah bee-yeh-'teh-rah)*
checkbook	**la chequera** *(lah cheh-'keh-rah)*
purse	**la bolsa** *(lah 'bohl-sah)*

• And how do you advertise? Note these items of interest:

It's in (the) . . .	**Está en . . .** *(ehs-'tah ehn)*
advertisement	**el anuncio** *(ehl ah-'noon-see-oh)*
article	**el artículo** *(ehl ahr-'tee-koo-loh)*
brochure	**el folleto** *(ehl foh-'yeh-toh)*
catalogue	**el catálogo** *(ehl kah-'tah-loh-goh)*
magazine	**la revista** *(lah reh-'vees-tah)*
news	**las noticias** *(lahs noh-'tee-see-ahs)*
newspaper	**el periódico** *(ehl peh-ree-'oh-dee-koh)*

• Talking about business includes the use of effective descriptive words. You will probably need this vocabulary at your next meeting with a Spanish speaker:

| It's (the) . . . | **Es . . .** *(ehs)* |
| confidential | **confidencial** *(kohn-fee-dehn-see-'ahl)* |

domestic	**nacional** *(nah-see-'oh-nahl)*
foreign	**extranjero** *(eks-trahn-'heh-roh)*
global	**mundial** *(moon-dee-'ahl)*
interim	**provisional** *(proh-vee-see-oh-'nahl)*
internal	**interno** *(een-'tehr-noh)*
international	**internacional** *(een-tehr-nah-see-oh-'nahl)*
interstate	**interestatal** *(een-tehr-ehs-tah-'tahl)*
national	**nacional** *(nah-see-oh-'nahl)*
public	**público** *('poo-blee-koh)*
seasonal	**estacional** *(ehs-tah-see-oh-'nahl)*
universal	**universal** *(oo-nee-vehr-'sahl)*

• When things go wrong, listen for these terms:

It's (the) . . .	**Es . . .** *(ehs)*
audit	**la verificación contable** *(lah veh-ree-fee-kah-see-'ohn kohn-'tah-bleh)*
bankruptcy	**la bancarrota** *(lah bahn-kah-'rroh-tah)*
collection	**la cobranza** *(lah koh-'brahn-sah)*
debt	**la deuda** *(lah 'deh-oo-dah)*
delay	**la demora** *(lah deh-'moh-rah)*
error	**el error** *(ehl eh-'rrohr)*
expense	**el gasto** *(ehl 'gahs-toh)*
extortion	**la extorsión** *(lah ehks-tohr-see-'ohn)*
forgery	**la falsificación** *(lah fahl-see-fee-kah-see-'ohn)*
fraud	**el fraude** *(ehl 'frah-oo-deh)*
insufficient funds	**los fondos insuficientes** *(lohs 'fohn-dohs een-soo-fee-see-'ehn-tehs)*
liability	**la obligación** *(lah oh-blee-gah-see-'ohn)*
loss	**la pérdida** *(lah 'pehr-dee-dah)*
penalty	**la multa** *(lah 'mool-tah)*
reduction	**la reducción** *(lah reh-dook-see-'ohn)*
robbery	**el robo** *(ehl 'roh-boh)*

Did you meet someone who just moved to this country? Are they a bit confused about our language and culture? When you find the time, share a few insights on U.S. customs toward tipping, dress, dating, holidays, and social skills. Make them feel welcome by respecting their perspective, and watch your relationship grow!

Do you have insurance?
¿Tiene seguro? *(tee-'eh-neh seh-'goo-roh)*

Outreach organizations usually can offer discounts on a variety of products. If you sell insurance coverage, get what you need from the following:

It's insurance for . . .	**Es seguro de . . .** *(ehs seh-'goo-roh deh)*
accidents	**accidentes** *(ahk-see-'dehn-tehs)*
automobile	**automóvil** *(aw-toh-'moh-veel)*
disability	**incapacidad** *(een-kah-pah-see-'dahd)*
family	**familia** *(fah-'mee-lee-ah)*
health	**salud** *(sah-'lood)*
hospital	**hospital** *(ohs-pee-'tahl)*
life	**vida** *('vee-dah)*
medical	**médico** *('meh-dee-koh)*

We have . . .	**Tenemos . . .** *(teh-'neh-mohs)*
affordable payments	**pagos a su alcance** *('pah-gohs ah soo ahl-'kahn-seh)*
comprehensive coverage	**cobertura completa** *(koh-behr-'too-rah kohm-'pleh-tah)*
easy access	**una localidad conveniente** *('oo-nah loh-kah-lee-'dahd kohn-veh-nee-'ehn-teh)*

individual health plans	**planes de salud individuales** *('plah-nehs deh sah-'lood een-dee-vee-'dwah-lehs)*
special rates	**tarifas especiales** *(tah-'ree-fahs ehs-peh-see-'ah-lehs)*
statewide network	**una red interestatal** *('oo-nah rehd een-tehr-ehs-tah-'tahl)*
24-hour service	**servicio de veinte y cuatro horas** *(sehr-'vee-see-oh deh 'veh-een-teh ee 'kwah-troh 'oh-rahs)*
wide selection	**una amplia selección** *('oo-nah 'ahm-plee-ah seh-lehk-see-'ohn)*
It also includes . . .	**También Incluye . . .** *(tahm-bee-'ehn een-'kloo-yeh)*
ambulance service	**servicio de ambulancia** *(sehr-'vee-see-oh deh ahm-boo-'lahn-see-ah)*
convalescent clinics	**clínicas de convalescencia** *('klee-nee-kahs deh kohn-vah-lehs-'sehn-see-ah)*
examinations	**exámenes** *(ehk-'sah-meh-nehs)*
home health care	**cuidado médico en el hogar** *(kwee-'dah-doh 'meh-dee-koh ehn ehl oh-'gahr)*
immunizations	**vacunas** *(vah-'koo-nahs)*
major surgery	**cirugía mayor** *(see-roo-'hee-ah mah-'yohr)*

¡MÁS AYUDA!

• As you work with finances, these words will help you with the math:

to add	**sumar** *(soo-'mahr)*
average	**promedio** *(proh-'meh-dee-oh)*
to divide	**dividir** *(dee-vee-'deer)*
fraction	**fracción** *(frahk-see-'ohn)*

to multiply	**multiplicar** *(mool-tee-plee-'kahr)*
percent	**por ciento** *(pohr see-'ehn-toh)*
to subtract	**restar** *(rehs-'tahr)*

• Keep collecting words that are similar in both languages:

restriction	**la restricción** *(lah rehs-treek-see-'ohn)*
inflation	**la inflación** *(lah een-flah-see-'ohn)*
transaction	**la transacción** *(lah trahn-sahk-see-'ohn)*

• Refer to these items when you send some information by mail:

post office	**la oficina de correos**
	(lah oh-fee-'see-nah deh koh-'rreh-ohs)
air mail	**el correo aéreo** *(ehl koh-'rreh-oh ah-'eh-reh-oh)*
letter	**la carta** *(lah 'kahr-tah)*
stamps	**las estampillas** *(lahs ehs-tahm-'pee-yahs)*
mailbox	**el buzón** *(ehl boo-'sohn)*
envelope	**el sobre** *(ehl 'soh-breh)*
delivery	**la entrega** *(lah ehn-'treh-gah)*
package	**el paquete** *(ehl pah-'keh-teh)*

• A few terms are so specialized or typical of this country that Spanish speakers will understand you better if you leave them untranslated:

el IRA
el IRS
el Medicare

 ¡ L A C U L T U R A !

Does everyone understand U.S. currency? New immigrants could get confused about our bills and coins, especially when debating the difference between a cent and a penny:

| cent, penny | **el centavo** *(ehl sehn-'tah-voh)* |
| dime | **diez centavos** *(dee-'ehs sehn-'tah-vohs)* |

dollar	**el dólar** *(ehl 'doh-lahr)*
nickel	**cinco centavos** *('seen-koh sehn-'tah-vohs)*
quarter	**veinte y cinco centavos**
	('veh-een-teh ee 'seen-koh sehn-'tah-vohs)

¡ *N E C E S I T A   P R A C T I C A R* !

Translate into Spanish:

How many would you like?

_____

I'm sorry, we don't have any more.

_____

Let's talk about the special rates.

_____

He has a dollar and a dime.

_____

It's life insurance.

_____

Notice all the action words you'll need to discuss the world of business. Can you develop a sentence or two?

to approve	**aprobar** *(ah-proh-'bahr)*

Aprobamos el trabajo.

to authorize	**autorizar** *(aw-toh-ree-'sahr)*

_____

to borrow	**pedir prestado** *(peh-'deer prehs-'tah-doh)*

_____

to buy	**comprar** *(kohm-'prahr)*

_____

to calculate	**calcular** *(kahl-koo-'lahr)*
to cancel	**cancelar** *(kahn-seh-'lahr)*
to collect	**recaudar** *(reh-kah-oo-'dahr)*
to confirm	**confirmar** *(kohn-feer-'mahr)*
to contribute	**contribuir** *(kohn-tree-boo-'eer)*
to deliver	**repartir** *(reh-pahr-'teer)*
to deposit	**depositar** *(deh-poh-see-'tahr)*
to distribute	**distribuir** *(dees-tree-boo-'eer)*
to exchange	**cambiar** *(kahm-bee-'ahr)*
to expire	**vencer** *(vehn-'sehr)*
to get	**conseguir** *(kohn-seh-'geer)*
to grow	**crecer** *(kreh-'sehr)*
to invest	**invertir** *(een-vehr-'teer)*
to join	**unir** *(oo-'neer)*

to lose	**perder** *(pehr-'dehr)*
to notify	**notificar** *(noh-tee-fee-'kahr)*
to pay	**pagar** *(pah-'gahr)*
to rent	**alquilar** *(ahl-kee-'lahr)*
to save	**ahorrar** *(ah-oh-'rrahr)*
to sell	**vender** *(vehn-'dehr)*
to share	**compartir** *(kohm-pahr-'teer)*
to withdraw	**retirar** *(reh-tee-'rahr)*

The law
La ley *(lah 'leh-ee)*

Dealing with national projects can lead to legal concerns. Copy this vital selection of items, and then put them away for emergency use:

addendum	**el anexo** *(ehl ah-'nek-soh)*
affidavit	**el afidávit** *(ehl ah-fee-'dah-veet)*
allegation	**la acusación** *(lah ah-koo-sah-see-'ohn)*
antitrust	**el antimonopolio** *(ehl ahn-tee-moh-noh-'poh-lee-oh)*
case	**el caso** *(ehl 'kah-soh)*
code	**el código** *(ehl 'koh-dee-goh)*
conditions	**las condiciones** *(lahs kohn-dee-see-'oh-nehs)*
court	**el tribunal** *(ehl tree-boo-'nahl)*
defense	**la defensa** *(lah deh-'fehn-sah)*

demands	**las reclamaciones**
	(lahs reh-klah-mah-see-'oh-nehs)
evidence	**la evidencia** *(lah eh-vee-'dehn-see-ah)*
injunction	**el interdicto** *(ehl een-tehr-'deek-toh)*
investigation	**la investigación** *(lah een-vehs-tee-gah-see-'ohn)*
litigation	**el pleito** *(ehl 'pleh-ee-toh)*
plaintiff	**el demandante** *(ehl deh-mahn-'dahn-teh)*
prosecution	**el procesamiento**
	(ehl proh-seh-sah-mee-'ehn-toh)
rights	**los derechos** *(lohs deh-'reh-chohs)*
rule	**la regla** *(lah 'reh-glah)*
settlement	**el arreglo** *(ehl ah-'rreh-gloh)*
terms	**los términos** *(lohs 'tehr-mee-nohs)*
testimony	**el testimonio** *(ehl tehs-tee-'moh-nee-oh)*
violation	**la violación** *(lah vee-oh-lah-see-'ohn)*

Politics
La política *(lah poh-'lee-tee-kah)*

Decisions in the political arena could affect your outreach efforts:

It has to do with (the) . . .	**Tiene que ver con . . .**
	(tee-'eh-neh keh vehr kohn)
affirmative action	**la acción afirmativa**
	(lah ahk-see-'ohn ah-feer-mah-'tee-vah)
bilingual education	**la educación bilingüe**
	(lah eh-doo-kah-see-'ohn bee-'leen-gweh)
civil rights	**los derechos civiles**
	(lohs deh-'reh-chohs see-'vee-lehs)
election	**la elección** *(lah eh-lehk-see-'ohn)*
government	**el gobierno** *(ehl goh-bee-'ehr-noh)*

media	**los medios de comunicación** *(lohs 'meh-dee-ohs deh koh-moo-nee-kah-see-'ohn)*
population	**la población** *(lah poh-blah-see-'ohn)*
Congress	**el congreso** *(ehl kohn-'greh-soh)*
labor dispute	**la disputa laboral** *(lah dees-'poo-tah lah-boh-'rahl)*
governor	**el gobernador** *(ehl goh-behr-nah-'dohr)*
senator	**el senador** *(ehl seh-nah-'dohr)*
vote	**el voto** *(ehl 'voh-toh)*
political party	**el partido político** *(ehl pahr 'too doh poh 'loo too koh)*
ecology	**la ecología** *(lah eh-koh-loh-'hee-ah)*
republican	**el republicano** *(ehl reh-poo-blee-'kah-noh)*
democrat	**el demócrata** *(ehl deh-'moh-krah-tah)*
President	**el presidente** *(ehl preh-see-'dehn-teh)*

Prepare yourself for the negative. These expressions require no article.

There is/are . . .	**Hay . . .** *('ah-ee)*
alcoholism	**(el) alcoholismo** *(ahl-koh-oh-'lees-moh)*
crime rate	**(el) índice de crimen** *('een-dee-seh deh 'kree-mehn)*
disease	**(las) enfermedades** *(ehn-fehr-meh-'dah-dehs)*
domestic violence	**(la) violencia doméstica** *(vee-oh-'lehn-see-ah doh-'mehs-tee-kah)*
drug abuse	**(el) abuso de drogas** *(ah-'boo-soh deh 'droh-gahs)*
drug addiction	**(la) drogadicción** *(droh-gah-deek-see-'ohn)*
drug traffic	**(el) narcotráfico** *(nahr-koh-'trah-fee-koh)*
gangs	**(las) pandillas** *(pahn-'dee-yahs)*

homelessness	**(la) gente desamparada**
	('hehn-teh deh-sahm-pah-'rah-dah)
hunger	**(el) hambre** *('ahm-breh)*
juvenile delinquency	**(la) delincuencia juvenil**
	(deh-leen-'kwehn-see-ah hoo-veh-'neel)
poverty	**(la) pobreza** *(poh-'breh-sah)*
pollution	**(la) contaminación**
	(lah kohn-tah-mee-nah-see-'ohn)
racism	**(el) racismo** *(rah-'sees-moh)*
runaway children	**(los) niños fugitivos**
	('neen-yohs foo-hee-'tee-vohs)
segregation	**(la) segregación** *(seh-greh-gah-see-'ohn)*
teen suicide	**(el) suicidio de adolescentes**
	(swee-'see-dee-oh deh ah-doh-lehs-'sehn-tehs)
unemployment	**(el) desempleo** *(deh-sehm-'pleh-oh)*
violence	**(la) violencia** *(vee-oh-'lehn-see-ah)*
war	**(la) guerra** *('geh-rrah)*

¡MÁS AYUDA!

• Speaking of political opinions, you will need the following vocabulary, even if some concepts are a little tough to explain:

They speak of ...	**Hablan de ...** *('ah-blahn deh)*
freedom	**la libertad** *(lah lee-behr-'tahd)*
peace	**la paz** *(lah pahs)*
hate	**el odio** *(ehl 'oh-dee-oh)*
respect	**el respeto** *(ehl rehs-'peh-toh)*
hope	**la esperanza** *(lah ehs-peh-'rahn-sah)*
sacrifice	**el sacrificio** *(ehl sah-kree-'fee-see-oh)*
kindness	**la bondad** *(lah bohn-'dahd)*
security	**la seguridad** *(lah seh-goo-ree-'dahd)*
love	**el amor** *(ehl ah-'mohr)*
trust	**la confianza** *(lah kohn-fee-'ahn-sah)*

¡ Necesita Practicar !

Match these words according to their topic. Notice the example:

guerra . . . . paz
amor   hambre
enfermedad   dinero
comida   odio
pobreza   defensa
acusación   salud

Telecommunications
Las telecomunicaciones
(lahs teh-leh-koh-moo-nee-kah-see-'oh-nehs)

National outreach projects can only be successful when contributing organizations keep in touch with one another, which means communication tools:

The computer needs a . . .	La computadora necesita . . .
	(lah kohm-poo-tah-'doh-rah neh-seh-'see-tah)
cable	**el cable** *(ehl 'kah-bleh)*
database	**la base de datos**
	(lah 'bah-seh deh 'dah-tohs)
disk	**el disco** *(ehl 'dees-koh)*
drive	**el impulsor** *(ehl eem-pool-'sohr)*
e-mail	**el correo electrónico**
	(ehl koh-'rreh-oh eh-lehk-'troh-nee-koh)
hardware	**los elementos físicos**
	(lohs eh-leh-'mehn-tohs 'fee-see-kohs)
input	**la entrada de información**
	(lah ehn-'trah-dah deh een-fohr-mah-see-'ohn)

access	**el acceso** *(ehl ahk-'seh-soh)*
printer	**la impresora** *(lah eem-preh-'soh-rah)*
modem	**el módem** *(ehl 'moh-dehm)*
keyboard	**el teclado** *(ehl teh-'klah-doh)*
language	**el lenguaje** *(ehl lehn-'gwah-heh)*
memory	**la memoria** *(lah meh-'moh-ree-ah)*
microprocessor	**el microprocesador**
	(ehl mee-kroh-proh-seh-sah-'dohr)
monitor	**el monitor** *(ehl moh-nee-'tohr)*
mouse	**el ratón** *(ehl rah-'tohn)*
port	**la conección** *(lah koh-nehk-see-'ohn)*
program	**el programa** *(ehl proh-'grah-mah)*
scanner	**el escáner** *(ehl ehs-'kah-nehr)*
screen	**la pantalla** *(lah pahn-'tah-yah)*
software	**el programa** *(ehl proh-'grah-mah)*
terminal	**el terminal** *(ehl tehr-mee-'nahl)*
tower	**la torre** *(lah 'toh-'rreh)*
microphone	**el micrófono** *(ehl mee-'kroh-foh-noh)*
speakers	**los parlantes** *(lohs pahr-'lahn-tehs)*
word processing	**el procesamiento de textos**
	(ehl proh-seh-sah-mee-'ehn-toh deh
	'tehks-tohs)

¡ M á s   A y u d a !

• The Spanish world of computers is full of untranslated English terms:

el internet
el zip drive
el web site
el laptop
el CD-ROM
el floppy

The telephone

El teléfono *(ehl teh-'leh-foh-noh)*

I have (the) ...	**Tengo ...** *('tehn-goh)*
answering machine	**el contestador telefónico** *(ehl kohn-tehs-tah-'dohr teh-leh-'foh-nee-koh)*
answering service	**el servicio telefónico** *(ehl sehr-'vee-see-oh teh-leh-'foh-nee-koh)*
area code	**el código de área** *(ehl 'koh-dee-goh deh 'ah-reh-ah)*
beeper	**el bíper** *(ehl 'bee-pehr)*
cellular phone	**el teléfono celular** *(ehl teh-'leh-foh-noh seh-loo-'lahr)*
conference call	**la llamada de conferencia** *(lah yah-'mah-dah deh kohn-feh-'rehn-see-ah)*
800 number	**el número de ochocientos** *(ehl 'noo-meh-roh deh oh-choh-see-'ehn-tohs)*
extension	**la extensión** *(lah ehks-tehn-see-ohn)*
fax	**el facsímil, el fax** *(ehl fahk-'see-meel, ehl fahks)*
headset	**el auricular** *(ehl ow-ree-koo-'lahr)*

Making phone calls in Spanish is a tough task, but with the proper one-liners in hand, conversations are much more productive. For calls coming into your office, place the phrases you need alongside the phone, and then wait for the chance to practice:

Hello, is _____ there?
Aló, ¿está _____? *(ah-'loh ehs-tah)*

May I speak to _____ ?
¿Puedo hablar con _____? *('pweh-doh ah-'blahr kohn)*

Phone call for _____.
Llamada para _____. *(yah-'mah-dah 'pah-rah)*

I'm calling about _____.
Estoy llamando acerca de _____.
 (ehs-'toh-ee yah-'mahn-doh ah-'sehr-kah deh)

I'll transfer you to _____.
Le voy a transferir a _____. *(leh 'voh-ee ah trahns-feh-'reer ah)*

Tell him/her that _____.
Dígale que _____. *('dee-gah-leh keh)*

Don't forget to say "please":

More slowly, please.
Más despacio, por favor. *(mahs dehs-'pah-see-oh pohr fah-'vohr)*

Wait a moment, please.
Espere un momento, por favor.
 (ehs-'peh-reh oon moh-'mehn-toh pohr fah-'vohr)

Please, it's very urgent.
Por favor, es muy urgente. *(pohr fah-'vohr ehs 'moo-ee oor-hehn-teh)*

Your number, please.
Su número, por favor. *(soo 'noo-meh-roh pohr fah-'vohr)*

Your name, please.
Su nombre, por favor. *(soo 'nohm-breh pohr fah-'vohr)*

Could you please repeat that?
¿Puede repetirlo, por favor?
 ('pweh-deh reh-peh-'teer-loh pohr fah-'vohr)

Let's break your one-liners into vocabulary-specific sets:

Can you call later?
¿Puede llamar más tarde? *('pweh-deh yah-'mahr mahs 'tahr-deh)*

He/She will call you later.
Llamará más tarde. *(yah-mah-'rah mahs 'tahr-deh)*

I'll call back later.
Llamaré más tarde. *(yah-mah-'reh mahs 'tahr-deh)*

Do you want to leave a message?
¿Quiere dejar un recado? *(kee-'eh-reh deh-'hahr oon reh-'kah-doh)*

I'd like to leave a message.
Quisiera dejar un recado. *(kee-see-'eh-rah deh-'hahr oon reh-'kah-doh)*

I will give him/her your message.
Le voy a dejar su mensaje. *(leh 'voh-ee ah deh-'hahr soo mehn-'sah-heh)*

Is it long distance?
¿Es de larga distancia? *(ehs deh 'lahr-gah dees-'tahn-see-ah)*

Is it a local call?
¿Es una llamada local? *(ehs 'oo-nah yah-'mah-dah loh-'kahl)*

Is it a collect call.
¿Es una llamada con cobro revertido?
 (ehs 'oo-nah yah-'mah-dah koh 'koh-broh reh-vehr-'tee-doh)

Frustrations happen in any language. Here are a few examples:

He/She isn't here.
No está aquí. *(noh ehs-'tah ah-'kee)*

He/She doesn't work here.
No trabaja aquí. *(noh trah-'bah-hah ah-'kee)*

He/She can't come to the phone.
No puede contestar la llamada.
 (noh 'pweh-deh kohn-tehs-'tahr lah yah-'mah-dah)

He/She is busy.
Está ocupado(a). *(ehs-'tah oh-koo-'pah-doh, dah)*

Is this the correct number?
¿Es el número correcto? *(ehs ehl 'noo-meh-roh koh-'rrehk-toh)*

I have a wrong number.
Tengo un número equivocado.
  ('tehn-goh oon 'noo-meh-roh eh-kee-voh-'kah-doh)

You have a wrong number.
Tiene un número equivocado.
  (tee-'eh-neh oon 'noo-meh-roh eh-kee-voh-'kah-doh)

The number has been changed.
El número ha cambiado. *(ehl 'noo-meh-roh ah kahm-bee-'ah-doh)*

¡MÁS AYUDA!

• Sometimes there are technical difficulties:

The line is bad.
La línea está mala. *(lah 'lee-neh-ah ehs-'tah 'mah-lah)*

The line is busy.
La línea está ocupada. *(lah 'lee-neh-ah ehs-'tah oh-koo-'pah-dah)*

The line is disconnected.
La línea esta desconectada.
  (lah 'lee-neh-ah ehs-'tah dehs-koh-nehk-'tah-dah)

• Now direct others how to handle the calls:

Dial this number.
Marque este número. *('mahr-keh 'ehs-teh 'noo-meh-roh)*

Press this number.
Oprima este número. *(oh-'pree-mah 'ehs-teh 'noo-meh-roh)*

Ask for this number.
Pida este número. *('pee-dah 'ehs-teh 'noo-meh-roh)*

Hang up the phone.
Cuelgue el teléfono. *('kwehl-geh ehl teh-'leh-foh-noh)*

¡*L A   C U L T U R A !*

To get a feel for communication in Spanish, find time to observe a group of Hispanics in public or at a social gathering. Facial expressions, touch, changes in tone, and hand signals are a few of the many nonverbal differences between the Latin American and U.S. cultures.

¡*N E C E S I T A   P R A C T I C A R !*

List five words that relate to the world of computers:

_____   _____

Translate this phone conversation:

Hello, is José there? It's very urgent.

_____

No, I'm sorry. Do you want to leave a message?

_____

Yes , thank you. My name is Marta, and I'm calling about the sale.

_____

It's time to clean!
¡Es la hora de limpiar!
(ehs lah 'oh-rah deh leem-pee-'ahr)

Many federal and state programs involve trash collection, maintenance, and general cleanup activities. Practice naming everything in both languages.

| Bring the ... | **Traiga** ... *('trah-ee-gah)* |
| box | **la caja** *(lah 'kah-hah)* |

broom	**la escoba** *(lah ehs-'koh-bah)*
brush	**el cepillo** *(ehl seh-'pee-yoh)*
bucket	**el balde** *(ehl 'bahl-deh)*
dustpan	**la pala para recoger basura**
	(lah 'pah- lah 'pah-rah reh-koh-'hehr bah-'soo-rah)
feather duster	**el plumero** *(ehl ploo-'meh-roh)*
gloves	**los guantes** *(lohs 'gwahn-tehs)*
hose	**la manguera** *(lah mahn-'geh-rah)*
mask	**la máscara** *(lah 'mahs-kah-rah)*
mop	**el trapeador** *(ehl trah-peh-ah-'dohr)*
rag	**el trapo** *(ehl 'trah-poh)*
scouring pad	**el estropajo** *(ehl ehs-troh-'pah-hoh)*
scraper	**el raspador** *(ehl rahs-pah-'dohr)*
scrub brush	**el cepillo de fregar**
	(ehl seh-'pee-yoh deh freh-'gahr)
sponge	**la esponja** *(lah ehs-'pohn-hah)*
stepladder	**la escalera** *(lah ehs-kah-'leh-rah)*
towel	**la toalla** *(lah toh-'ah-yah)*
trashbag	**la bolsa de basura**
	(lah 'bohl-sah deh bah-'soo-rah)
trashcan	**el cesto de basura**
	(ehl 'cehs-toh deh bah-'soo-rah)
vacuum cleaner	**la aspiradora** *(lah ahs-pee-rah-'doh-rah)*
wastepaper basket	**el papelero** *(ehl pah-peh-'leh-roh)*

Cleaning supplies
Los productos para limpiar
(lohs proh-'dook-tohs 'pah-rah leem-pee-'ahr)

The following products can easily be identified by name brands, and sometimes all you have to mention is the color of the container. However, to avoid confusion, try to be as specific as you can:

Please use (the) . . .	**Favor de usar . . .** *(fah-'vohr deh oo-'sahr)*
ammonia	**el amoníaco** *(ehl ah-moh-'nee-ah-koh)*

bleach	**el blanqueador** *(ehl blahn-keh-ah-'dohr)*
cleaner	**el limpiador** *(ehl leem-pee-ah-'dohr)*
cleanser	**el agente de limpieza** *(ehl ah-'hehn-teh deh leem-pee-'eh-sah)*
cream	**la crema** *(lah 'kreh-mah)*
foam	**la espuma** *(lah ehs-'poo-mah)*
liquid	**el líquido** *(ehl 'lee-kee-doh)*
paste	**la pasta** *(lah 'pahs-tah)*
polish	**el lustrador** *(ehl loos-trah-'dohr)*
powder	**el polvo** *(ehl 'pohl-voh)*
soap	**el jabón** *(ehl hah-'bohn)*
spray	**el rociador** *(ehl roh-see-ah-'dohr)*
wax	**la cera** *(lah 'seh-rah)*

Can you guess what these words mean?

el detergente

_____

el desinfectante

_____

el jabón de platos

_____

¡MÁS AYUDA!

• Be specific in your instructions: combine the words that you have learned to get your point across.

cleaning powder	**el polvo para limpiar** *(ehl 'pohl-voh 'pah-rah leem-pee-'ahr)*
hot water	**el agua caliente** *(ehl 'ah-gwah kah-lee-'ehn-teh)*
liquid soap	**el jabón líquido** *(ehl hah-'bohn 'lee-kee-doh)*
paper towel	**la toalla de papel** *(lah toh-'ah-yah deh pah-'pehl)*

wet sponge	**la esponja mojada** *(lah ehs-'pohn-hah moh-hah-dah)*

It's dirty!
¡Está sucio! *(ehs-'tah 'soo-see-oh)*

Now that all your supplies are in order, it's time to learn about the job ahead of us. Check over this next list of "unclean" vocabulary. Think of different ways to describe the unpleasant sights around you!

There is (are) . . .	**Hay . . .** *('ah-ee)*
ash	**(la) ceniza** *(seh-'nee-sah)*
crumbs	**(las) migas** *('mee-gahs)*
dirt	**(la) tierra** *(tee-'eh-rrah)*
dust	**(el) polvo** *('pohl-voh)*
filth	**(la) suciedad** *(soo-see-eh-'dahd)*
fungi	**(los) hongos** *('ohn-gohs)*
grime	**(la) mugre** *('moo-greh)*
mold	**(el) moho** *('moh-hoh)*
mud	**(el) lodo** *('loh-doh)*
rust	**(la) herrumbre** *(eh-'room-breh)*
scum	**(el) desecho** *(deh-'seh-choh)*
sewage	**(el) desagüe** *(deh-'sah-gweh)*
silt	**(el) cieno** *(see-'eh-noh)*
soot	**(el) tizne** *('tees-neh)*
trash	**(la) basura** *(bah-'soo-rah)*
waste	**(los) desperdicios** *(dehs-pehr-'dee-see-ohs)*

It's . . .	**Está . . .** *(ehs-'tah)*
bent	**doblado** *(doh-'blah-doh)*
broken	**roto** *('roh-toh)*
burned	**quemado** *(keh-'mah-doh)*
contaminated	**contaminado** *(kohn-tah-mee-'nah-doh)*
corroded	**corroído** *(koh-rroh-'ee-doh)*
cracked	**trizado** *(tree-'sah-doh)*

cut	**cortado** *(kohr-'tah-doh)*
damaged	**dañado** *(dahn-'yah-doh)*
dirty	**sucio** *('soo-see-oh)*
dusty	**polvoriento** *(pohl-voh-ree-'ehn-toh)*
faded	**descolorido** *(dehs-koh-loh-'ree-doh)*
filthy	**muy sucio** *('moo-ee 'soo-see-oh)*
marked	**marcado** *(mahr-'kah-doh)*
rotten	**podrido** *(poh-'dree-doh)*
ruined	**arruinado** *(ah-rroo-ee-'nah-doh)*
rusty	**herrumbrado** *(eh-rroom-'brah-doh)*
scuffed	**rayado** *(rah-'yah-doh)*
spoiled	**estropeado** *(ehs-troh-peh-'ah-doh)*
stained	**manchado** *(mahn-'chah-doh)*
torn	**rasgado, roto** *(rahs-'gah-doh, 'roh-toh)*
warped	**torcido** *(tohr-'see-doh)*
wet	**mojado** *(moh-'hah-doh)*
worn	**gastado** *(gahs-'tah-doh)*
It's . . .	**Es . . .** *(ehs)*
dangerous	**peligroso** *(peh-lee-'groh-soh)*
poisonous	**venenoso** *(veh-neh-'noh-soh)*

¡MÁS AYUDA!

• Look all around you. Pull what you need from this selection of descriptive words:

He/she's . . .	**Está . . .** *(ehs-'tah)*
abandoned	**abandonado(a)** *(ah-bahn-doh-'nah-doh, dah)*
at risk	**en riesgo** *(ehn ree-'ehs-goh)*
isolated	**aislado(a)** *(ah-ees-'lah-doh, dah)*
malnourished	**desnutrido(a)** *(dehs-noo-'tree-doh, dah)*
neglected	**desatendido(a)** *(dehs-ah-tehn-'dee-doh, dah)*
unemployed	**desempleado(a)** *(dehs-ehm-pleh-'ah-doh, dah)*
very sick	**muy enfermo(a)** *('moo-ee ehn-'fehr-moh, mah)*

¡N E C E S I T A   P R A C T I C A R !

Delete the word that doesn't belong with the others:

el vendedor, el limpiador, el lustrador
la escoba, el trapeador, la entrevista
el polvo, la lechuga, la tierra

See the pattern, and fill in the blanks:

cortar	<u>Está cortado.</u>
quemar	_____.
doblar	_____.
arruinar	_____.
dañar	_____.
manchar	_____.

From room to room
De cuarto a cuarto *(deh 'kwahr-toh ah 'kwahr-toh)*

To learn the parts of the house, simply walk around pronouncing all the items you come into contact with. You can even call out the name of each room as you wander through it. In no time at all, you'll be remembering words easily, and won't have to depend on the labels any more! As you mention a particular item, make comments using various descriptive words similar to the examples shown here.

attic   **el desván** *(ehl dehs-'vahn)*
El desván es pequeño. *(ehl dehs-'vahn ehs peh-'kehn-yoh)*

basement   **el sótano** *(ehl 'soh-tah-noh)*
El sótano está sucio. *(ehl 'soh-tah-noh ehs-'tah 'soo-see-oh)*

bathroom   **el cuarto de baño** *(ehl 'kwahr-toh deh 'bahn-yoh)*
El cuarto de baño es nuevo.
  (ehl 'kwahr-toh deh 'bahn-yoh ehs 'nweh-voh)

bedroom   **el dormitorio** *(ehl dohr-mee-'toh-ree-oh)*
El dormitorio es grande. *(ehl dohr-mee-'toh-ree-oh ehs 'grahn-deh)*

dining room   **el comedor** *(ehl koh-meh-'dohr)*
El comedor es viejo. *(ehl koh-meh-'dohr ehs vee-'eh-hoh)*

garage   **el garaje** *(ehl gah-'rah-heh)*
El garaje está lleno. *(ehl gah-'rah-heh ehs-'tah 'yeh-noh)*

hallway   **el pasillo** *(ehl pah-'see-yoh)*
El pasillo está frío. *(ehl pah-'see-yoh ehs-'tah 'free-oh)*

kitchen   **la cocina** *(lah koh-'see-nah)*
La cocina está limpia. *(lah koh-'see-nah ehs-'tah 'leem-pee-ah)*

living room   **la sala** *(lah 'sah-lah)*
La sala es bonita. *(lah 'sah-lah ehs boh-'nee-tah)*

Now take your people outside and clean up these items, too:

Let's go to (the) . . .   **Vamos a . . .** *('vah-mohs ah)*
   backyard   **el patio** *(ehl 'pah-tee-oh)*
   chimney   **la chimenea** *(lah chee-meh-'neh-ah)*
   driveway   **la entrada para carros**
           (lah ehn-'trah-dah 'pah-rah 'kah-rrohs)
   fence   **la cerca** *(lah 'sehr-kah)*
   gate   **el portón** *(ehl pohr-'tohn)*
   pool   **la piscina** *(lah pee-'see-nah)*
   porch   **el portal** *(ehl pohr-'tahl)*

¡ *M Á S*   *A Y U D A !*

• Let everyone on the premises know where the emergency items are located. Memorize these essential words:

alarm   **la alarma** *(lah ah-'lahr-mah)*
fire extinguisher   **el extintor** *(ehl ehks-teen-'tohr)*

first-aid kit	**la caja de primeros auxilios**
	(lah 'kah-hah deh pree-'meh-rohs owk-'see-lee-ohs)
fuse box	**la caja de fusibles**
	(lah 'kah-hah deh foo-'see-blehs)
gas meter	**el medidor de gas** *(ehl meh-dee-'dohr deh gahs)*
water valve	**la válvula de agua**
	(lah 'vahl-voo-lah deh 'ah-gwah)
security system	**el sistema de seguridad**
	(ehl sees-'teh-mah deh seh-goo-ree-'dahd)

• Don't forget these important parts of the building:

air conditioning	**el aire acondicionado**
	(ehl 'ah-ee-reh ah-kohn-dee-see-oh-'nah-doh)
heating	**la calefacción** *(lah kah-leh-fahk-see-'ohn)*
plumbing	**la tubería** *(lah too-beh-'ree-ah)*

• When giving cleaning instructions to everyone, be sure to tell them about the restroom:

Please check (the) . . .	**Favor de revisar . . .**
	(fah-'vohr deh reh-vee-'sahr)
dispenser	**el distribuidor** *(ehl dees-tree-boo-ee-'dohr)*
mirror	**el espejo** *(ehl ehs-'peh-hoh)*
paper towel	**la toalla de papel**
	(lah toh-'ah-yah deh pah-'pehl)
sink	**el lavamanos** *(ehl lah-vah-'mah-nohs)*
soap	**el jabón** *(ehl hah-'bohn)*
toilet	**el excusado** *(ehl ehks-koo-'sah-doh)*
toilet paper	**el papel higiénico**
	(ehl pah-'pehl ee-hee-'eh-nee-koh)
urinal	**el orinal** *(ehl oh-ree-'nahl)*

The fixtures

Las instalaciones *(lahs eens-tah-lah-see-'oh-nehs)*

While learning the names for household fixtures, create practical phrases to use with Spanish speakers:

Where is the . . . ?	**¿Dónde está . . . ?** *('dohn-deh ehs-'tah)*
It's next to the . . .	**Está al lado de . . .** *(ehs-'tah ahl 'lah-doh deh)*
I'm cleaning . . .	**Estoy limpiando . . .**
	(ehs-'toh-ee leem-pee-'ahn-doh)
bathroom sink	**el lavabo** *(ehl lah-'vah-boh)*
bathtub	**la tina** *(lah 'tee-nah)*
cabinet	**el gabinete** *(ehl gah-bee-'neh-teh)*
closet	**el ropero** *(ehl roh-'peh-roh)*
counter	**el mostrador** *(ehl mohs-trah-'dohr)*
dresser	**el tocador** *(ehl toh-kah-'dohr)*
fireplace	**la chimenea** *(lah chee-meh-'neh-ah)*
kitchen sink	**el fregadero** *(ehl freh-gah-'deh-roh)*
medicine chest	**el botiquín** *(ehl boh-tee-'keen)*
shower	**la ducha** *(lah 'doo-chah)*
toilet	**el excusado** *(ehl ehks-koo-'sah-doh)*

¡LAS ORDENES!

• Cleanup projects require a unique set of Spanish command words.

carry	**lleve** *('yeh-veh)*

Lleve el balde. *('yeh-veh ehl 'bahl-deh)*

clean	**limpie** *('leem-pee-eh)*

Limpie el baño. *('leem-pee-eh ehl 'bahn-yoh)*

close	**cierre** *(see-'eh-rreh)*

Cierre la puerta. *(see-'eh-rreh lah 'pwehr-tah)*

dust	**desempolve** *(deh-sehm-'pohl-veh)*

Desempolve el gabinete. *(deh-sehm-'pohl-veh ehl gah-bee-'neh-teh)*

lift   **levante** *(leh-'vahn-teh)*
Levante la mesa. *(leh-'vahn-teh lah 'meh-sah)*

lower   **baje** *('bah-heh)*
Baje la escalera. *('bah-heh lah ehs-kah-'leh-rah)*

move   **mueva** *('mweh-vah)*
Mueva el sofá. *('mweh-vah ehl soh-'fah)*

open   **abra** *('ah-brah)*
Abra la ventana. *('ah-brah lah vehn-'tah-nah)*

pick up   **recoja** *(reh-'koh-hah)*
Recoja la tierra. *(reh-'koh-hah lah tee-'eh-rrah)*

put   **ponga** *('pohn-gah)*
Ponga la silla aquí. *('pohn-gah lah 'see-yah ah-'kee)*

sweep   **barra** *('bah-rrah)*
Barra el piso. *('bah-rrah ehl 'pee-soh)*

throw awa   **tire** *('tee-reh)*
Tire la basura. *('tee-reh lah bah-'soo-rah)*

turn off   **apague** *(ah-'pah-geh)*
Apague la luz. *(ah-'pah-geh lah loos)*

turn on   **prenda** *('prehn-dah)*
Prenda la aspiradora. *('prehn-dah lah ahs-pee-rah-'doh-rah)*

vacuum   **limpie con aspiradora**
                       ('leem-pee-eh kohn ahs-pee-rah-'doh-rah)
Limpie con aspiradora la sala.
   ('leem-pee-eh kohn ahs-pee-rah-'doh-rah lah 'sah-lah)

wash   **lave** *('lah-veh)*
Lave con el cepillo. *('lah-veh kohn ehl seh-'pee-yoh)*

• Here's a reminder. To say "don't," just put **no** in front of the command:

Don't turn off the light!
¡No apague la luz! *(noh ah-'pah-geh lah loos)*

¡ *M Á S   A Y U D A !*

• All of these should be memorized and practiced right away!

Be very careful	**Tenga mucho cuidado.** *('tehn-gah 'moo-choh kwee-'dah-doh)*
Do it by hand.	**Hágalo a mano.** *('ah-gah-loh ah 'mah-noh)*
Do not touch it.	**No lo toque.** *(noh loh 'toh-keh)*
It doesn't work.	**No funciona.** *(noh foon-see-'oh-nah)*
Like this.	**Así.** *(ah-'see)*
Remember this.	**Recuerde esto.** *(reh-'kwehr-deh 'ehs-toh)*
This is the procedure.	**Este es el procedimiento.** *('ehs-teh ehs ehl proh-seh-dee-mee-'ehn-toh)*
This is what I want.	**Esto es lo que quiero.** *('ehs-toh ehs loh keh kee-'eh-roh)*
This way.	**De esta manera.** *(deh 'ehs-tah mah-'neh-rah)*

¡ *N E C E S I T A   P R A C T I C A R !*

Finish the sentences with the correct vocabulary:

sala, dormitorio, baño

La ducha está en el _____.
La chimenea está en la _____.
El tocador está en la _____.

Electrical appliances
Los electrodomésticos
(lohs eh-lehk-troh-doh-'mehs-tee-kohs)

Appliances need cleaning and repair as well. Learn how to refer to them in Spanish:

I found (the) . . .	**Encontré . . .** *(ehn-kohn-'treh)*
air conditioner	**el acondicionador de aire** *(ehl ah-kohn-dee-see-oh-nah-'dohr deh 'ah-ee-reh)*
answering machine	**el contestador telefónico** *(ehl kohn-tehs-tah-'dohr teh-leh-'foh-nee-koh)*
clock	**el reloj** *(ehl reh-'loh)*
dishwasher	**el lavaplatos** *(ehl lah-vah-'plah-tohs)*
dryer	**la secadora** *(lah seh-kah-'doh-rah)*
fan	**el ventilador** *(ehl vehn-tee-lah-'dohr)*
freezer	**el congelador** *(ehl kohn-heh-lah-dohr)*
garage door opener	**el abridor de garajes** *(ehl ah-bree-dohr deh gah-'rah-hehs)*
hair dryer	**el secador de pelo** *(ehl seh-kah-'dohr deh 'peh-loh)*
heater	**el calentador** *(ehl kah-lehn-tah-'dohr)*
hot water heater	**el calentador de agua** *(ehl kah-lehn-tah-'dohr deh 'ah-gwah)*
lamp	**la lámpara** *(lah 'lahm-pah-rah)*
microwave	**el horno de microonda** *(ehl 'ohr-noh deh mee-kroh-'ohn-dah)*
oven	**el horno** *(ehl 'ohr-noh)*
radio	**el radio** *(ehl 'rah-dee-oh)*
refrigerator	**el refrigerador** *(ehl reh-free-geh-rah-'dohr)*
sewing machine	**la máquina de coser** *(lah 'mah-kee-nah deh koh-'sehr)*
smoke alarm	**el detector de humo** *(ehl deh-tehk-'tohr deh 'oo-moh)*
stereo	**el estéreo** *(ehl ehs-'teh-reh-oh)*

stove	**la estufa** *(lah ehs-'too-fah)*
thermostat	**el termostato** *(ehl tehr-mohs-'tah-toh)*
toaster	**la tostadora** *(lah tohs-tah-'doh-rah)*
washer	**la lavadora** *(lah lah-vah-'doh-rah)*

Many household items are also used as outreach equipment:

camcorder	**la videocámara** *(lah vee-deh-oh-'kah-mah-rah)*
CD player	**el tocador de discos compactos,**
	el tocadiscos *(ehl toh-kah-'dohr deh 'dees-kohs kohm-'pahk-tohs, ehl toh-kah-'dees-kohs)*
DVD player	**el tocador de DVD** *(ehl toh-kah-'dohr deh deh-veh-'deh)*
TV	**el televisor** *(ehl teh-leh-vee-'sohr)*
VCR	**la videocasetera** *(lah vee-deh-oh-kah-seh-'teh-rah)*

¡ M Á S   A Y U D A !

• The location words fit in with most home-related vocabulary, especially when you're asking someone to do something. For example:

Change the sheets in the room.
Cambie las sábanas en el cuarto. *('kahm-bee-eh lahs 'sah-bah-nahs ehn ehl 'kwahr-toh)*

Clean behind the sofa.
Limpie detrás del sofá. *('leem-pee-eh deh-'trahs dehl soh-'fah)*

Make the bed over there.
Haga la cama allá. *('ah-gah lah 'kah-mah ah-'yah)*

Sweep next to the stove.
Barra la lado de la estufa. *('bah-rrah ahl 'lah-doh deh lah ehs-'too-fah)*

Vacuum under the bed.
Limpie con aspiradora debajo de la cama. *('leem-pee-eh kohn ahs-pee-rah-'doh-rah deh-'ba-hoh deh lah 'kah-mah)*

The car wash

El lavado de carros *(ehl lah-'vah-doh deh 'kah-rrohs)*

Most Spanish speakers in the United States are able to translate the basic parts of an automobile from Spanish into English, so you shouldn't have too much trouble in dialogues about washing and taking care of a car. However, when you do get stuck, refer to this list of pertinent command words and vocabulary:

Clean (the) . . .	**Limpie** . . . *('leem-pee-eh)*
Wash (the) . . .	**Lave** . . . *('lah-veh)*
Wax (the) . . .	**Encere** . . . *(ehn-'seh-reh)*
Replace (the) . . .	**Reemplace** . . . *(reh-ehm-'plah-seh)*
Repair (the) . . .	**Repare** . . . *(reh-'pah-reh)*
axle	**el eje** *(ehl 'eh-heh)*
brakes	**los frenos** *(lohs 'freh-nohs)*
bumper	**el parachoques** *(ehl pah-rah-'choh-kehs)*
cab	**la cabina** *(lah kah-'bee-nah)*
dashboard	**el tablero** *(ehl tah-'bleh-roh)*
door	**la puerta** *(lah 'pwehr-tah)*
engine	**el motor** *(ehl moh-'tohr)*
fender	**el guardabarro** *(ehl gwahr-dah-'bah-rroh)*
gauge	**el indicador** *(ehl een-dee-kah-'dohr)*
glove compartment	**la guantera** *(lah gwahn-'teh-rah)*
hood	**la cubierta** *(lah koo-bee-'ehr-tah)*
horn	**la bocina** *(lah boh-'see-nah)*
hubcap	**el tapacubos** *(ehl tah-pah-'koo-bohs)*
lights	**las luces** *(lahs 'loo-sehs)*
part	**la pieza** *(lah pee-'eh-sah)*
mirror	**el espejo** *(ehl ehs-'peh-hoh)*
muffler	**el silenciador** *(ehl see-lehn-see-ah-'dohr)*
roof	**el techo** *(ehl 'teh-choh)*
seat	**el asiento** *(ehl ah-see-ehn-toh)*
shock absorber	**el amortiguador** *(ehl ah-mohr-tee-gwah-'dohr)*
spare tire	**el neumático de repuesto** *(ehl neh-oo-'mah-tee-koh deh reh-'pwehs-toh)*

steering wheel	**el volante** *(ehl voh-'lahn-teh)*
tire	**el neumático** *(ehl neh-oo-'mah-tee-koh)*
trunk	**la maletera** *(lah mah-leh-'teh-rah)*
windshield	**el parabrisas** *(ehl pah-rah-'bree-sahs)*

¡*Necesita Practicar!*

| Mention | **Mencione** *(mehn-see-'oh-neh)* |

Tres piezas de un carro _____

Tres muebles _____

Tres electrodomésticos _____

We are here to help you
Estamos aquí para ayudarle
(ehs-'tah-mohs ah-'kee 'pah-rah ah-yoo-'dahr-leh)

Outreach workers are also asked to help in cases of national emergencies and disasters. Here is a list of events that demands an immediate response:

We had a/an . . .	**Tuvimos . . .** *(too-'vee-mohs)*
assault	**un asalto** *(oon ah-'sahl-toh)*
blackout	**un apagón** *(oon ah-pah-'gohn)*
bomb	**una bomba** *('oo-nah 'bohm-bah)*
car accident	**un accidente de carro** *(oon ahk-see-'dehn-teh deh 'kah-rroh)*
chemical spill	**un derrame de sustancias químicas** *(oon deh-'rrah-meh deh soos-'tahn-see-ahs 'kee-mee-kahs)*
crime	**un delito** *(oon deh-'lee-toh)*
explosion	**una explosión** *('oo-nah ehks-ploh-see-'ohn)*
fire	**un incendio** *(oon een-'sehn-dee-oh)*
looting	**un saqueo** *(oon sah-'keh-oh)*

raid	**una incursión** *('oo-nah een-koor-see-'ohn)*
riot	**un disturbio** *(oon dees-'toor-bee-oh)*
robbery	**un robo** *(oon 'roh-boh)*
strike	**una huelga** *('oo-nah oo-'ehl-gah)*
suicide	**un suicidio** *(oon swee-'see-dee-oh)*

There is/are . . .	**Hay** . . . *('ah-ee)*
flames	**llamas** *('yah-mahs)*
fumes	**vapores** *(vah-'poh-rehs)*
gas	**gas** *(gahs)*
poison	**veneno** *(veh-'neh-noh)*
smoke	**humo** *('oo-moh)*
toxic materials	**materiales tóxicos**
	(mah-teh-ree-'ah-lehs 'tohk-see-kohs)

Check (the) . . .	**Revise** . . . *(reh-'vee-seh)*
chain	**la cadena** *(lah kah-'deh-nah)*
deadbolt	**el pestillo** *(ehl pehs-'tee-yoh)*
key	**la llave** *(lah 'yah-veh)*
latch	**el cerrojo** *(ehl seh-'rroh-hoh)*
lock	**la cerradura** *(lah seh-rrah-'doo-rah)*
padlock	**el candado** *(ehl kahn-'dah-doh)*
safe	**la caja fuerte** *(lah 'kah-hah 'fwehr-teh)*

Use (the) . . .	**Use** . . . *('oo-seh)*
binoculars	**los binoculares** *(lohs bee-noh-koo-'lah-rehs)*
candle	**la vela** *(lah 'veh-lah)*
cone	**el cono** *(ehl 'koh-noh)*
flare	**la luz de bengala** *(lah loos deh behn-'gah-lah)*
flashlight	**la linterna** *(lah leen-'tehr-nah)*
hydrant	**la boca de agua** *(lah 'boh-kah deh 'ah-gwah)*

Here's (the) . . .	**Aquí tiene** . . . *(ah-'kee tee-'eh-neh)*
bell	**la campana** *(lah kahm-'pah-nah)*
bulletin	**el anuncio** *(ehl ah-'noon-see-oh)*
buzzer	**el timbre** *(ehl 'teem-breh)*
code	**el código** *(ehl 'koh-dee-goh)*

drill	**el simulacro** *(ehl see-moo-'lahk-roh)*
horn	**la bocina** *(lah boh-'see-nah)*
report	**el reporte** *(ehl reh-'pohr-teh)*
signal	**la señal** *(lah sehn-'yahl)*
siren	**la sirena** *(lah see-'reh-nah)*
warning	**la advertencia** *(lah ahd-vehr-'tehn-see-ah)*
whistle	**el silbato** *(ehl seel-'bah-toh)*

• We don't expect you to memorize every Spanish word appearing on these pages. What we do is provide specific areas of interest that you should highlight with bright markers.

capacity	**la capacidad** *(lah kah-pah-see-'dahd)*
caution	**la advertencia** *(lah ahd-vehr-'tehn-see-ah)*
danger	**el peligro** *(ehl peh-'lee-groh)*
emergency	**la emergencia** *(lah eh-mehr-'hehn-see-ah)*
rescue	**el rescate** *(ehl rehs-'kah-teh)*
safety	**la seguridad** *(lah seh-goo-ree-'dahd)*
threat	**la amenaza** *(lah ah-meh-'nah-sah)*

¡MÁS AYUDA!

• Stick with an easy pattern:

It's the . . .	**Es la . . .** *(ehs lah)*
evacuation	**evacuación** *(eh-vah-kwah-see-'ohn)*
precaution	**precaución** *(preh-kah-oo-see-'ohn)*
preparation	**preparación** *(preh-pah-rah-see-'ohn)*
prevention	**prevención** *(preh-vehn-see-'ohn)*
protection	**protección** *(proh-tehk-see-'ohn)*

• Try to put the new words together:

emergency exit	**la salida de emergencia** *(lah sah-'lee-dah deh eh-mehr-'hehn-see-ah)*
evacuation procedure	**el plan de evacuación** *(ehl plahn deh eh-vah-kwah-see-'ohn)*

rescue team	**el equipo de rescate**
	(ehl eh-'kee-poh deh rehs-'kah-teh)
room capacity	**la capacidad de la sala**
	(lah kah-pah-see-'dahd deh lah 'sah-lah)
safety manual	**el manual de seguridad**
	(ehl mah-'nwahl deh seh-goo-ree-'dahd)
Let's talk about (the) . . .	**Vamos a hablar de . . .**
	('vah-mohs ah ah-'blahr deh)
exercise	**el ejercicio** *(ehl eh-her-'see-see-oh)*
instructions	**las instrucciones**
	(lahs eens-trook-see-'oh-nehs)
phases	**las etapas** *(lahs eh-'tah-pahs)*
procedures	**los procedimientos**
	(lohs proh-seh-dee-mee-'ehn-tohs)
plan	**el plan** *(ehl plahn)*
steps	**los pasos** *(lohs 'pah-sohs)*
system	**el sistema** *(ehl sees-'teh-mah)*

Security personnel
El personal de seguridad
(ehl pehr-soh-'nahl deh seh-goo-ree-dahd)

One of the first responsibilities of police, security guards, or even re-servists is to find out who everyone is.

Who is (the) . . . ?	**¿Quién es . . . ?** *(kee-'ehn ehs)*
bystander	**el espectador** *(ehl ehs-pehk-tah-'dohr)*
companion	**el compañero** *(ehl kohm-pah-'nyeh-roh)*
driver	**el chofer** *(ehl choh-'fehr)*
employee	**el empleado** *(ehl ehm-pleh-'ah-doh)*
friend	**el amigo** *(ehl ah-'mee-goh)*
guard	**el guardia** *(ehl 'gwahr-dee-ah)*
helper	**el ayudante** *(ehl ah-yoo-'dahn-teh)*
leader	**el líder** *(ehl 'lee-dehr)*

member	**el miembro** *(ehl mee-'ehm-broh)*
minor	**el menor de edad** *(ehl meh-nohr deh eh-'dahd)*
neighbor	**el vecino** *(ehl veh-'see-noh)*
owner	**el dueño** *(ehl 'dweh-nyoh)*
passenger	**el pasajero** *(ehl pah-sah-'heh-roh)*
pedestrian	**el peatón** *(ehl peh-ah-'tohn)*
soldier	**el soldado** *(ehl sohl-'dah-doh)*
stranger	**el desconocido** *(ehl dehs-koh-noh-'see-doh)*
visitor	**el visitante** *(ehl vee-see-'tahn-teh)*
volunteer	**el voluntario** *(ehl voh-loon-'tah-ree-oh)*

Now mention some of the folks who may create a problem.

I saw (the) . . .	**Yo ví . . .** *(yoh vee)*
criminal	**el criminal** *(ehl kree-mee-'nahl)*
delinquent	**el delincuente** *(ehl deh-leen-'kwehn-teh)*
drug addict	**el drogadicto** *(ehl droh-gah-'deek-toh)*
drug dealer	**el droguero** *(ehl droh-'geh-roh)*
drunkard	**el borracho** *(ehl boh-'rrah-choh)*
gang member	**el pandillero** *(ehl pahn-dee-'yeh-roh)*
loiterer	**el holgazán** *(ehl ohl-gah-'sahn)*
pickpocket	**el carterista** *(ehl kaher-teh-'rees-tah)*
prostitute	**la prostituta** *(lah prohs-tee-'too-tah)*
thief	**el ladrón** *(ehl lah-'drohn)*
vagrant	**el vagabundo** *(ehl vah-gah-'boon-doh)*

¡*M Á S   A Y U D A !*

• When you question suspicious characters, combine your question words to collect the data you need. Highlight these phrases, or write them down and have them handy.

What are you doing here?

¿Qué hace aquí? *(keh 'ah-seh ah-'kee)*

Where are you from?
¿De dónde es? *(deh 'dohn-deh ehs)*

Where do you live?
¿Dónde vive? *('dohn-deh 'vee-veh)*

Have you been drinking?
¿Ha estado tomando alcohol?
(ah ehs-'tah-doh toh-'mahn-doh ahl-koh-'ohl)

Have you been taking drugs?
¿Ha estado tomando drogas?
(ah ehs-'tah-doh toh-'mahn-doh 'droh-gahs)

The crime scene
La escena del crimen
(lah ehs-'seh-nah dehl 'kree-mehn)

If a crime is committed, adequate terminology will be required. Here's a quick overview of crime-related words and one-liners:

We are going to search you.	**Le vamos a registrar.**
	(leh-'vah-mohs ah reh-gees-'trahr)
I called the police.	**Llamé a la policía.**
	(yah-'meh ah lah poh-lee-'see-ah)
You are under arrest for . . .	**Está arrestado por . . .**
	(ehs-'tah ah-rrehs-'tah-doh pohr)
abuse	**(el) abuso** *(ah-'boo-soh)*
arson	**(el) incendio premeditado**
	(een-'sehn-dee-oh preh-meh-dee-'tah-doh)
assault	**(el) asalto** *(ah-'sahl-toh)*
battery	**(la) agresión** *(ah-greh-see-'ohn)*
drug sale	**(la) venta de drogas**
	('vehn-tah deh 'droh-gahs)

embezzling	**(el) desfalco** *(dehs-'fahl-koh)*
extortion	**(la) extorsión** *(ehks-tohr-see'ohn)*
fraud	**(el) fraude** *('frah-oo-deh)*
gambling	**(el) juego de apuestas** *('hweh-goh deh ah-poo-'ehs-tahs)*
graffiti	**(el) grafiti** *(grah-'fee-tee)*
hijacking	**(el) robo en tránsito** *('roh-boh ehn 'trahn-see-toh)*
kidnapping	**(el) secuestro** *(seh-'kwehs-troh)*
libel	**(la) difamación** *(dee-fah-mah-see-'ohn)*
looting	**(el) saqueo** *(sah-'keh-oh)*
murder	**(el) asesinato** *(uh-seh-see-'nah-toh)*
rape	**(la) violación** *(vee-oh-lah-see-'ohn)*
smuggling	**(el) contrabando** *(kohn-trah-'bahn-doh)*
stabbing	**apuñalar** *(ah-poon-yah-'lahr)*
stealing	**(el) robo** *('roh-boh)*
trespassing	**(la) intrusión** *(een-troo-see-'ohn)*
vandalism	**(el) vandalismo** *(vahn-dah-'lees-moh)*
Let's talk about (the) ...	**Hablaremos de ...** *(ah-blah-'reh-mohs deh)*
bail	**la fianza** *(lah fee-'ahn-sah)*
felony	**el delito mayor** *(ehl deh-'lee-toh mah-'yohr)*
firearm	**el arma de fuego** *(ehl 'ahr-mah deh 'fweh-goh)*
jail	**la cárcel** *(lah 'kahr-sehl)*
law	**la ley** *(lah 'leh-ee)*
lawsuit	**el pleito** *(ehl 'pleh-ee-toh)*
legal aid	**la ayuda legal** *(lah ah-'yoo-dah leh-'gahl)*
parole	**la libertad bajo palabra** *(lah lee-behr-tahd 'bah-hoh pah-'lah-brah)*

probation	**la libertad provisional**
	(lah lee-behr-'tahd proh-vee-see-oh-'nahl)
subpoena	**la citación** *(lah see-tah-see-'ohn)*
surveillance	**la vigilancia** *(lah vee-hee-'lahn-see-ah)*
warrant	**la orden de la corte**
	(lah 'ohr-dehn deh lah 'kohr-teh)

¡MÁS AYUDA!

• Ask around for the names of common drugs or alcoholic beverages:

There is/are . . .	**Hay . . .** *('ah-ee)*
alcohol	**alcohol** *(ahl-koh-'ohl)*
beer	**cerveza** *(sehr-'veh-sah)*
crack	**crac** *(krahk)*
heroin	**heroína** *(eh-roh-'ee-nah)*
liquor	**licor** *(lee-'kohr)*
marijuana	**marijuana** *(mah-ree-'hwah-nah)*
morphine	**morfina** *(mohr-'fee-nah)*
narcotics	**narcóticos** *(nahr-'koh-tee-kohs)*
pills	**píldoras** *('peel-doh-rahs)*
speed	**metanfetamina** *(meh-tahn-feh-tah-'mee-nah)*
wine	**vino** *('vee-noh)*

We know (the) . . .	**Conocemos a . . .** *(koh-noh-'seh-mohs ah)*
suspect	**el sospechoso** *(ehl sohs-peh-'choh-soh)*
victim	**la víctima** *(lah 'veek-tee-mah)*
witness	**el testigo** *(ehl tehs-'tee-goh)*

• Stay alert as you confront the suspects with the following command words. Notice how the words address more than one person:

Come here.	**Vengan aquí.** *('vehn-gahn ah-'kee)*
Sit down.	**Siéntense.** *(see-'ehn-tehn-seh)*
Turn around.	**Dense vuelta.** *('dehn-seh voo-'ehl-tah)*
Empty your pockets.	**Vacíen los bolsillos.**
	(vah-'see-ehn lohs bohl-'see-yohs)

Give it to me.   **Dénmelo.** *('dehn-meh-loh)*
Show me your hands.   **Muéstrenme las manos.**
                        ('mwehs-trehn-meh lahs 'mah-nohs)

• Don't try to handle any legal matter with the few words you have learned. After contacting the authorities, ask the nearest Spanish speaker to assist you. This pattern works well with the words and phrases below:

Tell them that . . .   **Dígales que . . .** *('dee-gah-lehs keh)*
  help is on its way   **la ayuda está en camino**
                            (lah ah-'yoo-dah ehs-'tah ehn kah-'mee-noh)

  they have to calm down   **tienen que calmarse**
                            (too 'oh nohn koh kahl-'mahr-seh)

  they need to be careful   **necesitan tener cuidado**
                            (neh-seh-'see-tahn teh-'nehr kwee-'dah-doh)

  they cannot do that   **no pueden hacer eso**
                            (noh 'pweh-dehn ah-'sehr 'eh-soh)

  it is an emergency   **es una emergencia**
                            (ehs 'oo-nah eh-mehr-'hehn-see-ah)

• And here's a pattern that requires more verb infinitives:

Make sure that you guys . . .   **Asegúrense de . . .**
                                (ah-seh-'goo-rehn-seh deh)
  ask me   **preguntarme** *(preh-goon-'tahr-meh)*
  call them   **llamarles** *(yah-'mahr-lehs)*
  read it   **leerlo** *(leh-'ehr-loh)*

 ¡ *L a   C u l t u r a !*

One of the most difficult things to discuss in a foreign language concerns social ethics and values. Your personal feelings, attitudes, and beliefs cannot be communicated in a few short sentences. Therefore, the only way to deal with any serious matter is through an interpreter.

¡*NECESITA PRACTICAR!*

Connect the words that are closely related:

chofer	campana
humo	criminal
timbre	llave
candado	evacuación
rescate	pasajero
ladrón	incendio

¡*ACCIÓN!*

Here's still another one of those incredible verb patterns that makes speaking Spanish so much easier. Combine your verbs with the forms of the verb "to can," or **poder**:

To CAN	**PODER** *(poh-'dehr)*
I can	**Puedo** *('pweh-doh)*
I can begin.	**Puedo comenzar.**
	('pweh-doh koh-mehn-'sahr)
You, he, she can	**Puede** *('pweh-deh)*
She can play.	**Puede jugar.** *('pweh-deh hoo-'gahr)*
You, they can	**Pueden** *('pweh-dehn)*
They can rest.	**Pueden descansar.**
	('pweh-dehn dehs-kahn-'sahr)
We can	**Podemos** *(poh-'deh-mohs)*
We can eat.	**Podemos comer.**
	(poh-'deh-mohs koh-'mehr)

Check out this new tense! The following three variations of **poder** indicate the conditional state: "could." These three can be coupled with the infinitives of just about any verb:

I, you, he, she could . . .	**Podría** . . . *(poh-'dree-ah)*
They could . . .	**Podrían** . . . *(poh-'dree-ahn)*
We could . . .	**Podríamos** . . . *(poh-'dree-ah-mohs)*

to arrive	**llegar** *(yeh-'gahr)*	**Podríamos llegar.**
to ask for	**pedir** *(peh-'deer)*	**Podríamos pedir.**
to bend	**doblar** *(doh-'blahr)*	**Podríamos doblar.**
to check	**revisar** *(reh-vee-'sahr)*	_____
to climb	**subir** *(soo-'beer)*	_____
to cut	**cortar** *(kohr-'tahr)*	_____
to explain	**explicar** *(ehks-plee-'kahr)*	_____
to learn	**aprender** *(ah-'prehn-dehr)*	_____
to let	**dejar** *(deh-'hahr)*	_____
to load	**cargar** *(kahr-'gahr)*	_____
to lose	**perder** *(pehr-'dehr)*	_____
to measure	**medir** *(meh-'deer)*	_____
to pass	**pasar** *(pah-'sahr)*	_____
to pile	**amontonar** *(ah-mohn-toh-'nahr)*	_____
to repair	**reparar** *(reh-pah-'rahr)*	_____
to spray	**rociar** *(roh-see-'ahr)*	_____
to study	**estudiar** *(ehs-too-dee-'ahr)*	_____
to touch	**tocar** *(toh-'kahr)*	_____
to try	**tratar** *(trah-'tahr)*	_____
to unload	**descargar** *(dehs-kahr-'gahr)*	_____

¡ M Á S   A Y U D A !

• The idea of "un-" is usually translated as **des-** in Spanish verbs.

| to hook | **enganchar** *(ehn-gahn-'chahr)* |
| to unhook | **desenganchar** *(dehs-ehn-gahn-'chahr)* |

to do	**hacer** *(ah-'sehr)*
to undo	**deshacer** *(dehs-ah-'sehr)*
to plug in	**enchufar** *(ehn-choo-'fahr)*
to unplug	**desenchufar** *(dehs-ehn-choo-'fahr)*

• Give suggestions or make a command:

You should (must) . . . **Debe** . . . *('deh-beh)*

To continue **continuar** *(kohn-tee-'nwahr)*
Debe continuar con su trabajo.

To cooperate **cooperar** *(koh-oh-peh-'rahr)*
Debe cooperar con la policía.

To coordinate **coordinar** *(koh-ohr-dee-'nahr)*

To develop **desarrollar** *(deh-sah-rroh-'yahr)*

To follow **seguir** *(seh-'geer)*

To improve **mejorar** *(meh-hoh-'rahr)*

To lead **dirigir** *(dee-ree-'heer)*

To prepare **preparar** *(preh-pah-'rahr)*

To promise **prometer** *(proh-meh-'tehr)*

To recognize **reconocer** *(reh-koh-noh-'sehr)*

To repeat **repetir** *(reh-peh-'teer)*

To review	**repasar** *(reh-pah-'sahr)*

To share	**compartir** *(kohm-pahr-'teer)*

For a more extensive list of Spanish verbs, check the English–Spanish Verb List at the end of the book.

¡LAS ORDENES!

Practice these commands with your family and friends. The word **-lo** or **-la** at the end of commands refer to something or somebody, **-lo** if the object is masculine, **-la** if it is feminine:

Get it	**Consígalo** *(kohn-'see-gah-loh)*
Look for it	**Búsquela** *('boos-keh-lah)*
Park it	**Estaciónelo** *(ehs-tah-see-'oh-neh-loh)*
Pay it	**Páguela** *('pah-geh-lah)*
Pick it up	**Recójalo** *(reh-'koh-hah-loh)*
Put it	**Póngala** *('pohn-gah-lah)*
Return it	**Devuélvala** *(deh-voo-'ehl-vah-lah)*
Sell it	**Véndalo** *('vehn-dah-loh)*
Send it	**Mándela** *('mahn-deh-lah)*
Take it	**Tómela** *('toh-meh-lah)*

Chapter Five

To Other Countries
A otros países
(ah 'oh-trohs pah-'ee-sehs)

International assistance
La ayuda internacional
(lah ah-'yoo-dah een-tehr-nah-see-oh-'nahl)

Hundreds of well-known outreach organizations assist people outside the United States. As you develop activities for foreign countries, learn to identify people in the world by race and nationality.

She's . . .	**Ella es . . .** *('eh-yah ehs)*
Asian	**asiática** *(ah-see-'ah-tee-kah)*
black	**negra** *('neh-grah)*
Hispanic	**hispana** *(ees-'pah-nah)*
Islamic	**islamita** *(ees-lah-'mee-tah)*
Latin	**latina** *(lah-'tee-nah)*
Middle Eastern	**del Oriente Medio**
	(dehl oh-ree-'ehn-teh 'meh-dee-oh)
Polynesian	**polinesia** *(poh-lee-'neh-see-ah)*
white	**blanca** *('blahn-kah)*
He's . . .	**El es . . .** *(ehl ehs)*
African-American	**afroamericano** *(ah-froh-ah-meh-ree-'kah-noh)*
Anglo-Saxon	**anglosajón** *(ahn-gloh-sah-'hohn)*

Asian-American	**asiaticoamericano**
	(ah-see-ah-tee-koh-ah-meh-ree-'kah-noh)
Latin American	**latinoamericano**
	(lah-tee-noh-ah-meh-ree-'kah-noh)
Native American	**amerindio** *(ah-meh-'reen-dee-oh)*

Here are frequently seen places of origin:

The man is . . .	**El hombre es . . .** *(ehl 'ohm-breh ehs)*
African	**africano** *(ah-free-'kah-noh)*
Arab	**árabe** *('ah-rah-beh)*
Australian	**australiano** *(ows-trah-lee-'ah-noh)*
Canadian	**canadiense** *(kah-nah-dee-'ehn-seh)*
Chinese	**chino** *('chee-noh)*
English	**inglés** *(een-'glehs)*
European	**europeo** *(eh-oo-roh-'peh-oh)*
French	**francés** *(frahn-'sehs)*
German	**alemán** *(ah-leh-'mahn)*
Greek	**griego** *(gree-'eh-goh)*
Irish	**irlandés** *(eer-lahn-'dehs)*
Italian	**italiano** *(ee-tah-lee-'ah-noh)*
Japanese	**japonés** *(hah-poh-'nehs)*
Portuguese	**portugués** *(pohr-too-'gehs)*
Russian	**ruso** *('roo-soh)*
Spanish	**español** *(ehs-pahn-'yohl)*
U.S. national	**norteamericano**
	(nohr-teh-ah-meh-ree-'kah-noh)
Vietnamese	**vietnamita** *(vee-eht-nah-'mee-tah)*

And how about south of the border?

I'm _____.	**Soy _____.**
Argentinian	**argentino(a)** *(ahr-hehn-'tee-noh, nah)*
Bolivian	**boliviano(a)** *(boh-lee-vee-'ah-noh, nah)*
Brazilian	**brasileño(a)** *(brah-see-'lehn-yoh, yah)*
Chilean	**chileno(a)** *(chee-'leh-noh, nah)*

Costa Rican	**costarricense** *(kohs-tah-rree-'sehn-seh)*
Cuban	**cubano(a)** *(koo-'bah-noh, nah)*
Dominican	**dominicano(a)** *(doh-mee-nee-'kah-noh, nah)*
Ecuadorian	**ecuatoriano(a)** *(eh-kwah-toh-ree-'ah-noh, nah)*
Guatemalan	**guatemalteco(a)** *(gwah-teh-mahl-'teh-koh, kah)*
Haitian	**haitiano(a)** *(ah-ee-tee-'ah-noh, nah)*
Honduran	**hondureño(a)** *(ohn-doo-'rehn-yoh, yah)*
Mexican	**mexicano(a)** *(meh-hee-'kah-noh, nah)*
Nicaraguan	**nicaragüense** *(nee-kah-rah-'gwehn-seh)*
Panamanian	**panameño(a)** *(pah-nah-'mehn-yoh, yah)*
Paraguayan	**paraguayo(a)** *(pah-rah-'gwah-yoh, yah)*
Peruvian	**peruano(a)** *(peh-roo-'ah-noh, nah)*
Puerto Rican	**puertorriqueño(a)** *(pwehr-toh-rree-'kehn-yoh, yah)*
Salvadorean	**salvadoreño(a)** *(sahl-vah-doh-'rehn-yoh, yah)*
Uruguayan	**uruguayo(a)** *(oo-roo-'gwah-yoh, yah)*
Venezuelan	**venezolano(a)** *(veh-neh-soh-'lah-noh)*

¡MÁS AYUDA!

• How would you explain your purpose for work overseas?

foreign service	**el servicio en países extranjeros** *(ehl sehr-'vee-see-oh ehn pah-'ee-sehs ehks-trahn-'heh-rohs)*
economic development	**el desarrollo económico** *(ehl deh-sah-'rroh-yoh eh-koh-'noh-mee-koh)*
international relief	**la ayuda internacional** *(lah ah-'yoo-dah een-tehr-nah-see-oh-'nahl)*

• How would you describe the world you're trying to reach?

I see a lot of . . .	**Veo mucho de . . .** *('veh-oh 'moo-choh-deh)*
affliction	**(la) aflicción** *(ahf-leek-see-'ohn)*
anguish	**(la) angustia** *(ahn-'goos-tee-ah)*
crisis situation	**(la) situación de crisis** *(see-twah-see-'ohn deh 'kree-sees)*
desperation	**(la) desesperación** *(deh-sehs-peh-rah-see-'ohn)*
difficult circumstances	**(las) circunstancias difíciles** *(seer-koohns-'tahn-see-ahs dee-'fee-see-lehs)*
doubt	**(la) duda** *('doo-dah)*
hardship	**(las) privaciones** *(pree-vah-see-'oh-nehs)*
injustice	**(la) injusticia** *(een-hoos-'tee-see-ah)*
loneliness	**(la) soledad** *(soh-leh-'dahd)*
misery	**(la) miseria** *(mee-'seh-ree-ah)*
obstacles	**(los) obtáculos** *(ohbs-'tah-koo-lohs)*
sadness	**(la) tristeza** *(trees-'teh-sah)*
suffering	**(el) sufrimiento** *(soo-free-mee-'ehn-toh)*

¡ *L A   C U L T U R A !*

When referring to others by name, it really helps if you are able to pronounce people's names correctly. Always remember that Spanish is pronounced the way it is written, regardless of country of origin.

¡ *N E C E S I T A   P R A C T I C A R !*

Fill in these nationalities in Spanish:

El __mexicano__ es de México.

El _____ es de Canadá.

El _____ es de Vietnam.

El _____ es de Costa Rica.

El _____ es de Brasil.

El _____ es de Nicaragua.

Let's travel

Vamos a viajar *('vah-mohs ah vee-ah-'hahr)*

Gather up your team of workers and go over your international travel plans.

How far?	**¿A qué distancia?**
	(ah keh dees-'tahn-see-ah)
Which bus?	**¿Cuál autobús?**
	(kwahl ow-toh-'boos)
Is there drinking water?	**¿Hay agua potable?**
	('ah-ee 'ah-gwah poh-'tah-bleh)
Can they help us?	**¿Pueden ayudarnos?**
	('pweh-dehn ah-yoo-'dahr-nohs)
Can we pay with this?	**¿Podemos pagar con esto?**
	(poh-'deh-mohs pah-'gahr koh 'ehs-toh)

And don't leave home without the following:

Where's the . . . ?	**¿Dónde está . . . ?** *('dohn-deh ehs-'tah)*
airport	**el aeropuerto** *(ehl ah-eh-roh-'pwehr-toh)*
bank	**el banco** *(ehl 'bahn-koh)*
border	**la frontera** *(lah frohn-'teh-rah)*
customs	**la aduana** *(lah ah-'dwah-nah)*
hospital	**el hospital** *(ehl ohs-pee-'tahl)*
hotel	**el hotel** *(ehl oh-'tehl)*
market	**el mercado** *(ehl mehr-'kah-doh)*
passport	**el pasaporte** *(ehl pah-sah-'pohr-teh)*
post office	**el correo** *(ehl koh-'rreh-oh)*
station	**la estación** *(lah ehs-tah-see-'ohn)*
travel agency	**la agencia de viajes**
	(lah ah-'hehn-see-ah deh vee-'ah-hehs)

travelers checks	**los cheques de viajero**
	(lohs 'cheh-kehs deh vee-ah-'heh-roh)
visa	**la visa** *(lah 'vee-sah)*

I need . . .	**Necesito . . .** *(neh-seh-'see-toh)*
bus	**el autobús** *(ehl ow-toh-'boos)*
camera	**la cámara** *(lah 'kah-mah-rah)*
map	**el mapa** *(ehl 'mah-pah)*
suitcase	**la maleta** *(lah mah-'leh-tah)*
telephone	**el teléfono** *(ehl teh-'leh-foh-noh)*

If your plans include a stay at a hotel, check this list of words and phrases:

Talk to (the) . . .	**Hable con . . .** *('ah-bleh kohn)*
bellboy	**el botones** *(ehl boh-'toh-nehs)*
concierge	**el conserje** *(ehl kohn-'sehr-heh)*
driver	**el chofer** *(ehl choh-'fehr)*
guide	**el guía** *(ehl 'gee-ah)*
interpreter	**el intérprete** *(ehl een-'tehr-preh-teh)*
maid	**la criada** *(lah kree-'ah-dah)*
manager	**el gerente** *(ehl heh-'rehn-teh)*
owner	**el dueño** *(ehl 'dwehn-yoh)*

I must . . .	**Debo . . .** *('deh-boh)*
make reservations	**hacer reservaciones**
	(ah-'sehr reh-sehr-vah-see-'oh-nehs)
charge it	**cargarlo** *(kahr-'gahr-loh)*
exchange it	**cambiarlo** *(kahm-bee-'ahr-loh)*
make a call	**hacer una llamada**
	(ah-'sehr 'oo-nah yah-'mah-dah)

I would like to order . . .	**Quisiera ordenar . . .**
	(kee-see-'eh-rah ohr-deh-'nahr)
the bill	**la cuenta** *(lah 'kwehn-tah)*
a drink	**una bebida** *('oo-nah beh-'bee-dah)*
a haircut	**un corte de pelo**
	(oon 'kohr-teh deh 'peh-loh)

more ice	**más hielo** *(mahs ee-'eh-loh)*
the key	**la llave** *(lah 'yah-veh)*
a room	**una habitación** *('oo-nah ah-bee-tah-see-'ohn)*
room service	**el servicio de habitación** *(ehl sehr-'vee-see-oh deh ah-bee-tah-see-'ohn)*
a taxi	**un taxi** *(oon 'tahk-see)*
more towels	**más toallas** *(mahs toh-'ah-yahs)*

On foreign land
En tierra extranjera
(ehn tee-'eh-rrah ehks-trahn-'heh-rah)

Not all of your work will take place in urban areas. Much of the world's population lives in remote towns and villages. After clearing customs, your team may have to go to one of these locations:

They live in/on/at (the) . . .	**Viven en . . .** *('vee-vehn ehn)*
beach	**la playa** *(lah 'plah-yah)*
coast	**la costa** *(lah 'kohs-tah)*
countryside	**el campo** *(ehl 'kahm-poh)*
desert	**el desierto** *(ehl deh-see-'ehr-toh)*
forest	**el bosque** *(ehl 'bohs-keh)*
hill	**el cerro** *(ehl 'seh-rroh)*
jungle	**la selva** *(lah 'sehl-vah)*
lagoon	**la laguna** *(lah lah-'goo-nah)*
lake	**el lago** *(ehl 'lah-goh)*
mountain	**la montaña** *(lah mohn-'tahn-yah)*
ocean	**el océano** *(ehl oh-'seh-ah-noh)*
river	**el río** *(ehl 'ree-oh)*
sea	**el mar** *(ehl mahr)*
stream	**el arroyo** *(ehl ah-'rroh-yoh)*
swamp	**el pantano** *(ehl pahn-'tah-noh)*
valley	**el valle** *(ehl 'vah-yeh)*

It's (a) . . .	**Es . . .** *(ehs)*
farm	**una finca** *('oo-nah 'feen-kah)*
ranch	**un rancho** *(oon 'rahn-choh)*
town	**un pueblo** *(oon 'pweh-bloh)*
village	**una aldea** *('oo-nah ahl-'deh-ah)*

Working outdoors
Trabajando al aire libre
(trah-bah-'hahn-doh ahl 'ah-ee-reh 'lee-breh)

These are the words you will need with Spanish speakers in the outdoors. Look at the three beginning sentences below and see which applies best to the vocabulary that follows.

We're working with (the) . . .	**Estamos trabajando con . . .**
	(ehs-'tah-mohs trah-bah-'hahn-doh kohn)
We're cleaning (the) . . .	**Estamos limpiando . . .**
	(ehs-'tah-mohs leem-pee-'ahn-doh)
We're removing(the) . . .	**Estamos sacando . . .**
	(ehs-'tah-mohs sah-'kahn-doh)
bark	**la corteza** *(lah kohr-'teh-sah)*
branch	**la rama** *(lah 'rah-mah)*
bud	**el botón** *(ehl boh-'tohn)*
bulb	**el bulbo** *(ehl 'bool-boh)*
bush	**el arbusto** *(ehl ahr-'boos-toh)*
clay	**la arcilla** *(lah ahr-'see-yah)*
dirt	**la tierra** *(lah tee-'eh-rrah)*
dust	**el polvo** *(ehl 'pohl-voh)*
flower	**la flor** *(lah flohr)*
foliage	**el follaje** *(ehl foh-'yah-heh)*
grass	**el pasto** *(ehl 'pahs-toh)*
land	**el terreno** *(ehl teh-'rreh-noh)*
lawn	**el césped** *(ehl 'sehs-pehd)*

leaf	**la hoja** *(lah 'oh-hah)*
mold	**el hongo** *(ehl 'ohn-goh)*
mud	**el lodo** *(ehl 'loh-doh)*
plant	**la planta** *(lah 'plahn-tah)*
rock	**la piedra** *(lah pee-'eh-drah)*
root	**la raíz** *(lah rah-'ees)*
sand	**la arena** *(lah ah-'reh-nah)*
seed	**la semilla** *(lah seh-'mee-yah)*
stem	**el tallo** *(ehl 'tah-yoh)*
tree	**el árbol** *(ehl 'ahr-bohl)*
trunk	**el tronco** *(ehl 'trohn-koh)*
water	**el agua** *(ehl 'ah-gwah)*
weeds	**la maleza** *(lah mah-'leh-sah)*

They have a . . .	**Tienen . . .** *(tee-'eh-nehn)*
crop	**la cosecha** *(lah koh-'seh-chah)*
flowerbed	**el arriate** *(ehl ah-rree-'ah-teh)*
greenhouse	**el invernadero** *(ehl een-vehr-nah-'deh-roh)*
grove	**la arboleda** *(lah ahr-boh-'leh-dah)*
nursery	**el criadero** *(ehl kree-ah-'deh-roh)*
orchard	**la huerta** *(lah oo-'ehr-tah)*

Horticulture
La horticultura *(lah ohr-tee-kool-'too-rah)*

Learn the following words for trees and plants in the area. You may be asked to assist in the farming activities:

TREES	**LOS ÁRBOLES** *(lohs 'ahr-boh-lehs)*
birch	**el abedul** *(ehl ah-beh-'dool)*
cedar	**el cedro** *(ehl 'seh-droh)*
elm	**el olmo** *(ehl 'ohl-moh)*
fir	**el abeto** *(ehl ah-'beh-toh)*
maple	**el arce** *(ehl 'ahr-seh)*

oak	**el roble** *(ehl 'roh-bleh)*
palm	**la palmera** *(lah pahl-'meh-rah)*
pine	**el pino** *(ehl 'pee-noh)*
walnut	**el nogal** *(ehl noh-'gahl)*
willow	**el sauce** *(ehl 'sah-oo-seh)*

FRUITS	**LAS FRUTAS** *(lahs 'froo-tahs)*
apple	**la manzana** *(lah mahn-'sah-nah)*
apricot	**el albaricoque** *(ehl ahl-bah-ree-'koh-keh)*
avocado	**el aguacate** *(ehl ah-gwah-'kah-teh)*
cherry	**la cereza** *(lah seh-'reh-sah)*
grape	**la uva** *(lah 'oo-vah)*
grapefruit	**la toronja** *(lah toh-'rohn-hah)*
lemon	**el limón** *(ehl lee-'mohn)*
lime	**la lima** *(lah 'lee-mah)*
nectarine	**el melocotón** *(ehl meh-loh-koh-'tohn)*
orange	**la naranja** *(lah nah-'rahn-hah)*
peach	**el durazno** *(ehl doo-'rahs-noh)*
pear	**la pera** *(lah 'peh-rah)*
tangerine	**la mandarina** *(lah mahn-dah-'ree-nah)*
watermelon	**la sandía** *(lah sahn-'dee-ah)*

 ¡NECESITA PRACTICAR!

Connect the words that relate to each other:

el árbol	**la arena**
la playa	**el tronco**
el rancho	**la finca**

Name three kinds of wood.
Name three kinds of terrain.
Name three kinds of fruit trees.

Special projects
Proyectos especiales
(pro-'yehk-tohs ehs-peh-see-'ah-lehs)

Landscaping, yard work, and farm maintenance are projects that involve lots of job-specific vocabulary. If the people who help you speak only Spanish, here are helpful one-liners:

Help me with (the) . . .	**Ayúdeme con** . . . *(ah-'yo-deh-meh kohn)*
channel	**el canal** *(ehl kah-'nahl)*
ditch	**la zanja** *(lah 'sahn-hah)*
divider	**el divisor** *(ehl dee-vee-'sohr)*
drainage	**el drenaje** *(ehl dreh-'nah-heh)*
fence	**la cerca** *(lah 'sehr-kah)*
furrow	**el surco** *(ehl 'soor-koh)*
hole	**el hoyo** *(ehl 'oh-yoh)*
irrigation	**la irrigación** *(lah ee-rree-gah-see-'ohn)*
path	**el sendero** *(ehl sehn-'deh-roh)*
pipe	**el tubo** *(ehl 'too-boh)*
post	**el poste** *(ehl 'pohs-teh)*
road	**el camino** *(ehl kah-'mee-noh)*
slope	**el declive** *(ehl deh-'klee-veh)*
sprinklers	**las rociadoras** *(lahs roh-see-ah-'doh-rahs)*
stake	**la estaca** *(lah ehs-'tah-kah)*
stone	**la piedra** *(lah pee-'eh-drah)*
tunnel	**el túnel** *(ehl 'too-nehl)*

¡MÁS AYUDA!

• Working in an outdoor setting also requires a unique set of command words:

arrange	**arregle** *(ah-'rreh-gleh)*

Arregle las plantas. *(ah-'rreh-gleh lahs 'plahn-tahs)*

build   **construya** *(kohns-'troo-yah)*
Construya la cerca. *(kohns-'troo-yah lah 'sehr-kah)*

dig   **excave** *(ehks-'kah-veh)*
Excave una zanja. *(ehks-'kah-veh 'oo-nah 'sahn-hah)*

install   **instale** *(eens-'tah-leh)*
Instale el poste. *(eens-'tah-leh oon 'pohs-teh)*

kill   **mate** *('mah-teh)*
Mate los insectos. *('mah-teh lohs een-'sehk-tohs)*

load   **cargue** *('kahr-geh)*
Cargue el camión. *('kahr-geh ehl kah-mee-'ohn)*

mow   **corte** *('kohr toh)*
Corte el pasto hoy. *('kohr-teh ehl 'pahs-toh 'oh-ee)*

pile   **amontone** *(ah-mohn-'toh-neh)*
Amontone las hojas. *(ah-mohn-'toh-neh lahs 'oh-hahs)*

plant   **plante** *('plahn-teh)*
Plante el arbusto aquí. *('plahn-teh ehl ahr-'boos-toh ah-'kee)*

rake   **rastrille** *(rahs-'tree-yeh)*
Rastrille el jardín. *(rahs-'tree-yeh ehl hahr-'deen)*

spray   **rocíe** *(roh-'see-eh)*
Rocíe la huerta. *(roh-'see-eh lah oo-'ehr-tah)*

transplant   **trasplante** *(trahs-'plahn-teh)*
Trasplante el cacto. *(trahs-'plahn-teh ehl 'kahk-toh)*

trim   **pode** *('poh-deh)*
Pode el árbol. *('poh-deh ehl 'ahr-bohl)*

unload   **descargue** *(dehs-'kahr-geh)*
Descargue las cajas. *(dehs-'kahr-geh lahs 'kah-hahs)*

water   **riegue** *(rree-'eh-geh)*
Riegue el invernadero. *(rree-'eh-geh ehl een-vehr-nah-'deh-roh)*

carry   **lleve** *('yeh-veh)*
Lleve la maleza. *('yeh-veh lah mah-'leh-sah)*

change   **cambie** *('kahm-bee-eh)*
Cambie las flores. *(kahm-bee-eh lahs 'floh-rehs)*

clean   **limpie** *('leem-pee-eh)*
Limpie el patio. *('leem-pee-eh ehl 'pah-tee-oh)*

dump   **tire** *('tee-reh)*
Tire la basura. *('tee-reh lah bah-'soo-rah)*

sweep   **barra** *('bah-rrah)*
Barra la tierra. *('bah-rrah lah tee-'eh-rrah)*

Garden tools
Las herramientas de jardín
(lahs eh-rrah-mee-'ehn-tahs deh hahr-'deen)

To use specific tools and supplies, here is a list for you:

You have to use (the) . . .	**Tiene que usar . . .**
	(tee-'eh-neh keh oo-'sahr)
ax	**el hacha** *(ehl 'ah-chah)*
bag	**la bolsa** *(lah 'bohl-sah)*
blower	**el soplador** *(ehl soh-plah-'dohr)*
chainsaw	**la motosierra** *(lah moh-toh-see-'eh-rrah)*
clippers	**las tijeras podadoras**
	(lahs tee-'heh-rahs poh-dah-'doh-rahs)
fertilizer	**el abono** *(ehl ah-'boh-noh)*
gloves	**los guantes** *(los 'gwahn-tehs)*
hoe	**el azadón** *(ehl ah-sah-'dohn)*
hose	**la manguera** *(lah mahn-'geh-rah)*
insecticide	**el insecticida** *(ehl een-sehk-tee-'see-dah)*
lawn mower	**la cortadora de césped**
	(lah kohr-tah-'doh-rah deh 'sehs-pehd)

manure	**el estiércol** *(ehl ehs-tee-'ehr-kohl)*
pick	**el pico** *(ehl 'pee-koh)*
pitchfork	**la horquilla** *(lah ohr-'kee-yah)*
poison	**el veneno** *(ehl veh-'neh-noh)*
potting soil	**la tierra abonada**
	(lah tee-'eh-rrah ah-boh-'nah-dah)
rake	**el rastrillo** *(ehl rahs-'tree-yoh)*
rope	**la soga** *(lah 'soh-gah)*
rototiller	**el aflojador de tierra**
	(ehl ah-floh-hah-'dohr deh tee-'eh-rrah)
seeder	**la sembradora** *(lah sehm-brah-'doh-rah)*
shovel	**la pala** *(lah 'pah-lah)*
sprayer	**el rociador** *(ohl roh-see-uh-'dohr)*
tractor	**el tractor** *(ehl trahk-'tohr)*
trimmer	**el podador** *(ehl poh-dah-'dohr)*
trowel	**el desplantador**
	(ehl dehs-plahn-tah-'dohr)
wheelbarrow	**la carretilla** *(lah kah-rreh-'tee-yah)*
transplanter	**el trasplantador**
	(ehl trahs-plahn-tah-'dohr)

¡MÁS AYUDA!

• These verbs will allow you to make sentences with the vocabulary we have seen:

to cultivate	**cultivar** *(kool-tee-'vahr)*

Estamos cultivando flores.

to develop	**desarrollar** *(deh-sah-rroh-'yahr)*

_____.

to dissolve	**disolver** *(dee-sohl-'vehr)*

_____.

to ferment	**fermentar** *(fehr-mehn-'tahr)*

_____.

to level	**nivelar** *(nee-veh-'lahr)*

_____.

to mix	**mezclar** *(mehs-'klahr)*

_____.

to nurse	**criar** *(kree-'ahr)*

_____.

to plant	**plantar** *(plahn-'tahr)*

_____.

to prepare	**preparar** *(preh-pah-'rahr)*

_____.

to prevent	**prevenir** *(preh-veh-'neer)*

_____.

to produce	**producir** *(proh-doo-'seer)*

_____.

to reach	**alcanzar** *(ahl-kahn-'sahr)*

_____.

to reproduce	**reproducir** *(reh-proh-doo-'seer)*

_____.

to ripen	**madurar** *(mah-doo-'rahr)*

_____.

to sow	**sembrar** *(sehm-'brahr)*

_____.

to transplant	**trasplantar** *(trahs-plahn-'tahr)*

_____.

to water	**regar** *(reh-'gahr)*

_____.

¡N E C E S I T A P R A C T I C A R !

Insert the right word:

el canal, maduro, el rastrillo

El durazno está _____.

_____ **es una herramienta.**

Hay agua en _____.

¡M Á S A Y U D A !

• What do these words mean?

> **la germinación**
> **la plantación**
> **el desarrollo**

Insects

Los insectos *(lohs een-'sehk-tohs)*

Bugs and the outdoors go hand-in-hand, so study this next list whenever you go outside:

Kill the . . .	**Mate . . .** *('mah-teh)*
There's the . . .	**Allí está . . .** *(ah-'yee ehs-'tah)*
ant	**la hormiga** *(lah ohr-'mee-gah)*
bee	**la abeja** *(lah ah-'beh-hah)*
beetle	**el escarabajo** *(ehl ehs-kah-rah-'bah-hoh)*
butterfly	**la mariposa** *(lah mah-ree-'poh-sah)*
cricket	**el grillo** *(ehl 'gree-yoh)*
dragonfly	**la libélula** *(lah lee-'beh-loo-lah)*
flea	**la pulga** *(lah 'pool-gah)*

fly	**la mosca** *(lah 'mohs-kah)*
hornet	**el avispón** *(ehl ah-vees-'pohn)*
ladybug	**la mariquita** *(lah mah-ree-'kee-tah)*
locust	**la langosta** *(lah lahn-'gohs-tah)*
mosquito	**el zancudo** *(ehl sahn-'koo-doh)*
moth	**la polilla** *(lah poh-'lee-yah)*
scorpion	**el escorpión** *(ehl ehs-kohr-pee-'ohn)*
slug	**la babosa** *(lah bah-'boh-sah)*
snail	**el caracol** *(ehl kah-rah-'kohl)*
spider	**la araña** *(lah ah-'rahn-yah)*
wasp	**la avispa** *(lah ah-'vees-pah)*

Raising animals
La cría de animales
(lah 'kree-ah deh ah-nee-'mah-lehs)

When relief efforts include animal care, try communicating with a couple of these:

We lost (the) . . .	**Perdimos . . .** *(pehr-'dee-mohs)*
Give food to (the) . . .	**Dé comida a . . .**
	(deh koh-'mee-dah ah)
The _____ needs water.	**El/la _____ necesita agua.**
	(ehl, lah neh-seh-'see-tah 'ah-gwah)
bull	**el toro** *(ehl 'toh-roh)*
cat	**el gato** *(ehl 'gah-toh)*
chicken	**la gallina** *(lah gah-'yee-nah)*
cow	**la vaca** *(lah 'vah-kah)*
dog	**el perro** *(ehl 'peh-rroh)*
donkey	**el burro** *(ehl 'boo-rroh)*
fish	**el pez** *(ehl pehs)*
goat	**el chivo** *(ehl 'chee-voh)*
hog	**el cerdo** *(ehl 'sehr-doh)*
horse	**el caballo** *(ehl kah-'bah-yoh)*

mule	**la mula** *(lah 'moo-lah)*
ox	**el buey** *(ehl 'bweh-ee)*
parakeet	**el perico** *(ehl peh-'ree-koh)*
rabbit	**el conejo** *(ehl koh-'neh-hoh)*
sheep	**la oveja** *(lah oh-'veh-hah)*
turtle	**la tortuga** *(lah tohr-'too-gah)*

Put it in the . . .	**Póngalo(a) en . . .** *('pohn-gah-loh, lah ehn)*
barn	**el granero** *(ehl grah-'neh-roh)*
box	**la caja** *(lah 'kah-hah)*
cage	**la jaula** *(lah 'hah-oo-lah)*
coop	**el gallinero** *(ehl gah-yee-'neh-roh)*
field	**el campo** *(ehl 'kahm-poh)*
house	**la casa** *(lah 'kah-sah)*
nest	**el nido** *(ehl 'nee-doh)*
pen	**el corral** *(ehl koh-'rrahl)*
stable	**el establo** *(ehl ehs-'tah-bloh)*
sty	**la pocilga** *(lah poh-'seel-gah)*
yard	**el patio** *(ehl 'pah-tee-oh)*

It's a female.	**Es hembra.** *(ehs 'ehm-brah)*
It's a male.	**Es macho.** *(ehs 'mah-choh)*
It's friendly.	**Es amistoso(a).** *(ehs ah-mees-'toh-soh, sah)*
It's savage.	**Es salvaje.** *(ehs sahl-'vah-heh)*

It needs a vet.   **Necesita un veterinario.**
(neh-seh-'see-tah oon veh-teh-ree-'nah-ree-oh)

It has a mate.   **Tiene una pareja.**
(tee-'eh-neh 'oo-nah pah-'reh-hah)

It likes to bite.	**Le gusta morder.** *(leh 'goos-tah mohr-'dehr)*
It eats hay.	**Come heno.** *('koh-meh 'eh-noh)*
It uses a feeder.	**Usa un alimentador.**

('oo-sah oon ah-lee-mehn-tah-'dohr)

¡MÁS AYUDA!

• The job assignments may involve a variety of specialists. Make sure everyone understands their area of expertise:

I understand . . .	**Entiendo . . .** *(ehn-tee-'ehn-doh)*
animal nutrition	**la nutrición de animales**
	(lah noo-tree-see-'ohn deh ah-nee-'mah-lehs)
agricultural techniques	**las técnicas agrícolas**
	(lahs 'tehk-nee-kahs ah-'gree-koh-lahs)
food production	**la producción de alimentos**
	(lah pro-dook-see-'ohn deh ah-lee-'mehn-tohs)
I teach . . .	**Enseño . . .** *(ehn-'sehn-yoh)*
masonry	**(la) albañilería** *(alh-bah-nee-leh-'ree-ah)*
hunting	**(la) caza** *('kah-sah)*
fishing	**(la) pesca** *('pehs-kah)*
Let's . . .	**Vamos a . . .** *('vah-mohs ah)*
dig wells	**excavar pozos** *(ehks-kah-'vahr 'poh-sohs)*
level land	**nivelar el terreno**
	(nee-veh-'lahr ehl teh-'rreh-noh)
build bridges	**construir puentes**
	(kohns-troo-'eer 'pwehn-tehs)
repair dams	**reparar represas**
	(reh-pah-'rahr reh-'preh-sahs)
rebuild homes	**reconstruir casas**
	(reh-kohns-troo-'eer 'kah-sahs)

¡ LA CULTURA !

Remember that people in rural areas often have a unique appreciation of domestic animals, and already know a great deal concerning feeding habits, breeding, and general care. The same holds true for any horticultural project. It's probably wise to listen carefully to their suggestions.

Natural disasters
Los desastres naturales
(lohs deh-'sahs-trehs nah-too-'rah-lehs)

Relief efforts are often disrupted by Mother Nature. When you have to battle the elements, talk about the situation **en español**:

It was (the) . . .	**Fue . . .** *(foo-'eh)*
drought	**la sequía** *(ah seh-'kee-ah)*
earthquake	**el terremoto** *(ehl teh-rreh-'moh-toh)*
flood	**la inundación** *(lah ee-noon-dah-see-'ohn)*
frost	**la escarcha** *(lah ehs-'kahr-chah)*
hail	**el granizo** *(ehl grah-'nee-soh)*
hurricane	**el huracán** *(ehl oo-rah-'kahn)*
ice	**el hielo** *(ehl ee-'eh-loh)*
landslide	**la avalancha** *(lah ah-vah-'lahn-chah)*
rain	**la lluvia** *(lah 'yoo-vee-ah)*
sleet	**el aguanieve** *(ehl ah-gwah-nee-'eh-veh)*
snow	**la nieve** *(lah nee-'eh-veh)*
storm	**la tormenta** *(lah tohr-'mehn-tah)*
tornado	**el tornado** *(ehl tohr-'nah-doh)*
volcano	**el volcán** *(ehl vohl-'kahn)*
wind	**el viento** *(ehl vee-'ehn-toh)*

When foul weather strikes, you may have to mention a few medical concerns:

It's ...   **Es** ... *(ehs)*

  dehydration   **(la) deshidratación**
                                       (dehs-ee-drah-tah-see-'ohn)

  exhaustion   **(la) postración** *(pohs-trah-see-'ohn)*

  frostbite   **(el) congelamiento**
                                       (kohn-heh-lah-mee-'ehn-toh)

  gangrene   **(la) gangrena** *(gahn-'greh-nah)*

  sunstroke   **(la) insolación** *(een-soh-lah-see-'ohn)*

¡MÁS AYUDA!

War-torn areas also need aid; you might as well arrive with the necessary Spanish skills:

There were ...   **Había** ... *(ah-'bee-ah)*

  booby traps   **(las) trampas explosivas**
                                       ('trahm-pahs ehks-ploh-'see-vahs)

  bullets   **(las) balas** *('bah-lahs)*

  rockets   **(los) cohetes** *(koh-'eh-tehs)*

  cannons   **(los) cañones** *(kahn-'yoh-nehs)*

  bombs   **(las) bombas** *('bohm-bahs)*

  guns   **(las) armas** *('ahr-mahs)*

  helicopters   **(los) helicópteros** *(eh-lee-'kohp-teh-rohs)*

  tanks   **(los) tanques** *('tahn-kehs)*

  troops   **(las) tropas** *('troh-pahs)*

We saw ...   **Vimos** ... *('vee-mohs)*

  panic   **(el) pánico** *('pah-nee-koh)*

  misery   **(la) miseria** *(mee-'seh-ree-ah)*

  chaos   **(el) caos** *('kah-ohs)*

  guerrillas   **(las) guerrillas** *(geh-'rree-yahs)*

  hostages   **(los) rehenes** *(reh-'eh-nehs)*

  soldiers   **(los) soldados** *(sohl-'dah-dos)*

| terrorists | **(los) terroristas** *(teh-rroh-'rees-tahs)* |
| rebellion | **la rebelión** *(lah reh-beh-lee-'ohn)* |

¡NECESITA PRACTICAR!

Match the related vocabulary:

la avispa	el zorro
el lobo	la abeja
el cisne	el chivo
la oveja	el pato
el corral	el macho
la hembra	el establo
la bala	el arma

Repair and restoration
La reparación y la restauración
(lah reh-pah-rah-see-'ohn ee lah rehs-tah-oo-rah-see-'ohn)

Buildings often get damaged or destroyed when disasters strike. As groups move in to help repair, restore, and rebuild, use these Spanish words to get the job done:

I need (the) . . .	**Necesito** . . . *(neh-seh-'see-toh)*
Bring (the) . . .	**Traiga** . . . *('trah-ee-gah)*
bit	**el taladro** *(ehl tah-'lah-droh)*
blade	**la cuchilla** *(lah koo-'chee-yah)*
bolt	**el perno** *(ehl 'pehr-noh)*
chain	**la cadena** *(lah kah-'deh-nah)*
chisel	**el cincel** *(ehl seen-'sehl)*
clamp	**la abrazadera** *(lah ah-brah-sah-'deh-rah)*
compressor	**el compresor de aire**
	(ehl kohm-preh-'sohr deh 'ah-ee-reh)
drill	**el taladro** *(ehl tah-'lah-droh)*

electric cord	**el cordón eléctrico**
	(ehl kohr-'dohn eh-'lehk-tree-koh)
file	**la lima** *(lah 'lee-mah)*
glue	**el pegamento** *(ehl peh-gah-'mehn-toh)*
hacksaw	**la sierra para cortar metal**
	(lah see-'eh-rrah 'pah-rah kohr-'tahr meh-'tahl)
hammer	**el martillo** *(ehl mahr-'tee-yoh)*
jack	**el gato** *(ehl 'gah-toh)*
ladder	**la escalera** *(lah ehs-kah-'leh-rah)*
level	**el nivel** *(ehl nee-'vehl)*
measuring tape	**la cinta para medir**
	(lah 'seen-tah 'pah-rah meh-'deer)
nail	**el clavo** *(ehl 'klah-voh)*
nut	**la tuerca** *(lah 'twehr-kah)*
paint	brush **la brocha de pintar**
	(lah 'broh-chah deh peen-'tahr)
paint	**la pintura** *(lah peen-'too-rah)*
plan	**el plano** *(ehl 'plah-noh)*
plane	**el cepillo** *(ehl seh-'pee-yoh)*
pliers	**las pinzas** *(lahs 'peen-sahs)*
ramp	**la rampa** *(lah 'rahm-pah)*
roller	**el rodillo** *(ehl roh-'dee-yoh)*
safety glasses	**los lentes de seguridad**
	(lohs 'lehn-tehs deh seh-goo-ree-'dahd)
sandpaper	**el papel de lija** *(ehl pah-'pehl deh 'lee-hah)*
saw	**el serrucho** *(ehl seh-'rroo-choh)*
scaffold	**el andamio** *(ehl ahn-'dah-mee-oh)*
scraper	**el raspador** *(ehl rahs-pah-'dohr)*
screw	**el tornillo** *(ehl tohr-nee-yoh)*
screwdriver	**el atornillador** *(ehl ah-tohr-nee-yah-'dohr)*
staple	**la grapa** *(lah 'grah-pah)*
tape	**la cinta** *(lah 'seen-tah)*
tape measure	**la cinta para medir**
	(lah 'seen-tah 'pah-rah meh-'deer)
tongs	**las tenazas** *(lahs teh-'nah-sahs)*

toolbox	**la caja de herramientas**
	(lah 'kah-hah deh eh-rrah-mee-'ehn-tahs)
trowel	**la llana** *(lah 'yah-nah)*
washer	**la arandela** *(lah ah-rahn-'deh-lah)*
wire	**el alambre** *(ehl ah-'lahm-breh)*
wrench	**la llave inglesa** *(lah 'yah-veh een-'gleh-sah)*
Let's install (the) . . .	**Vamos a instalar . . .**
	('vah-mohs ah eens-tah-'lahr)
block	**el bloque** *(ehl 'bloh-keh)*
brace	**el grapón** *(ehl grah-'pohn)*
duct	**el conducto** *(ehl kohn-'dook-toh)*
drains	**los desagües** *(lohs des-'ah-gwehs)*
footing	**el pie** *(ehl pee-'eh)*
foundation	**la fundación** *(lah foon-dah-see-'ohn)*
frame	**la armadura** *(lah ahr-mah-'doo-rah)*
hinges	**las bisagras** *(lahs bee-'sah-grahs)*
gutters	**las canaletas** *(lahs kah-nah-'leh-tahs)*
tank	**el tanque** *(ehl 'tahn-keh)*
insulation	**el aislamiento** *(ehl ah-ees-lah-mee-'ehn-toh)*
joint	**la unión** *(lah oo-nee-'ohn)*
rafter	**la viga** *(lah 'vee-gah)*
railing	**la baranda** *(lah bah-'rahn-dah)*
shingles	**las tablillas** *(lahs tah-'blee-yahs)*
stud	**el poste** *(ehl 'pohs-teh)*
trim	**la moldura** *(lah mohl-'doo-rah)*
It goes in (the) . . .	**Va en . . .** *(vah ehn)*
corner	**la esquina** *(lah ehs-'kee-nah*
edge	**el borde** *(ehl 'bohr-deh)*
end	**la punta** *(lah 'poon-tah)*
front	**el frente** *(ehl 'frehn-teh)*
middle	**el medio** *(ehl 'meh-dee-oh)*
opening	**la abertura** *(lah ah-behr-'too-rah)*

The materials
Los materiales *(lohs mah-teh-ree-'ah-lehs)*

Make sure you've got everything you need to get the job done:

We need more . . .	**Necesitamos más . . .**
	(neh-seh-see-'tah-mohs mahs)
Unload (the) . . .	**Descargue . . .** *(dehs-'kahr-geh)*
aluminum	**el aluminio** *(ehl ah-loo-'mee-nee-oh)*
asbestos	**el asbesto** *(ehl ahs-'behs-toh)*
asphalt	**el asfalto** *(ehl ahs-'fahl-toh)*
brass	**el latón** *(ehl lah-'tohn)*
brick	**el ladrillo** *(ehl lah-'dree-yoh)*
bronze	**el bronce** *(ehl 'brohn-seh)*
canvas	**la lona** *(lah 'loh-nah)*
cardboard	**el cartón** *(ehl kahr-'tohn)*
cement	**el cemento** *(ehl seh-'mehn-toh)*
clay	**la arcilla** *(lah ahr-'see-yah)*
cloth	**la tela** *(lah 'teh-lah)*
glass	**el vidrio** *(ehl 'vee-dree-oh)*
gravel	**la grava** *(lah 'grah-vah)*
iron	**el hierro** *(ehl ee-'eh-rroh)*
linoleum	**el linóleo** *(ehl lee-'noh-leh-oh)*
marble	**el mármol** *(ehl 'mahr-mohl)*
mortar	**el mortero** *(ehl mohr-'teh-roh)*
pavement	**el pavimento** *(ehl pah-vee-'mehn-toh)*
pipe	**el tubo** *(ehl 'too-boh)*
plaster	**el yeso** *(ehl 'yeh-soh)*
plastic	**el plástico** *(ehl 'plahs-tee-koh)*
plywood	**la madera terciada**
	(lah mah-'deh-rah tehr-see-'ah-dah)
putty	**la masilla** *(lah mah-'see-yah)*
screen	**el mosquitero** *(ehl mohs-kee-'teh-roh)*
slab	**la losa** *(lah 'loh-sah)*
steel	**el acero** *(ehl ah-'seh-roh)*
stone	**la piedra** *(lah pee-'eh-drah*

stucco	**el estuco** *(ehl ehs-'too-koh)*
tar	**la brea** *(lah 'breh-ah)*
tile	**la baldosa** *(lah bahl-'doh-sah)*
wallpaper	**el empapelado** *(ehl ehm-pah-peh-'lah-doh)*
wire mesh	**la malla de acero**
	(lah 'mah-yah deh ah-'seh-roh)
wood	**la madera** *(lah mah-'deh-rah)*

Use the following materials to insert verbs and create phrases of your own:

coal	**el carbón** *(ehl kahr-'bohn)*	<u>Usamos el carbón.</u>
copper	**el cobre** *(ehl 'koh-breh)*	_____
cotton	**el algodón**	_____
	(ehl ahl-goh-'dohn)	
fuel	**el combustible**	_____
	(ehl kohm-boos-'tee-bleh)	
glue	**el pegamento**	_____
	(ehl peh-gah-'mehn-toh)	
gold	**el oro** *(ehl 'oh-roh)*	_____
grease	**la grasa** *(lah 'grah-sah)*	_____
ice	**el hielo** *(ehl ee-'eh-loh)*	_____
leather	**el cuero** *(ehl 'kweh-roh)*	_____
metal	**el metal** *(ehl meh-'tahl)*	_____
oil	**el aceite** *(ehl ah-'seh-ee-teh)*	_____
rubber	**la goma** *(lah 'goh-mah)*	_____
sand	**la arena** *(lah ah-'reh-nah)*	_____
silver	**la plata** *(lah 'plah-tah)*	_____
string	**la cuerda** *(lah 'kwehr-dah)*	_____
thread	**el hilo** *(ehl 'ee-loh)*	_____
wool	**la lana** *(lah 'lah-nah)*	_____

¡MÁS AYUDA!

• Descriptions will be needed on the worksite, so get started today:

It's . . .	Está . . . *(ehs-'tah)*
out of service	**fuera de servicio** *('fweh-rah deh sehr-'vee-see-oh)*
stuck	**pegado** *(peh-'gah-doh)*
defective	**defectuoso** *(deh-fehk-too-'oh-soh)*
lost	**perdido** *(pehr-'dee-doh)*
inoperative	**inoperable** *(ee-noh-peh-'rah-bleh)*
prohibited	**prohibido** *(proh-ee-'bee-doh)*
restricted	**restringido** *(rehs-treen-'hee-doh)*

• Always try to practice descriptions as opposites:

I think it's . . .	Creo que está . . . *('kreh-oh keh ehs-'tah)*
twisted	**torcido** *(tohr-'see-doh)*
straight	**recto** *('rehk-toh)*
loose	**suelto** *('swehl-toh)*
tight	**apretado** *(ah-preh-'tah-doh)*
heavy	**pesado** *(peh-'sah-doh)*
light	**ligero** *(lee-'heh-roh)*
clean	**limpio** *('leem-pee-oh)*
dirty	**sucio** *('soo-see-oh)*

¡NECESITA PRACTICAR!

Connect the words that belong together:

el martillo	**el acero**
el hielo	**la plata**
la pintura	**la nieve**
el oro	**la brocha**
el hierro	**el clavo**

Measure it!
¡Mídalo! *('mee-dah-loh)*

Discussing measurements is a daily routine on all repair projects:

It's a/an . . .	Es . . . *(ehs)*
bunch	**un racimo** *(oon rah-'see-moh)*
centimeter	**un centímetro** *(oon sehn-'tee-meh-troh)*
cup	**una taza** *('oo-nah 'tah-sah)*
foot	**un pie** *(oon pee-'eh)*
gallon	**un galón** *(oon gah-'lohn)*
gram	**un gramo** *(oon 'grah-moh)*
gross	**una gruesa** *('oo-nah groo-'eh-sah)*
inch	**una pulgada** *('oo nah pool 'gah-dah)*
kilogram	**un kilo** *(oon 'kee-loh)*
liter	**un litro** *(oon 'lee-troh)*
meter	**un metro** *(oon 'meh-troh)*
millimeter	**un milímetro** *(oon mee-'lee-meh-troh)*
ounce	**una onza** *('oo-nah 'ohn-sah)*
pint	**una pinta** *('oo-nah 'peen-tah)*
pound	**una libra** *('oo-nah 'lee-brah)*
quart	**un cuarto** *(oon 'kwahr-toh)*
ton	**una tonelada** *('oo-nah toh-neh-'lah-dah)*
truckload	**una camionada** *('oo-nah kah-mee-oh-'nah-dah)*
yard	**una yarda** *('oo-nah 'yahr-dah)*

It's . . .	Está . . . *(ehs-'tah)*
parallel	**paralelo** *(pah-rah-'leh-loh)*
straight	**derecho** *(deh-'reh-choh)*
uneven	**desigual** *(deh-see-'gwahl)*

What is the . . . ?	¿Cuál es . . . ? *(kwahl ehs)*
angle	**el ángulo** *(ehl 'ahn-goo-loh)*
circle	**el círculo** *(ehl 'seer-koo-loh)*
groove	**la muesca** *(lah 'mwehs-kah)*
height	**la altura** *(lah ahl-'too-rah)*
length	**el largo** *(ehl 'lahr-goh)*

line	**la línea** *(lah 'lee-neh-ah)*
point	**la punta** *(lah 'poon-tah)*
shape	**la forma** *(lah 'fohr-mah)*
size	**el tamaño** *(ehl tah-'mahn-yoh)*
square	**el cuadro** *(ehk 'kwah-droh)*
weight	**el peso** *(ehl 'peh-soh)*
width	**la anchura** *(lah ahn-'choo-rah)*

¡ MÁS AYUDA !

• Look who's on your work crew:

Call the . . .	**Llame a . . .** *('yah-meh ah)*
architect	**el arquitecto** *(ehl ahr-kee-'tehk-toh)*
carpenter	**el carpintero** *(ehl kahr-peen-'teh-roh)*
contractor	**el contratista** *(ehl kohn-trah-'tees-tah)*
electrician	**el electricista** *(ehl eh-lehk-tree-'sees-tah)*
engineer	**el ingeniero** *(ehl een-heh-nee-'eh-roh)*
laborer	**el obrero** *(ehl oh-'breh-roh)*
painter	**el pintor** *(ehl peen-'tohr)*
plumber	**el plomero** *(ehl ploh-'meh-roh)*
roofer	**el tejador** *(ehl teh-hah-'dohr)*
stonemason	**el albañil** *(ehl ahl-bahn-'yeel)*

• And in the kitchen, here's a little Spanish for volunteer cooks:

Take out (the) . . .	**Saque . . .** *('sah-keh)*
Wash (the) . . .	**Lave . . .** *('lah-veh)*
Dry (the) . . .	**Seque . . .** *('seh-keh)*
Put away (the) . . .	**Guarde . . .** *('gwahr-deh)*
bowl	**el plato hondo** *(ehl 'plah-toh 'ohn-doh)*
coffeepot	**la cafetera** *(lah kah-feh-'teh-rah)*
cup	**la taza** *(lah 'tah-sah)*
fork	**el tenedor** *(ehl teh-neh-'dohr)*
glass	**el vaso** *(ehl 'vah-soh)*

grill	**la parrilla** *(lah pah-'rree-yah)*
knife	**el cuchillo** *(ehl koo-'chee-yoh)*
napkin	**la servilleta** *(lah sehr-vee-'yeh-tah)*
pan	**la sartén** *(lah sahr-'tehn)*
pepper shaker	**el pimentero** *(ehl pee-mehn-'teh-roh)*
plate	**el plato** *(ehl 'plah-toh)*
platter	**la fuente** *(lah 'fwehn-teh)*
pot	**la olla** *(lah 'oh-yah)*
salt shaker	**el salero** *(ehl sah-'leh-roh)*
saucer	**el platillo** *(ehl plah-'tee-yoh)*
spoon	**la cuchara** *(lah koo-'chah-rah)*
tablecoth	**el mantel** *(ehl mahn-'tehl)*

 ¡ *N E C E S I T A   P R A C T I C A R !*

Translate!

La mitad de una tonelada es mil libras.
¿Cuántas onzas hay en dos galones?
La anchura del cuadro son doce pulgadas.
El contratista habla con el carpintero.
El perno y el tornillo no están derechos.

The warehouse
El almacén *(ehl ahl-mah-'sehn)*

Walk around a local warehouse, factory, or workshop, and you're bound to see most of the items below. Practice with these commands:

Bring (the) . . .	**Traiga** . . . *('trah-ee-gah)*
Use (the) . . .	**Use** . . . *('oo-seh)*
Move (the) . . .	**Mueva** . . . *('mweh-vah)*
cart	**la carretilla** *(lah kah-rreh-'tee-yah)*
cast	**el molde** *(ehl 'mohl-deh)*

dolly	**el travelín** *(ehl trah-veh-'leen)*
filter	**el filtro** *(ehl 'feel-troh)*
hoist	**el montacargas** *(ehl mohn-tah-'kahr-gahs)*
crane	**la grúa** *(lah 'groo-ah)*
hook	**el gancho** *(ehl 'gahn-choh)*
hose	**la manguera** *(lah mahn-'geh-rah)*
ladle	**el cucharón** *(ehl koo-chah-'rohn)*
net	**la red** *(lah rehd)*
pallet	**el soporte de madera**
	(ehl soh-'pohr-teh deh mah-'deh-rah)
plate	**la plancha** *(lah 'plahn-chah)*
pulley	**la polea** *(lah poh-'leh-ah)*
scale	**la báscula** *(lah 'bahs-koo-lah)*
scrap	**el desecho** *(ehl dehs-'eh-choh)*
stick	**el palo** *(ehl 'pah-loh)*
stool	**el banquillo** *(ehl bahn-'kee-yoh)*
tray	**la bandeja** *(lah bahn-'deh-hah)*
wheel	**la rueda** *(lah 'rweh-dah)*

¡MÁS AYUDA!

• Tell all the workers about certain safety items:

Put on (the) . . .**Póngase** . . . *('pohn-gah-seh)*

apron	**el delantal** *(ehl deh-lahn-'tahl)*
belt	**el cinturón de seguridad**
	(ehl seen-too-'rohn deh seh-goo-ree-'dahd)
boots	**las botas** *(las 'boh-tahs)*
earplugs	**los tapones para los oídos**
	(lohs tah-'poh-nehs 'pah-rah lohs oh-'ee-dohs)
gloves	**los guantes** *(lohs 'gwahn-tehs)*
hairnet	**la redecilla** *(lah reh-deh-'see-yah)*
helmet	**el casco** *(ehl 'kahs-koh)*
jacket	**la chaqueta** *(lah chah-'keh-tah)*

mask	**la máscara** *(lah 'mahs-kah-rah)*
mittens	**los mitones** *(lohs mee-'toh-nehs)*
overcoat	**el abrigo** *(ehl ah-'bre-goh)*
raincoat	**el impermeable** *(ehl eem-pehr-meh-'ah-bleh)*
safety glasses	**las gafas de seguridad** *(lahs 'gah-fahs deh seh-goo-ree-'dahd)*
strap	**la correa** *(lah koh-'rreh-ah)*
suit	**el traje** *(ehl 'trah-heh)*
uniform	**el uniforme** *(ehl oo-nee-'fohr-meh)*
vest	**el chaleco** *(ehl chah-'leh-koh)*

• A number of industries could get affected by major disasters. Here's a few international concerns:

There are problems with (the) . . .	**Hay problemas con . . .** *('ah-hee proh-'bleh-mahs kohn)*
airline	**la compañía aérea** *(lah kohm-pahn-'ee-ah ah-'eh-reh-ah)*
electrical power	**la energía eléctrica** *(lah eh-nehr-'hee-ah eh-'lehk-tree-kah)*
hydraulic energy	**la energía hidráulica** *(lah eh-nehr-'hee-ah ee-'drah-oo-lee-kah)*
ocean transport	**el transporte marítimo** *(ehl trahns-'pohr-teh mah-'ree-tee-moh)*
railway	**el ferrocarril** *(ehl feh-rroh-kah-'rreel)*
river transport	**el transporte fluvial** *(ehl trahn-'pohr-teh floo-vee-'ahl)*
road	**la carretera** *(lah kah-rreh-'teh-rah)*

Electrical equipment

El equipo eléctrico *(ehl eh-'kee-poh eh-'lehk-tree-koh)*

Add words to your list of electrical devices. This time, say **no**, using the following pattern:

Don't use (the) . . .	**No use** . . . *(noh 'oo-seh)*
battery	**la batería** *(lah bah-teh-'ree-ah)*
charger	**el cargador** *(ehl kahr-gah-'dohr)*
circuit	**el circuito** *(ehl seer-'kwee-toh)*
electrical cable	**el cable eléctrico**
	(ehl 'kah-bleh eh-'lehk-tree-koh)
electrical outlet	**el enchufe** *(ehl ehn-'choo-feh)*
extension cord	**el cable de extensión**
	(ehl 'kah-bleh deh ehks-tehn-see-'ohn)
generator	**el generador** *(ehl heh-neh-rah-'dohr)*
master switch	**el conmutador principal**
	(ehl kohn-moo-tah-'dohr preen-see-'pahl)
meter	**el medidor** *(ehl meh-dee-'dohr)*
switch	**el interruptor** *(ehl een-teh-rroop-'tohr)*
turbine	**la turbina** *(lah toor-'bee-nah)*
transformer	**el transformador** *(ehl trahns-fohr-mah-'dohr)*
wire	**el alambre** *(ehl ah-'lahm-breh)*
Don't press (the) . . .	**No oprima** . . . *(noh oh-'pree-mah)*
Don't move (the)	**No mueva** . . . *(noh 'mweh-vah)*
button	**el botón** *(ehl boh-'tohn)*
key	**la tecla** *(lah 'tehk-lah)*
knob	**el botón** *(ehl boh-'tohn)*
lever	**la palanca** *(lah pah-'lahn-kah)*
timer	**el contador** *(ehl kohn-tah-'dohr)*
Did you check (the) . . . ?	**¿Revisó** . . . ? *(reh-vee-'soh)*
AC	**la corriente alterna**
	(lah koh-rree-'ehn-teh ahl-'tehr-nah)
amps	**el amperaje** *(ehl ahm-peh-'rah-heh)*

DC	**la corriente continua**
	(lah koh-rree-'ehn-teh kohn-'tee-nwah)
high voltage	**el alto voltaje**
	(ehl 'ahl-toh vohl-'tah-heh)
horsepower	**los caballos de fuerza**
	(lohs kah-'bah-yohs deh 'fwehr-sah)
low voltage	**el bajo voltaje**
	(ehl 'bah-hoh vohl-'tah-heh)
wattage	**los vatios** *(lohs 'vah-tee-ohs)*

Common containers
Los recipientes comunes
(lohs reh-see-pee-'ehn-tehs koh-'moo-nehs)

Containers are everywhere. Tell your crew how to handle or carry the supplies and materials:

Fill the . . .	**Llene . . .** *('yeh-neh)*
Empty the . . .	**Vacíe . . .** *(vah-'see-eh)*
Carry the . . .	**Lleve . . .** *('yeh-veh)*
bag	**la bolsa** *(lah 'bohl-sah)*
barrel	**el barril** *(ehl bah-'rreel)*
basket	**la canasta** *(lah kah-'nahs-tah)*
bottle	**la botella** *(lah boh-'teh-yah)*
box	**la caja** *(lah 'kah-hah)*
bucket	**el balde** *(ehl 'bahl-deh)*
canister	**el recipiente** *(ehl reh-see-pee-'ehn-teh)*
container	**el contenedor** *(ehl kohn-teh-neh-'dohr)*
crate	**la caja para transporte**
	(lah 'kah-hah 'pah-rah trahns-'pohr-teh)
jar	**la jarra** *(lah 'hah-rrah)*
package	**el paquete** *(ehl pah-'keh-teh)*
tank	**el tanque** *(ehl 'tahn-keh)*
tube	**el tubo** *(ehl 'too-boh)*

¡L A   C U L T U R A !

What do you know about the metric system?

⁵/₈ mi.	=	**un kilómetro** *(oon kee-'loh-meh-troh)*
2.2 lbs.	=	**un kilogramo** *(oon kee-loh-'grah-moh)*
33° F	=	**0° C** *('seh-roh 'grah-doh 'sehl-see-oos)*

Important vehicles
Vehículos importantes
(veh-'ee-koo-lohs eem-pohr-'tahn-tehs)

Without appropriate rescue and reconstruction equipment, you'll be in trouble:

We need (the) . . .	**Necesitamos . . .** *(neh-seh-see-'tah-mohs)*
ambulance	**la ambulancia** *(lah ahm-boo-'lahn-see-ah)*
boxcar	**el vagón** *(ehl vah-'gohn)*
bulldozer	**la niveladora** *(lah nee-veh-lah-'doh-rah)*
cement truck	**el mezclador de cemento** *(ehl mehs-klah-'dohr deh seh-'mehn-toh)*
commercial vehicle	**el vehículo comercial** *(ehl veh-'ee-koo-loh koh-mehr-see-'ahl)*
delivery truck	**el camión de reparto** *(ehl kah-mee-'ohn deh reh-'pahr-toh)*
dump truck	**el volquete** *(ehl vohl-'keh-teh)*
flatbed truck	**el camión de plataforma** *(ehl kah-mee-'ohn deh plah-tah-'fohr-mah)*
helicopter	**el helicóptero** *(ehl eh-lee-'kohp-teh-roh)*
pick-up	**la camioneta** *(lah kah-mee-oh-'neh-tah)*
plane	**el avión** *(ehl ah-vee-'ohn)*
semitrailer	**el semirremolque** *(ehl seh-mee-rreh-'mohl-keh)*
ship	**el buque** *(ehl 'boo-keh)*

tank truck	**el camión cisterna** *(ehl kah-mee-'ohn sees-'tehr-nah)*
tow truck	**la grúa** *(lah 'groo-ah)*
tractor	**el tractor** *(ehl trahk-'tohr)*
tractor trailer	**el camión tractor** *(ehl kah-mee-'ohn trahk-'tohr)*
train	**el tren** *(ehl trehn)*
van	**la furgoneta** *(lah foor-goh-'neh-tah)*

 ¡*N E C E S I T A   P R A C T I C A R* !

In Spanish:

Name three pieces of safety equipment.
Name three pieces of electrical equipment.
Name three common containers.
Name three kinds of trucks.

Help me!
¡Ayúdenme! *(ah-'yoo-dehn-meh)*

Missions of mercy to foreign countries often involve encounters with sickness and death. Will you know enough Spanish to lend a hand?

He/She is . . .	**Está . . .** *(ehs-'tah)*
bleeding	**sangrando** *(sahn-'grahn-doh)*
choking	**asfixiándose** *(ahs-feek-see-'ahn-doh-seh)*
drowning	**ahogándose** *(ah-oh-'gahn-doh-seh)*
dying	**muriéndose** *(moo-ree-'ehn-doh-seh)*
unconscious	**inconsciente** *(een-kohn-see-'ehn-teh)*

Call the . . .	**Llame a . . .** *('yah-meh ah)*
ambulance	**la ambulancia** *(lah ahm-boo-'lahn-see-ah)*
clinic	**la clínica** *(lah 'klee-nee-kah)*
dentist	**el dentista** *(ehl dehn-'tees-tah)*

doctor	**el doctor** *(ehl dohk-'tohr)*
fire department	**el departamento de bomberos** *(ehl deh-pahr-tah-'mehn-toh deh bohm-'beh-rohs)*
hospital	**el hospital** *(ehl ohs-pee-'tahl)*
neighbor	**el vecino** *(ehl veh-'see-noh)*
operator	**la operadora** *(lah oh-peh-rah-'doh-rah)*
paramedic	**el paramédico** *(ehl pah-rah-'meh-dee-koh)*
police	**la policía** *(lah poh-lee-'see-ah)*
relative	**el pariente** *(ehl pah-ree-'ehn-teh)*

¡MÁS AYUDA!

• In extreme circumstances, use these command phrases:

Bring the stretcher!	**¡Traigan la camilla!** *('trah-ee-gahn lah kah-'mee-yah)*
Cover yourselves!	**¡Cúbranse!** *('koo-brahn-seh)*
Danger!	**¡Peligro!** *(peh-'lee-groh)*
Fire!	**¡Fuego!** *('fweh-goh)*
Get under the table!	**¡Pónganse bajo la mesa!** *('pohn-gahn-seh 'bah-hoh lah 'meh-sah)*
Help!	**¡Socorro!** *(soh-'koh-rroh)*
Run outside!	**¡Corran afuera!** *('koh-rrahn ah-'fweh-rah)*
Stay away from the windows!	**¡Quédense lejos de las ventanas!** *('keh-dehn-seh 'leh-hohs deh lahs vehn-'tah-nahs)*
Watch out!	**¡Cuidado!** *(kwee-'dah-doh)*

• Other rescue organizations may need to be contacted. Tell the community who's coming to help:

| Civil Defense | **la Defensa Civil** *(lah deh-'fehn-sah see-'veel)* |

National Guard   **la Guardia Nacional**
         (lah 'gwahr-dee-ah nah-see-oh-'nahl)
Red Cross   **la Cruz Roja** *(lah kroos 'roh-hah)*

What's the trouble?

¿Cuál es el problema? *(kwahl ehs ehl proh-'bleh-mah)*

Approach those on the scene, introduce yourself, and find out who needs emergency care:

Hi. I'm with _____.   **Hola, estoy con _____.**
                            ('oh-lah ehs-'toh-ee kohn)
Where are the victims?   **¿Dónde están las víctimas?**
                            ('dohn-deh ehs-'tahn lahs 'veek-tee-mahs)
Do you need help?   **¿Necesita ayuda?**
                            (neh-seh-'see-tah ah-'yoo-dah)
Where are you hurt?   **¿Dónde está lastimado?**
                            ('dohn-deh ehs-'tah lahs-tee-'mah-doh)
Are you OK?   **¿Está bien?** *(ehs-'tah bee-'ehn)*
Who is inside?   **¿Quién está adentro?**
                            (kee-ehn ehs-'tah ah-'dehn-troh)
Who is outside?   **¿Quién está afuera?**
                            (kee-'ehn ehs-'tah ah-'fweh-rah)

While everyone around you is trying to explain what happened, listen carefully for the words below. Repeat what you hear to make sure that there's absolutely no misunderstanding:

It's . . .   **Es . . .** *(ehs)*
  a bad fall   **una mala caída** *('oo-nah 'mah-lah kah-'ee-dah)*
  a convulsion   **una convulsión** *('oo-nah kohn-vool-see-'ohn)*
  the fatigue   **la fatiga** *(lah fah-'tee-gah)*
  a gunshot wound   **una herida de bala**
                        ('oo-nah eh-'ree-dah deh 'bah-lah)

a heart attack	**un ataque cardíaco**
	(oon ah-'tah-keh kahr-'dee-ah-koh)
an intoxication	**una intoxicación**
	('oo-nah een-tohk-see-kah-see-'ohn)
the malnutrition	**la desnutrición** *(lah dehs-noo-tree-see-'ohn)*
an overdose	**una sobredosis** *('oo-nah soh-breh-'doh-sees)*
a seizure	**un ataque** *(oon ah-'tah-keh)*
a shock	**una postración nerviosa**
	('oo-nah pohs-trah-see-'ohn nehr-vee-'oh-sah)
a snake bite	**una mordedura de culebra**
	('oo-nah mohr-deh-'doo-rah deh koo-'leh-brah)
a spasm	**un espasmo** *(oon ehs-'pahs-moh)*
a stabbing	**una puñalada** *('oo-nah poon-yah-'lah-dah)*
a strangulation	**un estrangulamiento**
	(oon ehs-trahn-goo-lah-mee-'ehn-toh)
a stroke	**un ataque fulminante**
	(oon ah-'tah-keh fool-mee-'nahn-teh)
a suffocation	**una sofocación** *('oo-nah soh-foh-kah-see-'ohn)*
a trauma	**un traumatismo** *(oon trah-oo-mah-'tees-moh)*

Now, move right in and calm the victim's fears:

I will help you.	**Le ayudaré.** *(leh ah-yoo-dah-'reh)*
You will be OK.	**Estará bien.** *(ehs-tah-'rah bee-'ehn)*
This will hurt a little.	**Esto dolerá un poco.**
	('ehs-toh doh-leh-'rah oon 'poh-koh)

¡MÁS AYUDA!

• Always be aware of any special problems with the victim:

He's . . .	**Es . . .** *(ehs)*
blind	**ciego(a)** *(see-'eh-goh, gah)*
deaf	**sordo(a)** *('sohr-doh, dah)*

disabled	**incapacitado(a)**
	(een-kah-pah-see-'tah-doh, dah)
farsighted	**présbita** *('prehs-bee-tah)*
handicapped	**minusválido(a)** *(mee-noos-'vah-lee-doh, dah)*
mute	**mudo(a)** *('moo-doh, dah)*
nearsighted	**miope** *(mee-'oh-peh)*

• While dealing with some people, keep an eye out for these little critters:

He has . . .	**Tiene . . .** *(tee-'eh-neh)*
fleas	**(las) pulgas** *('pool-gahs)*
lice	**(los) piojos** *(pee-'oh-hohs)*
ticks	**(las) garrapatas** *(gah-rruh-'puh-tahs)*
worms	**(los) gusanos** *(goo-'sah-nohs)*
parasites	**(los) parásitos** *(pah-'rah-see-tohs)*

Medical aid
La ayuda médica *(lah ah-'yoo-dah 'meh-dee-kah)*

All emergency healthcare workers and volunteers should memorize certain questions that require only a **sí** or a **no** for an answer:

Do you have (a) . . . ?	**¿Tiene . . . ?** *(tee-'eh-neh)*
backaches	**dolores de espalda**
	(doh-'loh-rehs deh ehs-'pahl-dah)
a blister	**una ampolla** *('oo-nah ahm-'poh-yah)*
a bruise	**una contusión** *('oo-nah kohn-too-see-'ohn)*
a cold	**un resfriado** *(oon rehs-free-'ah-doh)*
chills	**escalofríos** *(ehs-kah-loh-'free-ohs)*
constipation	**estreñimiento** *(ehs-trehn-ee-mee-'ehn-toh)*
convulsions	**convulsiones** *(kohn-vool-see-'oh-nehs)*
cough	**tos** *(tohs)*
cramps	**calambres** *(kah-'lahm-brehs)*
diarrhea	**diarrea** *(dee-ah-'rreh-ah)*

dizziness	**mareos** *(mah-'reh-ohs)*
fever	**fiebre** *(fee-'eh-breh)*
headaches	**dolores de cabeza**
	(doh-'loh-rehs deh kah-'beh-sah)
itching	**picazón** *(pee-kah-'sohn)*
menstruation	**menstruación** *(mehns-troo-ah-see-'ohn)*
nausea	**náuseas** *('now-seh-ahs)*
a numbness	**un adormecimiento**
	(oon ah-dohr-meh-see-mee-'ehn-toh)
phlegm	**flema** *('fleh-mah)*
seizures	**ataques** *(ah-'tah-kehs)*
stomachaches	**dolores de estómago**
	(doh-'loh-rehs deh ehs-'toh-mah-goh)
swelling	**hinchazón** *(een-chah-'sohn)*
toothache	**dolor de muelas** *(doh-'lohr deh 'mweh-lahs)*

Keep mentioning your concerns about their health:

It could be . . .	**Podría ser . . .** *(poh-'dree-ah sehr)*
an allergy	**una alergia** *('oo-nah ah-'lehr-hee-ah)*
a contagious disease	**una enfermedad contagiosa**
	('oo-nah ehn-fehr-meh-'dahd kohn-tah-hee-'oh-sah)
a dog bite	**una mordedura de perro**
	('oo-nah mohr-deh-'doo-rah deh 'peh-rroh)
high blood pressure	**la presión alta** *(lah preh-see-'ohn 'ahl-tah)*
the illness	**la enfermedad** *(lah ehn-fehr-meh-'dahd)*
an infection	**una infección** *('oo-nah een-fehk-see-'ohn)*
the injury	**la herida** *(lah eh-'ree-dah)*
an overdose	**una sobredosis** *('oo-nah soh-breh-'doh-sees)*
It's a . . .	**Es . . .** *(ehs)*
break	**una quebradura** *('oo-nah keh-brah-'doo-rah)*
burn	**una quemadura** *('oo-nah keh-mah-'doo-rah)*
cut	**una cortadura** *('oo-nah kohr-tah-'doo-rah)*
rash	**una erupción** *('oo-nah eh-roop-see-'ohn)*

| scratch | **un rasguño** *(oon rahs-'goon-yoh)* |
| sprain | **una torcedura** *('oo-nah tohr-seh-'doo-rah)* |

¡ *MÁS AYUDA!*

• Be sure to check on all illnesses. Has everyone had their shots?

Have you been inoculated against . . . ?	**¿Ha sido inoculado contra . . . ?** *(ah 'see-doh ee-noh-koo-'lah-doh 'kohn-trah)*
chicken pox	**la varicela** *(lah vah-ree-'seh-lah)*
diphtheria	**la difteria** *(lah deef-'teh-ree-ah)*
measles	**el sarampión** *(ehl sah-rahm-pee-'ohn)*
mumps	**las paperas** *(lahs pah-'peh-rahs)*
scarlet fever	**la escarlatina** *(lah ehs-kahr-lah-'tee-nah)*
tetanus	**el tétano** *(ehl 'teh-tah-noh)*
typhoid	**la fiebre tifoidea** *(lah fee-'eh-breh tee-foh-ee-'deh-ah)*

• These are spelled the same in both languages, but pronunciation may vary:

el cáncer *(ehl 'kahn-sehr)*
la diabetes *(lah dee-ah-'beh-tehs)*
la hepatitis *(lah eh-pah-'tee-tees)*
la influenza *(lah een-floo-'ehn-sah)*
la malaria *(lah mah-'lah-ree-ah)*
la meningitis *(lah meh-neen-'hee-tees)*
el polio *(ehl 'poh-lee-oh)*
la tuberculosis *(lah too-behr-koo-'loh-sees)*

Body parts

Las partes del cuerpo *(lahs 'pahr-tehs dehl 'kwehr-poh)*

You can't handle medical emergencies unless you learn the names for the body parts. Touch each one as you practice:

What happened to his/her____?	¿**Qué pasó con**_____? *(keh pah-'soh kohn)*
My _____ hurts.	**Me duele** _____. *(meh 'dweh-leh)*
ankle	**el tobillo** *(ehl toh-'bee-yoh)*
arm	**el brazo** *(ehl 'brah-soh)*
back	**la espalda** *(lah ehs-'pahl-dah)*
chest	**el pecho** *(ehl 'peh-choh)*
elbow	**el codo** *(ehl 'koh-doh)*
finger	**el dedo** *(ehl 'deh-doh)*
foot	**el pie** *(ehl pee-'eh)*
hand	**la mano** *(lah 'mah-noh)*
head	**la cabeza** *(lah kah-'beh-sah)*
hip	**la cadera** *(lah kah-'deh-rah)*
knee	**la rodilla** *(lah roh-'dee-yah)*
neck	**el cuello** *(ehl 'kweh-yoh)*
shoulder	**el hombro** *(ehl 'ohm-broh)*
stomach	**el estómago** *(ehl ehs-'toh-mah-goh)*
thigh	**el muslo** *(ehl 'moos-loh)*
throat	**la garganta** *(lah gahr-'gahn-tah)*
wrist	**la muñeca** *(lah moon-'yeh-kah)*

And what about this group of important features:

I hurt my _____.	**Me hice daño en** _____.
	(meh 'ee-seh 'dahn-yoh ehn)
cheek	**la mejilla** *(lah meh-'hee-yah)*
chin	**la barbilla** *(lah bahr-'bee-yah)*
ear	**la oreja** *(lah oh-'reh-hah)*
eye	**el ojo** *(ehl 'oh-hoh)*
face	**la cara** *(lah 'kah-rah)*

jaw	**la mandíbula** *(lah mahn-'dee-boo-lah)*
mouth	**la boca** *(lah 'boh-kah)*
nose	**la nariz** *(lah nah-'rees)*
tongue	**la lengua** *(lah lehn-gwah)*

I don't feel well
No me siento bien *(noh meh see-'ehn-toh bee-'ehn)*

Inquire about the victim's emotional status, and wait for a response:

Are you . . . ?	**¿Está . . . ?** *(ehs-'tah)*
alert	**alerta** *(ah-'lehr-tah)*
anxious	**ansioso** *('ahn-see-'oh-soh)*
awake	**despierto** *(dehs-pee-'ehr-toh)*
bad	**mal** *(mahl)*
better	**mejor** *(meh-'ohr)*
calm	**calmado** *(kahl-'mah-doh)*
comfortable	**cómodo** *('koh-moh-doh)*
confused	**confundido** *(kohn-foon-'dee-doh)*
dehydrated	**deshidratado** *(dehs-ee-drah-'tah-doh)*
dizzy	**mareado** *(mah-reh-'ah-doh)*
drunk	**borracho** *(boh-'rrah-choh)*
exhausted	**agotado** *(ah-goh-'tah-doh)*
fine	**bien** *(bee-'ehn)*
pleased	**satisfecho** *(sah-tees-'feh-choh)*
happy	**feliz** *(feh-'lees)*
hurt	**lastimado** *(lahs-tee-'mah-doh)*
injured	**herido** *(eh-'ree-doh)*
irritated	**irritado** *(ee-rree-'tah-doh)*
lost	**perdido** *(pehr-'dee-doh)*
nervous	**nervioso** *(nehr-vee-'oh-soh)*
numb	**adormecido** *(ah-dohr-meh-'see-doh)*
pregnant	**embarazada** *(ehm-bah-rah-'sah-dah)*
relaxed	**relajado** *(reh-lah-'hah-doh)*

restless	**inquieto** *(een-kee-'eh-toh)*
sad	**triste** *('trees-teh)*
sick	**enfermo** *(ehn-'fehr-moh)*
sore	**adolorido** *(ah-doh-loh-'ree-doh)*
strong	**fuerte** *('fwehr-teh)*
sweaty	**sudoroso** *(soo-doh-'roh-soh)*
tired	**cansado** *(kahn-'sah-doh)*
uncomfortable	**incómodo** *(een-'koh-moh-doh)*
upset	**molesto** *(moh-'lehs-toh)*
weak	**débil** *('deh-beel)*
worried	**preocupado** *(preh-oh-koo-'pah-doh)*
worse	**peor** *(peh-'ohr)*

¡MÁS AYUDA!

• We mentioned these emergency words earlier. Focus on the verb form:

Are you . . . ?	**¿Tiene . . . ?** *(tee-'eh-neh)*
I'm . . .	**Tengo . . .** *('tehn-goh)*
afraid	**miedo** *(mee-'eh-doh)*
cold	**frío** *('free-oh)*
hot	**calor** *(kah-'lohr)*
hungry	**hambre** *('ahm-breh)*
sleepy	**sueño** *('swehn-yoh)*
thirsty	**sed** *(sehd)*

Medications and treatment
Los medicamentos y el tratamiento
(lohs meh-dee-kah-'mehn-tohs ee ehl trah-tah-me-'ehn toh)

The doctor, nurse, or paramedic may advise the following:

He/She needs (the) . . .	**Necesita . . .** *(meh-seh-see-tah)*
Band-Aid	**la curita** *(lah koo-'ree-tah)*

bandage	**el vendaje** *(ehl vehn-'dah-heh)*
blanket	**la cobija** *(lah koh-'bee-hah)*
cane	**el bastón** *(ehl bahs-'tohn)*
cast	**la armadura de yeso** *(lah ahr-mah-'doo-rah deh 'yeh-soh)*
cough syrup	**el jarabe para la tos** *(ehl hah-'rah-beh 'pah-rah lah tohs)*
cream	**la crema** *(lah 'kreh-mah)*
crutches	**las muletas** *(lahs moo-'leh-tahs)*
disinfectant	**el desinfectante** *(ehl deh-seen-fehk-'tahn-teh)*
drops	**las gotas** *(lahs 'goh-tahs)*
glasses	**los lentes** *(lohs 'lehn-tehs)*
ice	**el hielo** *(ehl ee-'eh-loh)*
iodine	**el yodo** *(ehl 'yoh-doh)*
liniment	**el linimento** *(ehl lee-nee-'mehn-toh)*
lotion	**la loción** *(lah loh-see-'ohn)*
medication	**el medicamento** *(ehl meh-dee-kah-'mehn-toh)*
oxygen	**el oxígeno** *(ehl ohk-'see-heh-noh)*
penicillin	**la penicilina** *(lah peh-nee-see-lee-nah)*
powder	**el talco** *(ehl 'tahl-koh)*
prescription	**la receta** *(lah reh-'seh-tah)*
serum	**el suero** *(ehl 'sweh-roh)*
shot	**la inyección** *(lah een-yehk-see-'ohn)*
stitches	**las puntadas** *(lahs poon-'tah-dahs)*
surgery	**la cirugía** *(lah see-roo-'hee-ah)*
thermometer	**el termómetro** *(ehl tehr-'moh-meh-troh)*
Vaseline	**la vaselina** *(lah vah-seh-'lee-nah)*
vitamins	**las vitaminas** *(lahs vee-tah-'mee-nahs)*
wheelchair	**la silla de ruedas** *(lah 'see-yah deh 'rweh-dahs)*
X rays	**los rayos equis** *(lohs 'rah-yohs 'eh-kees)*

¡ M á s   A y u d a !

• Just as you did with previous lists, try to guess at the meaning of these:

antiácido *(ahn-tee-'ah-see-doh)*
antibiótico *(ahn-tee-bee-'oh-tee-koh)*
antídoto *(ahn-'tee-doh-toh)*
antihistamínicos *(ahn-tee-ees-tah-'mee-nee-kohs)*
antiséptico *(ahn-tee-'sehp-tee-koh)*
aspirina *(ahs-pee-'ree-nah)*
astringente *(ahs-treen-'hehn-teh)*
codeína *(koh-deh-'ee-nah)*
cortisona *(kohr-tee-'soh-nah)*
demerol *(deh-meh-'rohl)*
desinfectante *(deh-seen-fehk-'tahn-teh)*
insulina *(een-soo-'lee-nah)*
morfina *(mohr-'fee-nah)*
nitroglicerina *(nee-troh-glee-seh-'ree-nah)*
tranquilizante *(trahn-kee-lee-'sahn-teh)*

• These key words should be learned quickly. Combine them with those words that you use most often:

I have . . .	**Tengo . . .** *('tehn-goh)*
capsules	**las cápsulas** *(lahs 'kahp-soo-lahs)*
lozenges	**las pastillas** *(lahs pahs-'tee-yahs)*
pills	**las píldoras** *(lahs 'peel-doh-rahs)*
tablets	**las tabletas** *(lahs tah-'bleh-tahs)*
They're pills for . . .	**Son píldoras para . . .**
	(sohn 'peel-doh-rahs 'pah-rah)
birth control	**la anticoncepción**
	(lah ahn-tee-kohn-sehp-see-'ohn)
pain	**el dolor** *(ehl doh-'lohr)*
sleeping	**dormir** *(dohr-'meer)*

• Medical exams will probably be required. As before, the articles in parentheses should not be used with this particular sentence:

You need a/an ____ test. **Necesita un examen de _____.**

(neh-seh-'see-tah oon ehk-'sah-mehn deh)

AIDS	**(el) SIDA** *('see-dah)*
blood	**(la) sangre** *('sahn-greh)*
drug	**(las) drogas** *('droh-gahs)*
Pap smear	**Papinicolau** *(pah-pah-nee-koh-'lah-oo)*
pregnancy	**(el) embarazo** *(ehm-bah-'rah-soh)*
stool	**(los) excrementos** *(ehks-kreh-'mehn-tohs)*
urine	**(la) orina** *(oh-'ree-nah)*

• As usual, some remedies will be easy to remember. As a matter of fact, if you mention a drug in English they will probably understand what you're saying:

decongestant	**el descongestionante**
	(ehl dehs-kohn-hehs-tee-oh-'nahn-teh)
Epsom salts	**la sal de epsom** *(lah sahl deh 'ehp-sohm)*
laxative	**el laxante** *(ehl lahk-'sahn-teh)*
sedative	**el sedante** *(ehl seh-'dahn-teh)*
stimulant	**el estimulante** *(ehl ehs-tee-moo-'lahn-teh)*

 ¡ L A   C U L T U R A !

Throughout history, we have discovered that certain herbs and spices work wonders on common ailments. In Latin America, the practice of home remedies—**los remedios caseros** *(lohs reh-'meh-dee-ohs kah-'seh-rohs)*—is quite popular, so don't be surprised if your Hispanic friends offer to prepare something when someone gets sick or injured.

¡*NECESITA PRACTICAR*!

Choose the best word to complete each sentence below:

un avión, un paramédico, una oficina

El dentista tiene _____.
La ambulancia tiene _____.
El aeropuerto tiene _____.

List three major illnesses in Spanish:

_____ _____ _____

Fill in the word that belongs with the others:

tos, mudo, loción
ciego, sordo, _____
dolor de cabeza, fiebre, _____
crema, talco, _____

Practice with a friend:

¿Qué pasó?	**Hubo un accidente.**
¿Dónde está la víctima?	**Está en la calle.**
¿Qué tiene?	**Tiene una quebradura.**
¿Cómo se siente ahora?	**Está mejor.**

¡ A C C I Ó N !

Although there are many ways to state a past tense in Spanish, we will deal now with the more commonly used form. Read the following examples and, just as you did with present actions, make the changes in your verbs. You won't be perfect at first, but everyone will know what you're trying to say.

• **ar**-ending verbs

To Speak	**Hablar** *(ah-'blahr)*
I spoke	**Hablé** *(ah-'bleh)*

Hablé con el doctor. *(ah 'bloh kohn ehl dohk-'tohr)*

You/he/she spoke **Habló** *(ah-'bloh)*
Habló mucho. *(ah-'bloh 'moo-choh)*

You (pl.)/they spoke **Hablaron** *(ah-'blah-rohn)*
Hablaron en inglés. *(ah-'blah-rohn ehn een-'glehs)*

We spoke **Hablamos** *(ah-'blah-mohs)*
Hablamos después. *(ah-'blah-mohs dehs-'pwehs)*

• **er**-ending verbs

To Drink	**Beber** *(beh-'behr)*
I drank	**Bebí** *(beh-'bee)*

Bebí y hablé. *(beh-'bee ee ah-'bleh)*

You/he/she drank **Bebió** *(beh-bee-'oh)*
Ayer bebió mucho. *(ah-'yehr beh-bee-'oh 'moo-choh)*

You (pl.)/they drank **Bebieron** *(beh-bee-'eh-rohn)*
Bebieron y están muy mal. *(beh-bee-'eh-rohn ee ehs-'tahn 'moo-ee mahl)*

We drank **Bebimos** *(beh-'bee-mohs)*
Bebimos y estamos deshidratados.
  (beh-'bee-mohs ee ehs-'tah-mohs des-ee-drah-'tah-dohs)

• **ir**-ending verbs

To Leave	**Salir** *(sah-'leer)*
I left	**Salí** *(sah-'lee)*

Salí a las ocho. *(sah-'lee ah lahs 'oh-choh)*

You/he/she left	**Salió** *(sah-lee-'oh)*

Salió tarde. *(sah-lee-'oh 'tahr-deh)*

You (pl.)/they left	**Salieron** *(sah-lee-'eh-rohn)*

Salieron contentos. *(sah-lee-'eh-rohn kohn-'tehn-tohs)*

We left	**Salimos** *(sah-'lee-mohs)*

Salimos en el carro ayer. *(sah-'lee-mohs ehn ehl 'kah-rroh ah-'yehr)*

Some common verbs have irregular past tenses, so be on the lookout.

To Be	**Ser** *(sehr)*
I was	**fui** *(foo-'ee)*

Fui a la casa. *(foo-'ee ah lah 'kah-sah)*

You were; he/she was	**fue** *(foo-'eh)*

Fue un niño serio. *(fweh oon 'neen-yoh 'seh-ree-oh)*

You (pl.)/they were	**fueron** *(foo-'eh-rohn)*

Fueron dos niños felices. *(foo-'eh-rohn dohs 'neen-yohs 'feh-lee-sehs)*

We were	**fuimos** *(foo-'ee-mohs)*

Fuimos con mi hermano. *(foo-'ee-mohs kohn mee ehr-'mah-noh)*

Surprise! The past tense of "to go" is identical to the past tense of "to be": **fui, fue, fueron, fuimos.**

I went always.	**Fui siempre.** *(foo-'ee see-'ehm-preh)*
She went early.	**Ella fue temprano.**
	('eh-yah foo-'eh tehm-'prah-noh)
You (pl.) went once.	**Ustedes fueron una vez.**
	(oos-'teh-dehs foo-'eh-rohn 'oo-nah vehs)
We went sometimes.	**Fuimos a veces.** *(foo-'ee-mohs ah 'veh-sehs)*

To Have	**Tener** *(teh-'nehr)*

I had   **tuve** *('too-veh)*
Tuve una operación. *('too-veh 'oo-nah oh-peh-rah-see-'ohn)*

You/he/she had   **tuvo** *('too-voh)*
El tuvo frío. *(ehl 'too-voh 'free-oh)*

You (pl.)/they had   **tuvieron** *(too-vee-'eh-rohn)*
Ellos tuvieron calor. *('eh-yohs too-vee-'eh-rohn kah-'lohr)*

We had   **tuvimos** *(too-'vee-mohs)*
Tuvimos miedo. *(too-'vee-mohs mee-'eh-doh)*

¡ M á s A y u d a !

• Now let's check out another simple formula for changing basic verb forms to refer to past action. First, change all the verb endings to the **-ndo** ending, just as you did when you talked about current action:

tomar	**tomando** *(toh-'mahn-doh)*
comer	**comiendo** *(koh-mee-'ehn-doh)*
escribir	**escribiendo** *(ehs-kree-bee-'ehn-doh)*

Next, in place of the present tense of the verb **estar** (**estoy, está, están,** and **estamos**), use the past tense: **estaba, estaban,** and **estábamos** and combine them with the **-ndo** forms:

I was   **estaba** *(ehs-'tah-bah)*
Estaba hablando con el doctor.
   (ehs-'tah-bah ah-'blahn-doh kohn ehl dohk-'tohr)

You were; he/she was   **estaba** *(ehs-'tah-bah)*
Estaba tomando el agua.
   (ehs-'tah-bah toh-'mahn-doh ehl 'ah-gwah)

You (pl.)/they were   **estaban** *(ehs-'tah-bahn)*
Estaban abriendo las ventanas.
   (ehs-'tah-bahn ah-bree-'ehn-doh lahs vehn-'tah-nahs)

We were   estábamos *(ehs-'tah-bah-mohs)*

Estábamos comprando la medicina.

(ehs-'tah-bah-mohs kohm-'prahn-doh lah meh-dee-'see-nah)

¡*LAS ORDENES*!

As you know, command words in Spanish are derived from verb infinitives. Use the verb list in the back of the book to complete the following review exercise:

Carry	**Lleve** *('yeh-veh)*	<u>Llevar</u>
Clean	**Limpie** *('leem-pee-eh)*	<u>Limpiar</u>
Dry	**Seque** *('seh-keh)*	<u>Secar</u>
Empty	**Vacíe** *(vah-'see-eh)*	_____
Fill	**Llene** *('yeh-neh)*	_____
Lower	**Baje** *('bah-heh)*	_____
Move	**Mueva** *('mweh-vah)*	_____
Pick up	**Recoja** *(reh-'koh-hah)*	_____
Plug in	**Enchufe** *(ehn-'choo-feh)*	_____
Pull	**Jale** *('hah-leh)*	_____
Push	**Empuje** *(ehm-'poo-heh)*	_____
Put away	**Guarde** *('gwahr-deh)*	_____
Raise	**Levante** *(leh-'vahn-teh)*	_____
Throw away	**Tire** *('tee-reh)*	_____
Turn	**Voltee** *(vol-'teh-eh)*	_____
Turn off	**Apague** *(ah-'pah-geh)*	_____
Turn on	**Prenda** *('prehn-dah)*	_____
Unplug	**Desenchufe** *(dehs-ehn-'choo-feh)*	_____
Use	**Use** *('oo-seh)*	_____
Wash	**Lave** *('lah-veh)*	_____

¡MÁS AYUDA!

• The easiest shortcut to action in Spanish is to use infinitives as nouns. No special phrases are required. Look over these examples:

Off to work!	**¡A trabajar!** *(ah trah-bah-'hahr)*
Reading is important.	**Leer es importante.**
	(leh-'ehr ehs eem-pohr-'tahn-teh)
Shut the door when you leave.	**Al salir, cierre la puerta.**
	(ahl sah-'leer see-'eh-rreh lah 'pwehr-tah)

¡NECESITA PRACTICAR!

Follow the pattern below:

I speak	**Hablo**
I spoke	**Hablé**
I work	**Trabajo**
I worked	_____
I drive	**Manejo**
I drove	_____
I run	**Corro**
I ran	_____
I eat	**Como**
I ate	_____

Chapter Six

Capítulo Seis
(kah-'pee-too-loh 'seh-ees)

With the Children
Con los niños
(kohn lohs 'neen-yohs)

The little ones
Los niñitos *(lohs neen-'yee-tohs)*

Regardless of where you get involved with outreach, there are bound to be children nearby. Let's begin working with the youngest of all:

How's the baby's health?
¿Cómo está la salud del bebé?
('koh-moh ehs-'tah lah sah-'lood dehl beh-'beh)

The baby must drink the milk.
El bebé tiene que beber la leche.
(ehl beh-'beh tee-'eh-neh keh beh-'behr lah 'leh-cheh)

We have medicine for the children.
Tenemos medicina para los niños.
(teh-'neh-mohs meh-dee-'see-nah 'pah-rah lohs 'neen-yohs)

We're going to give him/her a shot.
Vamos a darle una inyección.
('vah-mohs ah 'dahr-leh 'oo-nah een-yehk-see-'ohn)

May I see the baby?
¿Puedo ver al bebé? *('pweh-doh vehr ahl beh-'beh)*

How much does he/she weigh?

¿Cuánto pesa? *('kwahn-toh 'peh-sah)*

She weighs nine pounds and three ounces.

Pesa nueve libras y tres onzas.

('peh-sah 'nweh-veh 'lee-brahs ee trehs 'ohn-sahs)

You will need a pediatrician.

Va a necesitar un pediatra.

(vah ah neh-seh-see-'tahr oon peh-dee-'ah-trah)

Now describe a baby girl:

She's . . .	Ella es . . . *('eh-yah ehs)*
blond	**rubia** *('roo-bee-ah)*
brunette	**morena** *(moh-'reh-nah)*
chubby	**gordita** *(gohr-'dee-tah)*
black	**negra** *('neh-grah)*
a twin	**una gemela** *('oo-nah heh-'meh-lah)*
pretty	**bonita** *(boh-'nee-tah)*
healthy	**sana** *('sah-nah)*
strong	**fuerte** *('fwehr-teh)*
happy	**feliz** *(feh-'lees)*
skinny	**flaquita** *(flah-'kee-tah)*
white	**blanca** *('blahn-kah)*

These words relate to infant care. Create your own sentences in the blank spaces:

blanket	**la cobija** *(lah koh-'bee-hah)*	**¡Traiga la cobija!**
milk	**la leche** *(lah 'leh-cheh)*	_____
diapers	**los pañales** *(lohs pahn-'yah-lehs)*	_____
nursing bottle	**el biberón** *(ehl bee-beh-'rohn)*	_____
pacifier	**el chupete** *(ehl choo-'peh-teh)*	_____
to cry	**llorar** *(yoh-'rahr)*	**¡Está llorando!**
to breastfeed	**amamantar** *(ah-mah-mahn-'tahr)*	_____
to burp	**eructar** *(eh-rook-'tahr)*	_____

| to crawl | **gatear** *(gah-teh-'ahr)* | _____ |
| to suck | **chupar** *(choo-'pahr)* | _____ |

¡*M á s A y u d a !*

• Remember that the easiest way to ask a Spanish speaker to help you is to start your phrase with **Favor de . . .** :

Please . . .	**Favor de . . .** *(fah-'vohr deh)*
bathe the children	**bañar a los niños**
	(bahn-'yahr ah lohs 'neen-yohs)
change their clothes	**cambiarles la ropa**
	(kahm-bee-'ahr-lehs lah 'roh-pah)
feed the children	**alimentar a los niños**
	(ah-lee-mehn-'tahr ah lohs 'neen-yohs)
leave it here	**dejarlo aquí** *(deh-'hahr-loh ah-'kee)*
wash their clothes	**lavar su ropa** *(lah-'vahr soo 'roh-pah)*

¡*L a C u l t u r a !*

Don't be afraid to touch the baby! In some Spanish-speaking countries, people believe that children can get sick if you stare at them without making physical contact. A brief stroke, hug, or light caress will make everyone feel more comfortable.

How cute!
¡Qué gracioso! *(keh grah-see-'oh-soh)*

This time, talk directly to the infant or toddler. Remember that friendly conversation and laughter are blended with your job-related language skills.

Come here!	**¡Ven acá!** *(vehn ah-'kah)*
Give me a hug!	**¡Dame un abrazo!** *('dah-meh oon ah-'brah-soh)*
It's for you!	**¡Es para ti!** *(ehs 'pah-rah tee)*

These phrases all mean "How cute!":

¡Qué bonito! *(keh boh-'nee-toh)*
¡Qué precioso! *(keh preh-see-'oh-soh)*
¡Qué lindo! *(keh 'leen-doh)*

Remember that the above phrases are for males. Change to **-a** endings when talking about females. And they can be added to any item:

What a cute . . .!	**¡Qué bonita . . .!** *(keh boh-'nee-tah)*
face	**cara** *('kah-rah)*
smile	**sonrisa** *(sohn-'ree-sah)*
voice	**voz** *(vohs)*

Now learn some vocabulary for a baby's or young child's personal belongings:

Where is the . . . ?	**¿Dónde está . . . ?** *('dohn-deh ehs-'tah)*
bib	**el babero** *(ehl bahr-'beh-roh)*
cradle	**la cuna mecedora**
	(lah 'koo-nah meh-seh-'doh-rah)
crib	**la cuna** *(lah 'koo-nah)*
diaper	**el pañal** *(ehl pahn-'yahl)*
doll	**la muñeca** *(lah moon-'yeh-kah)*
game	**el juego** *(ehl 'hweh-goh)*
potty	**el orinal** *(ehl oh-ree-'nahl)*
rattle	**el sonajero** *(ehl soh-nah-'heh-roh)*
stroller	**el cochecillo** *(ehl koh-cheh-'see-yoh)*
stuffed animal	**el animal de peluche**
	(ehl ah-nee-'mahl deh peh-'loo-cheh)
toy	**el juguete** *(ehl hoo-'geh-teh)*

¡*MÁS AYUDA!*

• The word **tú** *(too)* is the informal way of saying "you" or "your" in Spanish. The informal form is also exchanged between family and friends. Here are some examples:

You are my friend.
Tú eres mi amigo. *(too 'eh-rehs mee ah-'mee-goh)*

It's your food.
Es tu comida. *(ehs too koh-'mee-dah)*

Your baby is all right.
Tu bebé está bien. *(too beh-'beh ehs-'tah bee-'ehn)*

Did you notice that "your" is **tu**, but without the accent?

• The command words take on a slightly different form when you address children, because you use the **tú** mode:

Say "ah."	**Di "ah."** *(dee ah)*
Open your mouth.	**Abre la boca.** *('ah-breh lah 'boh-kah)*
Go to sleep.	**Duérmete.** *('dwehr-meh-teh)*
Don't . . .	**No . . .** *(noh)*
be afraid	**tengas miedo** *('tehn-gahs mee-'eh-doh)*
be naughty	**seas malcriado** *('seh-ahs mahl-kree-'ah-doh)*
cry	**llores** *('yoh-rehs)*

• All verb forms require changes when you talk to kids, because of the implicit or explicit use of **tú**. Most can be recognized because they end in the letter **s**.

Do you have . . . ?	**¿Tienes . . . ?** *(tee-'eh-nehs)*
Do you want . . . ?	**¿Quieres . . . ?** *(kee-'eh-rehs)*
Do you need . . . ?	**¿Necesitas . . . ?** *(neh-seh-'see-tahs)*

• Learn all the common ailments related to child care:

rash	**la erupción** *(lah eh-roop-see-'ohn)*
colic	**el cólico** *(ehl 'koh-lee-koh)*
vomiting	**los vómitos** *(lohs 'voh-mee-tohs)*

 ¡ NECESITA PRACTICAR !

Picture a group of children as you practice:

How many do you have?	**¿Cuántos tienes?** *('kwahn-tohs tee-'eh-nehs)*
Which one do you like?	**¿Cuál quieres?** *(kwahl kee-'eh-rehs)*
What do you need?	**¿Qué necesitas?** *(keh neh-seh-'see-tahs)*

Translate:

¿Tú hablas español?

_____

¿Dónde está tu familia?

_____

¡Qué bonito!

_____

Es gordita y feliz.

_____

Ella tiene un animal de peluche.

_____

¿Cuánto pesa el niñito?

_____

Toys!

Los juguetes *(lohs hoo-'geh-tehs)*

Hand out donated toys to the needy children. Make sure there is no fighting!

Take (the) . . .	**Toma** . . . *('toh-mah)*
I have (the) . . .	**Tengo** . . . *('tehn-goh)*
Here's (the) . . .	**Aquí tienes** . . . *(ah-'kee tee-'eh-nehs)*
ball	**la pelota** *(lah peh-'loh-tah)*
balloon	**el globo** *(ehl 'gloh-boh)*
blocks	**los cubitos** *(lohs koo-'bee-tohs)*
coloring book	**el librito de dibujos** *(ehl lee-'bree-toh deh dee-'boo-hohs)*
colored pencils	**los lápices de colores** *(lohs 'lah-pee-sehs deh koh-'loh-rehs)*
crayons	**los gises** *(los 'hee-sehs)*
doll	**la muñeca** *(lah moon-'yeh-kah)*
jump rope	**la cuerda para brincar** *(lah 'kwehr-dah 'pah-rah breen-'kahr)*
kite	**la cometa** *(lah koh-'meh-tah)*
skateboard	**la patineta** *(lah pah-tee-'neh-tah)*
little car	**el carrito** *(ehl kah-'rree-toh)*
marbles	**las canicas** *(lahs kah-'nee-kahs)*
model	**el modelo** *(ehl moh-'deh-loh)*
monster	**el monstruo** *(ehl 'mohns-troo-oh)*
puppets	**los títeres** *(lohs 'tee-teh-rehs)*
puzzle	**el rompecabezas** *(ehl rohm-peh-kah-'beh-sahs)*
skates	**los patines** *(lohs pah-'tee-nehs)*
sled	**el trineo** *(ehl tree-'neh-oh)*
spaceship	**la nave espacial** *(lah 'nah-veh ehs-pah-see-'ahl)*
storybook	**el libro de cuentos** *(ehl 'lee-broh deh 'kwehn-tohs)*
top	**el trompo** *(ehl 'trohm-poh)*
tricycle	**el triciclo** *(ehl tree-'seek-loh)*

video	**el video** *(ehl vee-'deh-oh)*
wagon	**el vagón** *(ehl vah-'gohn)*
whistle	**el silbato** *(ehl seel-'bah-toh)*
The toy_____	_____**de juguete** *(deh hoo-'geh-teh)*
airplane	**El avión** *(ehl ah-vee-'ohn)*
boat	**El bote** *(ehl 'boh-teh)*
bugle	**La trompeta** *(lah trohm-'peh-tah)*
soldier	**El soldado** *(ehl sohl-'dah-doh)*
truck	**El camión** *(ehl kah-mee-'ohn)*
It's (made of) . . .	**Es de . . .** *(ehs deh)*
cardboard	**(el) cartón** *(kahr-'tohn)*
cloth	**(la) tela** *('teh-lah)*
metal	**(el) metal** *(meh-'tahl)*
modeling clay	**(la) plastilina** *(plahs-tee-'lee-nah)*
plastic	**(el) plástico** *('plahs-tee-koh)*
wood	**(la) madera** *(mah-'deh-rah)*

¡ *M Á S A Y U D A !*

• Most Spanish speakers know the English brand names of popular playthings:

el Nintendo
la Barbie
los Legos

• There are plenty of words that relate to child's play. Try these during your playtime activities:

Do you like . . . ?	**¿Te gustan . . . ?** *(teh 'goos-tahn)*
cartoons	**los dibujos animados**
	(lohs dee-'boo-hohs ah-nee-'mah-dohs)
games	**los juegos** *(lohs 'hweh-gohs)*
jokes	**los chistes** *(lohs 'chees-tehs)*
rhymes	**las rimas** *(lahs 'ree-mahs)*

| songs | **las canciones** *(lahs kahn-see-'oh-nehs)* |
| tricks | **los trucos** *(lohs 'troo-kohs)* |

• Some very popular games include:

checkers	**el juego de damas**
	(ehl 'hweh-goh deh 'dah-mahs)
chess	**el ajedrez** *(ehl ah-heh-'drehs)*
Monopoly	**El Monopolio** *(ehl moh-noh-'poh-lee-oh)*
pachisi	**el ludo** *(ehl 'loo-doh)*
playing cards	**la baraja de juguete**
	(lah bah-'rah-hah deh hoo-'geh-teh)

• And don't forget to pass out the stuffed animals:

monkey	**el mono** *(ehl 'moh-noh)*
puppy	**el perrito** *(ehl peh-'rree-toh)*
teddy bear	**el osito** *(ehl oh-'see-toh)*

¡ L A   C U L T U R A !

Young children are sacred creatures in most cultures. In some Hispanic homes, the traditions and rituals of child rearing are not easily changed. Many customs are centuries-old and may contradict your own practices. Keep these things in mind as you offer help to Spanish speakers.

More hobbies and fun
Más pasatiempos y diversión
(mahs pah-sah-tee-'ehm-pohs ee dee-vehr-see-'ohn)

Kids around the world often get involved in these activities at an early age. Use the following phrases to discuss a child's interests:

Do you prefer . . . ?	**¿Prefieres..?** *(preh-fee-'eh-rehs)*
I prefer . . .	**Prefiero . . .** *(preh-fee-'eh-roh)*
drawing	**el dibujo** *(ehl dee-'boo-hoh)*

dancing	**el baile** *(ehl 'bah-ee-leh)*
magic	**la magia** *(lah 'mah-ee-ah)*
movies	**las películas** *(lahs peh-'lee-koo-lahs)*
music	**la música** *(lah 'moo-see-kah)*
religion	**la religión** *(lah reh-lee-hee-'ohn)*
recreation	**la recreación** *(lah reh-kreh-ah-see-'ohn)*
video games	**los juegos de video**
	(lohs 'hweh-gohs deh vee-'deh-oh)

¡ M Á S   A y u d a !

• But bear in mind the child you're dealing with:

The child is . . .	**El niño . . .** *(ehl 'neen-yoh)*
destitute	**es indigente** *(ehs een-dee-'hehn-teh)*
orphaned	**es huérfano** *(ehs 'hwehr-fah-noh)*
handicapped	**es desvalido** *(ehs dehs-vah-'lee-doh)*
disabled	**es incapacitado** *(ehs een-kah-pah-see-'tah-doh)*
poor	**es pobre** *(ehs 'poh-breh)*
hungry	**está hambriento** *(ehs-'tah ahm-bree-'ehn-toh)*
dying	**está moribundo** *(ehs-'tah moh-ree-'boon-doh)*

Sports
Los deportes *(lohs deh-'pohr-tehs)*

One of the best ways to connect with children is to get physically involved in their favorite activity. Playing sports requires little or no language at all. As you read the following vocabulary, notice how many Spanish words resemble their equivalents in English:

Let's practice . . .	**Practiquemos . . .** *(prahk-tee-'keh-mohs)*
We're going to try . . .	**Vamos a tratar . . .** *('vah-mohs ah trah-'tahr)*
I really like . . .	**Me gusta mucho . . .** *(meh 'goos-tah 'moo-choh)*
baseball	**el béisbol** *(ehl 'beh-ees-'bohl)*

basketball	**el baloncesto** *(ehl bah-lohn-'sehs-toh)*
boxing	**el boxeo** *(ehl bohk-'seh-oh)*
football	**el fútbol americano**
	(ehl 'foot-bohl ah-meh-ree-'kah-noh)
gymnastics	**la gimnasia** *(lah heem-'nah-see-ah)*
handball	**el frontón de mano**
	(ehl frohn-'tohn deh 'mah-noh)
Ping Pong	**el pimpón** *(ehl peem-'pohn)*
roller hockey	**el hockey en patines**
	(ehl 'oh-kee ehn pah-'tee-nehs)
soccer	**el fútbol** *(ehl 'foot-bohl)*
softball	**el sófbol** *(ehl 'sohf-bohl)*
track and field	**el atletismo** *(ehl ah-tleh-'tees-moh)*
volleyball	**el vóleibol** *(ehl 'voh-leh-ee-bohl)*
wrestling	**la lucha libre** *(lah 'loo-chah 'lee-breh)*

Do you know how to . . . ?	**¿Sabes . . . ?** *('sah-behs)*
Let's . . .	**Vamos a . . .** *('vah-mohs ah)*
bounce	**rebotar** *(reh-boh-'tahr)*
catch	**agarrar** *(ah-gah-'rrahr)*
dance	**bailar** *(bah-ee-'lahr)*
fish	**pescar** *(pehs-'kahr)*
hit	**pegar** *(peh-'gahr)*
kick	**patear** *(pah-teh-'ahr)*
pass	**pasar** *(pah-'sahr)*
pitch	**lanzar** *(lahn-'sahr)*
run	**correr** *(koh-'rrehr)*
serve	**servir** *(sehr-'veer)*
shoot	**disparar** *(dees-pah-'rahr)*
skate	**patinar** *(pah-tee-'nahr)*
swim	**nadar** *(nah-'dahr)*
throw	**tirar** *(tee-'rahr)*

Some activities consist of more than one word in Spanish:

Do you want to . . . ?	**¿Quieres . . . ?** *(kee-'eh-rehs)*
jump rope	**saltar soga** *(sahl-'tahr 'soh-gah)*

lift weights	**levantar pesas** *(leh-vahn-'tahr 'peh-sahs)*
do aerobics	**hacer ejercicios aeróbicos**
	(ah-'sehr eh-hehr-'see-see-ohs ah-eh-'roh-bee-kohs)
go camping	**ir a acampar** *(eer ah ah-kahm-'pahr)*
ride bikes	**montar en bicicleta**
	(mohn-'tahr ehn bee-see-'kleh-tah)
surf	**correr tabla** *(koh-'rrehr 'tah-blah)*

Be sure to hand out the proper equipment:

You need (the) . . .	**Necesitas** . . . *(neh-seh-'see-tahs)*
ball	**la pelota** *(lah peh-'loh-tah)*
basket	**la canasta** *(lah kah-'nahs-tah)*
bat	**el bate** *(ehl 'bah-teh)*
mitt	**el guante** *(ehl 'gwahn-teh)*
net	**la red** *(lah rehd)*
racket	**la raqueta** *(lah rah-'keh-tah)*
weights	**las pesas** *(lahs 'peh-sahs)*

¡ *M á s   A y u d a !*

• Out on the playground, the little ones are playing on these:

jungle gym	**los ejercicios infantiles**
	(lohs eh-hehr-'see-see-ohs een-fahn-'tee-lehs)
merry-go-round	**los caballitos** *(lohs kah-bah-'yee-tohs)*
seesaw	**el subibaja** *(ehl soo-bee-'bah-hah)*
slide	**el resbalador** *(ehl rehs-bah-lah-'dohr)*
swing	**el columpio** *(ehl koh-'loom-pee-oh)*

• Here you have Spanish words related to playground activity:

You guys need . . .	**Necesitan** . . . *(neh-seh-'see-tahn)*
a captain	**un capitán** *(oon kah-pee-'tahn)*
a coach	**un entrenador** *(oon ehn-treh-nah-'dohr)*

a player	**un jugador** *(oon hoo-gah-'dohr)*
a team	**un equipo** *(oon eh-'kee-poh)*
rules	**reglas** *('reh-glahs)*
a score	**una cuenta** *('oo-nah 'kwehn-tah)*
a tournament	**un torneo** *(oon tohr-'neh-oh)*
uniforms	**uniformes** *(oo-nee-'fohr-mehs)*

• When exercise is the topic, be sure to explain the benefits:

It helps with . . .	**Ayuda para . . .** *(ah-'yoo-dah 'pah-rah)*
fitness	**el buen estado físico**
	(ehl bwehn ehs-'tah-doh 'fee-see-koh)
strength	**la fuerza** *(lah 'fwehr-sah)*
weight loss	**la pérdida de peso**
	(lah 'pehr-dee-dah deh 'peh-soh)

 ¡*NECESITA PRACTICAR*!

Name three toys in Spanish.
Name three sports in Spanish.
Name three hobbies.

Connect the related words:

el baloncesto	**el biberón**
el boxeo	**la pelota**
el dibujo	**la red**
la leche	**el guante**
el vóleibol	**el lápiz**

 ¡*LA CULTURA*!

What do you know about children's games from other countries? You may have to ask around for the equivalents to activities such as hopscotch, dodgeball, or tag. Their names generally differ from one country to the next.

¡MÁS AYUDA!

• And then it's time to rest:

snack time	**el descanso para comer** *(ehl dehs-'kahn-soh 'pah-rah koh-'mehr)*
recess	**el recreo** *(ehl reh-'kreh-oh)*
lunchtime	**la hora de almuerzo** *(lah 'oh-rah deh ahl-'mwehr-soh)*

Do you go to school?

¿Vas a la escuela? *(vahs ah lah ehs-'kweh-lah)*

Youngsters who are old enough to attend school have greater needs than food, clothing, and shelter. Most outreach programs offer some education for both children and adults, so this is a list that should be memorized:

book	**el libro** *(ehl 'lee-broh)*
class	**la clase** *(lah 'klah-seh)*
classroom	**el salón de clase** *(ehl sah-'lohn deh 'klah-seh)*
grade level	**el grado** *(ehl 'grah-doh)*
lesson	**la lección** *(lah lehk-see-'ohn)*
paper	**el papel** *(ehl pah-'pehl)*
pen	**el lapicero** *(ehl lah-pee-'seh-roh)*
pencil	**el lápiz** *(ehl 'lah-pees)*
school	**la escuela** *(lah ehs-'kweh-lah)*
student	**el, la estudiante** *(ehl, lah ehs-too-dee-'ahn-teh)*
subject	**la asignatura** *(lah ah-seeg-nah-'too-rah)*
teacher	**el maestro/la maestra** *(ehl mah-'ehs-troh, lah mah-'ehs-trah)*

Some words will be required for a more formal academic setting:

academic grade	**la nota** or **la calificación** *(la 'noh-tah, lah kah-lee-fee-kah-see-'ohn)*

attendance	**la asistencia** *(lah ah-sees-'tehn-see-ah)*
homework	**la tarea** *(lah tah-'reh-ah)*
notebook	**el cuaderno** *(ehl kwah-'dehr-noh)*
principal	**el director/la directora**
	(ehl dee-rehk-'tohr, lah dee-rehk-'toh-rah)
test	**el examen** *(ehl ehk-'sah-men)*

At times, outreach educators may need to gather personal information from everyone for orientation or registration purposes. Here's a set of common questions:

Where do you go to school?
¿Adónde vas a la escuela? *(ah-'dohn-deh vahs ah lah ehs-'kweh-lah)*

What grade are you in?
¿En qué grado estás? *(ehn keh 'grah-doh ehs-'tahs)*

What is your favorite class?
¿Cuál es tu clase favorita? *(kwahl ehs too 'klah-seh fah-voh-'ree-tah)*

Do you go to school everyday?
¿Vas a la escuela todos los días?
(vahs ah lah ehs-'kweh-lah 'toh-dohs lohs 'dee-ahs)

Are you a good student?
¿Eres un buen estudiante? *('eh-rehs oon bwehn ehs-too-dee-'ahn-teh)*

Do you have all the forms?
¿Tienes todos los formularios?
(tee-'eh-nehs 'toh-dohs lohs fohr-moo-'lah-ree-ohs)

Is there someone in the home who speaks English?
¿Hay alguien en casa que hable inglés?
('ah-ee 'ahl-gee-ehn ehn too 'kah-sah keh 'ah-bleh een-'glehs)

How old are you?
¿Cuántos años tienes? *('kwahn-tohs 'ahn-yohs tee-'eh-nehs)*

It doesn't cost anything.
No te cuesta nada. *(noh teh 'kwehs-tah 'nah-dah)*

You will have fun.
Te vas a divertir. *(teh vahs ah dee-vehr-'teer)*

You should attend the class.
Debes asistir a la clase. *('deh-behs ah-sees-'teer ah lah 'klah-seh)*

The grade school
La escuela primaria

You must learn Spanish to help newly arrived Hispanics with the new terminology they encounter in school. If you are abroad, you must learn the language to make yourself understood.

Look at (the) . , ,	**Mira** . . . *('moo rah)*
alarm	**la alarma** *(lah ah-'lahr-mah)*
bell	**la campana** *(lah kahm-'pah-nah)*
bench	**el banco** *(ehl 'bahn-koh)*
bulletin board	**el tablero de anuncios**
	(ehl tah-'bleh-roh deh ah-'noon-see-ohs)
cabinet	**el gabinete** *(ehl gah-bee-'neh-teh)*
chalkboard	**el pizarrón** *(ehl pee-sah-'rrohn)*
clock	**el reloj** *(ehl reh-'loh)*
flag	**la bandera** *(lah bahn-'deh-rah)*
loudspeaker	**el altoparlante** *(ehl ahl-toh-pahr-'lahn-teh)*
projector	**el proyector** *(ehl proh-yehk-'tohr)*
pencil sharpener	**el sacapuntas** *(ehl sah-kah-'poon-tahs)*
desk	**el escritorio** *(ehl ehs-kree-'toh-ree-oh)*
wastebasket	**el cesto de basura**
	(ehl 'sehs-toh deh bah-'soo-rah)
teacher	**el maestro, la maestra**
	(ehl mah-'ehs-troh, lah mah-'ehs-trah)

As the children move through the grade school level, a variety of classroom materials will be put to use during instruction. To learn these objects quickly, write their names on stickers and attach these to the objects.

Bring (the) . . .	**Trae** . . . *('trah-eh)*
Use (the) . . .	**Usa** . . . *('oo-sah)*
Pick up (the) . . .	**Recoge** . . . *(reh-'koh-heh)*
card	**la tarjeta** *(lah tahr-'heh-tah)*
chalk	**la tiza** *(lahj 'tee-sah)*
envelope	**el sobre** *(ehl 'soh-breh)*
eraser	**el borrador** *(ehl boh-rrah-'dohr)*
folder	**la libreta** *(lah lee-'breh-tah)*
glue	**el pegamento** *(ehl peh-gah-'mehn-toh)*
marker	**el marcador** *(ehl mahr-kah-'dohr)*
paint	**la pintura** *(lah peen-'too-rah)*
paper clip	**el clip** *(ehl kleep)*
pin	**el alfiler** *(ehl ahl-fee-'lehr)*
poster	**la pancarta** *(lah pahn-'kahr-tah)*
ruler	**la regla** *(lah 'reh-glah)*
sheet	**la hoja** *(lah 'oh-hah)*
sign	**el letrero** *(ehl leh-'treh-roh)*
stapler	**la engrapadora** *(lah ehn-grah-pah-'doh-rah)*
string	**el hilo** *(ehl 'ee-loh)*
thumbtack	**la tachuela** *(lah tah-choo-'eh-lah)*

Continue to give directions. Most of the time, all that's needed is a one-liner or two:

This way.	**De esta manera.** *(deh 'ehs-tah mah-'neh-rah)*
Like this.	**Así.** *(ah-'see)*
Keep going.	**Sigue.** *('see-geh)*

¡ *M* Á *s* *A* *Y* *U* *D* *A* !

• You may be asked to teach a little culture as well:

national anthem	**el himno nacional** *(ehl 'eem-noh nah-see-oh-'nahl)*
pledge of allegiance	**la promesa patriótica** *(lah proh-'meh-sah pah-tree-'oh-tee-kah)*

• This book attempts to use "neutral Spanish," that is, Spanish that covers the greatest geographical area in the world. However, not all Spanish-speaking countries agree on the vocabulary, and once in a while you will encounter words different from those you have learned. For example:

pen	**la pluma** *(lah 'ploo-mah)*
notebook	**la carpeta** *(lah kahr-'peh-tah)*

• Spanglish is OK with well-known trademarks:

> **el Whiteout**
> **el Gluestick**
> **el Scotch tape**

The educational program
El programa educativo
(ehl proh-'grah-mah eh-doo-kah-'tee-voh)

You may have to talk to the children and their families about the educational program you offer:

We teach . . .	**Enseñamos . . .** *(ehn-sehn-'yah-mohs)*
art	**el arte** *(ehl 'ahr-teh)*
culture	**la cultura** *(lah kool-'too-rah)*
farming	**la agricultura** *(lah ah-gree-kool-'too-rah)*
geography	**la geografía** *(lah heh-oh-grah-'fee-ah)*
history	**la historia** *(lah ees-'toh-ree-ah)*
language	**el lenguaje** *(ehl lehn-'gwah-heh)*
math	**la matemática** *(lah mah-teh-'mah-tee-kah)*
music	**la música** *(lah 'moo-see-kah)*
religion	**la religión** *(lah reh-lee-hee-'ohn)*
science	**la ciencia** *(lah see-'ehn-see-ah)*
sewing	**la costura** *(lah kohs-'too-rah)*
social studies	**los estudios sociales**
	(los ehs-'too-dee-ohs soh-see-'ah-lehs)

These topics should be covered, too:

behavior	**el comportamiento**
	(ehl kohm-pohr-tah-mee-'ehn-toh)
health	**la salud** *(lah sah-'lood)*
safety	**la seguridad** *(lah seh-goo-ree-'dahd)*

All sorts of valuable phrases will be exchanged when you teach or learn, so grab hold of tne most popular terms right away:

What's (the) . . . ?	**¿Cuál es . . . ?** *(kwahl ehs)*
chapter	**el capítulo** *(ehl kah-'pee-too-loh)*
date	**la fecha** *(lah 'feh-chah)*
letter	**la letra** *(lah 'leh-trah)*
number	**el número** *(ehl 'noo-meh-roh)*
page	**la página** *(lah 'pah-hee-nah)*
story	**el cuento** *(ehl 'kwehn-toh)*
title	**el título** *(ehl 'tee-too-loh)*
word	**la palabra** *(lah pah-'lah-brah)*

Throughout each lesson, stimulate responses using key Spanish words:

Let's do (the) . . .	**Vamos a hacer . . .** *('vah-mohs ah ah-'sehr)*
activity	**la actividad** *(lah ahk-tee-vee-'dahd)*
assignment	**la tarea** *(lah tah-'reh-ah)*
course	**el curso** *(ehl 'koor-soh)*
exercise	**el ejercicio** *(ehl eh-hehr-'see-see-oh)*
program	**el programa** *(ehl proh-'grah-mah)*

Do all of you	**¿Todos entienden . . . ?**
understand (the) . . . ?	*('toh-dohs ehn-tee-'ehn-dehn)*
announcement	**el anuncio** *(ehl ah-'noon-see-oh)*
answer	**la respuesta** *(lah rehs-'pwehs-tah)*
bulletin	**el boletín** *(ehl boh-leh-'teen)*
calendar	**el calendario** *(ehl kah-lehn-'dah-ree-oh)*
concept	**el concepto** *(ehl kohn-'sehp-toh)*

directions	**las instrucciones** *(lahs eens-trook-see-'oh-nehs)*
example	**el ejemplo** *(ehl eh-'hehm-ploh)*
exercise	**el ejercicio** *(ehl eh-hehr-'see-see-oh)*
explanation	**la explicación** *(lah ehks-plee-kah-see-'ohn)*
idea	**la idea** *(lah ee-'deh-ah)*
information	**la información** *(lah een-fohr-mah-see-'ohn)*
material	**el material** *(ehl mah-teh-ree-'ahl)*
meaning	**el significado** *(ehl seeg-nee-fee-'kah-doh)*
note	**la nota** *(lah 'noh-tah)*
principle	**el principio** *(ehl preen-'see-pee-oh)*
problem	**el problema** *(ehl proh-'bleh-mah)*
project	**el proyecto** *(ehl proh-'yehk-toh)*
question	**la pregunta** *(lah preh-'goon-tah)*
reason	**la razón** *(lah rah-'sohn)*
report	**el informe** *(ehl een-'fohr-meh)*
result	**el resultado** *(ehl reh-sool-'tah-doh)*
schedule	**el horario** *(ehl oh-'rah-ree-oh)*
secret	**el secreto** *(ehl seh-'kreh-toh)*
solution	**la solución** *(lah soh-loo-see-'ohn)*
story	**el cuento** *(ehl 'kwehn-toh)*
theme	**el tema** *(ehl 'teh-mah)*
topic	**el asunto** *(ehl ah-'soon-toh)*

¡MÁS AYUDA!

• During test-taking, you need to be sure students understand the instructions. These expressions will come in handy:

You have to . . .	**Tienes que . . .** *(tee-'eh-nehs keh)*
write definitions	**escribir las definiciones** *(ehs-kree-'beer lahs deh-fee-nee-see-'oh-nehs)*

listen to dictation	**escuchar el dictado**
	(ehs-koo-'chahr ehl deek-'tah-doh)
say true or false	**decir verdadero o falso**
	(deh-'seer vehr-dah-'deh-roh oh 'fahl-soh)
do multiple choice	**hacer elección múltiple**
	(ah-'sehr eh-lehk-see-'ohn 'mool-tee-pleh)
fill in the blank	**llenar el espacio vacío**
	(yeh-'nahr ehl ehs-'pah-see-oh vah-'see-oh)
find the opposite	**encontrar lo opuesto**
	(ehn-kohn-'trahr loh oh-poo-'ehs-toh)
match the words	**poner en pareja las palabras**
	(poh-nehr ehn pah-'reh-hah lahs pah-'lah-brahs)
answer the questions	**contestar las preguntas**
	(kohn-tehs-'tahr lahs preh-'goon-tahs)

• Reading tutors on outreach teams have to learn appropriate terminology:

We're going to(the) . . .	**Vamos a . . .** *('vah-mohs ah)*
library	**la biblioteca** *(lah bee-blee-oh-'teh-kah)*
resource room	**el salón de recursos**
	(ehl sah-'lohn deh reh-'koor-sohs)
study hall	**el salón de estudio**
	(ehl sah-'lohn deh ehs-'too-dee-oh)
We study (the) . . .	**Estudiamos . . .** *(ehs-too-dee-'ah-mohs)*
character	**el personaje** *(ehl pehr-soh-'nah-heh)*
novel	**la novela** *(lah noh-'veh-lah)*
plot	**el argumento** *(ehl ahr-goo-'mehn-toh)*
poetry	**la poesía** *(lah poh-eh-'see-ah)*
short story	**el cuento** *(ehl 'kwehn-toh)*
We're looking for . . .	**Buscamos . . .** *(boos-'kah-mohs)*
article	**el artículo** *(ehl ahr-'tee-koo-loh)*
author	**el autor** *(ehl ow-'tohr)*
bibliography	**la bibliografía** *(lah bee-blee-oh-grah-'fee-ah)*

biography	**la biografía** *(lah bee-oh-grah-'fee-ah)*
catalog	**el catálogo** *(ehl kah-'tah-loh-goh)*
dictionary	**el diccionario** *(ehl deek-see-oh-'nah-ree-oh)*
encyclopedia	**la enciclopedia** *(lah ehn-see-kloh-'peh-dee-ah)*
glossary	**el glosario** *(ehl glo-'sah-ree-oh)*
index	**el índice** *(ehl 'een-dee-seh)*
magazine	**la revista** *(lah reh-'vees-tah)*
newspaper	**el periódico** *(ehl peh-ree-'oh-dee-koh)*
reference	**la referencia** *(lah reh-feh-'rehn-see-ah)*
table of contents	**el contenido** *(ehl kohn-teh-'nee-doh)*
title	**el título** *(ehl 'tee-too-loh)*

 ¡*Necesita Practicar!*

Choose the best word to complete each sentence:

el índice, los libros, la tiza, la novela

El autor tiene _____

La biblioteca tiene _____

El pizarrón tiene _____

La enciclopedia tiene _____

Let's learn English
Vamos a aprender inglés
('vah-mohs ah ah-prehn-'dehr een-'glehs)

As lessons are being presented, emphasize the importance of learning English. Here are a few beginning skills:

We study (the) . . .	**Estudiamos . . .** *(ehs-too-dee-'ah-mohs)*
alphabet	**el alfabeto** *(ehl ahl-fah-'beh-toh)*
dialog	**el diálogo** *(ehl dee-'ah-loh-goh)*
grammar	**la gramática** *(lah grah-'mah-tee-kah)*
handwriting	**la caligrafía** *(lah kah-lee-grah-'fee-ah)*

printing	**la letra de imprenta**
	(lah 'leh-trah deh eem-'prehn-tah)
pronunciation	**la pronunciación**
	(lah proh-noon-see-ah-see-'ohn)
reading	**la lectura** *(lah lehk-'too-rah)*
sentence	**la oración** *(lah oh-rah-see-'ohn)*
sound	**el sonido** *(ehl soh-'nee-doh)*
spelling	**la ortografía** *(lah ohr-toh-grah-'fee-ah)*
vocabulary	**el vocabulario** *(ehl voh-kah-boo-'lah-ree-oh)*
word	**la palabra** *(lah pah-'lah-brah)*
It's called (the) . . .	**Se llama . . .** *(seh 'yah-mah)*
adjective	**el adjetivo** *(ehl ahd-heh-'tee-voh)*
adverb	**el adverbio** *(ehl ahd-'vehr-bee-oh)*
comma	**la coma** *(lah 'koh-mah)*
noun	**el sustantivo** *(ehl soos-tahn-'tee-voh)*
period	**el punto** *(ehl 'poon-toh)*
pronoun	**el pronombre** *(ehl pro-'nohm-breh)*
subject	**el sujeto** *(ehl soo-'heh-toh)*
syllable	**la sílaba** *(lah 'see-lah-bah)*
tense	**el tiempo** *(ehl tee-'ehm-poh)*
verb	**el verbo** *(ehl 'vehr-boh)*
vowel	**la vocal** *(lah voh-'kahl)*

¡ L A   C U L T U R A !

Before attempting any educational program in a foreign country, do plenty of research first. Governments usually maintain strict control of the school system, so any changes in teacher selection, academic requirements, and classroom materials probably will require outside review and approval.

Classroom conversation

La conversación en la clase *(lah kohn-vehr-sah-see-'ohn ehn lah 'klah-seh)*

Always use positive action words. Notice how the word **le** can refer to "you":

I would like to _____ you.	Quisiera _____ *(kee-see-'eh-rah)*
assure	**asegurarle** *(ah-seh-goo-'rahr-leh)*
commend	**alabarle** *(ah-lah-'bahr-leh)*
compliment	**felicitarle** *(feh-lee-see-'tahr-leh)*
encourage	**animarle** *(ah-nee-'mahr-leh)*
motivate	**motivarle** *(moh-tee-'vahr-leh)*
persuade	**persuadirle** *(pehr-soo-ah-'deer-leh)*
reward	**recompensarle** *(reh-kohm-pehn-'sahr-leh)*
support	**apoyarle** *(ah-poh-'yahr-leh)*
thank	**agradecerle** *(ah-grah-deh-'sehr-leh)*

Don't run out of things to say!

I'm going to . . .	Voy a . . . *('voh-ee)*
clarify	**aclarar** *(ah-klah-'rahr)*
confirm	**confirmar** *(kohn-feer-'mahr)*
explain	**explicar** *(ehks-plee-'kahr)*
identify	**identificar** *(ee-dehn-tee-fee-'kahr)*
suggest	**sugerir** *(soo-heh-'reer)*

When you need to reveal results, scores, or grades, try the following terms:

It's acceptable	**Es aceptable** *(ehs ah-sehp-'tah-bleh)*
It's unacceptable	**Es inaceptable** *(ehs ee-nah-sehp-'tah-bleh)*
It's adequate	**Es adecuado** *(ehs ah-deh-'kwah-doh)*
It's inadequate	**Es inadecuado** *(ehs een-ah-deh-'kwah-doh)*
It's appropriate	**Es apropiado** *(ehs ah-proh-pee-'ah-doh)*
It's inappropriate	**No es apropiado** *(no ehs ah-proh-pee-'ah-doh)*

It's approved	**Está aprobado** *(ehs-'tah ah-proh-'bah-doh)*
It's not approved	**No está aprobado** *(noh ehs-'tah ah-proh-'bah-doh)*
It's better	**Está mejor** *(ehs-'tah meh-'hohr)*
It's worse	**Está peor** *(ehs-'tah peh-'ohr)*
It's correct	**Está correcto** *(ehs-'tah koh-'rrehk-toh)*
It's incorrect	**Está incorrecto** *(ehs-'tah een-koh-'rrehk-toh)*
It's excellent	**Es excelente** *(ehs ehk-seh-'lehn-teh)*
It's bad	**Es malo** *(ehs 'mah-loh)*
It's satisfactory	**Es satisfactorio** *(ehs sah-tees-fahk-'toh-ree-oh)*
It's unsatisfactory	**Es insatisfactorio** *(ehs een-sah-tees-fahk-'toh-ree-oh)*
It's (the) ...	**Es ...** *(ehs)*
average	**el promedio** *(ehl proh-'meh-dee-oh)*
maximum	**el máximo** *(ehl 'mahk-see-moh)*
minimum	**el mínimo** *(ehl 'mee-nee-moh)*

¡MÁS AYUDA!

• The verb, "to make a mistake" is **equivocarse** *(eh-kee-voh-'kahr-seh)*:

You make mistakes sometimes.

A veces te equivocas. *(ah 'veh-sehs teh eh-kee-'voh-kahs)*

• Here are more words and phrase that deal with assessments:

I agree.	**Estoy de acuerdo.** *(ehs-'toh-ee deh ah-'kwehr-doh)*
It needs improvement.	**Necesita mejorar.** *(neh-seh-'see-tah meh-hoh-'rahr)*
There were a lot of mistakes.	**Había muchos errores.** *(ah-'bee-ah 'moo-chohs eh-'rroh-rehs)*

¡*NECESITA PRACTICAR!*

Translate:

Quisiera felicitarle. Usted es muy buen estudiante. Su trabajo es excelente, y no hay muchos errores en sus exámenes.

Discipline
La disciplina *(lah dees-see-'plee-nah)*

No one can learn if there is too much disruption. Here are a few guidelines for conduct that can be presented at the grammar school level to Spanish-speaking children and their parents:

They need to . . .	**Necesitan . . .** *(neh-seh-'see-tahn)*
attend school	**asistir a la escuela**
	(ah-sees-'teer ah lah ehs-'kweh-lah)
arrive on time	**llegar a tiempo**
	(yeh-'gahr ah tee-'ehm-poh)
behave well	**portarse bien** *(pohr-'tahr-seh bee-'ehn)*
do their assignments	**hacer sus tareas**
	(ah-'sehr soos tah-'reh-ahs)
study for tests	**estudiar para los exámenes**
	(ehs-too-dee-'ahr 'pah-rah lohs ehk-'sah-meh-nehs)
obey the rules	**obedecer las reglas**
	(oh-beh-deh-'sehr lahs 'reh-glahs)
raise their hands	**levantar las manos**
	(leh-vahn-'tahr lahs 'mah-nohs)
listen to the teacher	**escuchar al maestro**
	(ehs-koo-'chahr ahl mah-'ehs-troh)
participate in class	**participar en la clase**
	(pahr-tee-see-'pahr ehn lah 'klah-seh)

bring supplies

traer sus útiles
(trah-'ehr soos 'oo-tee-lehs)

respect school property

respetar la propiedad de la escuela
(rehs-peh-'tahr lah proh-pee-eh-'dahd deh lah ehs-'kweh-lah)

wear appropiate clothing

ponerse ropa apropiada
(poh-'nehr-seh 'roh-pah ah-proh-pee-'ah-dah)

clean up their mess

limpiar su basura
(leem-pee-'ahr soo bah-'soo-rah)

take care of their things

cuidar sus cosas
(kwee-'dahr soos 'koh-sahs)

Now, let everyone know what they're not allowed to do:

No . . .

No . . . *(noh)*

bothering others

molestar a los demás
(moh-lehs-'tahr ah lohs deh-'mahs)

cursing

decir groserías
(deh-'seer groh-seh-'ree-ahs)

cutting class

faltar a clases
(fahl-'tahr ah 'klah-sehs)

forgetting pencil and paper

olvidar papel y lápiz
(ohl-vee-'dahr pah-'pehl ee 'lah-pees)

gum chewing

masticar chicle
(mahs-tee-'kahr 'cheek-leh)

littering

tirar basura *(tee-'rahr bah-'soo-rah)*

loitering

holgazanear *(ohl-gah-sah-neh-'ahr)*

losing books

perder los libros
(pehr-'dehr lohs 'lee-brohs)

making obscene gestures

hacer señales groseras
(ah-'sehr sehn-'yah-lehs groh-'seh-rahs)

smoking

fumar *(foo-'mahr)*

threatening

amenazar *(ah-meh-nah-'sahr)*

throwing things

tirar cosas *(tee-'rahr 'koh-sahs)*

whistling

silbar *(seel-'bahr)*

¡ MÁS AYUDA !

• Remember these commands from your grammar school?

No . . .	No . . . *(noh)*
fighting	**pelear** *(peh-leh-'ahr)*
grabbing	**agarrar** *(ah-gah-'rrahr)*
hitting	**pegar** *(peh-'gahr)*
kicking	**patear** *(pah-teh-'ahr)*
pulling	**jalar** *(hah-'lahr)*
pushing	**empujar** *(ehm-poo-'hahr)*
spitting	**escupir** *(ehs-koo-'peer)*
tripping	**hacer tropezar** *(ah-'sehr troh-peh-sahr)*
wrestling	**luchar** *(loo-'chahr)*
yelling	**gritar** *(gree-'tahr)*

More control
Más control *(mahs kohn-'trohl)*

At some outreach sites, the crowds of children can be pretty tough to manage. That calls for large-group command phrases:

Stay in line.	**Quédense en fila.** *('keh-dehn-seh ehn 'fee-lah)*
Keep to the right.	**Quédense a la derecha.**
	('keh-dehn-seh ah lah deh-'reh-chah)
Remain quiet.	**Quédense quietos.** *('keh-dehn-seh kee-'eh-tohs)*
Don't push.	**No empujen.** *(noh ehm-'poo-hehn)*
Don't run.	**No corran.** *(noh 'koh-rrahn)*
Don't yell.	**No griten.** *(noh 'gree-tehn)*
Put those away.	**Guarden las cosas.**
	('gwahr-dehn lahs 'koh-sahs)
Hurry up.	**Apúrense.** *(ah-'poo-rehn-seh)*

| Wait for your turn. | **Esperen su turno.** *(ehs-'peh-rehn soo 'toor-noh)* |
| You are dismissed. | **Pueden irse.** *('pweh-dehn 'eer-seh)* |

Please pick them up.	**Recójalos, por favor.**
	(reh-'koh-hah-lohs pohr fah-'vohr)
Stop it.	**No hagan eso.** *(noh 'ah-gahn 'eh-soh)*

Come here.	**Vengan aquí.** *('vehn-gahn ah-'kee)*
Keep walking.	**Sigan caminando.**
	('see-gahn kah-mee-'nahn-doh)

¡MÁS AYUDA!

• When bikes are around, tell children to follow the rules:

Do not ride your bike here.
No montes tu bicicleta aquí.
(noh 'mohn-tehs too bee-see-'kleh-tah ah-'kee)

Lock your bike in the bike rack.
Asegura tu bicicleta en el bicicletero.
(ah-seh-'goo-rah too bee-see-'kleh-tah ehn ehl bee-see-kleh-'teh-roh)

Bikes are kept in the bicyle area.
Las bicicletas se guardan en la zona de bicicletas.
(lahs bee-see-'kleh-tahs seh 'gwahr-dahn ehn lah 'soh-nah deh bee-see-'kleh-tahs)

We are not responsible for robbery or damage to bikes.
No somos responsables por robo o daño a las bicicletas.
(noh 'soh-mohs rehs-pohn-'sah-blehs pohr 'roh-boh oh 'dahn-yoh ah lahs bee-see-'kleh-tahs)

You cannot carry passengers on a bicycle.
No puedes llevar pasajeros en la bicicleta. *(noh 'pweh-dehs yeh-'vahr pah-sah-'heh-rohs ehn lah bee-see-'kleh-tah)*

You need to wear a helmet.

Necesitas usar un casco. *(neh-seh-'see-tahs oo-'sahr oon 'kahs-koh)*

Walk your bike!

¡Camina con tu bicicleta! *(kah-'mee-nah kohn too bee-see-'kleh-tah)*

The older student
El estudiante mayor
(ehl ehs-too-dee-'ahn-teh mah-'yohr)

For older children, you may want to consider using some of the following terms to explain the rules and regulations:

Please do not bring . . .	**Favor de no traer . . .**
	(fah-'vohr deh noh trah-'ehr)
cassettes	**(los) casetes** *(kah-'seh-tehs)*
CDs	**(los) discos compactos**
	('dees-kohs kohm-'pahk-tohs)
cell phones	**(los) teléfonos celulares**
	(teh-'leh-foh-nohs seh-loo-'lah-rehs)
chains	**(las) cadenas** *(kah-'deh-nahs)*
fireworks	**(los) fuegos artificiales**
	('fweh-gohs ahr-tee-fee-see-'ah-lehs)
knives	**(los) cuchillos** *(koo-'chee-yohs)*
lighters	**(los) encendedores**
	(ehn-sehn-deh-'doh-rehs)
magazines	**(las) revistas** *(reh-'vees-tahs)*
pets	**(las) mascotas** *(mahs-'koh-tahs)*
radios	**(los) radios** *('rah-dee-ohs)*
razors	**(las) navajas** *(nah-'vah-hahs)*
stereos	**(los) estéreos** *(ehs-'teh-reh-ohs)*
tobacco	**(el) tabaco** *(tah-'bah-koh)*

- Always try to provide some explanation:

They are . . .	**Son** . . . *(sohn)*
dangerous	**peligrosos** *(peh-lee-'groh-sohs)*
unsafe	**inseguros** *(een-seh-'goo-rohs)*
illegal	**ilegales** *(ee-leh-'gah-lehs)*

It's a problem
Es un problema *(ehs oon proh-'bleh-mah)*

More and more outreach programs target the needs of kids with severe behavior problems. Do any of these sound familiar?

He has (the) . . .	**Tiene** . . . *(tee-'eh-neh)*
alcohol	**el alcohol** *(ehl ahl-koh-'ohl)*
contraband	**el contrabando** *(ehl kohn-trah-'bahn-doh)*
drug	**la droga** *(lah 'droh-gah)*
explosive	**el explosivo** *(ehl ehks-ploh-'see-voh)*
firearm	**el arma de fuego** *(ehl 'ahr-mah deh 'fweh-goh)*

It's . . .	**Es** . . . *(ehs)*
cheating	**el fraude** *(ehl 'frah-oo-deh)*
extortion	**la extorsión** *(lah ehks-tohr-see-'ohn)*
gambling	**el juego por dinero**
	(ehl hoo-eh-goh pohr dee-'neh-roh)
graffiti	**el grafiti** *(ehl grah-'fee-tee)*
harassment	**el acosamiento** *(ehl ah-koh-sah-mee-'ehn-toh)*
trespassing	**la intrusión** *(lah een-troo-see-'ohn)*

They are . . . each other!	**¡Se están** . . .**!** *(seh ehs-'tahn)*
hugging	**abrazando** *(ah-brah-'sahn-doh)*
kissing	**besando** *(beh-'sahn-doh)*
touching	**tocando** *(toh-'kahn-doh)*

She is . . .!	**¡Ella está . . .!** *('eh-yah ehs-'tah)*
carrying a dangerous object	**llevando un objeto peligroso** *(yeh-'vahn-doh oon ohb-'heh-toh peh-lee-'groh-soh)*
flashing gang signs	**mostrando las señales de la pandilla** *(mohs-'trahn-doh lahs sehn-'yah-lehs deh lah pahn-'dee-yah)*
threatening everyone	**amenazando a todos** *(ah-meh-nah-'sahn-doh ah 'toh-dohs)*

¡NECESITA PRACTICAR!

Delete the word that doesn't belong with each series:

besando, comiendo, abrazando
revista, droga, alcohol
basura, palabra, oración
adjetivo, verbo, derecho
pelear, descansar, luchar

¡LA CULTURA!

Latin American parents usually have a high respect for education, and you may expect their cooperation once you have explained the shortcomings of their child. To avoid extremes, discuss the disciplinary action to be taken and warn them of U.S. laws regarding child abuse.

¡ *A C C I Ó N !*

So far we have discovered that in order to converse about activities in the present and the past tense, it was necessary to change the ending of the verb. For example:

To Work	**Trabajar** *(trah-bah-'hahr)*
I'm working.	**Estoy trabajando.**
	(ehs-'toh-ee trah-bah-'hahn-doh)
I work.	**Trabajo.** *(trah-'bah-hoh)*
I worked.	**Trabajé.** *(trah-bah-'heh)*

However, to refer to future actions, that is, those activities that you will do, it is necessary to alter the verb's endings:

I will work.	**Trabajar é** *(trah-bah-hah-'reh)*
You, he, she will work	**Trabajar á** *(trah-bah-hah-'rah)*
You (pl.); they will work	**Trabajar án** *(trah-bah-hah-'rahn)*
We will work	**Trabajar emos** *(trah-bah-hah-'reh-mohs)*

The same patterns hold true for the **-er** and **-ir** verbs as well:

To Eat	**Comer** *(koh-'mehr)*
I'll eat.	**Comeré.** *(koh-meh-'reh)*
You, he, she will eat	**Comerá** *(koh-meh-'rah)*
You (pl.); they will eat	**Comerán** *(koh-meh-'rahn)*
We will eat	**Comeremos** *(koh-meh-'reh-mohs)*

To Live	**Vivir** *(vee-'veer)*
I'll live	**Viviré** *(vee-vee-'reh)*
You, he, she will live	**Vivirá** *(vee-vee-'rah)*
You (pl.); they will live	**Vivirán** *(vee-vee-'rahn)*
We will live	**Viviremos** *(vee-vee-'reh-mohs)*

To Serve	**Servir** *(sehr-'veer)*
I'll serve	**Serviré** *(sehr-vee-'reh)*
You, he, she will serve	**Servirá** *(sehr-vee-'rah)*
You (pl.); they will serve	**Servirán** *(sehr-vee-'rahn)*
We will serve	**Serviremos** *(sehr-vee-'reh-mohs)*

To Run	**Correr** *(koh-'rrehr)*
I'll run	**Correré** *(koh-rreh-'reh)*
You, he, she will run	**Correrá** *(koh-rreh-'rah)*
You (pl.); they will run	**Correrán** *(koh-rreh-'rahn)*
We will run	**Correremos** *(koh-rreh-'reh-mohs)*

¡ M Á S   A Y U D A !

• Let's learn another quick way in Spanish to discuss what's going to happen in the future. It's the same form used to talk about where you are going. These are the basic forms of the verb to go:

To Go	**Ir** *(eer)*
I'm going to . . .	**Voy a . . .** *('voh-ee ah)*
You're, he's, she's going to . . .	**Va a . . .** *(vah ah)*
You guys are, they're going to . . .	**Van a . . .** *(vahn ah)*
We're going to . . .	**Vamos a . . .** *('vah-mohs ah)*

Look how well it works! Notice that all these statements refer to future actions:

I'm going to the bathroom.	**Voy al baño.** *('voh-ee ahl 'bahn-yoh)*
I'm going to clean.	**Voy a limpiar.**
	('voh-ee ah leem-pee-'ahr)
She's going to the office.	**Va a la oficina.**
	(vah ah lah oh-fee-'see-nah)
She's going to call.	**Va a llamar.** *(vah ah yah-'mahr)*
They're going to the room.	**Van al cuarto.** *(vahn ahl 'kwahr-toh)*
They're going to read.	**Van a leer.** *(vahn ah leh-'ehr)*

We're going there.	**Vamos allí.** *('vah-mohs ah-'yee)*
We're going to eat.	**Vamos a comer.**
	('vah-mohs ah koh-'mehr)

¡LAS ORDENES!

Although the duties of outreach professionals vary, most of the following commands will meet your specific needs. Remember that these words tell someone what to do, and are usually combined with -**le**, which means "him," and -**la**, which means "her" (in certain cases -**le** applies both to him and her, see below).

Accompany	him/her	**Acompáñele(a)** *(ah-kohm-'pahn-yeh-leh, lah)*
Allow	him/her	**Permítale** *(pehr-'mee-tah-leh)*
Bathe	him/her	**Báñele(a)** *('bahn-yel-leh, lah)*
Call	him/her	**Llámele(a)** *('yah-meh-leh, lah)*
Dress	him/her	**Vístale(a)** *('vees-tah-leh, lah)*
Give	him/her	**Déle** *('deh-leh)*
Help	him/her	**Ayúdele(a)** *(ah-'yoo-deh-leh, lah)*
Keep	him/her	**Manténgale(a)** *(mahn-'tehn-gah-leh, lah)*
Let/Leave	him/her	**Déjele(a)** *('deh-heh-leh, lah)*
Pick up	him/her	**Recójale(a)** *(reh-'koh-hah-leh, lah)*
Put	him/her	**Póngale(a)** *('pohn-gah-leh, lah)*
Scold	him/her	**Regáñele(a)** *(reh-'gahn-yeh-leh, lah)*
Serve	him/her	**Sírvale(a)** *('seer-vah-leh, lah)*
Show	him/her	**Muéstrele(a)** *('mwehs-treh-leh, lah)*
Tell	him/her	**Dígale** *('dee-gah-leh)*
Undress	him/her	**Desvístale(a)** *(dehs-'vees-tah-leh, lah)*
Wake up	him/her	**Despiértele(a)** *(dehs-pee-'ehr-teh-leh, lah)*
Wash	him/her	**Lávele(a)** *('lah-veh-leh, lah)*

¡NECESITA PRACTICAR!

Follow the example given:

Estudiaré	<u>Voy a estudiar.</u>
Comeré	_____
Trabajaré	_____
Escribiré	_____
Ayudaré	_____

Chapter Seven

Capítulo Siete
(kah-'pee-too-loh see-'eh-teh)

One on One
Entre dos
('ehn-treh dohs)

Can we talk?
¿Podemos conversar?
(poh-'deh-mohs kohn-vehr-'sahr)

Up till now, you have learned how to ask questions, make comments and give commands to Spanish-speaking people you meet in the field of outreach. But what happens after you establish relationships and would like to counsel them on more personal matters? Obviously, all of your language skills will be in high demand.

Start off by naming places where people often have a chance to socialize:

Do you remember (the) . . . ?	¿Se acuerda de . . . ? *(seh ah-'kwehr-dah deh)*
appointment	**la cita** *(lah 'see-tah)*
banquet	**el banquete** *(ehl bahn-'keh-teh)*
ceremony	**la ceremonia** *(lah seh-reh-'moh-nee-ah)*
class	**la clase** *(lah 'klah-seh)*
conference	**la conferencia** *(lah kohn-feh-'rehn-see-ah)*
event	**el evento** *(ehl eh-'vehn-toh)*

flight	**el vuelo** *(ehl voo-'eh-loh)*
meeting	**la reunión** *(lah reh-oo-nee-'ohn)*
party	**la fiesta** *(lah fee-'ehs-tah)*
picnic	**la comida campestre**
	(lah koh-'mee-dah kahm-'pehs-treh)
program	**el programa** *(ehl proh-'grah-mah)*
service	**el servicio** *(ehl sehr-'vee-see-oh)*
trip	**el viaje** *(ehl vee-'ah-heh)*
visit	**la visita** *(lah vee-'see-tah)*
wedding	**la boda** *(lah 'boh-dah)*

Once alone, be sure all of your Spanish comes out:

Hi!	**¡Hola!** *('oh-luh)*
How is everything?	**¿Cómo está todo?**
	('koh-moh ehs-'tah 'toh-doh)
Tell me about it.	**Dígame todo.** *('dee-gah-meh 'toh-doh)*
I want to talk to you.	**Quiero hablar con usted.**
	(kee-'eh-roh ah-'blahr kohn oos-'tehd)
I have something to tell you.	**Tengo algo que decirle.**
	('tehn-goh 'ahl-goh keh deh-'seer-leh)
Can we talk now?	**¿Podemos conversar ahora?**
	(poh-'deh-mohs kohn-vehr-'sahr ah-'oh-rah)
Let's sit down.	**Vamos a sentarnos.**
	('vah-mohs ah sehn-'tahr-nohs)
What's the trouble?	**¿Cuál es el problema?**
	(kwahl ehs ehl proh-'bleh-mah)

As you've done before, listen for any key area of concern.

Does it have to do with (the) . . . ?	**¿Tiene que ver con . . . ?**
	(tee-'eh-neh keh vehr kohn)
car	**el carro** *(ehl 'kah-rroh)*
church	**la iglesia** *(lah eeg-'leh-see-ah)*
family	**la familia** *(lah fah-'mee-lee-ah)*

health	**la salud** *(lah sah-'lood)*
house	**la casa** *(lah 'kah-sah)*
law	**la ley** *(lah 'leh-ee)*
school	**la escuela** *(lah ehs-'kweh-lah)*
work	**el trabajo** *(ehl trah-'bah-hoh)*

Is it a problem with (the) . . . ?	**¿Es un problema con . . . ?** *(ehs oon proh-'bleh-mah kohn)*
children	**los niños** *(lohs 'neen-yohs)*
friends	**los amigos** *(lohs ah-'mee-gohs)*
marriage	**el matrimonio** *(ehl mah-tree-'moh-nee-oh)*
neighbors	**los vecinos** *(lohs veh-'see-nohs)*
relatives	**los parientes** *(lohs pah-ree-'ehn-tehs)*

Sensitive issues

Los temas delicados *(lohs 'teh-mahs deh-lee-'kah-dos)*

Learn to discuss any sensitive issue, but be sure that a fluent Spanish-speaking professional is there to assist you.

Do you have information?
¿Tiene información? *(tee-'eh-neh een-fohr-mah-see-'ohn)*

How can I help you?
¿Cómo puedo ayudarle? *('koh-moh 'pweh-doh ah-yoo-'dahr-leh)*

What do you want to do?
¿Qué quiere hacer? *(keh kee-'eh-reh ah-'sehr)*

Notice the position of the suffix, **-me** *(meh)*:

Do you want to show me?
¿Quiere mostrarme? *(kee-'eh-reh mohs-'trahr-meh)*

Do you wish to talk to me?
¿Desea hablarme? *(deh-'seh-ah ah-'blahr-meh)*

Can you tell me?
¿Puede decirme? *('pweh-deh deh-'seer-meh)*

See how these verb forms refer to past actions:

What happened?
¿Qué pasó? *(keh pah-'soh)*

Where did it happen?
¿Dónde pasó? *('dohn-deh pah-'soh)*

Who saw what happened?
¿Quién vio lo que pasó? *(kee-'ehn vee-'oh loh keh pah-'soh)*

When did it happen?
¿Cuándo pasó eso? *('kwahn-doh pah-'soh 'eh-soh)*

How did it happen?
¿Cómo pasó eso? *('koh-moh pah-'soh 'eh-soh)*

Listen to their concerns:

I need (the) . . .	**Necesito . . .** *(neh-seh-'see-toh)*
clothing	**(la) ropa** *('roh-pah)*
food	**(la) comida** *(koh-'mee-dah)*
help	**(la) ayuda** *(ah-'yoo-dah)*
medicine	**(la) medicina** *(meh-dee-'see-nah)*
money	**(el) dinero** *(dee-'neh-roh)*
I want to talk about (the) . . .	**Quiero hablar de . . .** *(kee-'eh-roh ah-'blahr deh)*
alcohol	**el alcohol** *(ehl ahl-koh-'ohl)*
conflict	**el conflicto** *(ehl kohn-'fleek-toh)*
drugs	**las drogas** *(lahs 'droh-gahs)*
illness	**la enfermedad** *(lah ehn-fehr-meh-'dahd)*
injury	**la herida** *(lah eh-'ree-dah)*

¡MÁS AYUDA!

• Personal concerns often involve serious matters, so learn the following terms:

abandonment	**el abandono** *(ehl ah-bahn-'doh-noh)*
abortion	**el aborto** *(ehl ah-'bohr-toh)*
abuse	**el abuso** *(ehl ah-'boo-soh)*
addiction	**la adicción** *(lah ah-deek-see-'ohn)*
crime	**el crimen** *(ehl 'kree-mehn)*
death	**la muerte** *(lah 'mwehr-teh)*
discrimination	**la discriminación**
	(lah dees-kree-mee-nah-see-'ohn)
divorce	**el divorcio** *(ehl dee-'vohr-see-oh)*
failure	**el fracaso** *(ehl frah-'kah-soh)*
homosexuality	**la homosexualidad**
	(lah oh-moh-sehk-soo-ah-lee-'dahd)
loneliness	**la soledad** *(lah soh-leh-'dahd)*
pregnancy	**el embarazo** *(ehl ehm-bah-'rah-soh)*
sexual relations	**las relaciones sexuales**
	(lahs reh-lah-see-'oh-nehs sehk-soo-'ah-lehs)
violence	**la violencia** *(lah vee-oh-'lehn-see-ah)*

• Now, ask the right questions. Keep things brief:

Are you OK?	**¿Está bien?** *(ehs-'tah bee-'ehn)*
Are you sick?	**¿Está enfermo?** *(ehs-'tah ehn-'fehr-moh)*
Are you injured?	**¿Está lastimado?** *(ehs-'tah lahs-tee-'mah-doh)*

¡NECESITA PRACTICAR!

Translate into Spanish:

I want to talk about the fights and the abuse.
It has to do with food and clothing.
When and where did it happen?

Remember that most social events require the attendance of all family members. Here's a brief list of common activities within the Hispanic community:

anniversary	**el aniversario** *(ehl ah-nee-vehr-'sah-ree-oh)*
birth	**el nacimiento** *(ehl nah-see-mee-'ehn-toh)*
birthday	**el cumpleaños** *(ehl koom-pleh-'ahn-yohs)*
coming-out party of 15-year-old daughter	**la quinceañera** *(lah keen-seh-ahn-'yeh-rah)*
engagement	**el compromiso** *(ehl kohm-proh-'mee-soh)*
funeral	**el funeral** *(ehl foo-neh-'rahl)*
shower	**el shower** *(ehl 'chah-wehr)*
wedding	**el casamiento** *(ehl kah-sah-mee-'ehn-toh)*

Relationships
Las relaciones *(lahs reh-lah-see-'oh-nehs)*

Anyone who lives with family or friends will have struggles sooner or later. If the topic is in Spanish, listen for all the related vocabulary that will help you lend advice:

We had a/an ...	**Tuvimos ...** *(too-'vee-mohs)*
argument	**un argumento** *(oon ahr-goo-'mehn-toh)*
disagreement	**un desacuerdo** *(oon deh-sah-'kwehr-doh)*
dispute	**una disputa** *('oo-nah dees-'poo-tah)*
divorce	**un divorcio** *(oon dee-'vohr-see-oh)*
fight	**una pelea** *('oo-nah peh-'leh-ah)*
separation	**una separación** *('oo-nah seh-pah-rah-see-'ohn)*
It has to do with ...	**Tiene que ver con ...** *(tee-'eh-neh keh vehr kohn)*
gossip	**el chisme** *(ehl 'chees-meh)*
jealousy	**los celos** *(lohs 'seh-lohs)*

lies	**las mentiras** *(lahs mehn-'tee-rahs)*
promises	**las promesas** *(lahs proh-'meh-sahs)*

We are . . .	**Somos . . .** *('soh-mohs)*
a couple	**una pareja** *('oo-nah pah-'reh-hah)*
buddies	**amiguetes** *(ah-mee-'gheh-tehs)*
engaged	**novios** *('noh-vee-ohs)*
good friends	**buenos amigos** *('bweh-nohs ah-'mee-gohs)*
married	**casados** *(kah-'sah-dohs)*
partners	**socios** *('soh-see-ohs)*
relatives	**parientes** *(pah-ree-'ehn-tehs)*
roommates	**compañeros de cuarto**
	(kohm-pahn-'yeh-rohs deh 'kwahr-toh)

Now, keep your advice brief and to the point:

You should . . .	**Debes . . .** *('deh-behs)*
talk to him (her) again	**hablar con él (ella) de nuevo**
	(ah-'blahr kohn ehl, 'eh-yah, deh 'nweh-voh)
discuss it with a priest	**conversarlo con un cura**
	(kohn-vehr-'sahr-loh kohn oon 'koo-rah)
see a counselor	**ver un consejero**
	(vehr oon kohn-seh-'heh-roh)
try to resolve it	**tratar de resolverlo**
	(trah-'tahr deh reh-sohl-'vehr-loh)
work on the relationship	**trabajar en la relación**
	(trah-bah-'hahr ehn lah reh-lah-see-'ohn)

¡*MÁS AYUDA!*

• If the topic is **el amor** *(ehl ah-'mohr)*, focus on the other person:

He's or She's	**Es . . .** *(ehs)*
affectionate	**cariñoso(a)** *(kah-reen-'yoh-soh, sah)*
charming	**encantador(a)** *(ehn-kahn-tah-'dohr, rah)*

considerate	**considerado(a)** *(kohn-see-deh-'rah-doh, dah)*
faithful	**fiel** *(fee-'ehl)*
flirtatious	**coqueto(a)** *(koh-'keh-toh, tah)*
friendly	**amistoso(a)** *(ah-mees-'toh-soh, sah)*
handsome	**guapo(a)** *('gwah-poh, pah)*
honest	**honesto(a)** *(oh-'nehs-toh, tah)*
nice	**simpático(a)** *(seem-'pah-tee-koh, kah)*
passionate	**apasionado(a)** *(ah-pah-see-oh-'nah-doh, dah)*
pleasant	**agradable** *(ah-grah-'dah-bleh)*
respectful	**respetuoso(a)** *(rehs-peh-too-'oh-soh, sah)*
responsible	**responsable** *(rehs-pohn-'sah-bleh)*
romantic	**romántico(a)** *(roh-'mahn-tee-koh, kah)*
shy	**tímido(a)** *('tee-mee-doh, dah)*
sincere	**sincero(a)** *(seen-'seh-roh, rah)*
well-mannered	**educado(a)** *(eh-doo-'kah-doh, dah)*
wonderful	**maravilloso(a)** *(mah-rah-vee-'yoh-soh, sah)*
She is . . .	**Ella es . . .** *('eh-yah ehs)*
beautiful	**bella** *('beh-yah)*
lovely	**hermosa** *(ehr-'moh-sah)*
pretty	**bonita** *(boh-'nee-tah)*
seductive	**seductora** *(seh-dook-'toh-rah)*

• Family problems arise all the time. Study any new terminology:

child neglect	**el descuido del niño**
	(ehl dehs-'koo-ee-doh dehl 'neen-yoh)
child support	**la manutención** *(lah mah-noo-tehn-see-'ohn)*
domestic violence	**la violencia doméstica**
	(lah vee-oh-'lehn-see-ah doh-'mehs-tee-kah)
family conflict	**el conflicto familiar**
	(ehl kohn-'fleek-toh fah-mee-lee-'ahr)
fatherless child	**el niño sin padre**
	(ehl 'neen-yoh seen 'pah-dreh)
illegitimate child	**el niño ilegítimo**
	(ehl 'neen-yoh ee-leh-'hee-tee-moh)

infant mortality	**la mortalidad infantil**
	(lah mohr-tah-lee-'dahd een-fahn-'teel)
runaway child	**el niño fugitivo**
	(ehl 'neen-yoh foo-hee-'tee-voh)
unplanned pregnancy	**el embarazo imprevisto**
	(ehl ehm-bah-'rah-soh eem-preh-'vees-toh)
unwed mother	**la madre soltera**
	(lah 'mah-dreh sohl-'teh-rah)

Tell me everything
Dígame todo *('dee-gah-meh 'toh-doh)*

When there's trouble, keep everything in confidence, but make sure the person speaks to the proper authorities. Do any of these words look familiar?

Tell (the) . . .	**Dígale a . . .** *('dee-gah-leh ah)*
Call (the) . . .	**Llame a . . .** *('yah-meh ah)*
administrator	**el administrador**
	(ehl ahd-mee-nees-trah-'dohr)
counselor	**el consejero** *(ehl kohn-seh-'heh-roh)*
director	**el director** *(ehl dee-rehk-'tohr)*
doctor	**el médico** *(ehl 'meh-dee-koh)*
family	**la familia** *(lah fah-'mee-lee-ah)*
nurse	**la enfermera** *(lah ehn-fehr-'meh-rah)*
officer	**el oficial** *(ehl oh-fee-see-'ahl)*
police	**la policía** *(lah poh-lee-'see-ah)*
priest	**el sacerdote** *(ehl sah-sehr-'doh-teh)*
psychiatrist	**el psiquiatra** *(ehl see-kee-'ah-trah)*
psychologist	**el psicólogo** *(ehl see-'koh-loh-goh)*
social worker	**el trabajador social**
	(ehl trah-bah-hah-'dohr soh-see-'ahl)
specialist	**el especialista** *(ehl ehs-peh-see-ah-'lees-tah)*
supervisor	**el supervisor** *(ehl soo-pehr-vee-'sohr)*

teacher	**el maestro** *(ehl mah-'ehs-troh)*
therapist	**el terapista** *(ehl teh-rah-'pees-tah)*
volunteer	**el voluntario** *(ehl voh-loon-'tah-ree-'oh)*

Obviously, for such serious matters you will need an interpreter, but you can gain a lot of ground by assessing the basic situation on your own. These next words delve into the heart of the matter:

How do you feel?	**¿Cómo se siente?** *(koh-moh seh see-'ehn-teh)*
It seems you are . . .	**Parece que está . . .** *(pah-'reh-seh keh ehs-'tah)*
afraid	**asustado(a)** *(ah-soos-'tah-doh, dah)*
angry	**molesto(a)** *(moh-'lehs-toh, tah)*
apathetic	**apático(a)** *(ah-'pah-tee-koh, kah)*
bitter	**amargado(a)** *(ah-mahr-'gah-doh, dah)*
distracted	**distraído(a)** *(dees-trah-'ee-doh, dah)*
frustrated	**frustrado(a)** *(froos-'trah-doh, dah)*
hostile	**hostil** *(ohs-'teel)*
in mourning	**de luto** *(deh 'loo-toh)*
nervous	**nervioso(a)** *(nehr-vee-'oh-soh, sah)*
sad	**triste** *('trees-teh)*
tense	**tenso(a)** *('tehn-soh, sah)*

The feelings of people are such a key element in your profession! One helpful method is to make a card with a list of different feelings in Spanish, and then ask the person to point to the word that best describes his or her emotions.

Do you feel . . . ?	**¿Se siente . . . ?** *(seh see-'ehn-teh)*
I feel . . .	**Me siento . . .** *(meh see-'ehn-toh)*
abused	**abusado(a)** *(ah-boo-'sah-doh, dah)*
anxious	**ansioso(a)** *(ahn-see-'oh-soh, sah)*
ashamed	**avergonzado(a)** *(ah-vehr-gohn-'sah-doh, dah)*
bored	**aburrido(a)** *(ah-boo-'rree-doh, dah)*
bothered	**molesto(a)** *(moh-'lehs-toh, tah)*
confused	**confundido(a)** *(kohn-foon-'dee-doh, dah)*
depressed	**deprimido(a)** *(deh-pree-'mee-doh, dah)*

desperate	**desesperado(a)** *(deh-sehs-peh-'rah-doh, dah)*
embarrassed	**turbado(a)** *(toor-'bah-doh, dah)*
exhausted	**agotado(a)** *(ah-goh-'tah-doh, dah)*
fed up	**harto(a)** *('ahr-toh, tah)*
furious	**furioso(a)** *(foo-ree-'oh-soh, sah)*
guilty	**culpable** *(kool-'pah-bleh)*
hated	**odiado(a)** *(oh-dee-'ah-doh, dah)*
impatient	**impaciente** *(eem-pah-see-'ehn-teh)*
inferior	**inferior** *(een-feh-ree-'ohr)*
insecure	**inseguro(a)** *(een-seh-'goo-roh, rah)*
jealous	**celoso(a)** *(ceh-'loh-soh, sah)*
overloaded	**sobrecargado(a)**
	(soh-breh-kahr-'gah-doh, dah)
resentful	**resentido(a)** *(reh-sehn-'tee-doh, dah)*
restless	**inquieto(a)** *(een-kee-'eh-toh, tah)*
sensitive	**sensible** *(sehn-'see-bleh)*
strange	**raro(a)** *('rah-roh, rah)*
trapped	**atrapado(a)** *(ah-trah-'pah-doh, dah)*
uncomfortable	**incómodo(a)** *(een-'koh-moh-doh, dah)*
unhappy	**descontento(a)** *(dehs-kohn-'tehn-toh, tah)*
worried	**preocupado(a)** *(preh-oh-koo-'pah-doh, dah)*

¡MÁS AYUDA!

• You'll hear these words all the time:

fault	**la culpa** *(lah 'kool-pah)*
guilt	**la culpabilidad** *(lah kool-pah-bee-lee-'dahd)*
shame	**la vergüenza** *(lah vehr-'gwehn-sah)*

• Keep altering your descriptive words to reflect the feelings of females:

La muchacha está preocupada y confundida.
(lah moo-'chah-chah ehs-'tah preh-oh-koo-'pah-dah ee kohn-foon-'dee-dah)

• Deeper emotions are a little tougher to describe:

suicidal tendencies	**las tendencias suicidas**
	(lahs tehn-'dehn-see-ahs swee-'see-dahs)
emotional instability	**la inestabilidad emocional**
	(lah een-ehs-tah-bee-lee-'dahd eh-moh-see-oh-'nahl)
violent behavior	**el comportamiento violento**
	(ehl kohm-pohr-tah-mee-'ehn-toh vee-oh-'lehn-toh)

• Some words will trigger the need for immediate action:

incest	**el incesto** *(ehl een-'sehs-toh)*
pornography	**la pornografía** *(lah pohr-noh-grah-'fee-ah)*
rape	**la violación** *(lah vee-oh-lah-see-'ohn)*
molestation	**el acoso sexual** *(ehl ah-'koh-soh sehk-soo-'ahl)*

• Can you guess what these words mean?

fobia *('foh-bee-ah)*
trauma *('trah-oo-mah)*
tragedia *(trah-'heh-dee-ah)*

Physical problems
Los problemas físicos
(lohs proh-'bleh-mahs 'fee-see-kohs)

Emotional disturbances often are connected with physical problems.

I have problems with (the) . . .	**Tengo problemas con . . .** *('tehn-goh proh-'bleh-mahs kohn)*
balance	**el equilibrio** *(ehl eh-kee-'lee-bree-oh)*
breathing	**la respiración** *(lah rehs-pee-rah-see-'ohn)*
hearing	**la audición** *(lah ow-dee-see-'ohn)*
nerves	**los nervios** *(lohs 'nehr-vee-ohs)*

sight	**la vista** *(lah 'vees-tah)*
speech	**el habla** *(ehl 'ah-blah)*

Is/are there . . . ?	**¿Hay . . . ?** *('ah-ee)*
bad dreams	**sueños malos** *('swehn-yohs 'mah-lohs)*
convulsions	**convulsiones** *(kohn-vool-see-'oh-nehs)*
headaches	**dolores de cabeza**
	(doh-'loh-rehs deh kah-'beh-sah)
insomnia	**insomnio** *(een-'sohm-nee-oh)*
loss of memory	**falta de memoria**
	('fahl-tah deh meh-'moh-ree-ah)
numbness	**adormecimiento**
	(ah-dohr-meh-see-mee-'ehn-toh)
seizures	**ataques** *(ah-'tah-kehs)*

Check the medical file on the person. Is there any cause for special attention or alarm?

It's (the) . . .	**Es . . .** *(ehs)*
abnormality	**la anormalidad** *(lah ah-nohr-mah-lee-'dahd)*
disability	**la minusvalía** *(lah mee-noos-vah-'lee-ah)*
disease	**la enfermedad** *(lah ehn-fehr-meh-'dahd)*
disorder	**el desorden** *(ehl deh-'sohr-dehn)*
handicap	**la incapacidad** *(lah een-kah-pah-see-'dahd)*
syndrome	**el síndrome** *(ehl 'seen-droh-meh)*

¡ M Á S   A Y U D A !

• A few specific sentences may help you with emotional health topics:

Are you eating and sleeping OK?
¿Está comiendo y durmiendo bien?
(ehs-'tah koh-mee-'ehn-doh ee door-mee-'ehn-doh bee-'ehn)

Are you worried about anything?
¿Está preocupado por algo?
(ehs-'tah preh-oh-koo-'pah-doh pohr 'ahl-goh)

Do you have good relations with your relatives and friends?

¿Tiene buenas relaciones con sus parientes y amigos?

(tee-'eh-neh 'bweh-nahs reh-lah-see'oh-nehs kohn soos pah-ree-'ehn-tehs ee ah-'mee-gohs)

What illnesses and operations have you had?

¿Qué enfermedades y operaciones ha tenido?

(keh ehn-fehr-meh-'dah-des ee oh-peh-rah-see-'oh-nehs ah teh-'nee-doh)

When did the problem start?

¿Cuándo empezó el problema?

('kwahn-doh ehm-peh-'soh ehl proh-'bleh-mah)

- There's no . . .   **No hay . . .** *(noh 'ah-ee)*
  danger   **peligro** *(peh-'leeg-roh)*
  harm   **daño** *('dahn-yoh)*
  obstacle   **obstáculo** *(ohbs-'tah-koo-loh)*
  pain   **dolor** *(doh-'lohr)*
  risk   **riesgo** *(ree-'ehs-goh)*

- Say these easy-to-remember words aloud:

It's a _____ illness.   **Es una enfermedad _____.**

(ehs 'oo-nah ehn-fehr-meh-'dahd)

chronic   **crónica** *('kroh-nee-kah)*
terminal   **terminal** *(tehr-mee-'nahl)*
mental   **mental** *(mehn-'tahl)*

Advice

Los consejos *(lohs kohn-'seh-hohs)*

Now that you've heard about the concern, how about offering a little advice. Open with one-liners that get everyone to settle down.

You should . . .   **Debe . . .** *('deh-beh)*
  breathe deeply   **respirar profundamente**

(rehs-pee-'rahr proh-foon-dah-'mehn-teh)

calm down	**calmarse** *(kahl-'mahr-seh)*
come back later	**regresar más tarde**
	(reh-greh-'sahr mahs 'tahr-deh)
lower your voice	**bajar la voz** *(bah-'hahr lah vohs)*
pay attention	**prestar atención**
	(prehs-'tahr ah-tehn-see-'ohn)
relax	**relajarse** *(reh-lah-'hahr-seh)*
rest	**descansar** *(dehs-kahn-'sahr)*

Keep your comments short as you provide advice:

You need to . . .	**Necesita . . .** *(neh-seh-'see-tah)*
call your doctor	**llamar a su doctor**
	(yah-'mahr ah soo dohk-'tohr)
get more sleep	**dormir más** *(dohr-'meer mahs)*
see a specialist	**ver un especialista**
	(vehr oon ehs-peh-see-ah-'lees-tah)
take your medication	**tomar su medicamento**
	(toh-'mahr soo meh-dee-kah-'mehn-toh)
tell your family	**decirle a su familia**
	(deh-'seer-leh ah soo fah-'mee-lee-ah)
manage your stress	**controlar su estrés**
	(kohn-troh-'lahr soo ehs-'trehs)

Continue to get help from the right professionals:

Talk to (the) . . .	**Hable con . . .** *('ah-bleh kohn)*
Go to (the) . . .	**Vaya a . . .** *('vah-yah ah)*
allergist	**el alergista** *(ehl ah-lehr-'hees-tah)*
chiropractor	**el quiropractor** *(ehl kee-roh-'prahk-tohr)*
dentist	**el dentista** *(ehl dehn-'tees-tah)*
gynecologist	**el ginecólogo** *(ehl hee-neh-'koh-loh-goh)*
ophthalmologist	**el oftalmólogo** *(ehl ohf-tahl-'moh-loh-goh)*
optometrist	**el optometrista** *(ehl ohp-toh-meh-'trees-tah)*
orthodontist	**el ortodontista** *(ehl ohr-toh-dohn-'tees-tah)*
pediatrician	**el pediatra** *(ehl peh-dee-'ah-trah)*
physician	**el médico** *(ehl 'meh-dee-koh)*

And keep mentioning solutions or suggestions:

We offer (the) . . .	**Ofrecemos . . .** *(oh-freh-'seh-mohs)*
different classes	**diferentes clases**
	(dee-feh-'rehn-tehs 'klah-sehs)
individualized plans	**planes individuales**
	('plah-nehs een-dee-vee-'dwah-lehs)
intensive therapy	**terapia intensiva**
	(teh-'rah-pee-ah een-tehn-'see-vah)
personal contracts	**contratos personales**
	(kohn-'trah-tohs pehr-soh-'nah-lehs)
recovery groups	**grupos de recuperación**
	('groo-pohs deh reh-koo-peh-rah-see-'ohn)
rehabilitation	**rehabilitación** *(reh-ah-bee-lee-tah-see-'ohn)*
sign language	**lenguaje de sordomudos**
	(lehn-gwah-heh deh sohr-doh-'moo-dohs)
special programs	**programas especiales**
	(proh-'grah-mahs ehs-peh-see-'ah-lehs)
tutoring	**tutoría** *(too-toh-'ree-ah)*
The program is . . .	**El programa es . . .** *(ehl proh-'grah-mah ehs)*
free	**gratis** *('grah-tees)*
adaptive	**adaptivo** *(ah-dahp-'tee-voh)*
educational	**educativo** *(eh-doo-kah-'tee-voh)*
for home study	**para estudiar en casa**
	('pah-rah ehs-too-dee-'ahr ehn 'kah-sah)
private	**privado** *(pree-'vah-doh)*
vocational	**vocacional** *(voh-kah-see-oh-'nahl)*

¡MÁS AYUDA!

• Get involved in the appropiate activity:

You should attend (the) . . .	**Debe asistir a . . .** *('deh-beh ah-sees-'teer ah)*
class	**la clase** *(lah 'klah-seh)*

conference	**la conferencia** *(lah kohn-feh-'rehn-see-ah)*
committee	**el comité** *(ehl koh-mee-'teh)*
discussion	**la discusión** *(lah dees-koo-see-'ohn)*
meeting	**la reunión** *(lah reh-oo-nee-'ohn)*
seminar	**el seminario** *(ehl seh-mee-'nah-ree-oh)*

• Interject key words that are easy to remember:

You should read (the) . . .	**Debe leer . . .** *('deh-beh leh-'ehr)*
instructions	**las instrucciones**
	(lahs eens-trook-see-'oh-nehs)
recommendations	**las recomendaciones**
	(lahs reh-koh-mehn-dah-see-'oh-nehs)
questions and answers	**las preguntas y respuestas**
	(lahs preh-'goon-tahs ee rehs-'pwehs-tahs)
solutions	**las soluciones** *(lahs soh-loo-see-'oh-nehs)*
suggestions	**las sugerencias**
	(lahs soo-heh-'rehn-see-ahs)

 ¡*NECESITA PRACTICAR!*

Name three emotional feelings.

Name three outreach professionals.

Connect the words that relate:

mareado	dentista
reunión	furioso
molesto	comité
médico	débil
peligro	daño

The pregnancy

El embarazo *(ehl ehm-bah-'rah-soh)*

Pregnant women often don't have money to pay for medical help. Many outreach programs offer free services that inform them about family planning, childbirth, child care, and related issues. When assisting Spanish speakers during pregnancy, remember that most of their medical advice will come from family and friends.

Our program offers . . .	**Nuestro programa ofrece . . .**
	('nwehs-troh proh-'grah-mah oh-'freh-seh)
classes for mothers	**clases para las madres**
	('klah-sehs 'pah-rah lahs 'mah-drehs)
exercise classes	**clases para ejercicios**
	('klah-sehs 'pah-rah eh-hehr-'see-see-ohs)
food stamps	**cupones de comida**
	(koo-'poh-nehs deh koh-'mee-dah)
services for teenage pregnancies	**servicios para adolescentes embarazadas** *(sehr-'vee-see-ohs 'pah-rah ah-doh-leh-'sehn-tehs ehm-bah-rah-'sah-dahs)*
social services	**servicios sociales**
	(sehr-'vee-see-ohs soh-see-'ah-lehs)
welfare	**bienestar social**
	(bee-eh-nehs-'tahr soh-see-'ahl)
We talk about (the) . . .	**Hablamos de . . .** *(ah-'blah-mohs deh)*
abortion	**el aborto** *(ehl ah-'bohr-toh)*
adoption	**la adopción** *(lah ah-dohp-see-'ohn)*
AIDS	**el SIDA** *(ehl 'see-dah)*
birth control	**la anticoncepción** *(lah ahn-tee-kohn-sehp-see-'ohn)*
child care	**el cuidado del niño** *(ehl koo-ee-'dah-doh dehl 'neen-yoh)*

family planning	**la planificación familiar**
	(lah plah-nee-fee-kah-see-'ohn fah-mee-lee-'ahr)
prenatal care	**el cuidado prenatal**
	(ehl koo-ee-'dah-doh preh-nah-'tahl)
reproductive system	**el sistema reproductor**
	(ehl sees-'teh-mah reh-proh-dook-'tohr)
sexual relations	**las relaciones sexuales**
	(lahs reh-lah-see-'oh-nehs sehk-soo-'ah-lehs)

Sex and pregnancy can be handled as all other topics: see how basic questions and statements are formed, add pertinent vocabulary, and you'll hear yourself talk:

condom	**el condón** *(ehl kohn-'dohn)*
hormones	**las hormonas** *(lahs ohr-'moh-nahs)*
intercourse	**el coito** *(ehl 'koh-ee-toh)*
menstrual period	**la regla** *(lah 'reh-glah)*
pregnancy test	**el examen de embarazo**
	(ehl ehk-'sah-mehn deh ehm-bah-'rah-soh)
venereal disease	**la enfermedad venérea**
	(lah ehn-fehr-meh-'dahd veh-'neh-reh-ah)

Gather all the information that you can using basic question words:

How many children do you have?
¿Cuántos niños tiene? *('kwahn-tohs 'neen-yohs tee-'eh-neh)*

Who is the father?
¿Quién es el padre? *(kee-'ehn ehs ehl 'pah-dreh)*

When is the due date?
¿Cuándo es la fecha de nacimiento?
('kwahn-doh ehs lah 'feh-chah deh nah-see-mee-'ehn-toh)

What is your doctor's name?
¿Cómo se llama su doctor? *('koh-moh seh 'yah-mah soo dohk-'tohr)*

How much pain do you have?
¿Cuánto dolor tiene? *('kwahn-toh doh-'lohr tee-'eh-neh)*

Do you have . . . ?	**¿Tiene . . . ?** *(tee-'eh-neh)*
contractions	**contracciones** *(kohn-trahk-see-'oh-nehs)*
cramps	**calambres** *(kah-'lahm-brehs)*
discharges	**descargas** *(dehs-'kahr-gahs)*
labor pains	**dolores de parto** *(doh-'loh-rehs deh 'pahr-toh)*
nausea	**náusea** *('nah-oo-seh-ah)*
swelling	**hinchazón** *(een-chah-'sohn)*

If the big moment has arrived, here are a few emergency commands:

Breathe deeply.	**Respire profundamente.**
	(rehs-'pee-reh proh-foon-dah-'mehn-teh)
Grab my hand.	**Agarre mi mano.** *(ah-'gah-rreh mee 'mah-noh)*
Rest.	**Descanse.** *(dehs-'kahn-seh)*

 ¡NECESITA PRACTICAR!

Translate into Spanish:

We talk about family planning and child care.
Our program offers services for teenage pregnancies.
Do you have cramps and nausea?

Trouble at work
Los problemas en el trabajo
(lohs proh-'bleh-mahs ehn ehl trah-'bah-hoh)

In addition to personal health, work-related issues also will send Hispanics looking for help. At times, they may want to discuss such matters on a one-on-one basis. Once you ask how he or she is doing at work, be prepared for some of these concerns:

I got fired.
Me despidieron. *(meh dehs-pee-dee-'eh-rohn)*

I'm working less hours.
Estoy trabajando menos horas.
 (ehs-'toh-ee trah-bah-'hahn-doh 'meh-nohs 'oh-rahs)

They're going to transfer me.
Me van a transferir. *(meh vahn ah trahns-feh-'reer)*

They hired someone else.
Contrataron a otra persona.
 (kohn-trah-'tah-rohn ah 'oh-trah pehr-'soh-nah)

There's no more work.
No hay más trabajo. *(noh 'ah-ee mahs trah-'bah-hoh)*

They gave me a warning.
Me dieron una advertencia.
 (meh dee-'eh-rohn 'oo-nah ahd-vehr-'tehn-see-ah)

There were some changes.
Hubo algunos cambios. *('oo-boh ahl-'goo-nohs 'kahm-bee-ohs)*

I'll have to resign.
Tendré que renunciar. *(tehn-'dreh keh reh-noon-see-'ahr)*

People lose their jobs for a number of reasons:

I didn't finish it.	**No lo terminé.** *(noh loh tehr-mee-'neh)*
I missed work.	**Falté al trabajo.** *(fahl-'teh ahl trah-'bah-hoh)*
I arrived late.	**Llegué tarde.** *(yeh-'geh 'tahr-deh)*

What exactly is the problem? Ask them:

Is there a problem with . . .	**Hay un problema con . . .** *('ah-ee oon proh-'bleh-mah kohn)*
lack of transportation	**la falta de transporte** *(lah 'fahl-tah deh trahns-'pohr-teh)*
language proficiency	**la competencia en el lenguaje** *(lah kohm-peh-'tehn-see-ah ehn ehl lehn-'gwah-heh)*

personality differences	**las diferencias de personalidad**
	(lahs dee-feh-'rehn-see-ahs deh pehr-soh-nah-lee-'dahd)
insubordination	**la insubordinación**
	(lah een-soo-bohr-dee-nah-see-'ohn)
lack of cooperation	**la falta de cooperación**
	(lah 'fahl-tah deh koh-oh-peh-rah-see-'ohn)
misconduct	**la mala conducta**
	(lah 'mah-lah kohn-'dook-tah)
procrastination	**las dilaciones** *(lahs dee-lah-see-'oh-nehs)*
poor attitude	**la actitud negativa**
	(lah ahk-tee-'tood neh-gah-'tee-vah)

Some issues are much more serious:

discrimination	**la discriminación**
	(lah dees-kree-mee-nah-see-'ohn)
sexual harassment	**el acosamiento sexual**
	(ehl ah-koh-sah-mee-'ehn-toh sehk-soo-'ahl)
physical abuse	**el abuso físico** *(ehl ah-'boo-soh 'fee-see-koh)*
racial conflict	**el conflicto racial**
	(ehl kohn-'fleek-toh rah-see-'ahl)
violent behavior	**el comportamiento violento**
	(ehl kohm-pohr-tah-mee-'ehn-toh vee-oh-'lehn-toh)

¡MÁS AYUDA!

• These work-related conditions affect everyone:

downsize	**la reducción de empleados**
	(lah reh-dook-see-'ohn deh ehm-pleh-'ah-dohs)
turnover	**la rotación de personal**
	(lah roh-tah-see-'ohn deh pehr-soh-'nahl)
shortage	**la escasez de personal**
	(lah ehs-kah-'sehs deh pehr-soh-'nahl)

Effective phrases

Las frases eficaces *(lahs 'frah-sehs eh-fee-'kah-sehs)*

If you would like to be helpful, remember that some one-liners get people to open up immediately:

Can you explain what caused the problem?
¿Puede explicar qué causó el problema?
('pweh-deh ehks-plee-'kahr keh kow-'soh ehl proh-'bleh-mah)

Are you aware there is a problem?
¿Está consciente de que hay un problema?
(ehs-'tah kohn-see-'ehn-teh deh keh 'ah-ee oon proh-'bleh-mah)

Can you tell me why this occurred?
¿Puede decirme por qué ocurrió esto?
('pweh-deh deh-'seer-meh pohr keh oh-koo-rree-'oh 'ehs-toh)

What can we do to correct the mistake?
¿Qué podemos hacer para corregir el error?
(keh poh-'deh-mohs ah-'sehr 'pah-rah koh-rreh-'heer ehl eh-'rrohr)

I think you should . . .	**Creo que debe . . .** *('kreh-oh keh 'deh-beh)*
get professional help	**buscar ayuda profesional**
	(boos-'kahr ah-yoo-dah proh-feh-see-oh-'nahl)
call your lawyer	**llamar a su abogado**
	(yah-'mahr ah soo ah-boh-'gah-doh)
stay home until they call you	**quedarse en casa hasta que le llamen**
	(keh-'dahr-seh ehn 'kah-sah 'ahs-tah keh leh 'yah-mehn)
look for another job	**buscar otro trabajo**
	(boos-'kahr 'oh-troh trah-'bah-hoh)
talk to the union	**hablar con el sindicato**
	(ah-'blahr kohn ehl seen-dee-'kah-toh)
read the contract	**leer el contrato** *(leh-'ehr ehl kohn-'trah-toh)*
know your rights	**saber sus derechos**
	(sah-'behr soos deh-'reh-chohs)
have more training	**tener más entrenamiento**
	(teh-'nehr mahs ehn-treh-nah-mee-'ehn-toh)

¡ M Á S   A y u d a !

• Every year, thousands of drug recovery groups are set up by outreach organizations. Learn a few key words and phrases:

drug dependency	**la dependencia de las drogas** *(lah deh-pehn-'dehn-see-ah deh lahs 'dro-gahs)*
therapy	**la terapia** *(lah teh-'rah-pee-ah)*
treatment	**el tratamiento** *(ehl trah-tah-mee-'ehn-toh)*
addiction	**la adicción** *(lah ah-deek-see-'ohn)*
recovery	**la recuperación** *(lah reh-koo-peh-rah-see-'ohn)*
detoxification	**la desintoxicación** *(lah doh seen-tohk-see-kah-see-'ohn)*
relapse	**la recaída** *(lah reh-kah-'ee-dah)*
rehabilitation	**la rehabilitación** *(lah reh-ah-bee-lee-tah-see-'ohn)*
counseling	**el asesoramiento** *(ehl ah-seh-soh-rah-mee-'ehn-toh)*
probation	**la libertad condicional** *(lah lee-behr-'tahd kohn-dee-see-oh-'nahl)*
12-step program	**el programa de doce pasos** *(ehl proh-'grah-mah deh 'doh-seh 'pah-sohs)*

Looking for work
La búsqueda de trabajo
(lah 'boos-keh-dah deh trah-'bah-hoh)

Outreach organizations often work with local businesses in an effort to hire and train potential employees. If you are involved in the process, practice with the pattern below:

I would like . . .	**Quisiera . . .** *(kee-see-'eh-rah)*
to hire you	**contratarle** *(kohn-trah-'tahr-leh)*

to explain the test	**explicar la prueba**
	(ehks-plee-'kahr lah proo-'eh-bah)
to read your resume	**leer su curriculum**
	(leh-'ehr soo koo-'rree-koo-loom)
to send you something	**mandarle algo**
	(mahn-'dahr-leh 'ahl-goh)
to describe the position	**describir el puesto**
	(dehs-kree-'beer ehl 'pwehs-toh)
to offer you a job	**ofrecerle un trabajo**
	(oh-freh-'sehr-leh oon trah-'bah-hoh)
to know if you're interested	**saber si está interesado**
	(sah-'behr see ehs-'tah een-teh-reh-'sah-doh)
to see if you're available	**ver si está disponible**
	(vehr see ehs-'tah dees-poh-'neeb-leh)
to have more information	**tener más información**
	(teh-'nehr mahs een-fohr-mah-see-'ohn)
to interview you	**hacerle una entrevista**
	(ah-'sehr-leh 'oo-nah ehn-treh-'vees-tah)
to talk to your boss	**hablar con su jefe**
	(ah-'blahr kohn soo 'heh-feh)
to call you later	**llamarle más tarde**
	(yah-'mahr-leh mahs 'tahr-deh)
to give you the opportunity	**darle la oportunidad**
	('dahr-leh lah oh-pohr-too-nee-'dahd)
to train you	**entrenarle** *(ehn-treh-'nahr-leh)*
to teach you	**enseñarle** *(ehn-sehn-'yahr-leh)*
to discuss the details	**discutir los detalles**
	(dees-koo-'teer lohs deh-'tah-yehs)
to recommend a place	**recomendar un sitio**
	(reh-koh-mehn-'dahr oon 'see-tee-oh)

to check these references	**verificar estas referencias** *(veh-ree-fee-'kahr 'ehs-tahs reh-feh-'rehn-see-ahs)*
to have a second interview	**tener una segunda entrevista** *(teh-'nehr 'oo-nah seh-'goon-dah ehn-treh-'vees-tah)*

You can't be of much help until you know much about the candidate. Continue collecting information with more question words.

What's your . . . ?	**¿Cuál es su . . . ?** *(kwahl ehs soo)*
field	**campo de trabajo** *('kahm-poh deh trah-'bah-hoh)*
level	**nivel** *(nee 'vehl)*
preference	**preferencia** *(preh-feh-'rehn-see-ah)*
skill	**habilidad** *(ah-bee-lee-'dahd)*
specialty	**especialidad** *(ehs-peh-see-ah-lee-'dahd)*
talent	**talento** *(tah-'lehn-toh)*
title	**título** *('tee-too-loh)*
Who's your . . . ?	**¿Quién es su . . . ?** *(kee-'ehn ehs soo)*
boss	**jefe** *('heh-feh)*
closest relative	**pariente más cercano** *(pah-ree-'ehn-teh mahs sehr-'kah-noh)*
family physician	**médico familiar** *('meh-dee-koh fah-mee-lee-'ahr)*
friend	**amigo** *(ah-'mee-goh)*
manager	**gerente** *(heh-'rehn-teh)*
neighbor	**vecino** *(veh-'see-noh)*
previous employer	**empleador previo** *(ehm-pleh-ah-'dohr 'preh-vee-oh)*
reference	**referencia** *(reh-feh-'rehn-see-ah)*
spouse	**esposo(a)** *(ehs-'poh-soh, sah)*
supervisor	**supervisor** *(soo-pehr-vee-'sohr)*

How much . . . ?	**¿Cuánto/a . . . ?** *('kwahn-toh, tah)*
do you earn	**¿Cuánto gana?** *('kwahn-toh 'gah-nah)*
education do you have	**¿Cuánta educación tiene?** *('kwahn-tah eh-doo-kah-see-'ohn tee-'eh-neh)*
experience do you have	**¿Cuánta experiencia tiene?** *('kwahn-tah ehks-peh-ree-'ehn-see-ah tee-'eh-neh)*
training do you have	**¿Cuánto entrenamiento tiene?** *('kwahn-toh ehn-treh-nah-mee-'ehn-toh tee-'eh-neh)*
When . . . ?	**¿Cuándo . . . ?** *('kwahn-doh)*
can you meet	**puede reunirse** *('pweh-deh reh-oo-'neer-seh)*
can you start	**puede empezar** *('pweh-deh ehm-peh-'sahr)*
can you work	**puede trabajar** *('pweh-deh trah-bah-'hahr)*
did you finish	**terminó** *(tehr-mee-'noh)*
did you leave	**salió** *(sah-lee-'oh)*
did you quit	**renunció** *(reh-noon-see-'oh)*
did you start	**empezó** *(ehm-peh-'soh)*
did you work there	**trabajó ahí** *(trah-bah-'hoh ah-'ee)*
Where . . . ?	**¿Dónde . . . ?** *('dohn-deh)*
did you study	**estudió** *(ehs-too-dee-'oh)*
did you work before	**trabajó antes** *(tra-bah-'hoh 'ahn-tehs)*
do you live	**vive** *('vee-veh)*
do you work now	**trabaja ahora** *(trah-'bah-hah ah-'oh-rah)*
were you born	**nació** *(nah-see-'oh)*
Why . . . ?	**¿Por qué . . . ?** *(pohr keh)*
aren't you working	**no está trabajando** *(noh ehs-'tah trah-bah-'hahn-doh)*
are you applying	**está solicitando trabajo** *(ehs-'tah soh-lee-see-'tahn-doh trah-'bah-hoh)*
are you quitting	**está renunciando** *(ehs-'tah reh-noon-see-'ahn-doh)*

should I hire you   **debiera contratarle**
                       (deh-bee-'eh-rah kohn-trah-'tahr-leh)

were you fired   **le despidieron** *(leh dehs-pee-dee-'eh-rohn)*

¡ *Más Ayuda!*

• You must ask about this topic:

Are you a U.S. citizen?

¿Es usted un ciudadano (una ciudadana) de los Estados Unidos?
(ehs oos-'tehd oon see-oo-dah-'dah-noh, 'oo-nah see-oo-dah-'dah-nah, deh lohs ehs-'tah-dohs oo-'nee-dohs)

Do you have a green card?
¿Tiene una tarjeta de residencia permanente?
(tee-'eh-neh 'oo-nah tahr-'heh-tah deh reh-see-'dehn-see-ah pehr-mah-'nehn-teh)

What's your resident number?
¿Cuál es su número de residente?
(kwahl ehs soo 'noo-meh-roh deh reh-see-'dehn-teh)

Are you a naturalized citizen?
¿Es usted un ciudadano naturalizado (una ciudadana naturalizada)? *(ehs oos-'tehd oon see-oo-dah-'dah-noh nah-too-rah-lee-'sah-doh, 'oo-nah see-oo-dah-'dah-nah nah-too-rah-lee-'sah-dah)*

Do you have a work permit?
¿Tiene un permiso de trabajo?
(tee-'eh-neh oon pehr-'mee-soh deh trah-'bah-hoh)

Questions for you
Preguntas para usted
(preh-'goon-tahs 'pah-rah oos-'tehd)

The potential employee has lots of questions, so prepare yourself with the basic terminology:

How much do you pay?
¿Cuánto paga usted? *('kwahn-toh 'pah-gah oos-'tehd)*

When can I start?
¿Cuándo puedo empezar? *('kwahn-doh 'pweh-doh ehm-peh-'sahr)*

Is it part-time or full-time?
¿Es tiempo completo o tiempo parcial?
(ehs tee-'ehm-poh kohm-'pleh-toh oh tee-'ehm-poh pahr-see-'ahl)

How are the benefits?
¿Cómo son los beneficios? *('koh-moh sohn lohs beh-neh-'fee-see-ohs)*

What's my shift?
¿Cuál es mi turno de trabajo?
(kwahl ehs mee 'toor-noh deh trah-'bah-hoh)

What are my days off?
¿Cuáles son mis días de descanso? *('kwah-lehs son mees 'dee-ahs deh dehs-'kahn-soh)*

How many hours a week?
¿Cuántas horas por semana? *('kwahn-tahs 'oh-rahs pohr seh-'mah-nah)*

When will you be hiring?
¿Cuándo estarán contratando?
('kwahn-doh ehs-tah-'rahn kohn-trah-'tahn-doh)

What skills do I need?
¿Qué habilidades necesito? *(keh ah-bee-lee-'dah-dehs neh-seh-'see-toh)*

When can I get a raise?
¿Cuándo recibiré un aumento?
('kwahn-doh reh-see-bee-'reh oon ow-'mehn-toh)

¡ M á s   A y u d a !

• If you plan to sit down with your Spanish-speaking candidates or staff members and brief them on financial matters, this list of terms will allow you to elaborate:

It's (the) . . .	**Es . . .** *(ehs)*
hourly pay	**el pago por hora** *(ehl 'pah-goh pohr 'oh-rah)*
monthly salary	**el salario por mes** *(ehl sah-'lah-ree-oh pohr mehs)*
weekly wage	**el sueldo por semana** *(ehl 'swehl-doh pohr seh-'mah-nah)*
base pay	**el sueldo inicial** *(ehl 'swehl-doh ee-nee-see-'ahl)*
payday	**el día de paga** *(ehl 'dee-ah deh 'pah-gah)*
pay period	**el período de paga** *(ehl peh-'ree-oh-doh deh 'pah-gah)*
minimum wage	**el salario mínimo** *(ehl sah-'lah-ree-oh 'mee-nee-moh)*
overtime rate	**el salario por sobretiempo** *(ehl sah-'lah-ree-oh pohr soh-breh-tee-'ehm-poh)*
time and a half	**el salario por tiempo y medio** *(ehl sah-'lah-ree-oh pohr tee-'ehm-poh ee 'meh-dee-oh)*
cost of living increase	**el aumento del costo de vida** *(ehl ow-'mehn-toh dehl 'kohs-toh deh 'vee-dah)*
pay cut	**la reducción de sueldo** *(lah reh-dook-see-'ohn deh 'swehl-doh)*
pay hike	**el aumento de sueldo** *(ehl ow-'mehn-toh deh 'swehl-doh)*
gross income	**los ingresos brutos** *(lohs een-'greh-sohs 'broo-tohs)*

net income	**los ingresos netos** *(lohs een-'greh-sohs 'neh-tohs)*
Let's talk about (the) . . .	**Hablaremos sobre . . .** *(ah-blah-'reh-mohs 'soh-breh)*
advance	**el anticipo** *(ehl ahn-tee-'see-poh)*
amount	**la suma** *(lah 'soo-mah)*
balance	**el saldo** *(ehl 'sahl-doh)*
cost	**el costo** *(ehl 'kohs-toh)*
credit	**el crédito** *(ehl 'kreh-dee-toh)*
expenditures	**los gastos** *(lohs 'gahs-tohs)*
fee	**el honorario** *(ehl oh-noh-'rah-ree-oh)*
funds	**los fondos** *(lohs 'fohn-dohs)*
investments	**las inversiones** *(lahs een-vehr-see-'oh-nehs)*
loans	**los préstamos** *(lohs 'prehs-tah-mohs)*
mortgage	**la hipoteca** *(lah ee-poh-'teh-kah)*
property	**la propiedad** *(lah proh-pee-eh-'dahd)*
savings	**los ahorros** *(lohs ah-'oh-rrohs)*

• Try this pattern:

On this date, you receive (the) . . .	**En esta fecha, recibe usted . . .** *(ehn 'ehs-tah 'feh-chah reh-'see-beh oos-'tehd)*
check	**el cheque** *(ehl 'cheh-keh)*
commission	**la comisión** *(lah koh-mee-see-'ohn)*
earnings	**las ganancias** *(lahs gah-'nahn-see-ahs)*
paycheck	**la paga** *(lah 'pah-gah)*
payment	**el pago** *(ehl 'pah-goh)*
raise	**el aumento** *(ehl ow-'mehn-toh)*
salary	**el salario** *(ehl sah-'lah-ree-oh)*
tips	**las propinas** *(lahs proh-'pee-nahs)*
wages	**el sueldo** *(ehl 'swehl-doh)*

Job placement
La asignación de trabajo
(lah ah-seeg-nah-see-'ohn deh trah-'bah-hoh)

In order to answer work-related questions and then complete the job placement process, all this vocabulary should be put to good use:

Lets's talk about (the) . . .	**Vamos a hablar de . . .** *('vah-mohs ah ah-'blahr deh)*
appointment	**la cita** *(lah 'see-tah)*
approval	**la aprobación** *(lah ah-proh-bah-see'ohn)*
employment	**el empleo** *(ehl ehm-'pleh-oh)*
experience	**la experiencia** *(lah ehks-peh-ree-'ehn-see-ah)*
interview	**la entrevista** *(lah ehn-treh-'vees-tah)*
knowledge	**el conocimiento** *(ehl koh-noh-see-mee-'ehn-toh)*
location	**el lugar** *(ehl loo-'gahr)*
meeting	**la reunión** *(lah reh-oo-nee-'ohn)*
qualifications	**las calificaciones** *(lahs kah-lee-fee-kah-see-'oh-nehs)*
training	**el entrenamiento** *(ehl ehn-treh-nah-mee-'ehn-toh)*
I have (the) . . .	**Tengo . . .** *('tehn-goh)*
application	**la solicitud** *(lah soh-lee-see-'tood)*
card	**la tarjeta** *(lah tahr-'heh-tah)*
certificate	**el certificado** *(ehl sehr-tee-fee-'kah-doh)*
contract	**el contrato** *(ehl kohn-'trah-toh)*
diploma	**el diploma** *(ehl dee-'ploh-mah)*
driver's license	**la licencia de manejar** *(lah lee-'sehn-see-ah deh mah-neh-'hahr)*
equipment	**el equipo** *(ehl eh-'kee-poh)*
form	**el formulario** *(ehl fohr-moo-'lah-ree-oh)*
identification	**la identificación** *(lah ee-dehn-tee-fee-kah-see-'ohn)*
insurance	**el seguro** *(ehl seh-'goo-roh)*
record	**el registro** *(ehl reh-'hees-troh)*

references	**las referencias** *(lahs reh-feh-'rehn-see-ahs)*
requirements	**los requisitos** *(lohs reh-kee-'see-tohs)*
results	**los resultados** *(los reh-sool-'tah-dohs)*
resume	**el currículum, el resumé**
	(ehl koo-'rree-koo-loom, ehl reh-soo-'meh)
schedule	**el horario** *(ehl oh-'rah-ree-oh)*
tools	**las herramientas** *(lahs eh-rrah-mee-'ehn-tahs)*
transcripts	**las transcripciones**
	(lahs trahns-kreep-see-'oh-nehs)
uniform	**el uniforme** *(ehl oo-nee-'fohr-meh)*

¡ M á s   A y u d a !

• One tense of the verb **haber** allows you to ask what the applicant has or has not done in the past. Be careful with your pronunciation as you try out the pattern below:

Have you . . . ?	**¿Ha . . . ?** *(ah)*
been looking for a job	**estado buscando un trabajo**
	(ehs-'tah-doh boos-'kahn-doh oon trah-'bah-hoh)
completed high school	**terminado la escuela secundaria**
	(tehr-mee-'nah-doh lah ehs-'kweh-lah seh-koon-'dah-ree-ah)
had experience	**tenido experiencia**
	(teh-'nee-doh ehks-peh-ree-'ehn-see-ah)
had training	**tenido entrenamiento**
	(teh-'nee-doh ehn-treh-nah-mee-'ehn-toh)
seen the classified ad	**visto el anuncio clasificado**
	('vees-toh ehl ah-'noon-see-oh klah-see-fee-'kah-doh)
taken special courses	**tomado cursos especiale**
	(toh-'mah-doh 'koor-sohs ehs-peh-see-'ah-lehs)

worked here before **trabajado aquí antes**
       (trah-bah-'hah-doh ah-'kee 'ahn-tehs)

• Break down the job into pieces:

It's (the) . . .	**Es . . .** *(ehs)*
chore	**la faena** *(lah fah-'eh-nah)*
duty	**la obligación** *(lah oh-blee-gah-see-'ohn)*
errand	**el encargo** *(ehl ehn-'kahr-goh)*
job	**el trabajo** *(ehl trah-'bah-hoh)*
service	**el servicio** *(ehl sehr-'vee-see-oh)*
task	**la tarea** *(lah tah-'reh-ah)*

How's your . . . ?	**¿Cómo está su . . . ?** *('koh-moh ehs-'tah soo)*
attitude	**(la) actitud** *(ahk-tee-'tood)*
behavior	**(el) comportamiento**
	(kohm-pohr-tah-mee-'ehn-toh)
health	**(la) salud** *(sah-'lood)*
personality	**(la) personalidad** *(pehr-soh-nah-lee-'dahd)*

Let's discuss (the) . . .	**Vamos a discutir . . .**
	('vah-mohs ah dees-koo-'teer)
appearance	**el aspecto** *(ehl ahs-'pehk-toh)*
grades in school	**las notas en la escuela**
	(lahs 'noh-tahs ehn lah ehs-'kweh-lah)
language proficiency	**la competencia en el lenguaje**
	(lah kohm-peh-'tehn-see-ah ehn ehl lehn-'gwah-heh)
military service	**el servicio militar**
	(ehl sehr-'vee-see-oh mee-lee-'tahr)
physical requirements	**los requisitos físicos**
	(lohs reh-kee-'see-tohs 'fee-see-kohs)

¡Necesita Practicar!

Translate, and then practice these two dialogues:

Me despidieron ayer.	¿Puede decirme por qué?
Sí. Falté al trabajo mucho.	¿Qué pasó? ¿Ha estado enfermo?
Sí, y ahora no tengo dinero.	Creo que debo buscar otro trabajo.
¿Cuál es su campo de trabajo?	Soy carpintero.
¿Dónde trabajó antes?	En Miami, Florida.
Bien. Tengo su aplicación y quisiera llamarle más tarde.	Gracias. ¿Cuándo estarán contratando?
En dos semanas.	

Students in trouble
Los estudiantes con problemas
(lohs ehs-too-dee-'ahn-tehs kohn proh-'bleh-mahs)

Adults aren't the only ones who run into trouble. Young people may also want to discuss their age- and school-related problems with someone, so let's take a look at those words and expressions that refer to counseling kids:

I'm here to help you.
Estoy aquí para ayudarte.
(ehs-'toh-ee ah-'kee 'pah-rah ah-yoo-'dahr-teh)

Everything is confidential.
Todo es confidencial. *('toh-doh ehs kohn-fee-dehn-see-'ahl)*

It says here that you have a problem with . . .
Dice aquí que tienes un problema con . . .
('dee-seh ah-'kee keh tee-'eh-nehs oon proh-'bleh-mah kohn)

defiance of authority	**oposición a la autoridad** (*oh-poh-see-see-'ohn ah lah ow-toh-ree-'dahd*)
disruptive behavior	**desorden** (*deh-'sohr-dehn*)
incomplete assignments	**tareas incompletas** (*tah-'reh-ahs een-kohm-'pleh-tahs*)
poor work habits	**malos hábitos de estudio** (*'mah-lohs 'ah-bee-tohs deh ehs-'too-dee-oh*)
tardiness	**tardanzas** (*tahr-'dahn-sahs*)

Ask this question carefully. Notice the informal verb form:

How did you behave?	**¿Cómo te portaste?** (*'koh-moh teh pohr-'tahs-teh*)
Were you . . . ?	**Fuiste . . . ?** (*'fwees-teh*)
careless	**descuidado(a)** (*dehs-kwee-'dah-doh, dah*)
critical	**crítico(a)** (*'kree-tee-koh, kah*)
cruel	**cruel** (*kroo'ehl*)
dishonest	**deshonesto(a)** (*dehs-oh-'nehs-toh, tah*)
disrespectful	**irrespetuoso(a)** (*ee-rrehs-peh-too-'oh-soh, sah*)
forgetful	**olvidadizo(a)** (*ohl-vee-dah-'dee-soh, sah*)
incompetent	**incompetente** (*een-kohm-peh-'tehn-teh*)
lazy	**perezoso(a)** (*peh-reh-'soh-soh, sah*)
negligent	**negligente** (*neh-glee-'gehn-teh*)
restless	**inquieto(a)** (*een-kee-'eh-toh, tah*)
sarcastic	**sarcástico(a)** (*sahr-'kahs-tee-koh, kah*)
sassy	**fresco(a)** (*'frehs-koh, kah*)
selfish	**egoísta** (*eh-goh-'ees-tah*)
Now you have to deal with . . .	**Ahora debes tratar con . . .** (*ah-'oh-rah 'deh-behs trah-'tahr kohn*)
detention	**la detención** (*lah deh-tehn-see-'ohn*)
discipline	**la disciplina** (*lah dee-see-'plee-nah*)
expulsion	**la expulsión** (*lah ehks-pool-see-'ohn*)
formal report	**el reporte formal** (*ehl reh-'pohr-teh fohr-'mahl*)

home phone call	**la llamada a la casa** *(lah yah-'mah-dah ah lah 'kah-sah)*
juvenile court	**el tribunal de menores** *(ehl tree-boo-'nahl deh meh-'noh-rehs)*
legal contract	**el contrato legal** *(ehl kohn-'trah-toh leh-'gahl)*
official transfer	**la transferencia oficial** *(lah trahns-feh-'rehn-see-ah oh-fee-see-'ahl)*
parent conference	**la reunión con los padres** *(lah reh-oo-nee-'ohn kohn lohs 'pah-drehs)*
personal intervention	**la intervención personal** *(lah een-tehr-vehn-see-'ohn pehr-soh-'nahl)*
punishment	**el castigo** *(ehl kahs-'tee-goh)*
reprimand	**la reprensión** *(lah reh-prehn-see-'ohn)*
suspension	**la suspensión** *(lah soos-pehn-see-'ohn)*
warning	**la advertencia** *(lah ahd-vehr-'tehn-see-ah)*

¡ *M Á S   A Y U D A* !

• Ask each student about the lack of homework. Notice the past tense verb form:

Did you turn it in?	**¿Lo entregaste?** *(loh ehn-treh-'gahs-teh)*
Did you lose it?	**¿Lo perdiste?** *(loh pehr-'dees-teh)*
Did you finish it?	**¿Lo terminaste?** *(loh tehr-mee-'nahs-teh)*
Did you do it?	**¿Lo hiciste?** *(loh ee-'sees-teh)*
Did you understand it?	**¿Lo entendiste?** *(loh ehn-tehn-'dees-teh)*

Family conference
La reunión con la familia
(lah reh-oo-nee-'ohn kohn lah fah-'mee-lee-ah)

One of the most effective ways to help out kids with problems is to include the family during the process. Although you are far from ready to hold your own in a conversation in Spanish, the following sentences will clearly state the problem. Your interpreter will take care of the details.

We are worried because your son (daughter) . .	**Estamos preocupados porque su hijo(a)** . . . *(ehs-'tah-mohs preh-oh-koo-'pah-dohs 'pohr-keh soo 'ee-hoh, hah)*
isn't interested	**no está interesado(a)** *(noh ehs-'tah een-teh-reh-'sah-doh, dah)*
doesn't study	**no estudia** *(noh ehs-'too-dee-ah)*
doesn't participate	**no participa** *(noh pahr-tee-'see-pah)*
always arrives late	**siempre llega tarde** *(see-'ehm-preh 'yeh-gah 'tahr-deh)*
misses school	**falta a la escuela** *('fahl-tah ah lah ehs-'kweh-lah)*
likes to fight	**le gusta pelear** *(leh 'goos-tah peh-leh-'ahr)*
is failing classes	**está fallando en sus clases** *(ehs-'tah fah-'yahn-doh ehn soos 'klah-sehs)*
What do you think about his/her . . .	**¿Qué piensa usted de . . . ?** *(keh pee-'ehn-sah oos-'tehd deh)*
assignments	**sus tareas** *(soos tah-'reh-ahs)*
problem	**su problema** *(soo proh-'bleh-mah)*
friends	**sus amigos** *(soos ah-'mee-gohs)*
class	**su clase** *(soo 'klah-seh)*
work	**su trabajo** *(soo trah-'bah-hoh)*
grades	**sus notas** *(soos 'noh-tahs)*
behavior	**su comportamiento** *(soo kohm-pohr-tah-mee-'ehn-toh)*

• Yes, **su** means "his" or "her" singular, and **sus** means "his" or "her" plural.

Do you help him/her?	**¿Le/la ayuda?** *(leh, lah ah-'yoo-dah)*
Do you praise him/her?	**¿Le/la alaba?** *(leh, lah ah-'lah-bah)*
Do you punish him/her?	**¿Le/la castiga?** *(leh, lah kahs-'tee-gah)*

What kind of student is he/she?	**¿Qué tipo de estudiante es?**
	(keh 'tee-poh deh ehs-too-dee-'ahn-teh ehs)
average	**promedio** *(proh-'meh-dee-oh)*
bad	**malo(a)** *('mah-loh, lah)*
better	**mejor** *(meh-'hohr)*
outstanding	**destacado(a)**
	(dehs-tah-'kah-doh, dah)
satisfactory	**satisfactorio(a)**
	(sah-tees-fak-'toh-ree-oh, rah)

Key comments
Los comentarios claves
(lohs koh-mehn-'tah-ree-ohs 'klah-vehs)

Be clear and direct as you express what you think:

Students need . . .	**Los estudiantes necesitan . . .**
	(los ehs-too-dee-'ahn-tehs neh-seh-'see-tahn)
counseling	**asesoramiento** *(ah-seh-soh-rah-mee-'ehn-toh)*
discipline	**disciplina** *(dee-see-'plee-nah)*
independence	**independencia** *(een-deh-pehn-'dehn-see-ah)*
praise	**alabanzas** *(ah-lah-'bahn-sahs)*
support	**apoyo** *(ah-'poh-yoh)*
It has to do with (the) . . .	**Tiene que ver con . . .**
	(tee-'eh-neh keh vehr kohn)
honesty	**la honestidad** *(lah oh-nehs-tee-'dahd)*
responsibility	**la responsabilidad**
	(lah rehs-pohn-sah-bee-lee-'dahd)
trust	**la confianza** *(lah kohn-fee-'ahn-sah)*

And don't forget your command phrases:

Ask your son what he learned.

Pregunte a su hijo qué aprendió.

(preh-'goon-teh ah soo 'ee-hoh keh ah-prehn-dee-'oh)

Come to the parent meetings.

Venga a las reuniones de los padres.

('vehn-gah ah lahs reh-oo-nee-'oh-nehs deh lohs 'pah-drehs)

Call us if there is a problem.

Llámenos si hay un problema.

('yah-meh-nohs see 'ah-ee oon proh-'bleh-mah)

¡ *M Á S   A Y U D A !*

• Sometimes counseling sessions don't go exactly as planned:

It's cancelled.

Está cancelada. *('ehs-'tah kahn-seh-'lah-dah)*

I'm going to postpone it.

Voy a posponerla. *('voh-ee ah pohs-poh-'nehr-lah)*

They changed it.

La han cambiado. *(lah ahn kahm-bee-'ah-doh)*

I have to go to a meeting.

Tengo que ir a una reunión.

('tehn-goh keh eer ah 'oo-nah reh-oo-nee-'ohn)

I can't have a meeting now.

No puedo tener una reunión ahora.

(noh 'pweh-doh teh-'nehr 'oo-nah reh-oo-nee-'ohn ah-'oh-rah)

• Be careful about discussing some activities:

to gossip	**chismear** *(chees-meh-'ahr)*	
to lie	**mentir** *(mehn-'teer)*	
to steal	**robar** *(roh-'bahr)*	

Words of encouragement
Palabras de ánimo *(pah-'lah-brahs deh 'ah-nee-moh)*

Personal problems can be helped once the comment focuses on the positive. The following list of questions asks the Spanish speaker to come up with practical solutions. Have an interpreter at your side as you provide much-needed support.

I'd like to hear your ideas.
Quisiera escuchar tus ideas.
 (kee-see-'eh-rah ehs-koo-'chahr toos ee-'deh-ahs)

What other possibilities do you see?
¿Qué otras posibilidades ves?
 (keh 'oh-trahs poh-see-bee-lee-'dah-dehs vehs)

What steps would you take to correct the problem?
¿Qué medidas tomarías para corregir el problema?
 (keh meh-'dee-dahs toh-mah-'ree-ahs 'pah-rah koh-rreh-'heer ehl proh-'bleh-mah)

Are you convinced that this is the best solution?
¿Estás seguro de que ésta es la mejor solución?
 (ehs-'tahs seh-'goo-roh deh keh 'ehs-tah ehs lah meh-'hohr soh-loo-see-'ohn)

What do you think about it?
¿Qué piensas acerca de eso?
 (keh pee-'ehn-sahs ah-'sehr-kah deh 'eh-soh)

Let's analyze and solve the problem.
Vamos a analizar y a resolver el problema.
 ('vah-mohs ah ah-nah-lee-'sahr ee ah reh-sohl-'vehr ehl proh-'bleh-mah)

I'd like to hear	**Quisiera escuchar tu . . .**
your . . .	*(kee-see-'eh-rah ehs-koo-'chahr too)*
comment	**comentario** *(koh-mehn-'tah-ree-oh)*
idea	**idea** *(ee-'deh-ah)*
interpretation	**interpretación** *(een-tehr-preh-tah-see-'ohn)*

opinion	**opinión** *(oh-pee-nee-'ohn)*
response	**respuesta** *(rehs-'pwehs-tah)*

• Sometimes you will have the pleasure of praising . . .

You have . . .	**Tú tienes . . .** *(too tee-'eh-nehs)*
This/These is/are . . .	**Hay . . .** *('ah-ee)*
excellent achievements	**logros excelentes**
	('loh-grohs ehk-seh-'lehn-tehs)
fast development	**desarrollo rápido**
	(deh-sah-'rroh-yoh 'rah-pee-doh)
good effort	**buen esfuerzo** *(bwehn ehs-'fwehr-soh)*
good self-motivation	**buena automotivación**
	('bweh-nah ow-toh-moh-tee-vah-see-'ohn)
great potential	**gran potencial** *(grahn poh-tehn-see-'ahl)*
lots of desire	**mucho deseo** *('moo-choh deh-'seh-oh)*
more success	**más éxito** *(mahs 'ehk-see-toh)*
obvious progress	**progreso obvio**
	(proh-'greh-soh ohb-vee-'oh)
outstanding conduct	**conducta destacada**
	(kohn-'dook-tah dehs-tah-'kah-dah)
sense of accomplishment	**sentimiento de logro**
	(sehn-tee-mee-'ehn-toh deh 'loh-groh)

• At other times you must put your foot down . . .

I see . . .	**Yo veo . . .** *(yoh 'veh-oh)*
inadequate behavior	**conducta inadecuada**
	(kohn-'dook-tah ee-nah-deh-'kwah-dah)
insufficient potential	**potencial insuficiente**
	(poh-tehn-see-'ahl een-soo-fee-see-'ehn-teh)
less success	**menos éxito** *('meh-nohs 'ehk-see-toh)*
little desire	**poco deseo** *('poh-koh deh-'seh-oh)*
little effort	**poco esfuerzo** *('poh-koh ehs-'fwehr-soh)*
no progress	**ningún progreso**
	(neen-'goon proh-'greh-soh)

poor achievement	**logros deficientes**
	('loh-grohs deh-fee-see-'ehn-tehs)
scanty self-motivation	**escasa automotivación**
	(ehs-'kah-sah ow-toh-moh-tee-vah-see-'ohn)
sense of failure	**sentimiento de fracaso**
	(sehn-tee-mee-'ehn-toh deh frah-kah-soh)
slow development	**desarrollo lento**
	(deh-sah-'rroh-yoh 'lehn-toh)

Now say something else that will raise their self esteem:

You are . . .	**Tú eres . . .** *(too 'eh-rehs)*
attentive	**atento(a)** *(ah-'tehn-toh, tah)*
bright	**brillante** *(bree-'yahn-teh)*
capable	**capaz** *(kah-'pahs)*
clever	**listo(a)** *('lees-toh, tah)*
confident	**seguro(a)** *(seh-'goo-roh, rah)*
cooperative	**cooperador(a)** *(koh-oh-peh-rah-dohr, rah)*
courageous	**valiente** *(vah-lee-'ehn-teh)*
ethical	**ético(a)** *('eh-tee-koh, kah)*
fair	**justo(a)** *('hoos-toh, tah)*
friendly	**amistoso(a)** *(ah-mees-'toh-soh, sah)*
healthy	**sano(a)** *('sah-noh, nah)*
helpful	**servicial** *(sehr-vee-see-'ahl)*
honest	**honesto(a)** *(oh-'nehs-toh, tah)*
intelligent	**inteligente** *(een-teh-lee-'hehn-teh)*
kind	**amable** *(ah-'mah-bleh)*
loved	**querido(a)** *(keh-'ree-doh, dah)*
nice	**simpático(a)** *(seem-'pah-tee-koh, kah)*
patient	**paciente** *(pah-see-'ehn-teh)*
polite	**cortés** *(kohr-'tehs)*
respectful	**respetuoso(a)** *(rehs-peh-too-'oh-soh)*
responsible	**responsable** *(rehs-pohn-'sah-bleh)*
thoughtful	**considerado(a)** *(kohn-see-deh-'rah-doh, dah)*

He/She is very . . .	**Es muy . . .** *(ehs 'moo-ee)*
artistic	**artístico(a)** *(ahr-'tees-tee-koh, kah)*
athletic	**atlético(a)** *(aht-'leh-tee-koh, kah)*
clean	**limpio(a)** *('leem-pee-oh, ah)*
obedient	**obediente** *(oh-beh-dee-'ehn-teh)*
organized	**organizado(a)** *(ohr-gah-nee-'sah-doh, dah)*
punctual	**puntual** *(poon-too-'ahl)*
studious	**aplicado(a)** *(ah-plee-'kah-doh, dah)*

He/She is . . .	**Es . . .** *(ehs)*
dirty	**sucio(a)** *('soo-see-oh, ah)*
disobedient	**desobediente** *(deh-soh-beh-dee-'ehn-teh)*
disorganized	**desorganizado(a)** *(deh-sohr-gah-nee-'sah-doh, dah)*
irresponsible	**irresponsable** *(ee-rrehs-pohn-'sah-bleh)*
lazy	**perezoso(a)** *(peh-reh-'soh-soh, sah)*

Planning for the future
La planificación para el futuro
(lah plah-nee-fee-kah-see-'ohn 'pah-rah ehl foo-'too-roh)

Guidance and career counselors take on special duties as they deal with people out of work. These sample phrases should help:

There is/are . . .	**Hay . . .** *('ah-ee)*
job opportunities	**oportunidades para trabajar** *(oh-pohr-too-nee-'dah-dehs 'pah-rah trah-bah-'hahr)*
job placement	**asignación de trabajo** *(ah-seeg-nah-see-'ohn deh trah-'bah-hoh)*
job requirements	**requisitos para el trabajo** *(reh-kee-'see-tohs 'pah-rah ehl trah-'bah-hoh)*

Let's talk about (the) . . .	**Vamos a hablar de . . .** *('vah-mohs ah ah-'blahr deh)*
career planning	**la planificación de carreras** *(lah plah-nee-fee-kah-see-'ohn deh kah-'rreh-rahs)*
remedial program	**el programa de refuerzo** *(ehl proh-'grah-mah deh reh-foo-'ehr-soh)*
summer school	**la escuela de verano** *(lah ehs-'kweh-lah deh veh-'rah-noh)*
technical training	**el entrenamiento técnico** *(ehl ehn-treh-nah-mee-'ehn-toh 'tehk-nee-koh)*
work experience	**la experiencia en el trabajo** *(lah ehks-peh-ree-'ehn-see-ah ehn ehl trah-'bah-hoh)*
Here's information about (the) . . .	**Aquí tienes información sobre . . .** *(ah-'kee tee-'eh-nehs een-fohr-mah-see-'ohn 'soh-breh)*
application	**la solicitud** *(lah soh-lee-see-'tood)*
armed forces	**las fuerzas armadas** *(lahs 'fwehr-sahs ahr-'mah-dahs)*
degree	**la licenciatura** *(lah lee-sehn-see-ah-'too-rah)*
electives	**la materia optativa** *(lah mah-'teh-ree-ah ohp-tah-'tee-vah)*
entrance exams	**los exámenes de admisión** *(lohs ehk-'sah-meh-nehs deh ahd-mee-see-'ohn)*
financial aid	**la ayuda financiera** *(lah ah-'yoo-dah fee-nahn-see-'eh-rah)*
funding	**la obtención de fondos** *(lah ohb-tehn-see-'ohn deh 'fohn-dohs)*
letters of recommendation	**las cartas de recomendación** *(lahs 'kahr-tahs deh reh-koh-mehn-dah-see-'ohn)*
loan	**el préstamo** *(ehl 'prehs-tah-moh)*

prerequisites	**los prerrequisitos**
	(lohs preh-rreh-kee-'see-tohs)
registration	**la registración** *(lah reh-hees-trah-see-'ohn)*
scholarship	**la beca** *(lah 'beh-kah)*
testing	**los exámenes** *(lohs ehk-'sah-meh-nehs)*
transcripts	**la copia de los certificados**
	(lah 'koh-pee-ah deh lohs sehr-tee-fee-'kah-dohs)

It's a program for	**Es un programa para . . .**
(the) . . .	*(ehs oon proh-'grah-mah 'pah-rah)*
Bachelor of Arts	**la licenciatura de letras**
	(lah lee-sehn-see-ah-'too-rah deh 'leh-trahs)
Bachelor of Science	**la licenciatura de ciencias**
	(lah lee-sehn-see-ah-'too-rah deh see-'ehn-see-ahs)
Doctorate Degree	**el doctorado** *(ehl dohk-toh-'rah-doh)*
Master of Arts	**la maestría en letras**
	(lah mah-ehs-'tree-ah ehn 'leh-trahs)
Master of Science	**la maestría en ciencias**
	(lah mah-ehs-'tree-ahehn see-'ehn-see-ahs)
Ph.D.	**el doctorado en humanidades**
	(ehl dohk-toh-'rah-doh ehn oo-mah-nee-'dah-dehs)

We can help you

Podemos ayudarle *(poh-'deh-mohs ah-yoo-'dahr-leh)*

We have (the) . . .	**Tenemos . . .** *(teh-'neh-mohs)*
alternatives	**las alternativas** *(lahs ahl-tehr-nah-'tee-vahs)*
goals	**las metas** *(lahs 'meh-tahs)*
instructions	**las instrucciones** *(lahs eens-trook-see-'oh-nehs)*
objectives	**los objetivos** *(lohs ohb-heh-'tee-vohs)*
recommendations	**las recomendaciones**
	(lahs reh-koh-mehn-dah-see-'oh-nehs)

requirements	**los requisitos** *(lohs reh-kee-'see-tohs)*
research	**la investigación** *(lah een-vehs-tee-gah-see-'ohn)*
solutions	**las soluciones** *(lahs soh-loo-see-'oh-nehs)*
suggestions	**las sugerencias** *(lahs soo-heh-'rehn-see-ahs)*

Let the person know that your organization is there to help. Mention what you are willing to do:

We offer (the) . . .	**Ofrecemos . . .** *(oh-freh-'seh-mohs)*
day care center	**(la) guardería infantil**
	(gwahr-deh-'ree-ah een-fahn-'teel)
donation	**(la) donación** *(doh-nah-see-'ohn)*
food stamps	**(los) cupones de alimentos**
	(koo-'poh-nehs deh ah-lee-'mehn-tohs)
housing	**(la) vivienda** *(vee-vee-'ehn-dah)*
insurance	**(el) seguro** *(seh-'goo-roh)*
legal service	**(el) servicio legal** *(sehr-'vee-see-oh leh-'gahl)*
medical care	**(el) cuidado médico**
	(kwee-'dah-doh 'meh-dee-koh)
vaccination	**(la) vacunación** *(vah-koo-nah-see-'ohn)*
welfare	**(el) bienestar social**
	(bee-eh-nehs-'tahr soh-see-'ahl)

¡MÁS AYUDA!

• Keep the family's needs on target:

assistance	**la ayuda** *(lah ah-'yoo-dah)*
resource	**el recurso** *(ehl reh-'koor-soh)*
shelter	**el amparo** *(ehl ahm-'pah-roh)*
support	**el apoyo** *(ehl ah-'poh-yoh)*
therapy	**la terapia** *(lah teh-'rah-pee-ah)*

• Few could survive without the following expressions:

| Above all . . . | **Sobre todo . . .** *('soh-breh 'toh-doh)* |
| At first . . . | **Al principio . . .** *(ahl preen-'see-pee-oh)* |

At last . . .	**Por fin** . . . *(pohr feen)*
At least . . .	**Por lo menos** . . . *(pohr loh 'meh-nohs)*
By the way . . .	**A propósito** . . . *(ah proh-'poh-see-toh)*
For example . . .	**Por ejemplo** . . . *(pohr eh-'hehm-ploh)*
In general . . .	**En general** . . . *(ehn heh-neh-'rahl)*
In other words . . .	**En otras palabras** . . .
	(ehn 'oh-trahs pah-'lah-brahs)
On the other hand . . .	**En cambio** . . . *(ehn 'kahm-bee-oh)*
That is . . .	**Es decir** . . . *(ehs deh-'seer)*

Try some:

En general, estoy bien. *(ehn heh-neh-'rahl ehs-'toh-ee bee-'ehn)*
A propósito, mañana no hay trabajo.
 (ah proh-'poh-see-toh mahn-'yah-nah noh 'ah-ee trah-'bah-hoh)
Al principio, vengan a la oficina.
 (ahl preen-'see-pee-oh 'vehn-gahn ah lah oh-fee-'see-nah)

¡*Necesita Practicar!*

Connect the opposites:

aplicado	**obediente**
sucio	**incompetente**
egoísta	**servicial**
desobediente	**perezoso**
listo	**limpio**

Translate into English:

Favor de no hablar sin permiso.
Los estudiantes necesitan alabanzas.
¿Por qué piensa usted que está fallando?
Pregunte a su hijo qué aprendió.
Ella tiene buenos modales y se porta bien.
Aquí tiene información sobre el bienestar social.

The missionary

El misionero *(ehl mee-see-oh-'neh-roh)*

Here are some words that will help out anyone working in a church ministry or religious organization. Use the new vocabulary to create your own sentences:

angel	**el ángel** *(ehl 'ahn-hehl)*	<u>**Hay ángeles en el cielo.**</u>
baptism	**el bautismo** *(ehl bow-'tees-moh)*	<u>**Fui al bautismo.**</u>
belief	**la creencia** *(lah kreh-'ehn-see-ah)*	<u>**Tengo una creencia.**</u>

believer   **el, la creyente** *(ehl, lah kreh-'yehn-teh)*

_____

atheist   **el, la ateo(a)** *(ehl, lah ah-'teh-oh, ah)*

_____

blessing   **la bendición** *(lah behn-dee-see-'ohn)*

_____

church   **la iglesia** *(lah eeg-'leh-see-ah)*

_____

confession   **la confesión** *(lah kohn-feh-see-'ohn)*

_____

creation   **la creación** *(lah kreh-ah-see'ohn)*

_____

cross   **la cruz** *(lah kroos)*

_____

death   **la muerte** *(lah 'mwehr-teh)*

_____

devil   **el diablo** *(ehl dee-'ah-bloh)*

_____

disciple	**el, la discípulo(a)** *(ehl, lah dee-'see-poo-loh, lah)*
eternity	**la eternidad** *(lah eh-tehr-nee-'dahd)*
faith	**la fe** *(lah feh)*
fasting	**el ayuno** *(ehl ah-'yoo-noh)*
grace	**la gracia** *(lah 'grah-see-ah)*
heaven	**el cielo** *(ehl see-'eh-loh)*
hell	**el infierno** *(ehl een-fee-'ehr-noh)*
hope	**la esperanza** *(lah ehs-peh-'rahn-sah)*
joy	**la alegría** *(lah ah-leh-'gree-ah)*
judgment	**el juicio** *(ehl hoo-'ee-see-oh)*
life	**la vida** *(lah 'vee-dah)*
love	**el amor** *(ehl ah-'mohr)*
meditation	**la meditación** *(lah meh-dee-tah-see-'ohn)*

mercy	**la misericordia** *(lah mee-seh-ree-'kohr-dee-ah)*
message	**el mensaje** *(ehl mehn-'sah-heh)*
miracle	**el milagro** *(ehl mee-'lah-groh)*
pastor	**el, la pastor(a)** *(ehl, lah pahs-'tohr, rah)*
peace	**la paz** *(lah pahs)*
prayer	**la oración** *(lah oh-rah-see-'ohn)*
religion	**la religión** *(lah reh-lee-hee-'ohn)*
sacrifice	**el sacrificio** *(ehl sah-kree-'fee-see-oh)*
salvation	**la salvación** *(lah sahl-vah-see-'ohn)*
service	**el servicio** *(ehl sehr-'vee-see-oh)*
sin	**el pecado** *(ehl peh-kah-doh)*
sinner	**el, la pecador(a)** *(ehl, lah peh-kah-'dohr, rah)*
soul	**el alma** *(ehl 'ahl-mah)*

suffering   el **sufrimiento** *(ehl soo-free-mee-'ehn-toh)*

temptation   la **tentación** *(lah tehn-tah-see-'ohn)*

testimony   el **testimonio** *(ehl tehs-tee-'moh-nee-oh)*

Keep going:

Ascension	la **Ascención** *(lah ah-sehn-see-'ohn)*
Bible	la **Biblia** *(lah 'bee-blee-ah)*
Communion	la **Comunión** *('lah koh-moo-nee-'ohn)*
Easter	la **Pascua** *(lah 'pahs-kwah)*
God	**Dios** *(dee-'ohs)*
Holy Spirit	el **Espíritu Santo** *(ehl ehs-'pee-ree-too 'sahn-toh)*
Jehovah	**Jehová** *(heh-oh-'vah)*
Jesus Christ	**Jesucristo** *(heh-soo-'krees-toh)*
The Lord	el **Señor** *(ehl sehn-'yohr)*
New Testament	el **Nuevo Testamento** *(ehl 'nweh-voh tehs-tah-'mehn-toh)*
Old Testament	el **Antiguo Testamento** *(ehl ahn-'tee-gwoh tehs-tah-'mehn-toh)*
Pentecost	el **Pentecostés** *(ehl pehn-teh-kohs-'tehs)*
Resurrection	la **Resurrección** *(lah reh-soo-rrehk-see-'ohn)*
Sacred Scriptures	las **Sagradas Escrituras** *(lahs sah-'grah-dahs ehs-kree-'too-rahs)*
Savior	el **Salvador** *(ehl sahl-vah-'dohr)*
Son of God	el **Hijo de Dios** *(ehl 'ee-hoh deh dee-'ohs)*

The Church Service
El servicio religioso
(ehl sehr-'vee-see-oh reh-lee-hee-'oh-soh)

Read this service-related vocabulary and then create short sentences:

mass	**la misa** *(lah 'mee-sah)*	<u>**El sacerdote está en misa.**</u>
pew	**el banco** *(ehl 'bahn-koh)*	<u>**Siéntese en el banco.**</u>
hymn	**el himno** *(ehl 'eem-noh)*	<u>**Me gusta el himno.**</u>
hymnal	**el himnario** *(ehl eem-'nah-ree-oh)*	<u>**Abra el himnario.**</u>

activity   **la actividad** *(lah ahk-tee-vee-'dahd)*

_____

meeting   **la reunión** *(lah reh-oo-nee-'ohn)*

_____

announcement   **el anuncio** *(ehl ah-'noon-see-oh)*

_____

service   **el servicio** *(ehl sehr-'vee-see-oh)*

_____

choir   **el coro** *(ehl 'koh-roh)*

_____

program   **el programa** *(ehl proh-'grah-mah)*

_____

schedule   **el horario** *(ehl oh-'rah-ree-oh)*

_____

group   **el grupo** *(ehl 'groo-poh)*

_____

celebration   **la celebración** *(lah seh-leh-brah-see'ohn)*

_____

song	**la canción** *(lah kahn-see-'ohn)*
request	**la petición** *(lah peh-tee-see-'ohn)*
tithe	**el diezmo** *(ehl dee-'ehs-moh)*
congregation	**la congregación** *(lah kohn-greh-gah-see-'ohn)*
sermon	**el sermón** *(ehl sehr-'mohn)*
gospel	**el evangelio** *(ehl eh-vahn-'heh-lee-oh)*

¡ *L A   C U L T U R A !*

Most of Spain and Latin America is Roman Catholic, so you may notice the religious influence during your association with Hispanics during a crisis. Using the word **Dios** in conversation, attending daily mass, or observing Catholic traditions are constant signs of their faith. Remember that respect and sensitivity are always in demand when topics center around cultural and religious beliefs.

Working with the elderly
Trabajando con la gente mayor
(trah-bah-'hahn-doh kohn lah 'hehn-teh mah-'yohr)

Another group of people in need of attention is sometimes the most forgotten. Although most Hispanic families in the world provide for their own elderly relatives, there is still a demand for outreach Spanish at convalescent homes, hospitals, and home care facilities. The best way to acquire the phrases you'll need is to study the topics separately. First, make contact:

How are you feeling today?
¿Cómo se siente hoy? *('koh-moh seh see-'ehn-teh 'oh-ee)*

Is there anything you need?
¿Hay algo que necesita? *('ah-ee 'ahl-goh keh neh-seh-'see-tah)*

Did you talk to the doctor?
¿Habló con el doctor? *(ah-'bloh kohn ehl dohk-'tohr)*

What would you like to do today?
¿Qué quiere hacer hoy? *(keh kee-'eh-reh ah-'sehr 'oh-ee)*

Did you eat?	**¿Comió?** *(koh-mee-'oh)*
Did you sleep?	**¿Durmió?** *(door-mee-'oh)*
Did you take your medicine?	**¿Tomó su medicina?**
	(toh-'moh soo meh-dee-'see-nah)

Heart problems affect many of the elderly:

Do you have . . . ?	**¿Tiene . . . ?** *(tee-'eh-neh)*
chest pains	**dolores en el pecho**
	(doh-'loh-rehs ehn ehl 'peh-choh)
heart murmurs	**murmullos en el corazón**
	(moor-'moo-yohs ehn ehl koh-rah-'sohn)
shortness of breath	**falta de aliento** *('fahl-tah deh ah-lee-'ehn- toh)*

Have you ever had a heart attack?
¿Ha tenido alguna vez un ataque cardíaco?
(ah teh-'nee-doh ahl-'goo-nah vehs oon ah-'tah-keh kahr-'dee-ah-koh)

Your blood pressure is very high.
Su presión es muy alta. *(soo preh-see-'ohn ehs 'moo-ee 'ahl-tah)*

You are overweight.
Tiene sobrepeso. *(tee-'eh-neh soh-breh-'peh-soh)*

Your case is (not) serious.
Su caso (no) es grave. *(soo 'kah-soh noh ehs 'grah-veh)*

Your pulse is very fast.
Su pulso es muy rápido. *(soo 'pool-soh ehs 'moo-ee 'rah-pee-doh)*

You need complete bed rest for now.
Por ahora, necesita completo descanso en cama.
(pohr ah-'oh-rah neh-seh-'see-tah kohm-'pleh-toh dehs-'kahn-soh ehn 'kah-mah)

We're going to change your diet.
Vamos a cambiar su dieta.
('vah-mohs ah kahm-bee-'ahr soo dee-'eh-tah)

I'm sick
Estoy enfermo *(ehs-'toh -ee ehn-'fehr-moh)*

This next set of words and one-liners relates to illness and surgery.

You need (the) . . .	**Necesita . . .** *(neh-seh-'see-tah)*
cane	**el bastón** *(ehl bahs-'tohn)*
crutches	**las muletas** *(lahs moo-'leh-tahs)*
guide dog	**el perro lazarillo** *(ehl 'peh-rroh lah-sah-'ree-yoh)*
hearing aids	**los audífonos** *(lohs ow-'dee-foh-nohs)*
injection	**la inyección** *(lah een-yehk-see-'ohn)*
MRI	**la imagen por resonancia magnética** *(lah ee-'mah-hehn pohr reh-soh-'nahn-see-ah mahg-'neh-tee-kah)*
operation	**la operación** *(lah oh-peh-rah-see-'ohn)*
results	**los resultados** *(lohs reh-sool-'tah-dohs)*
specialist	**el especialista** *(ehl ehs-peh-see-ah-'lees-tah)*
surgery	**la cirugía** *(lah see-roo-'hee-ah)*
test	**el examen** *(ehl ehk-'sah-mehn)*
treatment	**el tratamiento** *(ehl trah-tah-mee-'ehn-toh)*

wheelchair	**la silla de ruedas**
	(lah 'see-yah deh 'rweh-dahs)
X ray	**la radiografía** *(lah rah-dee-oh-grah-'fee-ah)*

You're going to . . .	**Va a . . .** *(vah ah)*
feel tired and weak	**sentirse cansado y débil**
	(sehn-'teer-seh kahn-'sah-doh ee 'deh-beel)
have nausea, vomiting,	**tener naúsea, vómitos, diarrea y**
diarrhea, and constipation	**estreñimiento** *(teh-'nehr 'now-seh-ah*
	'voh-mee-tohs dee-ah-'rreh-ah ee ehs-
	trehn-ee-mee-'ehn-toh)
have some side effects	**tener algunos efectos secundarios**
	(teh-'nehr ahl-'goo-nohs eh-'fehk-tohs
	seh-koon-'dah-ree-ohs)

Older people and signs of nervous or psychological disorders are closely related. Your knowledge of key words may become invaluable in a crisis:

Have you had . . . ?	**¿Ha tenido . . . ?** *(ah teh-'nee-doh)*
some paralysis	**parálisis parcial**
	(pah-'rah-lee-sees pahr-see-'ahl)
convulsions	**convulsiones** *(kohn-vool-see-'oh-nehs)*
discharge	**secreción** *(seh-kreh-see-'ohn)*
dizziness	**mareos** *(mah-'reh-ohs)*
emotional problems	**problemas emocionales**
	(proh-'bleh-mahs eh-moh-see-oh-'nah-lehs)
fainting spells	**desmayos** *(dehs-'mah-yohs)*
headaches	**dolores de cabeza**
	(doh-'loh-rehs deh kah-'beh-sah)
problems with balance	**problemas con su equilibrio**
	(proh-'bleh-mahs kohn soo eh-kee-'lee-bree-oh)
blurred vision	**visión borrosa** *(vee-see-'ohn boh-'rroh-sah)*

double vision	**visión doble** *(vee-see-'ohn 'doh-bleh)*
numbness	**adormecimiento**
	(ah-dohr-meh-see-mee-'ehn-toh)
sensitivity	**sensibilidad** *(sehn-see-bee-lee-'dahd)*
tingling	**hormigueo** *(ohr-mee-'geh-oh)*
weakness	**debilidad** *(deh-bee-lee-'dahd)*

And listen to them explain:

I have . . .	**Tengo** . . . *('tehn-goh)*
anxiety	**ansiedad** *(ahn-see-eh-'dahd)*
bad dreams	**sueños malos** *('swehn-yohs 'mah-lohs)*
confusion	**confusión** *(kohn-foo-see-'ohn)*
depression	**desánimo** *(dehs-'ah-nee-moh)*
fear	**miedo** *(mee-'eh-doh)*
hysteria attacks	**histerias** *(ees-'teh-ree-ahs)*
insomnia	**insomnio** *(een-'sohm-nee-oh)*
loss of memory	**falta de memoria**
	('fahl-tah deh meh-'moh-ree-ah)
seizures	**ataques** *(ah-'tah-kehs)*
visions	**visiones** *(vee-see-'oh-nehs)*

¡ M Á S   A Y U D A !

• As you may have guessed, some terms sound a lot like English:

She is a(n) . . .	**Ella es una** . . . *('eh-yah ehs 'oo-nah)*
alcoholic	**alcohólica** *(ahl-koh-'oh-lee-kah)*
drug addict	**drogadicta** *(droh-gah-'deek-tah)*
epileptic	**epiléptica** *(eh-pee-'lehp-tee-kah)*
manic depressive	**maniacodepresiva**
	(mah-nee-ah-koh-deh-preh-'see-vah)
paranoid	**paranoica** *(pah-rah-'noh-ee-kah)*
schizophrenic	**esquizofrénica** *(ehs-kee-soh-'freh-nee-kah)*

• Now, tell the people you're caring for what they cannot do:

For now, you can't drive a car.
Por ahora, no puede manejar un carro.
  (pohr ah-'oh-rah noh 'pweh-deh mah-neh-'hahr oon 'kah-rroh)

You can't do strenuous exercise.
No puede hacer mucho ejercicio físico.
  (noh 'pweh-deh ah-'sehr 'moo-choh eh-hehr-'see-see-oh 'fee-see-koh)

You can't have a lot of stress or tension.
No puede tener mucho estrés o tensión.
  (noh 'pweh-deh teh-'nehr 'moo-choh ehs-'trehs oh tehn-see-'ohn)

• If they need a favor, maybe you will want to offer your help. These errands are pretty common:

Do you want me to . . . ?	**¿Desea que yo . . . ?**
	(deh-'seh-ah keh yoh)
buy you something	**le compre algo** *(leh 'kohm-preh 'ahl-goh)*
call your family	**llame a su familia**
	('yah-meh ah soo fah-'mee-lee-ah)
pick them up	**los recoja** *(lohs reh-'koh-hah)*
rent a video	**alquile un video** *(ahl-'kee-leh oon vee-'deh-oh)*
send this by mail	**envíe ésto por correo**
	(ehn-'vee-eh 'ehs-toh pohr koh-'rreh-oh)
stop at the cleaners	**pare en la tintorería**
	('pah-reh ehn lah teen-toh-reh-'ree-ah)
walk the dog	**camine el perro**
	(kah-'mee-neh ehl 'peh-rroh)

 ¡ N E C E S I T A   P R A C T I C A R !

Translate into English:

¿Tiene usted murmullos en el corazón?
Necesita completo descanso en cama.
¿Ha tenido adormecimiento en las piernas?

Ella es una paranoica y tiene un problema emocional.
No puede hacer mucho ejercicio físico.

• When death strikes, expressions of sympathy given in the grievers'
native language would be appreciated:

I'm very sorry.	**Lo siento mucho.** *(loh see-'ehn-toh 'moo-choh)*	
We are very sorry.	**Lo sentimos mucho.**	
	(loh sehn-'tee-mohs 'moo-choh)	

casket	**el ataúd** *(ehl ah-tah-'ood)*	<u>El ataúd es negro.</u>
funeral	**el funeral** *(ehl foo-neh-'rahl)*	<u>Voy al funeral.</u>
mortuary	**la funeraria**	<u>La funeraria es excelente</u>.
	(lah foo-neh-'rah-ree-ah)	

burial	**el entierro** *(ehl ehn-tee-'eh-rroh)*

---

ceremony	**la ceremonia** *(lah seh-reh-'moh-nee-ah)*

---

cremation	**la cremación** *(lah kreh-mah-see-'ohn)*

---

dead	**el, la muerto(a)** *(ehl, lah 'mwehr-toh, tah)*

---

death	**la muerte** *(lah 'mwehr-teh)*

---

grief	**el dolor** *(ehl doh-'lohr)*

---

hearse	**el coche fúnebre** *(ehl 'koh-che 'foo-neh-breh)*

---

loss	**la pérdida** *(lah 'pehr-dee-dah)*

---

mourning	**el duelo** *(ehl 'dweh-loh)*

---

tombstone	**la lápida** *(lah 'lah-pee-dah)*

---

wake	**el velatorio** *(ehl veh-lah-'toh-ree-oh)*

• Note how verbs can be used:

TO BE IN MOURNING **ESTAR DE DUELO**
(ehs-'tahr deh 'dweh-loh)
La familia está de duelo. *(lah fah-'mee-lee-ah ehs-'tah deh 'dweh-loh)*

TO SYMPATHIZE **EXPRESAR SIMPATÍA**
(ehks-preh-'sahr seem-pah-'tee-ah)
Ana expresa simpatía a José.
('ah-nah ehks-'preh-sah seem-pah-'tee-ah ah hoh-'seh)

TO DIE **MORIR** *(moh-'reer)*
El abuelo va a morir. *(ehl ah-'bweh-loh vah ah moh-'reer)*

TO CONSOLE **CONSOLAR** *(kohn-soh-'lahr)*
El padre consoló a su hija. *(ehl 'pah-dreh kohn-soh-'loh ah soo 'ee-hah)*

TO SUFFER **SUFRIR** *(soo-'freer)*
Ella va a sufrir mucho. *('eh-yah vah ah soo-'freer 'moo-choh)*

TO CRY **LLORAR** *(yoh-'rahr)*
Nosotros lloramos en la ceremonia.
(noh-'soh-trohs yoh-'rah-mohs ehn lah seh-reh-'moh-nee-ah)

<h1 style="text-align:center">¡ A C C I Ó N !</h1>

To ask if anyone "has had" something before, you must use the tense **Ha tenido**, which translates as "Have you had . . . ?" or "Has he or she had . . . ?" Try it:

Have you had a problem?
¿Ha tenido un problema? *(ah teh-'nee-doh oon proh-'bleh-mah)*

Have you had the illness?
¿Ha tenido la enfermedad? *(ah teh-'nee-doh lah ehn-fehr-meh-'dahd)*

Have you had fear?
¿Ha tenido miedo? *(ah teh-'nee-doh mee-'eh-doh)*

• Study this double-verb pattern. It's important because it refers to actions that have already taken place. Practice these examples:

Have you had this pain before?
¿Ha tenido este dolor antes? *(ah teh-'nee-doh 'ehs-teh doh-'lohr 'ahn-tehs)*

Have you spoken with the doctor?
¿Ha hablado con el doctor? *(ah ah-'blah-doh kohn ehl dohk-'tohr)*

• Here is what you need to get started:

I have . . .	**he** *(eh)*	had	**tenido** *(teh-'nee-doh)*
You, he, or she has . . .	**ha** *(ah)*	eaten	**comido** *(koh-'mee-doh)*
They or you (pl.) have . . .	**han** *(ahn)*	taken	**tomado** *(toh-'mah-doh)*
We have . . .	**hemos** *('eh-mohs)*	gone	**ido** *('ee-doh)*

This next series is an overview of actions that have happened. Read them aloud:

Has he/she had an accident?
¿Ha tenido un accidente? *(ah teh-'nee-doh oon ahk-see-'dehn-teh)*

Has he/she taken any medicines?
¿Han tomado alguna medicina?
(ah toh-'mah-doh ahl-'goo-nah meh-dee-'see-nah)

Has he/she slept?
¿Ha dormido? *(ah dohr-'mee-doh)*

¡ MÁS AYUDA !

• Another fast and effective way to tell someone that an activity was just completed is to use the verb "to finish," **acabar** *(ah-kah-'bahr)* plus **de** *(deh)* plus the infinitive of any verb you wish to use:

TO FINISH	**ACABAR DE** *(ah-kah-'bahr deh)*
I just finished . . .	**Acabo de . . .** *(ah-'kah-boh deh)*
I just finished working.	**Acabo de trabajar.** *(ah-'kah-boh deh trah-bah-'hahr)*
You, he, she just finished . . .	**Acaba de . . .** *(ah-'kah-bah deh)*
He just finished running.	**Acaba de correr.** *(ah-'kah-bah deh koh-'rrehr)*
They, you (pl.) just finished . . .	**Acaban de . . .** *(ah-'kah-bahn deh)*
They just finished talking.	**Acaban de hablar.** *(ah-'kah-bahn deh ah-'blahr)*
We just finished . . .	**Acabamos de . . .** *(ah-kah-'bah-mohs deh)*
We just finished eating.	**Acabamos de comer.** *(ah-kah-'bah-mohs deh koh-'mehr)*

- By the way, **acabar** can be used as a regular action word:

I'm finishing now.	**Estoy acabando ahora.**
	(ehs-'toh-ee ah-kah-'bahn-doh ah-'oh-rah)
I finish at five.	**Acabo a las cinco.**
	(ah-'kah-boh ah lahs 'seen-koh)
I was finishing.	**Estaba acabando.**
	(ehs-'tah-bah ah-kah-'bahn-doh)
I'll finish with the job.	**Acabaré con el trabajo.**
	(ah-kah-bah-'reh kohn ehl trah-'bah-hoh)

¡*LAS ORDENES!*

Memorize each of these as if they were single words. Then use the vocabulary you have learned to shape your own sentences:

Bring it to me.	**Tráigamelo.** *('trah-ee-gah-meh-loh)*
Close it.	**Ciérrelo.** *(see-'eh-rreh-loh)*
Do it.	**Hágalo.** *('ah-gah-loh)*
Follow me.	**Sígame.** *('see-gah-meh)*
Give it to me.	**Démelo.** *('deh-meh-loh)*
Help me.	**Ayúdeme.** *(ah-'yoo-deh-meh)*
Lift them up.	**Levántelos.** *(leh-'vahn-teh-lohs)*
Look at me.	**Míreme.** *('mee-reh-meh)*
Lower them.	**Bájelos.** *('bah-heh-lohs)*
Show it to me.	**Muéstremelo.** *('mwehs-treh-meh-loh)*
Take it away.	**Quítelo.** *('kee-teh-loh)*
Take it out.	**Sáquelo.** *('sah-keh-loh)*
Tell it to me.	**Dígamelo.** *('dee-gah-meh-loh)*
Throw it to me.	**Tíremelo.** *('tee-reh-meh-loh)*
Turn around.	**Dése vuelta.** *('deh-seh voo-'ehl-tah)*
Turn it off.	**Apáguelo.** *(ah-'pah-geh-loh)*
Turn it on.	**Préndalo.** *('prehn-dah-loh)*
Write it.	**Escríbalo.** *(ehs-'kree-bah-loh)*

¡ *M Á S   A Y U D A !*

• Watch the Spanish channels on your TV. The more exposure to Spanish you have, the faster you'll pick it up.

• Continue selecting objects in your house, writing their Spanish names on stickers, and affixing the stickers to them. Then, every time you pass close to those objects, peek at their stickers.

• Don't overstress pronunciation or grammar skills. Both will repair themselves as more Spanish is spoken.

• Try children's songs in Spanish. Their simplicity will make you understand a lot, and the music will make learning fun.

• An excellent technique is giving or receiving commands and then following them with proper physical action. Such exercises seem to accelerate the language acquisition process.

• Exchange lots of questions and answers. By focusing on the primary question words, beginners learn practical ways to speak survival Spanish.

• Regular exchanges of friendly greetings, courteous remarks, and ordinary expressions encourage non-Spanish speakers to participate in conversations and speak up on their own.

• Repetition of any Spanish word helps people remember it. For any key vocabulary item, say it clearly more than once. When possible, say it to a Spanish speaker and have him repeat it back to you.

• Always have a Spanish-English/English-Spanish paperback dictionary nearby. Keep a second one in your car.

¡ *L A   C U L T U R A !*

Many Americans work with new immigrants who are unfamiliar with local, state, or federal laws and regulations. If you plan to establish a long-term relationship, you can prevent potential problems by giving them as much legal information as possible. By contacting a variety of service agencies, one can pick up literature in Spanish concerning citizenship, taxes, health care, education, transportation, and residence, as well as personal rights and privileges.

Final words
Las últimas palabras
(lahs 'ool-tee-mahs pah-'lah-brahs)

After you've read through this guidebook, go back and review those words and phrases that you thought were the most important. Don't try to take in too much at one sitting! Be patient with yourself, and practice your new skills as often as you can. If possible, keep a record of what you've learned, and share the information with family, friends, or co-workers. Have fun while you learn, relax, and always pay special attention to any cultural differences.

¡Buena suerte, amigos! *('bweh-nah soo-'ehr-teh ah-'mee-gohs)*

Su profesor, Bill *(soo proh-feh-'sohr beel)*

English—Spanish Verb List

Memorize any verb that you need, highlight those of secondary importance. Be sure to pronounce each syllable correctly:

to accept	**aceptar** *(ah-sehp-'tahr)*
to accommodate	**acomodar** *(ah-koh-moh-'dahr)*
to accompany	**acompañar** *(ah-kohm-pahn-'yahr)*
to accrue	**acumular** *(ah-koo-moo-'lahr)*
to achieve	**lograr** *(loh-'grahr)*
to adapt	**adaptar** *(ah-dahp-'tahr)*
to add	**añadir** *(ahn-yah-'deer)*
to adjust	**ajustar** *(ah-hoos-'tahr)*
to allow	**permitir** *(pehr-mee-'teer)*
to analyze	**analizar** *(ah-nah-lee-sahr)*
to answer	**contestar** *(kohn-tehs-'tahr)*
to antagonize	**antagonizar** *(ahn-tah-goh-nee-'sahr)*
to appreciate	**apreciar** *(ah-preh-see-'ahr)*
to approve	**aprobar** *(ah-proh-'bahr)*
to argue	**discutir** *(dees-koo-'teer)*
to arrange	**arreglar** *(ah-rreh-'glahr)*
to arrive	**llegar** *(yeh-'gahr)*
to ask	**pedir** *(peh-'deer)*
to ask	**preguntar** *(preh-goon-'tahr)*
to assemble	**armar** *(ahr-'mahr)*
to assure	**asegurar** *(ah-seh-goo-'rahr)*
to attach	**unir** *(oo-'neer)*
to attend	**asistir** *(ah-sees-'teer)*
to authorize	**autorizar** *(ow-toh-ree-'sahr)*
to bathe oneself	**bañarse** *(bahn-'yahr-seh)*
to be	**ser/estar** *(sehr, ehs-'tahr)*
to beat up	**golpear** *(gohl-peh-'ahr)*
to begin	**empezar** *(ehm-peh-'sahr)*
to believe	**creer** *(kreh-'ehr)*
to bend	**doblar** *(doh-'blahr)*
to bite	**morder** *(mohr-'dehr)*
to borrow	**pedir prestado** *(peh-'deer prehs-'tah-doh)*
to bother	**molestar** *(moh-lehs-'tahr)*
to bounce	**rebotar** *(reh-boh-'tahr)*
to break	**romper** *(rohm-'pehr)*
to bring	**traer** *(trah-'ehr)*
to build	**construir** *(kohns-troo-'eer)*
to calculate	**calcular** *(kahl-koo-'lahr)*
to call	**llamar** *(yah-'mahr)*
to cancel	**cancelar** *(kahn-seh-'lahr)*
to carry	**llevar** *(yeh-'vahr)*
to carry out	**cumplir** *(koom-'pleer)*
to change	**cambiar** *(kahm-bee-'ahr)*
to charge	**cobrar** *(koh-'brahr)*
to check	**averiguar** *(ah-veh-ree-'gwahr)*
to clarify	**aclarar** *(ah-klah-'rahr)*
to clean	**limpiar** *(leem-pee-'ahr)*

to climb	**subir** *(soo-'beer)*
to close	**cerrar** *(seh-'rrahr)*
to collect	**recolectar** *(reh-koh-lehk-'tahr)*
to come	**venir** *(veh-'neer)*
to comfort	**confortar** *(kohn-fohr-'tahr)*
to commend	**alabar** *(ah-lah-'bahr)*
to commit oneself	**comprometerse** *(kohm-proh-meh-'tehr-seh)*
to communicate	**comunicar** *(koh-moo-nee-'kahr)*
to complain	**quejarse** *(keh-'hahr-seh)*
to compliment	**felicitar** *(feh-lee-see-'tahr)*
to compromise	**comprometer** *(kohm-proh-meh-'tehr)*
to confirm	**confirmar** *(kohn-feer-'mahr)*
to connect	**conectar** *(koh-nehk-'tahr)*
to consult	**consultar** *(kohn-sool-'tahr)*
to continue	**continuar** *(kohn-teen-'wahr)*
to contribute	**contribuir** *(kohn-tree-'bweer)*
to converse	**conversar** *(kohn-vehr-'sahr)*
to cooperate	**cooperar** *(koh-oh-peh-'rahr)*
to coordinate	**coordinar** *(koh-ohr-dee-'nahr)*
to correct	**corregir** *(koh-rreh-'heer)*
to cost	**costar** *(kohs-'tahr)*
to counsel	**aconsejar** *(ah-kohn-seh-'hahr)*
to count	**contar** *(kohn-'tahr)*
to cover	**cubrir** *(koo-'breer)*
to cry	**llorar** *(yoh-'rahr)*
to cultivate	**cultivar** *(kool-tee-'vahr)*
to cure	**curar** *(koo-'rahr)*
to curse	**maldecir** *(mahl-deh-'seer)*
to cut	**cortar** *(kohr-'tahr)*
to debate	**debatir** *(deh-bah-'teer)*
to defend	**defender** *(deh-fehn-'dehr)*
to deliver	**repartir** *(reh-pahr-'teer)*
to demand	**demandar** *(deh-mahn-'dahr)*
to demonstrate	**demostrar** *(deh-mohs-'trahr)*
to deny	**negar** *(neh-'gahr)*
to deposit	**depositar** *(deh-poh-see-'tahr)*
to detect	**detectar** *(deh-tehk-'tahr)*
to develop	**desarrollar** *(deh-sah-rroh-'yahr)*
to die	**morir** *(moh-'reer)*
to dig	**excavar** *(ehks-kah-'vahr)*
to distribute	**distribuir** *(dees-tree-'bweer)*
to do	**hacer** *(ah-'sehr)*
to donate	**donar** *(doh-'nahr)*
to dress oneself	**vestirse** *(vehs-'teer-seh)*
to drill	**taladrar** *(tah-lah-'drahr)*
to drink	**beber, tomar** *(beh-'behr, toh-'mahr)*
to drive	**manejar** *(mah-neh-'hahr)*
to dry	**secar** *(seh-'kahr)*
to earn	**ganar** *(gah-'nahr)*
to eat	**comer** *(koh-'mehr)*
to empty	**vaciar** *(vah-see-'ahr)*
to encourage	**animar** *(ah-nee-'mahr)*
to enjoy oneself	**divertirse** *(dee-vehr-'teer-seh)*
to enroll	**matricular** *(mah-tree-koo-'lahr)*
to enter	**entrar** *(ehn-'trahr)*
to establish	**establecer** *(ehs-tah-bleh-'sehr)*
to evaluate	**evaluar** *(eh-vah-loo-'ahr)*
to exceed	**sobrepasar** *(soh-breh-pah-'sahr)*

to exchange	**intercambiar** *(een-tehr-kahm-bee-'ahr)*
to exhibit	**exhibir** *(ehks-ee-'beer)*
to expire	**vencer** *(vehn-'sehr)*
to explain	**explicar** *(ehks-plee-'kahr)*
to exploit	**explotar** *(ehks-ploh-'tahr)*
to fail	**fallar** *(fah-'yahr)*
to fall	**caer** *(kah-'ehr)*
to feed	**alimentar** *(ah-lee-mehn-'tahr)*
to fight	**pelear** *(peh-leh-'ahr)*
to file	**archivar** *(ahr-chee-'vahr)*
to fill	**llenar** *(yeh-'nahr)*
to find	**encontrar** *(ehn-kohn-'trahr)*
to finish	**terminar** *(tehr-mee-'nahr)*
to fix	**arreglar** *(ah-rreh-'glahr)*
to focus	**enfocar** *(ehn-foh-'kahr)*
to follow	**seguir** *(seh-'geer)*
to forgive	**perdonar** *(pehr-doh-'nahr)*
to gather	**recoger** *(reh-koh-'hehr)*
to get	**conseguir** *(kohn-seh-'geer)*
to get up	**levantarse** *(leh-vahn-'tahr-seh)*
to give	**dar** *(dahr)*
to give away	**regalar** *(reh-gah-'lahr)*
to glue	**pegar** *(peh-'gahr)*
to go	**ir** *(eer)*
to grab	**agarrar** *(ah-gah-'rrahr)*
to grow	**crecer** *(kreh-'sehr)*
to guarantee	**garantizar** *(gah-rahn-tee-'sahr)*
to hang	**colgar** *(kohl-'gahr)*
to harvest	**cosechar** *(koh-seh-'chahr)*
to have	**tener/haber** *(teh-'nehr, ah-'behr)*
to heal	**sanar** *(sah-'nahr)*
to hear	**oír** *(oh-'eer)*
to heat	**calentar** *(kah-lehn-'tahr)*
to help	**ayudar** *(ah-yoo-'dahr)*
to hide	**esconder** *(ehs-kohn-'dehr)*
to hire	**contratar** *(kohn-trah-'tahr)*
to hit	**pegar** *(peh-'gahr)*
to hurry oneself	**apurarse** *(ah-poo-'rahr-seh)*
to identify	**identificar** *(ee-dehn-tee-fee-'kahr)*
to immunize	**inmunizar** *(een-moo-nee-'sahr)*
to improve	**mejorar** *(meh-hoh-'rahr)*
to inspect	**inspeccionar** *(eens-pehk-see-oh-'nahr)*
to install	**instalar** *(eens-tah-'lahr)*
to interfere	**interferir** *(een-tehr-feh-'reer)*
to intervene	**intervenir** *(een-tehr-veh-'neer)*
to invest	**invertir** *(een-vehr-'teer)*
to join	**juntar** *(hoon-'tahr)*
to joke	**bromear** *(broh-meh-'ahr)*
to jump	**saltar** *(sahl-'tahr)*
to keep	**guardar** *(gwahr-'dahr)*
to kick	**patear** *(pah-teh-'ahr)*
to kill	**matar** *(mah-'tahr)*
to know (person)	**conocer** *(koh-noh-'sehr)*
to know (something)	**saber** *(sah-'behr)*
to laugh	**reír** *(reh-'eer)*
to lead	**dirigir** *(dee-ree-'heer)*
to learn	**aprender** *(ah-prehn-'dehr)*
to leave	**salir** *(sah-'leer)*

to let	**dejar** *(deh-'hahr)*
to level	**nivelar** *(nee-veh-'lahr)*
to lie	**mentir** *(mehn-'teer)*
to lift	**levantar** *(leh-vahn-'tahr)*
to listen	**escuchar** *(ehs-koo-'chahr)*
to live	**vivir** *(vee-'veer)*
to load	**cargar** *(kahr-'gahr)*
to loan	**prestar** *(prehs-'tahr)*
to lock	**cerrar con llave** *(seh-'rrahr kohn 'yah-veh)*
to look	**mirar** *(mee-'rahr)*
to look for	**buscar** *(boos-'kahr)*
to lose	**perder** *(pehr-'dehr)*
to love	**amar** *(ah-'mahr)*
to lower	**bajar** *(bah-'hahr)*
to maintain	**mantener** *(mahn-teh-'nehr)*
to make	**hacer** *(ah-'sehr)*
to manage	**manejar** *(mah-neh-'hahr)*
to mark	**marcar** *(mahr-'kahr)*
to measure	**medir** *(meh-'deer)*
to mix	**mezclar** *(mehs-'klahr)*
to monitor	**controlar** *(kohn-troh-'lahr)*
to motivate	**motivar** *(moh-tee-'vahr)*
to move	**mover** *(moh-'vehr)*
to need	**necesitar** *(neh-seh-see-'tahr)*
to negotiate	**negociar** *(neh-goh-see-'ahr)*
to notice	**fijarse** *(fee-'hahr-seh)*
to notify	**notificar** *(noh-tee-fee-'kahr)*
to nurse	**criar** *(kree-'ahr)*
to obey	**obedecer** *(oh-beh-deh-'sehr)*
to observe	**observar** *(ohb-sehr-'vahr)*
to offer	**ofrecer** *(oh-freh-'sehr)*
to open	**abrir** *(ah-'breer)*
to organize	**organizar** *(ohr-gah-nee-'sahr)*
to overcome	**superar** *(soo-peh-'rahr)*
to paint	**pintar** *(peen-'tahr)*
to park	**estacionar** *(ehs-tah-see-'oh-nahr)*
to pass	**pasar** *(pah-'sahr)*
to pay	**pagar** *(pah-'gahr)*
to perceive	**percibir** *(pehr-see-'beer)*
to persuade	**persuadir** *(pehr-'swah-deer)*
to pick up	**recoger** *(reh-koh-'hehr)*
to pile	**amontonar** *(ah-mohn-toh-'nahr)*
to plan	**planear** *(plah-neh-'ahr)*
to plant	**plantar** *(plahn-'tahr)*
to play	**jugar** *(hoo-'gahr)*
to plug in	**enchufar** *(ehn-choo-'fahr)*
to practice	**practicar** *(prahk-tee-'kahr)*
to pray	**rezar** *(reh-'sahr)*
to preach	**predicar** *(preh-dee-'kahr)*
to prepare	**preparar** *(preh-pah-'rahr)*
to prescribe	**prescribir** *(prehs-kree-'beer)*
to press	**presionar** *(preh-see-oh-'nahr)*
to prevent	**prevenir** *(preh-veh-'neer)*
to process	**procesar** *(proh-seh-'sahr)*
to produce	**producir** *(proh-doo-'seer)*
to promise	**prometer** *(proh-meh-'tehr)*
to protect	**proteger** *(proh-teh-'hehr)*
to prove	**probar** *(proh-'bahr)*

to pull	**jalar** *(ahh-'lahr)*
to punish	**castigar** *(kahs-tee-'gahr)*
to purify	**purificar** *(poo-ree-fee-'kahr)*
to push	**empujar** *(ehm-poo-'hahr)*
to put	**poner** *(poh-'nehr)*
to put away	**guardar** *(gwahr-'dahr)*
to put in	**meter** *(meh-'tehr)*
to rain	**llover** *(yoh-'vehr)*
to reach	**alcanzar** *(ahl-kahn-'sahr)*
to read	**leer** *(leh-'ehr)*
to receive	**recibir** *(reh-see-'beer)*
to recognize	**reconocer** *(reh-koh-noh-'sehr)*
to recommend	**recomendar** *(reh-koh-mehn-'dahr)*
to record	**documentar** *(doh-koo-mehn-'tahr)*
to recuperate	**recuperar** *(reh-koo-peh-'rahr)*
to reinforce	**reforzar** *(reh-fohr-'sahr)*
to reject	**rechazar** *(reh-chah-'sahr)*
to relieve	**aliviar** *(ah-lee-vee-'ahr)*
to remember	**recordar** *(reh-kohr-'dahr)*
to remove	**sacar** *(sah-'kahr)*
to rent	**alquilar** *(ahl-kee-'lahr)*
to repair	**reparar** *(reh-pah-'rahr)*
to repeat	**repetir** *(reh-peh-'teer)*
to replace	**reemplazar** *(reh-ehm-plah-'sahr)*
to represent	**representar** *(reh-preh-sehn-'tahr)*
to reproduce	**reproducir** *(reh-proh-doo-'seer)*
to rescue	**rescatar** *(rehs-kah-'tahr)*
to resolve	**resolver** *(reh-sohl-'vehr)*
to respect	**respetar** *(rehs-peh-'tahr)*
to rest	**descansar** *(dehs-kahn-'sahr)*
to restrain	**restringir** *(rehs-treen-'heer)*
to return	**regresar** *(reh-greh-'sahr)*
to review	**repasar** *(reh-pah-'sahr)*
to reward	**recompensar** *(reh-kohm-pehn-'sahr)*
to ride	**montar** *(mohn-'tahr)*
to roll	**rodar** *(roh-'dahr)*
to run	**correr** *(koh-'rrehr)*
to sand	**limar** *(lee-'mahr)*
to save	**ahorrar** *(ah-oh-'rrahr)*
to scrub	**fregar** *(freh-'gahr)*
to search	**registrar** *(reh-hees-'trahr)*
to see	**ver** *(vehr)*
to send	**enviar** *(ehn-vee-'ahr)*
to serve	**servir** *(sehr-'veer)*
to shake	**sacudir** *(sah-koo-'deer)*
to share	**compartir** *(kohm-pahr-'teer)*
to shave oneself	**afeitarse** *(ah-feh-ee-'tahr-seh)*
to show	**mostrar** *(mohs-'trahr)*
to sign	**firmar** *(feer-'mahr)*
to sit	**sentarse** *(sehn-'tahr-seh)*
to sleep	**dormir** *(dohr-'meer)*
to smoke	**fumar** *(foo-'mahr)*
to snow	**nevar** *(neh-'vahr)*
to sow	**sembrar** *(sehm-'brahr)*
to speak	**hablar** *(ah-'blahr)*
to spend	**gastar** *(gahs-'tahr)*
to spray	**rociar** *(roh-see-'ahr)*
to stand	**pararse** *(pah-'rahr-seh)*

to stay	**quedarse** *(keh-'dahr-seh)*
to stop	**parar** *(pah-'rahr)*
to struggle	**esforzarse** *(ehs-fohr-'sahr-seh)*
to study	**estudiar** *(ehs-too-dee-'ahr)*
to suffer	**sufrir** *(soo-'freer)*
to suggest	**sugerir** *(soo-heh-'reer)*
to support	**apoyar** *(ah-poh-'yahr)*
to suspend	**suspender** *(soos-pehn-'dehr)*
to sweep	**barrer** *(bah-'rrehr)*
to take	**tomar** *(toh-'mahr)*
to take away	**quitar** *(kee-'tahr)*
to take care	**cuidar** *(kwee-'dahr)*
to tease	**burlarse** *(boor-'lahr-seh)*
to tell	**decir** *(deh-'seer)*
to test	**examinar** *(ehk-sah-mee-'nahr)*
to thank	**agradecer** *(ah-grah-deh-'sehr)*
to think	**pensar** *(pehn-'sahr)*
to throw	**tirar** *(tee-'rahr)*
to throw away	**botar** *(boh-'tahr)*
to touch	**tocar** *(toh-'kahr)*
to transfer	**transferir** *(trahns-feh-'reer)*
to transform	**transformar** *(trahns-fohr-'mahr)*
to transplant	**trasplantar** *(trahs-plahn-'tahr)*
to trim	**podar** *(poh-'dahr)*
to trip	**tropezar** *(troh-peh-sahr)*
to try	**tratar** *(trah-tahr)*
to turn	**dar vuelta** *(dahr voo-'ehl-tah)*
to turn off	**apagar** *(ah-pah-'gahr)*
to turn on	**prender** *(prehn-'dehr)*
to understand	**entender** *(ehn-tehn-'dehr)*
to undress oneself	**desvestirse** *(dehs-vehs-'teer-seh)*
to unload	**descargar** *(dehs-kahr-'gahr)*
to unplug	**desenchufar** *(dehs-ehn-choo-'fahr)*
to use	**usar** *(oo-'sahr)*
to vacuum	**aspirar** *(ahs-pee-'rahr)*
to verify	**verificar** *(veh-ree-fee-'kahr)*
to visit	**visitar** *(vee-see-'tahr)*
to vote	**votar** *(voh-'tahr)*
to wait	**esperar** *(ehs-peh-'rahr)*
to wake up	**despertarse** *(dehs-pehr-'tahr-seh)*
to walk	**caminar** *(kah-mee-'nahr)*
to wash oneself	**lavarse** *(lah-'vahr-seh)*
to water	**regar** *(reh-'gahr)*
to wax	**encerar** *(ehn-seh-'rahr)*
to weigh	**pesar** *(peh-'sahr)*
to weld	**soldar** *(sohl-'dahr)*
to win	**ganar** *(gah-'nahr)*
to withdraw	**sacar** *(sah-'kahr)*
to work	**trabajar** *(trah-bah-'hahr)*
to wrestle	**luchar** *(loo-'chahr)*
to write	**escribir** *(ehs-kree-'beer)*
to yell	**gritar** *(gree-'tahr)*

Spanish—English Verb List

Memorize any verb that you need, highlight those of secondary importance. Be sure to pronounce each syllable correctly:

abrir *(ah-'breer)*	to open
aceptar *(ah-sehp-'tahr)*	to accept
aclarar *(ah-klah-'rahr)*	to clarify
acomodar *(ah-koh-moh-'dahr)*	to accommodate
acompañar *(ah-kohm-pahn-'yahr)*	to accompany
aconsejar *(ah-kohn-seh-'hahr)*	to counsel
acumular *(ah-koo-moo-'lahr)*	to accrue
adaptar *(ah-dahp-'tahr)*	to adapt
afeitarse *(ah-feh-ee-'tahr-seh)*	to shave oneself
agarrar *(ah-gah-'rrahr)*	to grab
agradecer *(ah-grah-deh-'sehr)*	to thank
ahorrar *(ah-oh-'rrahr)*	to save
ajustar *(ah-hoos-'tahr)*	to adjust
alabar *(ah-lah-'bahr)*	to commend
alcanzar *(ahl-kahn-'sahr)*	to reach
alimentar *(ah-lee-mehn-'tahr)*	to feed
aliviar *(ah-lee-vee-'ahr)*	to relieve
alquilar *(ahl-kee-'lahr)*	to rent
amar *(ah-'mahr)*	to love
amontonar *(ah-mohn-toh-'nahr)*	to pile
añadir *(ahn-yah-'deer)*	to add
analizar *(ah-nah-lee-sahr)*	to analyze
animar *(ah-nee-'mahr)*	to encourage
antagonizar *(ahn-tah-goh-nee-'sahr)*	to antagonize
apagar *(ah-pah-'gahr)*	to turn off
apoyar *(ah-poh-'yahr)*	to support
apreciar *(ah-preh-see-'ahr)*	to appreciate
aprender *(ah-prehn-'dehr)*	to learn
aprobar *(ah-proh-'bahr)*	to approve
apurarse *(ah-poo-'rahr-seh)*	to hurry oneself
archivar *(ahr-chee-'vahr)*	to file
armar *(ahr-'mahr)*	to assemble
arreglar *(ah-rreh-'glahr)*	to arrange
arreglar *(ah-rreh-'glahr)*	to fix
asegurar *(ah-seh-goo-'rahr)*	to assure
asistir *(ah-sees-'teer)*	to attend
aspirar *(ahs-pee-'rahr)*	to vacuum
autorizar *(ow-toh-ree-'sahr)*	to authorize
averiguar *(ah-veh-ree-'gwahr)*	to check
ayudar *(ah-yoo-'dahr)*	to help
bajar *(bah-'hahr)*	to lower
bañarse *(bahn-'yahr-seh)*	to bathe oneself
barrer *(bah-'rrehr)*	to sweep
beber, tomar *(beh-'behr, toh-'mahr)*	to drink
botar *(boh-'tahr)*	to throw away
bromear *(broh-meh-'ahr)*	to joke
burlarse *(boor-'lahr-seh)*	to tease

buscar *(boos-'kahr)* — to look for
caer *(kah-'ehr)* — to fall
calcular *(kahl-koo-'lahr)* — to calculate
calentar *(kah-lehn-'tahr)* — to heat
cambiar *(kahm-bee-'ahr)* — to change
caminar *(kah-mee-'nahr)* — to walk
cancelar *(kahn-seh-'lahr)* — to cancel
cargar *(kahr-'gahr)* — to load
castigar *(kahs-tee-'gahr)* — to punish
cerrar *(seh-'rrahr)* — to close
cerrar con llave *(seh-'rrahr kohn 'yah-veh)* — to lock
cobrar *(koh-'brahr)* — to charge
colgar *(kohl-'gahr)* — to hang
comer *(koh-'mehr)* — to eat
compartir *(kohm-pahr-'teer)* — to share
comprometer *(kohm-proh-meh-'tehr)* — to compromise
comprometerse *(kohm-proh-meh-'tehr-seh)* — to commit oneself
comunicar *(koh-moo-nee-'kahr)* — to communicate
conectar *(koh-nehk-'tahr)* — to connect
confirmar *(kohn-feer-'mahr)* — to confirm
confortar *(kohn-fohr-'tahr)* — to comfort
conocer *('koh-noh-'sehr)* — to know (person)
conseguir *(kohn-seh-'geer)* — to get
construir *(kohns-troo-'eer)* — to build
consultar *(kohn-sool-'tahr)* — to consult
contar *(kohn-'tahr)* — to count
contestar *(kohn-tehs-'tahr)* — to answer
continuar *(kohn-teen-'wahr)* — to continue
contratar *(kohn-trah-'tahr)* — to hire
contribuir *(kohn-tree-'bweer)* — to contribute
controlar *(kohn-troh-'lahr)* — to monitor
conversar *(kohn-vehr-'sahr)* — to converse
cooperar *(koh-oh-peh-'rahr)* — to cooperate
coordinar *(koh-ohr-dee-'nahr)* — to coordinate
corregir *(koh-rreh-'heer)* — to correct
correr *(koh-'rrehr)* — to run
cortar *(kohr-'tahr)* — to cut
cosechar *(koh-seh-'chahr)* — to harvest
costar *(kohs-'tahr)* — to cost
crecer *(kreh-'sehr)* — to grow
creer *(kreh-'ehr)* — to believe
criar *(kree-'ahr)* — to nurse
cubrir *(koo-'breer)* — to cover
cuidar *(kwee-'dahr)* — to take care
cultivar *(kool-tee-'vahr)* — to cultivate
cumplir *(koom-'pleer)* — to carry out
curar *(koo-'rahr)* — to cure
dar *(dahr)* — to give
dar vuelta *(dahr voo-'ehl-tah)* — to turn
debatir *(deh-bah-'teer)* — to debate
decir *(deh-'seer)* — to tell
defender *(deh-fehn-'dehr)* — to defend
dejar *(deh-'hahr)* — to let
demandar *(deh-mahn-'dahr)* — to demand
demostrar *(deh-mohs-'trahr)* — to demonstrate
depositar *(deh-poh-see-'tahr)* — to deposit
desarrollar *(deh-sah-rroh-'yahr)* — to develop
descansar *(dehs-kahn-'sahr)* — to rest

descargar *(dehs-kahr-'gahr)*	to unload
desenchufar *(dehs-ehn-choo-'fahr)*	to unplug
despertarse *(dehs-pehr-'tahr-seh)*	to wake up
desvestirse *(dehs-vehs-'teer-seh)*	to undress oneself
detectar *(deh-tehk-'tahr)*	to detect
dirigir *(dee-ree-'heer)*	to lead
discutir *(dees-koo-'teer)*	to argue
distribuir *(dees-tree-'bweer)*	to distribute
divertirse *(dee-vehr-'teer-seh)*	to enjoy oneself
doblar *(doh-'blahr)*	to bend
documentar *(doh-koo-mehn-'tahr)*	to record
donar *(doh-'nahr)*	to donate
dormir *(dohr-'meer)*	to sleep
empezar *(ehm-peh-'sahr)*	to begin
empujar *(ehm-poo-'hahr)*	to push
encerar *(ehn-seh-'rahr)*	to wax
enchufar *(ehn-choo-'fahr)*	to plug in
encontrar *(ehn-kohn-'trahr)*	to find
enfocar *(ehn-foh-'kahr)*	to focus
entender *(ehn-tehn-'dehr)*	to understand
entrar *(ehn-'trahr)*	to enter
enviar *(ehn-vee-'ahr)*	to send
esconder *(ehs-kohn-'dehr)*	to hide
escribir *(ehs-kree-'beer)*	to write
escuchar *(ehs-koo-'chahr)*	to listen
esforzarse *(ehs-fohr-'sahr-seh)*	to struggle
esperar *(ehs-peh-'rahr)*	to wait
establecer *(ehs-tah-bleh-'sehr)*	to establish
estacionar *(ehs-tah-see-'oh-nahr)*	to park
estudiar *(ehs-too-dee-'ahr)*	to study
evaluar *(eh-vah-loo-ahr)*	to evaluate
examinar *(ehk-sah-mee-'nahr)*	to test
excavar *(ehks-kah-'vahr)*	to dig
exhibir *(ehks-ee-'beer)*	to exhibit
explicar *(ehks-plee-'kahr)*	to explain
explotar *(ehks-ploh-'tahr)*	to exploit
fallar *(fah-'yahr)*	to fail
felicitar *(feh-lee-see-'tahr)*	to compliment
fijarse *(fee-'hahr-seh)*	to notice
firmar *(feer-'mahr)*	to sign
fregar *(freh-'gahr)*	to scrub
fumar *(foo-'mahr)*	to smoke
ganar *(gah-'nahr)*	to earn
ganar *(gah-'nahr)*	to win
garantizar *(gah-rahn-tee-'sahr)*	to guarantee
gastar *(gahs-'tahr)*	to spend
golpear *(gohl-peh-'ahr)*	to beat up
gritar *(gree-'tahr)*	to yell
guardar *(gwahr-'dahr)*	to put away
guardar *(gwahr-'dahr)*	to keep
hablar *(ah-'blahr)*	to speak
hacer *(ah-'sehr)*	to do
hacer *(ah-'sehr)*	to make
identificar *(ee-dehn-tee-fee-'kahr)*	to identify
inmunizar *(een-moo-nee-'sahr)*	to immunize
inspeccionar *(eens-pehk-see-oh-'nahr)*	to inspect
instalar *(eens-tah-'lahr)*	to install
intercambiar *(een-tehr-kahm-bee-'ahr)*	to exchange

interferir *(een-tehr-feh-'reer)*	to interfere
intervenir *(een-tehr-veh-'neer)*	to intervene
invertir *(een-vehr-'teer)*	to invest
ir *(eer)*	to go
jalar *(ahh-'lahr)*	to pull
jugar *(hoo-'gahr)*	to play
juntar *(hoon-'tahr)*	to join
lavarse *(lah-'vahr-seh)*	to wash oneself
leer *(leh-'ehr)*	to read
levantar *(leh-vahn-'tahr)*	to lift
levantarse *(leh-vahn-'tahr-seh)*	to get up
limar *(lee-'mahr)*	to sand
limpiar *(leem-pee-'ahr)*	to clean
llamar *(yah-'mahr)*	to call
llegar *(yeh-'gahr)*	to arrive
llenar *(yeh-'nahr)*	to fill
llevar *(yeh-'vahr)*	to carry
llorar *(yoh-'rahr)*	to cry
llover *(yoh-'vehr)*	to rain
lograr *(loh-'grahr)*	to achieve
luchar *(loo-'chahr)*	to wrestle
maldecir *(mahl-deh-'seer)*	to curse
manejar *(mah-neh-'hahr)*	to manage
manejar *(mah-neh-'hahr)*	to drive
mantener *(mahn-teh-'nehr)*	to maintain
marcar *(mahr-'kahr)*	to mark
matar *(mah-'tahr)*	to kill
matricular *(mah-tree-koo-'lahr)*	to enroll
medir *(meh-'deer)*	to measure
mejorar *(meh-hoh-'rahr)*	to improve
mentir *(mehn-'teer)*	to lie
meter *(meh-'tehr)*	to put in
mezclar *(mehs-'klahr)*	to mix
mirar *(mee-'rahr)*	to look
molestar *(moh-lehs-'tahr)*	to bother
montar *(mohn-'tahr)*	to ride
morder *(mohr-'dehr)*	to bite
morir *(moh-'reer)*	to die
mostrar *(mohs-'trahr)*	to show
motivar *(moh-tee-'vahr)*	to motivate
mover *(moh-'vehr)*	to move
necesitar *(neh-seh-see-'tahr)*	to need
negar *(neh-'gahr)*	to deny
negociar *(neh-goh-see-'ahr)*	to negotiate
nevar *(neh-'vahr)*	to snow
nivelar *(nee-veh-'lahr)*	to level
notificar *(noh-tee-fee-'kahr)*	to notify
obedecer *(oh-beh-deh-'sehr)*	to obey
observar *(ohb-sehr-'vahr)*	to observe
ofrecer *(oh-freh-'sehr)*	to offer
oír *(oh-'eer)*	to hear
organizar *(ohr-gah-nee-'sahr)*	to organize
pagar *(pah-'gahr)*	to pay
parar *(pah-'rahr)*	to stop
pararse *(pah-'rahr-seh)*	to stand
pasar *(pah-'sahr)*	to pass
patear *(pah-teh-'ahr)*	to kick
pedir *(peh-'deer)*	to ask

pedir prestado *(peh-'deer prehs-'tah-doh)*	to borrow
pegar *(peh-'gahr)*	to glue
pegar *(peh-'gahr)*	to hit
pelear *(peh-leh-'ahr)*	to fight
pensar *(pehn-'sahr)*	to think
percibir *(pehr-see-'beer)*	to perceive
perder *(pehr-'dehr)*	to lose
perdonar *(pehr-doh-'nahr)*	to forgive
permitir *(pehr-mee-'teer)*	to allow
persuadir *(pehr-'swah-deer)*	to persuade
pesar *(peh-'sahr)*	to weigh
pintar *(peen-'tahr)*	to paint
planear *(plah-neh-'ahr)*	to plan
plantar *(plahn-'tahr)*	to plant
podar *(poh-'dahr)*	to trim
poner *(poh-'nehr)*	to put
practicar *(prahk-tee-'kahr)*	to practice
predicar *(preh-dee-'kahr)*	to preach
preguntar *(preh-goon-'tahr)*	to ask
prender *(prehn-'dehr)*	to turn on
preparar *(preh-pah-'rahr)*	to prepare
prescribir *(prehs-kree-'beer)*	to prescribe
presionar *(preh-see-oh-'nahr)*	to press
prestar *(prehs-'tahr)*	to loan
prevenir *(preh-veh-'neer)*	to prevent
probar *(proh-'bahr)*	to prove
procesar *(proh-seh-'sahr)*	to process
producir *(proh-doo-'seer)*	to produce
prometer *(proh-meh-'tehr)*	to promise
proteger *(proh-teh-'hehr)*	to protect
purificar *(poo-ree-fee-'kahr)*	to purify
quedarse *(keh-'dahr-seh)*	to stay
quejarse *(keh-'hahr-seh)*	to complain
quitar *(kee-'tahr)*	to take away
rebotar *(reh-boh-'tahr)*	to bounce
rechazar *(reh-chah-'sahr)*	to reject
recibir *(reh-see-'beer)*	to receive
recoger *(reh-koh-'hehr)*	to gather
recoger *(reh-koh-'hehr)*	to pick up
recolectar *(reh-koh-lehk-'tahr)*	to collect
recomendar *(reh-koh-mehn-'dahr)*	to recommend
recompensar *(reh-kohm-pehn-'sahr)*	to reward
reconocer *(reh-koh-noh-'sehr)*	to recognize
recordar *(reh-kohr-'dahr)*	to remember
recuperar *(reh-koo-peh-'rahr)*	to recuperate
reemplazar *(reh-ehm-plah-'sahr)*	to replace
reforzar *(reh-fohr-'sahr)*	to reinforce
regalar *(reh-gah-'lahr)*	to give away
regar *(reh-'gahr)*	to water
registrar *(reh-hees-'trahr)*	to search
regresar *(reh-greh-'sahr)*	to return
reír *(reh-'eer)*	to laugh
reparar *(reh-pah-'rahr)*	to repair
repartir *(reh-pahr-'teer)*	to deliver
repasar *(reh-pah-'sahr)*	to review
repetir *(reh-peh-'teer)*	to repeat
representar *(reh-preh-sehn-'tahr)*	to represent
reproducir *(reh-proh-doo-'seer)*	to reproduce

rescatar *(rehs-kah-'tahr)*	to rescue
resolver *(reh-sohl-'vehr)*	to resolve
respetar *(rehs-peh-'tahr)*	to respect
restringir *(rehs-treen-'heer)*	to restrain
rezar *(reh-'sahr)*	to pray
rociar *(roh-see-'ahr)*	to spray
rodar *(roh-'dahr)*	to roll
romper *(rohm-'pehr)*	to break
saber *(sah-'behr)*	to know (something)
sacar *(sah-'kahr)*	to remove
sacar *(sah-'kahr)*	to withdraw
sacudir *(sah-koo-'deer)*	to shake
salir *(sah-'leer)*	to leave
saltar *(sahl-'tahr)*	to jump
sanar *(sah-'nahr)*	to heal
secar *(seh-'kahr)*	to dry
seguir *(seh-'geer)*	to follow
sembrar *(sehm-'brahr)*	to sow
sentarse *(sehn-'tahr-seh)*	to sit
ser/estar *(sehr, ehs-'tahr)*	to be
servir *(sehr-'veer)*	to serve
sobrepasar *(soh-breh-pah-'sahr)*	to exceed
soldar *(sohl-'dahr)*	to weld
subir *(soo-'beer)*	to climb
sufrir *(soo-'freer)*	to suffer
sugerir *(soo-heh-'reer)*	to suggest
superar *(soo-peh-'rahr)*	to overcome
suspender *(soos-pehn-'dehr)*	to suspend
taladrar *(tah-lah-'drahr)*	to drill
tener/haber *(teh-'nehr, ah-'behr)*	to have
terminar *(tehr-mee-'nahr)*	to finish
tirar *(tee-'rahr)*	to throw
tocar *(toh-'kahr)*	to touch
tomar *(toh-'mahr)*	to take
trabajar *(trah-bah-'hahr)*	to work
traer *(trah-'ehr)*	to bring
transferir *(trahns-feh-'reer)*	to transfer
transformar *(trahns-fohr-'mahr)*	to transform
trasplantar *(trahs-plahn-'tahr)*	to transplant
tratar *(trah-tahr)*	to try
tropezar *(troh-peh-sahr)*	to trip
unir *(oo-'neer)*	to attach
usar *(oo-'sahr)*	to use
vaciar *(vah-see-'ahr)*	to empty
vencer *(vehn-'sehr)*	to expire
venir *(veh-'neer)*	to come
ver *(vehr)*	to see
verificar *(veh-ree-fee-'kahr)*	to verify
vestirse *(vehs-'teer-seh)*	to dress oneself
visitar *(vee-see-'tahr)*	to visit
vivir *(vee-'veer)*	to live
votar *(voh-'tahr)*	to vote

English-Spanish Glossary

The gender of nouns is indicated by the use of the articles **el** ("the," masc.) or **la** ("the," fem.). When the noun can be both feminine and masculine (**el artista, la artista**), this is indicated by the combination "**el/la**."

Most Spanish adjectives and pronouns are either masculine or feminine; for example, "a bad boy" is **un niño malo**, whereas "a bad girl" is **una niña mala**. Simplicity and space constraints rule out having both masculine and feminine forms here; instead, we present the masculine form only, with the understanding that you should change the **-o** ending to an **-a** ending in order to change to the feminine form. Exceptions to this rule (**el lápiz azul, la casa azul**) are handled by indicating "masc. & fem." after the word.

a (fem.)	una	*('oo-nah)*
a (masc.)	un	*(oon)*
a (fem. pl.)	unas	*('oo-nahs)*
a (masc. pl.)	unos	*('oo-nohs)*
A.M.	de la mañana	*(deh lah mahn-'yah-nah)*
abortion	aborto, el	*(ehl ah-'bohr-toh)*
above	encima	*(ehn-'see-mah)*
abuse	abuso, el	*(ehl ah-'boo-soh)*
acquaintance	compañero, el	*(ehl kohm-pahn-'yeh-roh)*
addict	adicto, el	*(ehl ah-'deek-toh)*
addiction	adicción, la	*(lah ah-deek-see-'ohn)*
address	dirección, la	*(lah dee-rehk-see-'ohn)*
administrator	administrador, el	*(ehl ahd-mee-nees-trah-'dohr)*
adoption	adopción, la	*(lah ah-dohp-see-'ohn)*
advice	consejos, los	*(lohs kohn-'seh-hohs)*
after	después	*(dehs-'pwehs)*
again	otra vez	*('oh-trah vehs)*
age	edad, la	*(lah eh-'dahd)*
agency	agencia, la	*(lah ah-'hehn-see-ah)*
AIDS	SIDA, el	*(ehl 'see-dah)*
airport	aeropuerto, el	*(ehl ah-eh-roh-'pwehr-toh)*
alarm	alarma, la	*(lah ah-'lahr-mah)*
alcohol	alcohol, el	*(ehl ahl-koh-'ohl)*
all	todos	*('toh-dohs)*
alphabet	alfabeto, el	*(ehl ahl-fah-'beh-toh)*
already	ya	*(yah)*

always	siempre	*(see-'ehm-preh)*
ambitious	ambicioso	*(ahm-bee-see-'oh-soh)*
amount	cantidad, la	*(lah kahn-tee-'dahd)*
angel	ángel, el	*(ehl 'ahn-hehl)*
angry	molesto	*(moh-'lehs-toh)*
ankle	tobillo, el	*(ehl toh-'bee-yoh)*
anniversary	aniversario, el	*(ehl ah-nee-vehr-'sah-ree-oh)*
answer	respuesta, la	*(lah rehs-'pwehs-tah)*
ant	hormiga, la	*(lah ohr-'mee-gah)*
anxious	ansioso	*(ahn-see-'oh-soh)*
anyone	cualquiera	*(kwahl-kee-'eh-rah)*
anything	cualquier cosa	*(kwahl-kee-'ehr 'koh-sah)*
anywhere	en cualquier parte	*(ehn kwahl-kee-'ehr 'pahr-teh)*
apartment	apartamento, el	*(ehl ah-pahr-tah-'mehn-toh)*
apple	manzana, la	*(lah mahn-'sah-nah)*
appliance	electrodoméstico, el	*(ehl eh-lehk-troh-doh-'mehs-tee-koh)*
application	solicitud, la	*(lah soh-lee-see-'tood)*
appointment	cita, la	*(lah 'see-tah)*
April	abril	*(ah-'breel)*
apron	delantal, el	*(ehl deh-lahn-'tahl)*
architect	arquitecto, el	*(ehl ahr-kee-'tehk-toh)*
area	área, el	*(ehl 'ah-reh-ah)*
argument	argumento, el	*(ehl ahr-goo-'mehn-toh)*
arm	brazo, el	*(ehl 'brah-soh)*
armchair	sillón, el	*(ehl see-'yohn)*
around	alrededor	*(ahl-reh-deh-'dohr)*
arrow	flecha, la	*(lah 'fleh-chah)*
article	artículo, el	*(ehl ahr-'tee-koo-loh)*
artist	artista, el/la	*(ehl, lah ahr-'tees-tah)*
assistance	asistencia, la	*(lah ah-sees-'tehn-see-ah)*
assistant	asistente, el	*(ehl ah-sees-'tehn-teh)*
associate	asociado, el	*(ehl ah-soh-see-'ah-doh)*
association	asociación, la	*(lah ah-soh-see-ah-see-'ohn)*
at	en	*(ehn)*
attendance	asistencia, la	*(lah ah-sees-'tehn-see-ah)*
attic	desván, el	*(ehl dehs-'vahn)*
attitude	actitud, la	*(lah ahk-tee-'tood)*
August	agosto	*(ah-'gohs-toh)*
aunt	tía, la	*(lah 'tee-ah)*
author	autor, el	*(ehl ow-'tohr)*
available	disponible	*(dees-poh-'nee-bleh)*
average	promedio, el	*(ehl proh-'meh-dee-oh)*
awake	despierto	*(dehs-pee-'ehr-toh)*
baby	bebé, el/la	*(ehl, lah beh-'beh)*
babysitter	niñero, el	*(ehl neen-'yeh-roh)*
back	espalda, la	*(lah ehs-'pahl-dah)*
bacon	tocino, el	*(ehl toh-'see-noh)*

bad	mal	*(mahl)*
ball	pelota, la	*(lah peh-'loh-tah)*
banana	plátano, el	*(ehl 'plah-tah-noh)*
bank	banco, el	*(ehl 'bahn-koh)*
banquet	banquete, el	*(ehl bahn-'keh-teh)*
baptism	bautismo, el	*(ehl bow-'tees-moh)*
bar	bar, el	*(ehl bahr)*
bargain	ganga, la	*(lah 'gahn-gah)*
barn	granero, el	*(ehl grah-'neh-roh)*
bartender	cantinero, el	*(ehl kahn-tee-'neh-roh)*
basement	sótano, el	*(ehl 'soh-tah-noh)*
basketball	baloncesto, el	*(ehl bah-lohn-'sehs-toh*
bathing suit	traje de baño, el	*(ehl 'trah-heh deh 'bahn-yoh)*
bathrobe	bata de baño, la	*(lah 'bah-tah deh 'bahn-yoh)*
bathroom	cuarto de baño, el	*(ehl 'kwahr-toh deh 'bahn-yoh)*
bathtub	tina, la	*(lah 'tee-nah)*
battery	batería, la	*(lah bah-teh-'ree-ah)*
beach	playa, la	*(lah 'plah-yah)*
beans	frijoles, los	*(lohs free-'hoh-lehs)*
bear	oso, el	*(ehl 'oh-soh)*
beautiful	bello	*('beh-yoh)*
beauty salon	salón de belleza, el	*(ehl sah-'lohn deh beh-'yeh-sah)*
bed	cama, la	*(lah 'kah-mah)*
bedroom	dormitorio, el	*(ehl dohr-mee-'toh-ree-oh)*
bee	abeja, la	*(lah ah-'beh-hah)*
beef	carne, la	*(lah 'kahr-neh)*
beer	cerveza, la	*(lah sehr-'veh-sah)*
beetle	escarabajo, el	*ehl ehs-kah-rah-'bah-hoh)*
before	antes	*('ahn-tehs)*
behavior	comportamiento, el	*(ehl kohm-pohr-tah-mee-'ehn-toh)*
behind	detrás	*(deh-'trahs)*
belief	creencia, la	*(lah kreh-'ehn-see-ah)*
believer	creyente, el/la	*(ehl, lah kreh-'yehn-teh)*
bellhop	botones, el/la	*(ehl, lah boh-'toh-nehs)*
belt	correa, la	*(lah koh-'rreh-ah)*
bench	banco, el	*(ehl 'bahn-koh)*
better	mejor	*(meh-'hohr)*
between	entre	*('ehn-treh)*
Bible	Biblia, la	*(lah 'bee-blee-ah)*
bicycle	bicicleta, la	*(lah bee-see-'kleh-tah)*
big	grande	*('grahn-deh)*
bill	cuenta, la	*(lah 'kwehn-tah)*
billboard	letrero, el	*(ehl leh-'treh-roh)*
billfold	billetera, la	*(lah bee-yeh-'teh-rah)*
bird	pájaro, el	*(ehl 'pah-hah-roh)*
birth	nacimiento, el	*(ehl nah-see-mee-'ehn-toh)*
birthday	cumpleaños, el	*(ehl koom-pleh-'ahn-yohs)*

black	negro	*('neh-groh)*
blanket	cobija, la	*(lah koh-'bee-hah)*
bleach	blanqueador, el	*(ehl blahn-keh-ah-'dohr)*
blessing	bendición, la	*(lah behn-dee-see-'ohn)*
blind	ciego	*(see-'eh-goh)*
blind person	el ciego	*(ehl see-'eh-goh)*
blood	sangre, la	*(lah 'sahn-greh)*
blouse	blusa, la	*(lah 'bloo-sah)*
blue	azul (masc. & fem.)	*(ah-'sool)*
body	cuerpo, el	*(ehl 'kwehr-poh)*
bomb	bomba, la	*(lah 'bohm-bah)*
book	libro, el	*(ehl 'lee-broh)*
bookshelf	librero, el	*(ehl lee-'breh-roh)*
bookstore	librería, la	*(lah lee-breh-'ree-ah)*
boots	botas, las	*(lahs 'boh-tahs)*
border	frontera, la	*(lah frohn-'teh-rah)*
bored	aburrido	*(ah-boo-'rree-doh)*
boss	jefe, el	*(ehl 'heh-feh)*
boss	patrón, el	*(ehl pah-'trohn)*
bottom	fondo, el	*(ehl 'fohn-doh)*
bowl	plato hondo, el	*(ehl 'plah-toh 'ohn-doh)*
box	caja, la	*(lah 'kah-hah)*
boy	niño, el	*(ehl 'neen-yoh)*
boyfriend	novio, el	*(ehl 'noh-vee-oh)*
brain	cerebro, el	*(ehl seh-'reh-broh)*
brakes	frenos, los	*(lohs 'freh-nohs)*
brand	marca, la	*(lah 'mahr-kah)*
brassiere	sostén, el	*(ehl sohs-'tehn)*
brave	valiente (masc. & fem.)	*(vah-lee-'ehn-teh)*
bread	pan, el	*(ehl pahn)*
breakfast	desayuno, el	*(ehl deh-sah-'yoo-noh)*
brick	ladrillo, el	*(ehl lah-'dree-yoh)*
bridge	puente, el	*(ehl 'pwehn-teh)*
bright	despierto	*(dehs-pee-'ehr-toh)*
brochure	folleto, el	*(ehl foh-'yeh-toh)*
broken	roto	*('roh-toh)*
broom	escoba, la	*(lah ehs-'koh-bah)*
broth	caldo, el	*(ehl 'kahl-doh)*
brother	hermano, el	*(ehl ehr-'mah-noh)*
brown	café (masc. & fem.)	*(kah-'feh)*
bruise	contusión, la	*(lah kohn-too-see-'ohn)*
brunette	morena	*(moh-'reh-nah)*
brush	cepillo, el	*(ehl seh-'pee-yoh)*
bucket	balde, el	*(ehl 'bahl-deh)*
bugs	insectos, los	*(lohs een-'sehk-tohs)*
building	edificio, el	*(ehl eh-dee-'fee-see-oh)*
bulldozer	niveladora, la	*(lah nee-veh-lah-'doh-rah)*

burned	quemado	*(keh-'mah-doh)*
bus	autobús, el	*(ehl ow-toh-'boos)*
bus station	estación de autobús, la	*(lah ehs-tah-see-'ohn deh ow-toh-'boos)*
bus stop	parada de autobús, la	*(lah pah-'rah-dah deh ow-toh-'boos)*
bush	arbusto, el	*(ehl ahr-'boos-toh)*
business	negocio, el	*(ehl neh-'goh-see-oh)*
busy	ocupado	*(oh-koo-'pah-doh)*
butter	mantequilla, la	*(lah mahn-teh-'kee-yah)*
button	botón, el	*(ehl boh-'tohn)*
cabbage	repollo, el	*(ehl reh-'poh-yoh)*
cabinet	gabinete, el	*(ehl gah-bee-'neh-teh)*
cafeteria	cafetería, la	*(lah kah-feh-teh-'ree-ah)*
cage	jaula, la	*(lah 'how-lah)*
cake	torta, la	*(lah 'tohr-tah)*
calendar	calendario, el	*(ehl kah-lehn-'dah-ree-oh)*
calm	calmado	*(kahl-'mah-doh)*
camera	cámara, la	*(lah 'kah-mah-rah)*
campgrounds	campamento, el	*(ehl kahm-pah-'mehn-toh)*
candle	vela, la	*(lah 'veh-lah)*
candy	dulce, el	*(ehl 'dool-seh)*
cane	bastón, el	*(ehl bahs-'tohn)*
cantaloupe	melón, el	*(ehl meh-'lohn)*
cap	gorra, la	*(lah 'goh-rrah)*
car	carro, el	*(ehl 'kah-rroh)*
car lot	lote de carros, el	*(ehl 'loh-teh deh 'kah-rrohs)*
card	tarjeta, la	*(lah tahr-'heh-tah)*
cardboard	cartón, el	*(ehl kahr-'tohn)*
care	cuidado, el	*(ehl 'kwee-dah-doh)*
carpenter	carpintero, el	*(ehl kahr-peen-'teh-roh)*
carpet	alfombra, la	*(lah ahl-'fohm-brah)*
carpeting	alfombrado, el	*(ehl ahl-fohm-'bra-doh)*
carrot	zanahoria, la	*(lah sah-nah-'oh-ree-ah)*
cart	carreta, la	*(lah kah-'rreh-tah)*
case	caso, el	*(ehl 'kah-soh)*
cash	efectivo, el	*(ehl eh-fehk-'tee-voh)*
cashier	cajero, el	*(ehl kah-'heh-roh)*
cat	gato, el	*(ehl 'gah-toh)*
catalogue	catálogo, el	*(ehl kah-'tah-loh-goh)*
cause	causa, la	*(lah 'kah-oo-sah)*
ceiling	cielo raso, el	*(ehl see-'eh-loh 'rah-soh)*
celebration	celebración, la	*(lah seh-leh-brah-see-'ohn)*
celery	apio, el	*(ehl 'ah-pee-oh)*
cement	cemento, el	*(ehl seh-'mehn-toh)*
cemetery	cementerio, el	*(ehl seh-mehn-'teh-ree-oh)*
center	centro, el	*(ehl 'sehn-troh)*
ceremony	ceremonia, la	*(lah seh-reh-'moh-nee-ah)*
chain	cadena, la	*(lah kah-'deh-nah)*

chair	silla, la	*(lah 'see-yah)*
chalkboard	pizarrón, el	*(ehl pee-sah-'rrohn)*
change	cambio, el	*(ehl 'kahm-bee-oh)*
chapel	capilla, la	*(lah kah-'pee-yah)*
charity	caridad, la	*(lah kah-ree-'dahd)*
cheap	barato	*(bah-'rah-toh)*
checks	cheques, los	*(lohs 'cheh-kehs)*
cheese	queso, el	*(ehl 'keh-soh)*
cherry	cereza, la	*(lah seh-'reh-sah)*
chest	pecho, el	*(ehl 'peh-choh)*
chest of drawers	cómoda, la	*(lah 'koh-moh-dah)*
chewing gum	chicle, el	*(ehl 'cheek-leh)*
chicken	pollo, el	*(ehl 'poh-yoh)*
chimney	chimenea, la	*(lah chee-meh-'neh-ah)*
choir	coro, el	*(ehl 'koh-roh)*
Christmas	Navidad, la	*(lah nah-vee-'dahd)*
church	iglesia, la	*(lah eey-'leh-see-ah)*
citizen	ciudadano, el	*(ehl see-oo-dah-'dah-noh)*
city	ciudad, la	*(lah see-oo-'dahd)*
city block	cuadra, la	*(lah 'kwah-drah)*
city hall	municipio, el	*(ehl moo-nee-'see-pee-oh)*
class	clase, la	*(lah 'klah-seh)*
classroom	salón de clase, el	*(ehl sah-'lohn deh 'klah-seh)*
clean	limpio	*('leem-pee-oh)*
clear	despejado	*(dehs-peh-'hah-doh)*
clerk	dependiente, el/la	*(ehl, lah deh-pehn-dee-'ehn-teh)*
client	cliente, el	*(ehl klee-'ehn-teh)*
clinic	clínica, la	*(lah 'klee-nee-kah)*
clock	reloj, el	*(ehl reh-'loh)*
closet	ropero, el	*(ehl roh-'peh-roh)*
cloth	tela, la	*(lah 'teh-lah)*
clothing	ropa, la	*(lah 'roh-pah)*
cloudy	nublado	*(noo-'blah-doh)*
club	club, el	*(ehl kloob)*
coach	entrenador, el	*(ehl ehn-treh-nah-'dohr)*
coal	carbón, el	*(ehl kahr-'bohn)*
coconut	coco, el	*(ehl 'koh-koh)*
code	código, el	*(ehl 'koh-dee-goh)*
coffee	café, el	*(ehl kah-'feh)*
coin	moneda, la	*(lah moh-'neh-dah)*
college	universidad, la	*(lah oo-nee-vehr-see-'dahd)*
cologne	colonia, la	*(lah koh-'loh-nee-ah)*
comb	peine, el	*(ehl 'peh-ee-neh)*
combination lock	candado, el	*(ehl kahn-'dah-doh)*
comfortable	cómodo	*('koh-moh-doh)*
committee	comité, el	*(ehl koh-mee-'teh)*
communion	comunión, la	*(lah koh-moo-nee-'ohn)*

community	comunidad, la	*(lah koh-moo-nee-'dahd)*
company	compañía, la	*(lah kohm-pah-'nee-ah)*
computer	computadora, la	*(lah kohm-poo-tah-'doh-rah)*
conditioner	acondicionador, el	*(ehl ah-kohn-dee-see-oh-nah-'dohr)*
condom	condón, el	*(ehl kohn-'dohn)*
conference	conferencia, la	*(lah kohn-feh-'rehn-see-ah)*
confession	confesión, la	*(lah kohn-feh-see-'ohn)*
confident	convencido	*(kohn-vehn-'see-doh)*
conflict	conflicto, el	*(ehl kohn-'fleek-toh)*
confused	confundido	*(kohn-foon-'dee-doh)*
congratulations	felicitaciones, las	*(lahs feh-lee-see-tah-see-'oh-nehs)*
congregation	congregación, la	*(lah kohn-greh-gah-see-'ohn)*
consultant	consultor, el	*(ehl kohn-sool-'tohr)*
content	contenido, el	*(ehl kohn-teh-'nee-doh)*
contract	contrato, el	*(ehl kohn-'trah-toh)*
contractor	contratista, el/la	*(ehl, lah kohn-trah-'tees-tah)*
contributions	contribuciones, las	*(lahs kohn-tree-boo-see-'oh-nehs)*
contributor	contribuyente, el/la	*(ehl, lah kohn-tree-boo-'yehn-teh)*
convalescent home	clínica de reposo, la	*(lah 'klee-nee-kah deh reh-'poh-soh)*
cook	cocinero, el	*(ehl koh-see-'neh-roh)*
cooked	cocinado	*(koh-see-'nah-doh)*
cookie	galleta, la	*(lah gah-'yeh-tah)*
cool	fresco	*('frehs-koh)*
coordinator	coordinador, el	*(ehl koh-ohr-dee-nah-'dohr)*
copy	copia, la	*(lah 'koh-pee-ah)*
corn	maíz, el	*(ehl mah-'ees)*
corner	esquina, la	*(lah ehs-'kee-nah)*
cosmetics	cosméticos, los	*(lohs kohs-'meh-tee-kohs)*
cost	costo, el	*(ehl 'kohs-toh)*
costume	disfraz, el	*(ehl dees-'frahs)*
cotton	algodón, el	*(ehl ahl-goh-'dohn)*
cough	tos, la	*(lah tohs)*
counseling	consejo, el	*(ehl kohn-'seh-hoh)*
counselor	consejero, el	*(ehl kohn-seh-'heh-roh)*
counter	mostrador, el	*(ehl mohs-trah-'dohr)*
county	condado, el	*(ehl kohn-'dah-doh)*
course	curso, el	*(ehl 'koor-soh)*
court	tribunal, el	*(ehl tree-boo-'nahl)*
courtesy	cortesía, la	*(lah kohr-teh-'see-ah)*
courtyard	patio, el	*(ehl 'pah-tee-oh)*
cousin	primo, el	*(ehl 'pree-moh)*
cow	vaca, la	*(lah 'vah-kah)*
crab	cangrejo, el	*(ehl kahn-'greh-hoh)*
cracker	galleta salada, la	*(lah gah-'yeh-tah sah-'lah-dah)*
cream	crema, la	*(lah 'kreh-mah)*
creation	creación, la	*(lah kreh-ah-see-'ohn)*
credit	crédito, el	*(ehl 'kreh-dee-toh)*

crew	tripulación, la	*(lah tree-poo-lah-see-'ohn)*
crib	cuna, la	*(lah 'koo-nah)*
crime	delito, el	*(ehl deh-'lee-toh)*
crop	cosecha, la	*(lah koh-'seh-chah)*
cross	cruz, la	*(lah kroos)*
crosswalk	cruce de peatones, el	*(ehl 'kroo-seh deh peh-ah-'toh-nehs)*
cruel	cruel (masc. & fem.)	*(kroo-'ehl)*
crutches	muletas, las	*(lahs moo-'leh-tahs)*
cucumber	pepino, el	*(ehl peh-'pee-noh)*
cup	taza, la	*(lah 'tah-sah)*
curtains	cortinas, las	*(lahs kohr-'tee-nahs)*
customer	cliente, el	*(ehl klee-'ehn-teh)*
customs	aduana, la	*(lah ah-'dwah-nah)*
cut	cortado	*(kohr-'tah-doh)*
damaged	dañado	*(dahn'yah-doh)*
dance	baile, el	*(ehl 'bah-ee-leh)*
dangerous	peligroso	*(peh-lee-'groh-soh)*
date	fecha, la	*(lah 'feh-chah)*
date of birth	fecha de nacimiento, la	*(lah 'feh-chah deh nah-see-mee-'ehn-toh)*
daughter	hija, la	*(lah 'ee-hah)*
day	día, el	*(ehl 'dee-ah)*
dead	muerto, el	*(ehl 'mwehr-toh)*
deaf	sordo	*('sohr-doh)*
death	muerte, la	*(lah 'mwehr-teh)*
debt	deuda, la	*(lah 'deh-oo-dah)*
December	diciembre	*(dee-see-'ehm-breh)*
deep	profundo	*(proh-'foon-doh)*
deer	venado, el	*(ehl veh-'nah-doh)*
degree	grado, el	*(ehl 'grah-doh)*
dehydrated	deshidratado	*(deh-see-drah-'tah-doh)*
delicious	delicioso	*(deh-lee-see-'oh-soh)*
delivery	reparto, el	*(ehl reh-'pahr-toh)*
dentist	dentista, el/la	*(ehl, lah dehn-'tees-tah)*
deodorant	desodorante, el	*(ehl deh-soh-doh-'rahn-teh)*
depressed	deprimido	*(deh-pree-'mee-doh)*
desert	desierto, el	*(ehl deh-see-'ehr-toh)*
desk	escritorio, el	*(ehl ehs-kree-'toh-ree-oh)*
dessert	postre, el	*(ehl 'pohs-treh)*
devil	diablo, el	*(ehl dee-'ah-bloh)*
dictionary	diccionario, el	*(ehl deek-see-oh-'nah-ree-oh)*
difficult	difícil	*(dee-'fee-seel)*
dining room	comedor, el	*(ehl koh-meh-'dohr)*
dinner	cena, la	*(lah 'seh-nah)*
directions	instrucciones, las	*(lahs eens-trook-see-'oh-nehs)*
dirt	tierra, la	*(lah tee-'eh-rrah)*
dirty	sucio	*('soo-see-oh)*
disabled	incapacitado	*(een-kah-pah-see-'tah-doh)*

disadvantaged	desfavorecido	*(dehs-fah-voh-reh-'see-doh)*
disciple	discípulo, el	*(ehl dee-'see-poo-loh)*
discipline	disciplina, la	*(lah dee-see-'plee-nah)*
discount	descuento, el	*(ehl dehs-'kwehn-toh)*
disease	enfermedad, la	*(lah ehn-fehr-meh-'dahd)*
dishwasher	lavaplatos, el	*(ehl lah-vah-'plah-tohs)*
distance	distancia, la	*(lah dees-'tahn-see-ah)*
district	distrito, el	*(ehl dees-'tree-toh)*
divorce	divorcio, el	*(ehl dee-'vohr-see-oh)*
divorced	divorciado	*(dee-vohr-see-'ah-doh)*
dizzy	mareado	*(mah-reh-'ah-doh)*
doctor	doctor, el	*(ehl dohk-'tohr)*
dog	perro, el	*(ehl 'peh-rroh)*
doll	muñeca, la	*(lah moon-'yeh-kah)*
dollar	dólar, el	*(ehl 'doh-lahr)*
donation	donación, la	*(lah doh-nah-see-'ohn)*
donkey	burro, el	*(ehl 'boo-rroh)*
donor	donador, el	*(ehl doh-nah-'dohr)*
door	puerta, la	*(lah 'pwehr-tah)*
double	doble, el	*(ehl 'doh-bleh)*
down	abajo	*(ah-'bah-hoh)*
downtown	centro, el	*(ehl 'sehn-troh)*
dozen	docena, la	*(lah doh-'seh-nah)*
drain	desagüe, el	*(ehl deh-'sah-gweh)*
drawer	cajón, el	*(ehl kah-'hohn)*
dress	vestido, el	*(ehl vehs-'tee-doh)*
dresser	tocador, el	*(ehl toh-kah-'dohr)*
drill	taladro, el	*(ehl tah-'lah-droh)*
driver	chofer, el	*(ehl choh-'fehr)*
driver's license	licencia de manejar, la	*(lah lee-'sehn-see-ah deh mah-neh-'hahr)*
drug	droga, la	*(lah 'droh-gah)*
drunk	borracho	*(boh-'rrah-choh)*
dry	seco	*('seh-koh)*
dryer	secadora, la	*(lah seh-kah-'doh-rah)*
duck	pato, el	*(ehl 'pah-toh)*
dust	polvo, el	*(ehl 'pohl-voh)*
ear	oreja, la	*(lah oh-'reh-hah)*
early	temprano	*(tehm-'prah-noh)*
earthquake	terremoto, el	*(ehl teh-rreh-'moh-toh)*
east	este, el	*(ehl 'ehs-teh)*
Easter	Pascua, la	*(lah 'pahs-kwah)*
easy	fácil	*('fah-seel)*
ecology	ecología, la	*(lah eh-koh-loh-'hee-ah)*
education	educación, la	*(lah eh-doo-kah-see-'ohn)*
educator	educador, el	*(ehl eh-doo-kah-'dohr)*
effort	esfuerzo, el	*(ehl ehs-foo-'ehr-soh)*
egg	huevo, el	*(ehl 'hweh-voh)*

eight	ocho	('oh-choh)
eighteen	dieciocho	(dee-eh-see-'oh-choh)
eighth	octavo	(ohk-'tah-voh)
eighty	ochenta	(oh-'chehn-tah)
elbow	codo, el	(ehl 'koh-doh)
elevator	ascensor, el	(ehl ah-sehn-'sohr)
eleven	once	('ohn-seh)
emergency	emergencia, la	(lah eh-mehr-'hehn-see-ah)
employee	empleado, el	(ehl ehm-pleh-'ah-doh)
employer	empresario, el	(ehl ehm-preh-'sah-ree-oh)
employment	empleo, el	(ehl ehm-'pleh-oh)
endorsement	endoso, el	(ehl ehn-'doh-soh)
engine	motor, el	(ehl moh'tohr)
engineer	ingeniero, el	(ehl een-heh-nee-'eh-roh)
entrance	entrada, la	(lah ehn-'trah-dah)
envelope	sobre, el	(ehl 'soh-breh)
equipment	equipo	(ehl eh-'kee-poh)
eraser	borrador, el	(ehl boh-rrah-'dohr)
eternity	eternidad, la	(lah eh-tehr-nee-'dahd)
event	evento, el	(ehl eh-'vehn-toh)
everyone	todos	('toh-dohs)
everything	todo	('toh-doh)
everywhere	por todas partes	(pohr 'toh-dahs 'pahr-tehs)
evidence	evidencia, la	(lah eh-vee-'dehn-see-ah)
example	ejemplo, el	(ehl eh-'hehm-ploh)
excellent	excelente	(ehk-seh-'lehn-teh)
excited	emocionado	(eh-moh-see-oh-'nah-doh)
executive	ejecutivo, el	(ehl eh-heh-koo-'tee-voh)
exercise	ejercicio, el	(ehl eh-hehr-'see-see-oh)
exhausted	agotado	(ah-goh-'tah-doh)
exit	salida, la	(lah sah-'lee-dah)
expensive	caro	('kah-roh)
explosive	explosivo, el	(ehl ehks-ploh-'see-voh)
eye	ojo, el	(ehl 'oh-hoh)
face	cara, la	(lah 'kah-rah)
factory	fábrica, la	(lah 'fah-bree-kah)
failure	fracaso, el	(ehl frah-'kah-soh)
fair	feria, la	(lah 'feh-ree-ah)
faith	fe, la	(lah feh)
fall	otoño, el	(ehl oh-'tohn-yoh)
family	familia, la	(lah fah-'mee-lee-ah)
famous	famoso	(fah-'moh-soh)
fan	ventilador, el	(ehl vehn-tee-lah-'dohr)
far	lejos	('leh-hohs)
farm	finca, la	(lah 'feen-kah)
farmer	campesino, el	(ehl kahm-peh-'see-noh)
farming	cultivo, el	(ehl kool-'tee-voh)

fast	rápido	*('rah-pee-doh)*
fat	gordo	*('gohr-doh)*
father	padre, el	*(ehl 'pah-dreh)*
fault	culpa, la	*(lah 'kool-pah)*
fax	fax, el	*(ehl fahks)*
fear	miedo, el	*(ehl mee-'eh-doh)*
February	febrero	*(feh-'breh-roh)*
feeling	sentimiento, el	*(ehl sehn-tee-mee-'ehn-toh)*
feminine	femenino	*(feh-meh-'nee-noh)*
fence	cerca, la	*(lah 'sehr-kah)*
fertile	fértil (masc. & fem.)	*('fehr-teel)*
fever	fiebre, la	*(lah fee-'eh-breh)*
few	pocos	*('poh-kohs)*
field	campo, el	*(ehl 'kahm-poh)*
fifteen	quince	*('keen-seh)*
fifth	quinto	*('keen-toh)*
fifty	cincuenta	*(seen-'kwehn-tah)*
fight	pelea, la	*(lah peh-'leh-ah)*
file cabinet	archivo, el	*(ehl ahr-'chee-voh)*
finance	finanzas, las	*(lahs fee-'nahn-sahs)*
fine	bien	*(bee-'ehn)*
finger	dedo, el	*(ehl 'deh-doh)*
fire	incendio, el	*(ehl een-'sehn-dee-oh)*
fire department	cuartel de bomberos, el	*(ehl kwahr-'tehl deh bohm-'beh-rohs)*
fire extinguisher	extintor, el	*(ehl ehks-teen-'tohr)*
firefighter	bombero, el	*(ehl bohm-'beh-roh)*
fireplace	chimenea, la	*(lah chee-meh-'neh-ah)*
first	primero	*(pree-'meh-roh)*
fish (caught)	pescado, el	*(ehl pehs-'kah-doh)*
fish (in water)	pez, el	*(ehl pehs)*
fishing	pesca, la	*(lah 'pehs-kah)*
five	cinco	*('seen-koh)*
flashlight	linterna, la	*(lah leen-'tehr-nah)*
flight	vuelo, el	*(ehl voo-'eh-loh)*
floor	piso, el	*(ehl 'pee-soh)*
flour	harina, la	*(lah ah-'ree-nah)*
flower	flor, la	*(lah flohr)*
fly	mosca, la	*(lah 'mohs-kah)*
food	comida, la	*(lah koh-'mee-dah)*
food stamps	cupones de alimentos, los	*(lohs koo-'poh-nehs deh ah-lee-'mehn-tohs)*
foot	pie, el	*(ehl pee-'eh)*
for	para, por	*('pah-rah, pohr)*
foreigner	extranjero, el	*(ehl ehks-irahn-'heh-roh)*
foreman	capataz, el/la	*(ehl, lah kah-pah-'tahs)*
forest	bosque, el	*(ehl 'bohs-keh)*
fork	tenedor, el	*(ehl teh-neh-'dohr)*
form	formulario, el	*(ehl fohr-moo-'lah-ree-oh)*

forty	cuarenta	*(kwah-'rehn-tah)*
forward	adelante	*(ah-deh-'lahn-teh)*
foundation	fundación, la	*(lah foon-dah-see-'ohn)*
fountain	fuente, la	*(lah foo-'ehn-teh)*
four	cuatro	*('kwah-troh)*
fourteen	catorce	*(kah-'tohr-seh)*
fourth	cuarto	*('kwahr-toh)*
fox	zorro, el	*(ehl 'soh-rroh)*
free	gratis	*('grah-tees)*
freedom	libertad, la	*(lah lee-behr-'tahd)*
freezer	congelador, el	*(ehl kohn-heh-lah-'dohr)*
freezing	helado	*(eh-'lah-doh)*
fresh	fresco	*('frehs-koh)*
Friday	viernes	*(vee-'ehr-nehs)*
friend	amigo, el	*(ehl ah-'mee-goh)*
friendly	amistoso	*(ah-mees-'toh-soh)*
from	de	*(deh)*
front	frente, el	*(ehl 'frehn-teh)*
frost	escarcha, la	*(lah ehs-'kahr-chah)*
frozen	congelado	*(kohn-heh-'lah-doh)*
fruit	fruta, la	*(lah 'froo-tah)*
fuel	combustible, el	*(kohm-boos-'tee-bleh)*
fun	divertido	*(dee-vehr-'tee-doh)*
fundraising	colección de fondos, la	*(lah koh-lehk-see-'ohn deh 'fohn-dohs)*
funeral	funeral, el	*(ehl foo-neh-'rahl)*
funny	chistoso	*(chees-'toh-soh)*
furious	furioso	*(foo-ree-'oh-soh)*
gallon	galón, el	*(ehl gah-'lohn)*
game	juego, el	*(ehl 'hweh-goh)*
gang	pandilla, la	*(lah pahn-'dee-yah)*
garage	garaje, el	*(ehl gah-'rah-heh)*
gardener	jardinero, el	*(ehl hahr-dee-'neh-roh)*
garlic	ajo, el	*(ehl 'ah-hoh)*
gas station	gasolinera, la	*(lah gah-soh-lee-'neh-rah)*
gate	portón, el	*(ehl pohr-'tohn)*
gathering	junta, la	*(lah 'hoon-tah)*
gift	regalo, el	*(ehl reh-'gah-loh)*
girdle	faja, la	*(lah 'fah-hah)*
girl	niña, la	*(lah 'neen-yah)*
girlfriend	novia, la	*(lah 'noh-vee-ah)*
glass	vidrio, el	*(ehl vee-dree-'oh)*
glass (drinking)	vaso, el	*(ehl 'vah-soh)*
glasses	lentes, los	*(lohs 'lehn-tehs)*
glove	guante, el	*(ehl 'gwahn-teh)*
glue	pegamento, el	*(ehl peh-gah-'mehn-toh)*
goal	meta, la	*(lah 'meh-tah)*
God	Dios	*(dee-'ohs)*

good	bueno	*('bweh-noh)*
Good evening	Buenas noches	*('bweh-nahs 'noh-chehs)*
Good-bye	Adiós	*(ah-dee-'ohs)*
gospel	evangelio, el	*(ehl eh-vahn-'heh-lee-oh)*
government	gobierno, el	*(ehl goh-bee-'ehr-noh)*
governor	gobernador, el	*(ehl goh-behr-nah-'dohr)*
grace	gracia, la	*(lah 'grah-see-ah)*
granddaughter	nieta, la	*(lah nee-'eh-tah)*
grandfather	abuelo, el	*(ehl ah-'bweh-loh)*
grandmother	abuela, la	*(lah ah-'bweh-lah)*
grandson	nieto, el	*(ehl nee-'eh-toh)*
grape	uva, la	*(lah 'oo-vah)*
grapefruit	toronja, la	*(lah toh-'rohn-hah)*
grass	pasto, el	*(ehl 'pahs-toh)*
green	verde (masc. & fem.)	*('vehr-deh)*
greeting cards	tarjetas de saludo, las	*(lahs tahr-'heh-tahs deh sah-'loo-doh)*
group	grupo, el	*(ehl 'groo-poh)*
guard	guardia, el/la	*(ehl, lah 'gwahr-dee-ah)*
guidance	orientación, la	*(lah oh-ree-ehn-tah-see-'ohn)*
guide	guía, el/la	*(ehl, lah 'gee-ah)*
guilt	culpa, la	*(lah 'kool-pah)*
guitar	guitarra, la	*(lah gee-'tah-rrah)*
gun	arma, el	*(ehl 'ahr-mah)*
gym	gimnasio, el	*(ehl heem-'nah-see-oh)*
hail	granizo, el	*(ehl grah-'nee-soh)*
hairbrush	cepillo, el	*(ehl seh-'pee-yoh)*
hairspray	laca, la	*(lah 'lah-kah)*
half	mitad, la	*(lah mee-'tahd)*
hallway	pasillo, el	*(ehl pah-'see-yoh)*
ham	jamón, el	*(ehl hah-'mohn)*
hamburger	hamburguesa	*(lah ahm-boor-'geh-sah)*
hammer	martillo, el	*(ehl mahr-'tee-yoh)*
hand	mano, la	*(lah 'mah-noh)*
handicapped	minusválido, el	*(ehl mee-noos-'vah-lee-doh)*
handkerchief	pañuelo, el	*(ehl pahn-yoo-'eh-loh)*
handsome	guapo	*('gwah-poh)*
happiness	felicidad, la	*(lah feh-lee-see-'dahd)*
happy	feliz (masc. & fem.)	*(feh-'lees)*
hard	duro	*('doo-roh)*
harm	daño, el	*(ehl 'dahn-yoh)*
hate	odio, el	*(ehl 'oh-dee-oh)*
he	él	*(ehl)*
head	cabeza, la	*(lah kah-'beh-sah)*
health	salud, la	*(lah sah-'lood)*
healthy	saludable (masc. & fem.)	*(sah-loo-'dah-bleh)*
heart	corazón, el	*(ehl koh-rah-'sohn)*
heater	calentador, el	*(ehl kah-lehn-tah-'dohr)*

heating	calefacción, la	*(lah kah-leh-fahk-see-'ohn)*
heaven	cielo, el	*(ehl see-'eh-loh)*
heavy	pesado	*(peh-'sah-doh)*
helicopter	helicóptero, el	*(ehl eh-lee-'kohp-teh-roh)*
hell	infierno, el	*(ehl een-fee-'ehr-noh)*
helmet	casco, el	*(ehl 'kahs-koh)*
helper	ayudante, el/la	*(ehl, lah ah-yoo-'dahn-teh)*
helpless	indefenso	*(een-deh-'fehn-soh)*
her	su	*(soo)*
here	aquí	*(ah-'kee)*
hers	suya	*('soo-yah)*
Hi	Hola	*('oh-lah)*
highway	carretera, la	*(lah kah-rreh-'teh-rah)*
hip	cadera, la	*(lah kah-'deh-rah)*
his	su, suyo	*(soo, 'soo-yoh)*
hoe	azadón, el	*(ehl ah-sah-'dohn)*
hole	hoyo, el	*(ehl 'oh-yoh)*
Holy Spirit	Espíritu Santo, el	*(ehl ehs-'pee-ree-too 'sahn-toh)*
home	hogar, el	*(ehl oh-'gahr)*
homeless	desamparado	*(deh-sahm-pah-'rah-doh)*
homework	tarea, la	*(lah tah-'reh-ah)*
homosexuality	homosexualidad, la	*(lah oh-moh-sek-soo-ah-lee-'dahd)*
honey	miel, la	*(lah mee-'ehl)*
hope	esperanza, la	*(lah ehs-peh-'rahn-sah)*
horse	caballo, el	*(ehl kah-'bah-yoh)*
hose	manguera, la	*(lah mahn-'geh-rah)*
hospital	hospital, el	*(ehl ohs-pee-'tahl)*
house	casa, la	*(lah 'kah-sah)*
housing	vivienda, la	*(lah vee-vee-'ehn-dah)*
how	cómo	*('koh-moh)*
how many	cuántos	*('kwahn-tohs)*
how much	cuánto	*('kwahn-toh)*
humility	humildad, la	*(lah oo-meel-'dahd)*
hunger	hambre, el	*(ehl 'ahm-breh)*
hurricane	huracán, el	*(ehl oo-rah-'kahn)*
hurt	lastimado	*(lahs-tee-'mah-doh)*
husband	esposo, el	*(ehl ehs-'poh-soh)*
hut	choza, la	*(lah 'choh-sah)*
hymn	himno, el	*(ehl 'eem-noh)*
I	yo	*(yoh)*
ice	hielo, el	*(ehl ee-'eh-loh)*
ice cream	helado, el	*(ehl eh-'lah-doh)*
identification	identificación, la	*(lah ee-dehn-tee-fee-kah-see-'ohn)*
immigrant	inmigrante, el/la	*(ehl, lah een-mee-'grahn-teh)*
important	importante (masc. & fem.)	*(eem-pohr-'tahn-teh)*
impoverished	empobrecido	*(ehm-poh-breh-'see-doh)*
in	en	*(ehn)*

inch	pulgada, la	*(lah pool-'gah-dah)*
industrious	trabajador	*(trah-bah-hah-'dohr)*
information	información, la	*(lah een-fohr-mah-see-'ohn)*
ingredients	ingredientes, los	*(lohs een-greh-dee-'ehn-tehs)*
injury	herida, la	*(lah eh-'ree-dah)*
ink	tinta, la	*(lah 'teen-tah)*
inside	adentro	*(ah-'dehn-troh)*
inside out	al revés	*(ahl reh-'vehs)*
institution	institución, la	*(lah eens-tee-too-see-'ohn)*
insurance	seguro, el	*(ehl seh-'goo-roh)*
intelligent	inteligente (masc. & fem.)	*(een-teh-lee-'hehn-teh)*
interested	interesado	*(een-teh-reh-'sah-doh)*
interesting	interesante (masc. & fem.)	*(een-teh-reh-'sahn-teh)*
interpreter	intérprete, el/la	*(ehl, lah een-'tehr-preh-teh)*
interview	entrevista, la	*(lah ehn-treh-'vees-tah)*
invoice	factura, la	*(lah fahk-'too-rah)*
iron	hierro, el	*(ehl ee-'eh-rroh)*
jacket	chaqueta, la	*(lah chah-'keh-tah)*
jail	cárcel, la	*(lah 'kahr-sehl)*
janitor	conserje, el/la	*(ehl, lah kohn-'sehr-heh)*
January	enero	*(eh-'neh-roh)*
jar	jarra, la	*(lah 'hah-rrah)*
Jesus Christ	Jesucristo	*(heh-soo-'krees-toh)*
job	trabajo, el	*(ehl trah-'bah-hoh)*
joy	gozo, el	*(ehl 'goh-soh)*
juice	jugo, el	*(ehl 'hoo-goh)*
July	julio	*('hoo-lee-oh)*
June	junio	*('hoo-nee-oh)*
jungle	selva, la	*(lah 'sehl-vah)*
just	apenas	*(ah-'peh-nahs)*
key	llave, la	*(lah 'yah-veh)*
keyboard	teclado, el	*(ehl tehk-'lah-doh)*
kindness	bondad, la	*(lah bohn-'dahd)*
kitchen	cocina, la	*(lah koh-'see-nah)*
knee	rodilla, la	*(lah roh-'dee-yah)*
knife	cuchillo, el	*(ehl koo-chee-yoh)*
knob	tirador, el	*(ehl tee-rah-'dohr)*
knowledge	conocimiento, el	*(ehl koh-noh-see-mee-'ehn-toh)*
label	etiqueta, la	*(lah eh-tee-'keh-tah)*
laborer	obrero, el	*(ehl oh-'breh-roh)*
ladder	escalera, la	*(lah ehs-kah-'leh-rah)*
lake	lago, el	*(ehl 'lah-goh)*
lamb	cordero, el	*(ehl kohr-'deh-roh)*
lamp	lámpara, la	*(lah 'lahm-pah-rah)*
language	lenguaje, el	*(ehl lehn-'gwah-heh)*
late	tarde	*('tahr-deh)*
later	más tarde	*(mahs 'tahr-deh)*

law	ley, la	*(lah 'leh-ee)*
lawn	césped, el	*(ehl 'sehs-pehd)*
lawsuit	pleito, el	*(ehl 'pleh-ee-toh)*
lawyer	abogado, el	*(ehl ah-boh-'gah-doh)*
lazy	perezoso	*(peh-reh-'soh-soh)*
leader	líder, el/la	*(ehl, lah 'lee-dehr)*
league	liga, la	*(lah 'lee-gah)*
leather	cuero, el	*(ehl 'kweh-roh)*
left	izquierda, la	*(lah ees-'kee-'ehr-dah)*
lemon	limón, el	*(ehl lee-'mohn)*
lemonade	limonada, la	*(lah lee-moh-'nah-dah)*
less	menos	*('meh-nohs)*
lesson	lección, la	*(lah lehk-see-'ohn)*
letter	carta, la	*(lah 'kahr-tah)*
lettuce	lechuga, la	*(lah leh-'choo-gah)*
library	biblioteca, la	*(lah bee-blee-oh-'teh-kah)*
life	vida, la	*(lah 'vee-dah)*
light	luz, la	*(lah loos)*
light bulb	foco, el	*(ehl 'foh-koh)*
lightning	relámpago, el	*(ehl reh-'lahm-pah-goh)*
line	línea, la	*(lah 'lee-neh-ah)*
liquid	líquido, el	*(ehl 'lee-kee-doh)*
list	lista, la	*(lah 'lees-tah)*
little	poco	*('poh-koh)*
living room	sala, la	*(lah 'sah-lah)*
lobby	vestíbulo, el	*(ehl vehs-'tee-boo-loh)*
lobster	langosta, la	*(lah lahn-'gohs-tah)*
lock	cerradura, la	*(lah seh-rrah-'doo-rah)*
lodging	alojamiento, el	*(ehl ah-loh-hah-mee-'ehn-toh)*
loneliness	soledad, la	*(lah soh-leh-'dahd)*
loose	suelto	*('swehl-toh)*
Lord	Señor, el	*(ehl sehn-'yohr)*
loss	pérdida, la	*(lah 'pehr-dee-dah)*
lost	perdido	*(pehr-'dee-doh)*
love	amor, el	*(ehl ah-'mohr)*
luck	suerte, la	*(lah 'swehr-teh)*
luggage	equipaje, el	*(ehl eh-kee-'pah-heh)*
lunch	almuerzo, el	*(ehl ahl-'mwehr-soh)*
lung	pulmón, el	*(ehl pool-'mohn)*
machine	máquina, la	*(lah 'mah-kee-nah)*
machinery	maquinaria, la	*(lah mah-kee-'nah-ree-ah)*
magazine	revista, la	*(lah reh-'vees-tah)*
maid	criada, la	*(lah kree-'ah-dah)*
mail	correo, el	*(ehl koh-'rreh-oh)*
mail carrier	cartero, el	*(ehl kahr-'teh-roh)*
maintenance	mantenimiento, el	*(ehl mahn-teh-nee-mee-'ehn-toh)*
makeup	maquillaje, el	*(ehl mah-kee-'yah-heh)*

male	masculino	*(mahs-koo-'lee-noh)*
man	hombre, el	*(ehl 'ohm-breh)*
manager	gerente, el	*(ehl heh-'rehn-teh)*
many	muchos	*('moo-chohs)*
map	mapa, el	*(ehl 'mah-pah)*
March	marzo	*('mahr-soh)*
market	mercado, el	*(ehl mehr-'kah-doh)*
marriage	matrimonio, el	*(ehl mah-tree-'moh-nee-oh)*
married	casado	*(kah-'sah-doh)*
mask	máscara, la	*(lah 'mahs-kah-rah)*
matches	fósforos, los	*(lohs 'fohs-foh-rohs)*
mattress	colchón, el	*(ehl kohl-'chohn)*
mature	maduro	*(mah-'doo-roh)*
May	mayo	*('mah-yoh)*
maybe	quizás	*(kee-'sahs)*
mayonnaise	mayonesa, la	*(lah mah-yoh-'neh-sah)*
meals	comidas, las	*(lahs koh-'mee-dahs)*
meat	carne, la	*(lah 'kahr-neh)*
mechanic	mecánico, el/la	*(ehl, lah meh-'kah-nee-koh)*
medicine	medicina, la	*(lah meh-dee-'see-nah)*
meeting	reunión, la	*(lah reh-oo-nee-'ohn)*
member	miembro, el/la	*(ehl, lah mee-'ehm-broh)*
merchandise	mercancía, la	*(lah mehr-kahn-'see-ah)*
mercy	misericordia, la	*(lah mee-seh-ree-'kohr-dee-ah)*
message	mensaje, el	*(ehl mehn-'sah-heh)*
microphone	micrófono, el	*(ehl mee-'kroh-foh-noh)*
microwave	horno de microonda, el	*(ehl 'ohr-noh deh mee-kroh-'ohn-dah)*
milk	leche, la	*(lah 'leh-cheh)*
mine	mío	*('mee-oh)*
minister	pastor, el	*(ehl pahs-'tohr)*
ministry	ministerio, el	*(ehl mee-nees-'teh-ree-oh)*
miracle	milagro, el	*(ehl mee-'lah-groh)*
mirror	espejo, el	*(ehl ehs-'peh-hoh)*
mission	misión, la	*(lah mee-see-'ohn)*
missionary	misionero, el	*(ehl mee-see-oh-'neh-roh)*
mittens	mitones, los	*(los mee-'toh-nehs)*
mold	moho, el	*(ehl 'moh-hoh)*
Monday	lunes	*('loo-nehs)*
money	dinero, el	*(ehl dee-'neh-roh)*
month	mes, el	*(ehl mehs)*
moon	luna, la	*(lah 'loo-nah)*
mop	trapeador, el	*(ehl trah-peh-ah-'dohr)*
more	más	*(mahs)*
mortgage	hipoteca, la	*(lah ee-poh-'teh-kah)*
mosquito	zancudo, el	*(ehl sahn-'koo-doh)*
moth	polilla, la	*(lah poh-'lee-yah)*
mother	madre, la	*(lah 'mah-dreh)*

motorcycle	motocicleta, la	*(lah moh-toh-see-'kleh-tah)*
mountain	montaña, la	*(lah mohn-'tahn-yah)*
mouse	ratón, el	*(ehl rah-'tohn)*
mouth	boca, la	*(lah 'boh-kah)*
movie theater	cine, el	*(ehl 'see-neh)*
much	mucho	*('moo-choh)*
mud	lodo, el	*(ehl 'loh-doh)*
muffler	silenciador, el	*(ehl see-lehn-see-ah-'dohr)*
museum	museo, el	*(ehl moo-'seh-oh)*
mushroom	hongo, el	*(ehl 'ohn-goh)*
music	música, la	*(lah 'moo-see-kah)*
musician	músico, el/la	*(ehl, lah 'moo-see-koh)*
mustard	mostaza, la	*(lah mohs-'tah-sah)*
my	mi	*(mee)*
nail	clavo, el	*(ehl 'klah-voh)*
napkin	servilleta, la	*(lah sehr-vee-'yeh-tah)*
narrow	estrecho	*(ehs-'treh-choh)*
nationality	nacionalidad, la	*(lah nah-see-oh-nah-lee-'dahd)*
neck	cuello, el	*(ehl 'kweh-yoh)*
necklace	collar, el	*(ehl koh-'yahr)*
needle	aguja, la	*(lah ah-'goo-hah)*
neighbor	vecino, el	*(ehl veh-'see-noh)*
neighborhood	vecindario, el	*(ehl veh-seen-'dah-ree-oh)*
nephew	sobrino, el	*(ehl soh-'bree-noh)*
nervous	nervioso	*(nehr-vee-'oh-soh)*
nest	nido, el	*(ehl 'nee-doh)*
net	red, la	*(lah rehd)*
never	nunca	*('noon-kah)*
new	nuevo	*('nweh-voh)*
news	noticias, las	*(lahs noh-'tee-see-ahs)*
newspaper	periódico, el	*(ehl peh-ree-'oh-dee-koh)*
next	próximo	*('prohk-see-moh)*
nice	simpático	*(seem-'pah-tee-koh)*
niece	sobrina, la	*(lah soh-'bree-nah)*
nine	nueve	*('nweh-veh)*
nineteen	diecinueve	*(dee-eh-see-'nweh-veh)*
ninth	noveno	*(noh-'veh-noh)*
ninety	noventa	*(noh-'vehn-tah)*
no one	nadie	*('nah-dee-eh)*
north	norte, el	*(ehl 'nohr-teh)*
nose	nariz, la	*(lah nah-'rees)*
notebook	cuaderno, el	*(ehl kwah-'dehr-noh)*
nothing	nada	*('nah-dah)*
November	noviembre	*(noh-vee-'ehm-breh)*
now	ahora	*(ah-'oh-rah)*
nowhere	por ninguna parte	*(pohr neen-'goo-nah 'pahr-teh)*
number	número, el	*(ehl 'noo-meh-roh)*

nun	monja, la	*(lah 'mohn-hah)*
nurse	enfermera, la	*(lah ehn-fehr-'meh-rah)*
nuts	nueces, las	*(lahs 'nweh-sehs)*
ocean	océano, el	*(ehl oh-'seh-ah-noh)*
October	octubre	*(ohk-'too-breh)*
offering	ofrenda, la	*(lah oh-'frehn-dah)*
office	oficina, la	*(lah oh-fee-'see-nah)*
official	oficial	*(oh-fee-see-'ahl)*
of	de	*(deh)*
oil	aceite, el	*(ehl ah-'seh-ee-teh)*
OK	Bueno	*('bweh-noh)*
old	viejo	*(vee-'eh-hoh)*
older	mayor (masc. & fem.)	*(mah-'yohr)*
on	en	*(ehn)*
once	una vez	*('oo-nah vehs)*
one	uno	*('oo-noh)*
one hundred	cien	*(see-'ehn)*
one thousand	mil	*(meel)*
onion	cebolla, la	*(lah seh-'boh-yah)*
operator	operador, el	*(ehl oh-peh-rah-'dohr)*
opinion	opinión, la	*(lah oh-pee-nee-'ohn)*
orange (color)	anaranjado	*(ah-nah-rahn-'hah-doh)*
orange (fruit)	naranja, la	*(lah nah-'rahn-hah)*
orchard	huerta, la	*(lah 'hwehr-tah)*
orphanage	orfanato, el	*(ehl ohr-fah-'nah-toh)*
ounce	onza, la	*(lah 'ohn-sah)*
outside	afuera	*(ah-foo-'eh-rah)*
outskirts	afueras, las	*(lahs ah-foo-'eh-rahs)*
outstanding	sobresaliente	*(soh-breh-sah-lee-'ehn-teh)*
oven	horno, el	*(ehl 'ohr-noh)*
over	sobre	*('soh-breh)*
overcoat	abrigo, el	*(ehl ah-'bree-goh)*
owner	dueño, el	*(ehl 'dwehn-yoh)*
P.M.	de la noche	*(deh lah 'noh-cheh)*
package	paquete, el	*(ahl pah-'keh-teh)*
packaging	embalaje, el	*(ehl ehm-bah-'lah-heh)*
page	página, la	*(lah 'pah-hee-nah)*
pain	dolor, el	*(ehl doh-'lohr)*
paint	pintura, la	*(lah peen-'too-rah)*
painter	pintor, el	*(ehl peen-'tohr)*
painting	cuadro, el	*(ehl 'kwah-droh)*
pajamas	pijama, el	*(ehl pee-'yah-mah)*
pan	sartén, la	*(lah sahr-'tehn)*
panties	bragas, las	*(lahs 'brah-gahs)*
pants	pantalones, los	*(lohs pahn-tah-'loh-nehs)*
paper	papel, el	*(ehl pah-'pehl)*
parade	desfile, el	*(ehl dehs-'fee-leh)*

paramedic	paramédico, el	*(ehl pah-rah-'meh-dee-koh)*
parish	parroquia, la	*(lah pah-'rroh-kee-ah)*
parishioner	parroquiano, el	*(ehl pah-rroh-kee-'ah-noh)*
park	parque, el	*(ehl 'pahr-keh)*
parking lot	estacionamiento, el	*(ehl ehs-tah-see-oh-nah-mee-'ehn-toh)*
parking meter	parquímetro, el	*(ehl pahr-'kee-meh-troh)*
partner	socio, el	*(ehl 'soh-see-oh)*
party	fiesta, la	*(lah fee-'ehs-tah)*
passenger	pasajero, el	*(ehl pah-sah-'heh-roh)*
passport	pasaporte, el	*(ehl pah-sah-'pohr-teh)*
paste	pasta, la	*(lah 'pahs-tah)*
pastor	pastor, el	*(ehl pahs'tohr)*
path	camino, el	*(ehl kah-'mee-noh)*
patience	paciencia, la	*(lah pah-see-'ehn-see-ah)*
patient	paciente, el/la	*(ehl, lah pah-see-'ehn-teh)*
payment	pago, el	*(ehl 'pah-goh)*
peace	paz, la	*(lah pahs)*
peach	durazno, el	*(ehl doo-'rahs-noh)*
peak	pico, el	*(ehl 'pee-koh)*
peanut butter	crema de maní, la	*(lah 'kreh-mah deh mah-'nee)*
pear	pera, la	*(lah 'peh-rah)*
peas	arvejitas, las	*(lahs ahr-veh-'hee-tahs)*
pedestrian	peatón, el	*(ehl peh-ah-'tohn)*
pediatrician	pediatra, el/la	*(ehl, lah peh-dee-'ah-trah)*
pen	lapicero, el	*(ehl lah-pee-'seh-roh)*
penalty	multa, la	*(lah 'mool-tah)*
pencil	lápiz, el	*(ehl 'lah-pees)*
penicillin	penicilina, la	*(lah peh-nee-see-'lee-nah)*
penny	centavo, el	*(ehl sehn-'tah-voh)*
people	gente, la	*(lah 'hehn-teh)*
pepper	pimienta, la	*(lah pee-mee-'ehn-tah)*
percentage	porcentaje, el	*(ehl pohr-sehn-'tah-heh)*
performance	función, la	*(lah foon-see-'ohn)*
perfume	perfume, el	*(ehl pehr-'foo-meh)*
permanent	permanente	*(pehr-mah-'nehn-teh)*
permit	permiso, el	*(ehl pehr-'mee-soh)*
person	persona, la	*(lah pehr-'soh-nah)*
personality	personalidad, la	*(lah pehr-soh-nah-lee-dahd)*
pharmacy	farmacia, la	*(lah fahr-'mah-see-ah)*
phone call	llamada, la	*(lah yah-'mah-dah)*
picnic	merienda, la	*(lah meh-ree-'ehn-dah)*
pie	pastel, el	*(ehl pahs-'tehl)*
pier	muelle, el	*(ehl 'mweh-yeh)*
pig	cerdo, el	*(ehl 'sehr-doh)*
pill	píldora, la	*(lah 'peel-doh-rah)*
pilot	piloto, el/la	*(ehl, lah pee-'loh-toh)*
pin	alfiler, el	*(ehl ahl-fee-'lehr)*

pineapple	piña, la	*(lah 'peen-yah)*
pitcher	cántaro, el	*(ehl 'kahn-tah-roh)*
plane	avión, el	*(ehl ah-vee-'ohn)*
planet	planeta, el	*(ehl plah-'neh-tah)*
plastic	plástico, el	*(ehl 'plahs-tee-koh)*
plate	plato, el	*(ehl 'plah-toh)*
player	jugador, el	*(ehl hoo-gah-'dohr)*
Please	Por favor	*(pohr fah-'vohr)*
plumber	plomero, el	*(ehl plo-'meh-roh)*
plumbing	tubería, la	*(lah too-beh-'ree-ah)*
pocket	bolsillo, el	*(ehl bohl-'see-yoh)*
poisonous	venenoso	*(veh-neh-'noh-soh)*
police officer	policía, el/la	*(ehl, lah poh-lee-'see-ah)*
police station	estación de policía, la	*(lah ehs-tah-see-'ohn deh poh-lee-'see-ah)*
polish	lustrador, el	*(ehl loos-trah-'dohr)*
polite	cortés (masc. & fem.)	*(kohr-'tehs)*
pollution	contaminación, la	*(lah kohn-tah-mee-nah-see-'ohn)*
pool	piscina, la	*(lah pee-'see-nah)*
poor	pobre (masc. & fem.)	*('poh-breh)*
porch	portal, el	*(ehl pohr-'tahl)*
post office	oficina de correos, la	*(lah oh-fee-'see-nah deh koh-'rreh-ohs)*
postcard	tarjeta postal, la	*(lah tahr-'heh-tah pohs-'tahl)*
pot (flower)	maceta, la	*(lah mah-'seh-tah)*
pot (cooking)	olla, la	*(lah 'oh-yah)*
potato	papa, la	*(lah 'pah-pah)*
pound	libra, la	*(lah 'lee-brah)*
poverty	pobreza, la	*(lah poh-'breh-sah)*
powder	polvo, el	*(ehl 'pohl-voh)*
praise	alabanza, la	*(lah ah-lah-'bahn-sah)*
prayer	oración, la	*(lah oh-rah-see-'ohn)*
pregnancy	embarazo, el	*(ehl ehm-bah-'rah-soh)*
pregnant	embarazada	*(ehm-bah-rah-'sah-dah)*
prescription	receta, la	*(lah reh-'seh-tah)*
president	presidente, el	*(ehl preh-see-'dehn-teh)*
pretty	bonito	*(boh-'nee-toh)*
price	precio, el	*(ehl 'preh-see-oh)*
priest	sacerdote, el	*(ehl sah-sehr-'doh-teh)*
principal	director, el	*(ehl dee-rehk-'tohr)*
printer	impresora, la	*(lah eem-preh-'soh-rah)*
prison	prisión, la	*(lah pree-see-'ohn)*
prisoner	prisionero, el	*(ehl pree-see-oh-'neh-roh)*
private	privado	*(pree-'vah-doh)*
prize	premio, el	*(ehl 'preh-mee-oh)*
program	programa, el	*(ehl proh-'grah-mah)*
project	proyecto, el	*(ehl proh-'yehk-toh)*
property	propiedad, la	*(lah proh-pee-eh-'dahd)*
psychologist	psicólogo, el	*(ehl see-'koh-loh-goh)*

public	el público	*(ehl 'poo-blee-koh)*
pumpkin	calabaza, la	*(lah kah-lah-'bah-sah)*
purple	morado	*(moh-'rah-doh)*
purpose	propósito, el	*(ehl proh-'poh-see-toh)*
purse	bolsa, la	*(lah 'bohl-sah)*
quality	calidad, la	*(lah kah-lee-'dahd)*
quantity	cantidad, la	*(lah kahn-tee-'dahd)*
question	pregunta, la	*(lah preh-'goon-tah)*
quickly	rápidamente	*('rah-pee-dah-mehn-teh)*
quiet	quieto	*(kee-'eh-toh)*
rabbit	conejo, el	*(ehl koh-'neh-hoh)*
race	raza, la	*(lah 'rah-sah)*
rag	trapo, el	*(ehl 'trah-poh)*
railroad	ferrocarril, el	*(ehl feh-rroh-kah-'rreel)*
rain	lluvia, la	*(lah 'yoo-vee-ah)*
raincoat	impermeable, el	*(ehl eem-pehr-meh-'ah bleh)*
raisin	pasa, la	*(lah 'pah-sah)*
rake	rastrillo, el	*(ehl rahs-'tree-yoh)*
rape	violación, la	*(lah vee-oh-lah-see-'ohn)*
rat	rata, la	*(lah 'rah-tah)*
ready	listo	*('lees-toh)*
receipt	recibo, el	*(ehl reh-'see-boh)*
receiving	la recepción	*(lah reh-sehp-see-'ohn)*
record	registro, el	*(ehl reh-'hees-troh)*
recovery	recuperación, la	*(lah reh-koo-peh-rah-see-'ohn)*
recreation	recreación, la	*(lah reh-kreh-ah-see-'ohn)*
recycling	reciclaje, el	*(ehl reh-see-'klah-heh)*
red	rojo	*('roh-hoh)*
refrigerator	refrigerador, el	*(ehl reh-free-heh-rah-'dohr)*
refugee	refugiado, el	*(ehl reh-foo-hee-'ah-doh)*
refund	reembolso, el	*(ehl reh-ehm-'bohl-soh)*
rehabilitation	rehabilitación, la	*(lah reh-ah-bee-lee-tah-see-'ohn)*
relapse	recaída, la	*(lah reh-kah-'ee-dah)*
relative	pariente, el/la	*(ehl, lah pah-ree-'ehn-teh)*
relaxed	relajado	*(reh-lah-'hah-doh)*
relief	alivio, el	*(ehl ah-'lee-vee-oh)*
religion	religión, la	*(lah reh-lee-hee-'ohn)*
religious	religioso	*(reh-lee-hee-'oh-soh)*
repair	reparación, la	*(lah reh-pah-rah-see-'ohn)*
report	reporte, el	*(ehl reh-'pohr-teh)*
representative	representante, el/la	*(ehl, lah reh-preh-sehn-'tahn-teh)*
rescue	rescate, el	*(ehl rehs-'kah-teh)*
research	investigación, la	*(lah een-vehs-tee-gah-see-'ohn)*
resident	residente, el/la	*(ehl, lah reh-see-'dehn-teh)*
resource	recurso, el	*(ehl reh-'koor-soh)*
respect	respeto, el	*(ehl rehs-'peh-toh)*
responsible	responsable (masc. & fem.)	*(rehs-pohn-'sah-bleh)*

restroom	servicio, el	*(ehl sehr-'vee-see-oh)*
rice	arroz, el	*(ehl ah-'rrohs)*
rich	rico	*('ree-koh)*
right	derecho, el	*(deh-'reh-choh)*
ring	anillo, el	*(ehl ah-'nee-yoh)*
risk	riesgo, el	*(ehl ree-'ehs-goh)*
river	río, el	*(ehl 'ree-oh)*
road	camino, el	*(ahl kah-'mee-noh)*
roast beef	rosbif, el	*(ehl rohs-'beef)*
robbery	robo, el	*(ehl 'roh-boh)*
robe	bata, la	*(lah 'bah-tah)*
rock	piedra, la	*(lah pee-'eh-drah)*
roll	panecillo, el	*(ehl pah-neh-'see-yoh)*
roof	techo, el	*(ehl 'teh-choh)*
room	cuarto, el	*(ehl 'kwahr-toh)*
roommate	compañero de cuarto, el	*(ehl kohm-pahn-'yeh-roh deh 'kwahr-toh)*
rough	áspero	*('ahs-peh-roh)*
rubber	goma, la	*(lah 'goh-mah)*
rule	regla, la	*(lah 'reh-glah)*
sacrifice	sacrificio, el	*(ehl sah-kree-'fee-see-oh)*
sad	triste (masc. & fem.)	*('trees-teh)*
sadness	tristeza, la	*(lah trees-'teh-sah)*
safe	seguro	*(seh-'goo-roh)*
safety	seguridad, la	*(lah seh-goo-ree-'dahd)*
salad	ensalada, la	*(lah ehn-sah-'lah-dah)*
sale	venta, la	*(lah 'vehn-tah)*
salesperson	vendedor, el	*(ehl vehn-deh-'dohr)*
salt	sal, la	*(lah sahl)*
salvation	salvación, la	*(lah sahl-vah-see-'ohn)*
sample	muestra, la	*(lah 'mwehs-trah)*
sand	arena, la	*(lah ah-'reh-nah)*
sandals	sandalias, las	*(lahs sahn-'dah-lee-ahs)*
sanitation	saneamiento, el	*(ehl sah-neh-ah-mee-'ehn-toh)*
satellite	satélite, el	*(ehl sah-'teh-lee-teh)*
saturday	sábado	*('sah-bah-doh)*
sauce	salsa, la	*(lah 'sahl-sah)*
Savior	Salvador, el	*(ehl sahl-vah-'dohr)*
saw	serrucho, el	*(ehl seh-'rroo-choh)*
scale	báscula, la	*(lah 'bahs-koo-lah)*
scared	espantado	*(ehs-pahn-'tah-doh)*
scarf	bufanda, la	*(lah boo-'fahn-dah)*
schedule	horario, el	*(ehl oh-'rah-ree-oh)*
scholarship	beca, la	*(lah 'beh-kah)*
school	escuela, la	*(lah ehs-'kweh-lah)*
school bus	autobús escolar, el	*(ehl ow-toh-'boos ehs-koh-'lahr)*
scissors	tijeras, las	*(lahs tee-'heh-rahs)*
screen	pantalla, la	*(lah pahn-'tah-yah)*

screw	tornillo, el	*(ehl tohr-'nee-yoh)*
seafood	marisco, el	*(ehl mah-'rees-koh)*
seat	asiento, el	*(ehl ah-see-'ehn-toh)*
second	segundo	*(seh-'goon-doh)*
secretary	secretario, el	*(ehl seh-kreh-'tah-ree-oh)*
security	seguridad, la	*(lah seh-goo-ree-'dahd)*
seed	semilla, la	*(lah seh-'mee-yah)*
seminar	seminario, el	*(ehl seh-mee-'nah-ree-oh)*
sentence	oración, la	*(lah oh-rah-see-'ohn)*
separated	separado	*(seh-pah-'rah-doh)*
September	setiembre	*(seh-tee-'ehm-breh)*
serious	serio	*('seh-ree-oh)*
sermon	sermón, el	*(ehl sehr-'mohn)*
servant	criado, el	*(ehl kree-'ah-doh)*
service	servicio, el	*(ehl sehr-'vee-see-oh)*
session	sesión, la	*(lah seh-see-'ohn)*
seven	siete	*('see-'eh-teh)*
seventeen	diecisiete	*(dee-eh-see-see-'eh-teh)*
seventh	séptimo	*('sehp-tee-moh)*
seventy	setenta	*(seh-'tehn-tah)*
sewage	desagüe, el	*(ehl deh-'sah-gweh)*
shallow	bajo	*('bah-hoh)*
shampoo	champú, el	*(ehl chahm-'poo)*
shape	forma, la	*(lah 'fohr-mah)*
shaver	afeitadora, la	*(lah ah-feh-ee-tah-'doh-rah)*
she	ella	*('eh-yah)*
shed	cabaña, la	*(lah kah-'bahn-yah)*
sheet	sábana, la	*(lah 'sah-bah-nah)*
shelf	repisa, la	*(lah reh-'pee-sah)*
shelter	refugio, el	*(ehl reh-'foo-hee-oh)*
shipment	envío, el	*(ehl ehn-'vee-oh)*
shirt	camisa, la	*(lah kah-'mee-sah)*
shoe	zapato, el	*(ehl sah-'pah-toh)*
short (in height)	bajo	*('bah-hoh)*
shorts	calzoncillos, los	*(lohs kahl-sohn-'see-yohs)*
shoulder	hombro, el	*(ehl 'ohm-broh)*
shovel	pala, la	*(lah 'pah-lah)*
show	espectáculo, el	*(ehl ehs-pehk-'tah-koo-loh)*
shower	ducha, la	*(lah 'doo-chah)*
sick	enfermo	*(ehn-'fehr-moh)*
sidewalk	acera, la	*(lah ah-'seh-rah)*
sign	señal, la	*(lah sehn-'yahl)*
signature	firma, la	*(lah 'feer-'mah)*
silverware	cubiertos, los	*(lohs koo-bee-'ehr-tohs)*
sin	pecado, el	*(ehl peh-'kah-doh)*
single	soltero	*(sohl-'teh-roh)*
sink	lavamanos, el	*(ehl lah-vah-'mah-nohs)*

sinner	pecador, el	*(ehl peh-kah-'dohr)*
sister	hermana, la	*(lah ehr-'mah-nah)*
six	seis	*('seh-ees)*
sixteen	dieciséis	*(dee-ehs-ee-'seh-ees)*
sixth	sexto	*('sehks-toh)*
sixty	sesenta	*(seh-'sehn-tah)*
size	tamaño, el	*(ehl tah-'mahn-yoh)*
skill	habilidad, la	*(lah ah-bee-lee-'dahd)*
skirt	falda	*(lah 'fahl-dah)*
sky	cielo, el	*(ehl see-'eh-loh)*
slip	combinación, la	*(lah kohm-bee-nah-see-'ohn)*
slippers	zapatillas, las	*(lahs sah-pah-'tee-yahs)*
slow	lento	*('lehn-toh)*
slowly	lentamente	*(lehn-tah-'mehn-teh)*
small	pequeño	*(peh-'kehn-yoh)*
smile	sonrisa, la	*(lah sohn-'ree-sah)*
smoke	humo, el	*(ehl 'oo-moh)*
smooth	liso	*('lee-soh)*
snack	merienda, la	*(lah meh-ree-'ehn-dah)*
snail	caracol, el	*(ehl kah-rah-'kohl)*
snake	culebra, la	*(lah koo-'leh-brah)*
snow	nieve, la	*(lah nee-'eh-veh)*
soap	jabón, el	*(ehl hah-'bohn)*
social security	seguro social, el	*(ehl seh-'goo-roh soh-see-'ahl)*
sociologist	sociólogo, el	*(ehl soh-see-'oh-loh-goh)*
socks	calcetines, los	*(lohs kahl-seh-'tee-nehs)*
sofa	sofá, el	*(ehl soh-'fah)*
soft	suave (masc. & fem.)	*(soo-'ah-veh)*
soft drink	refresco, el	*(ehl reh-'frehs-koh)*
soldier	soldado, el/la	*(ehl, lah sohl-'dah-doh)*
someone	alguien	*('ahl-gee-ehn)*
something	algo	*('ahl-goh)*
sometimes	a veces	*(ah 'veh-sehs)*
somewhere	por alguna parte	*(pohr ahl-'goo-nah 'pahr-teh)*
son	hijo, el	*(ehl 'ee-hoh)*
song	canción, la	*(lah kahn-see-'ohn)*
soon	pronto	*('prohn-toh)*
soul	alma, el	*(ehl 'ahl-mah)*
soup	sopa, la	*(lah 'soh-pah)*
sour	agrio	*('ah-gree-oh)*
south	sur, el	*(ehl soor)*
space	espacio, el	*(ehl ehs-'pah-see-oh)*
specialist	especialista, el/la	*(ehl, lah ehs-peh-see-ah-'lees-tah)*
spicy	picante	*(pee-'kahn-teh)*
spider	araña, la	*(lah ah-'rahn-yah)*
spirit	espíritu, el	*(ehl ehs-'pee-ree-too)*
sponge	esponja, la	*(lah ehs-'pohn-hah)*

sponsor	patrocinador, el	*(ehl pah-troh-see-nah-'dohr)*
spoon	cuchara, la	*(lah koo-'chah-rah)*
sports	deportes, los	*(lohs deh-'pohr-tehs)*
sports coat	saco, el	*(ehl 'sah-koh)*
spring	primavera, la	*(lah pree-mah-'veh-rah)*
stable	establo, el	*(ehl ehs-'tah-bloh)*
stage	escenario, el	*(ehl ehs-seh-'nah-ree-oh)*
stairs	escalera, la	*(lah ehs-kah-'leh-rah)*
stamp	estampilla, la	*(lah ehs-tahm-'pee-yah)*
star	estrella, la	*(lah ehs-'treh-yah)*
state	estado, el	*(ehl ehs-'tah-doh)*
station	estación, la	*(lah ehs-tah-see-'ohn)*
statue	estatua, la	*(lah ehs-'tah-twah)*
steak	bistec, el	*(ehl bees-'tehk)*
stereo	estéreo, el	*(ehl ehs-'teh-reh-oh)*
stick	palo, el	*(ehl 'pah-loh)*
stomach	estómago, el	*(ehl ehs-'toh-mah-goh)*
stool	banquillo, el	*(ehl bahn-'kee-yoh)*
stop sign	señal de parada, la	*(lah sehn-'yahl deh pah-'rah-dah)*
storage	depósito, el	*(ehl deh-'poh-see-toh)*
store	tienda, la	*(lah tee-'ehn-dah)*
storm	tormenta, la	*(lah tohr-'mehn-tah)*
stove	estufa, la	*(lah ehs-'too-fah)*
straight	recto	*('rehk-toh)*
strange	raro	*('rah-roh)*
stranger	desconocido, el	*(ehl dehs-koh-noh-'see-doh)*
strawberry	fresa, la	*(lah 'freh-sah)*
street	calle, la	*(lah 'kah-yeh)*
strength	fuerza, la	*(lah 'fwehr-sah)*
stretcher	camilla, la	*(lah kah-'mee-yah)*
strong	fuerte (masc. & fem.)	*('fwehr-teh)*
student	estudiante, el/la	*(ehl, lah ehs-too-dee-'ahn-teh)*
subway	metro, el	*(ehl 'meh-troh)*
suffering	sufrimiento, el	*(ehl soo-free-mee-'ehn-toh)*
sugar	azúcar, el	*(ehl ah-'soo-kahr)*
suggestions	sugerencias, las	*(lahs soo-heh-'rehn-see-ahs)*
suicide	suicidio, el	*(ehl soo-ee-'see-dee-oh)*
suitcase	maleta, la	*(lah mah-'leh-tah)*
summer	verano, el	*(ehl veh-'rah-noh)*
sun	sol, el	*(ehl sohl)*
Sunday	domingo	*(doh-'meen-goh)*
sunglasses	lentes de sol, los	*(lohs 'lehn-tehs deh sohl)*
supplies	víveres, los	*(lohs 'vee-veh-rehs)*
support	apoyo, el	*(ehl ah-'poh-yoh)*
sure	seguro	*(seh-'goo-roh)*
surgeon	cirujano, el	*(ehl see-roo-'hah-noh)*
surgery	cirugía, la	*(lah see-roo-'hee-ah)*

surprised	sorprendido	*(sohr-prehn-'dee-doh)*
survivor	sobreviviente, el/la	*(ehl, lah soh-breh-vee-vee-'ehn-teh)*
suspect	sospechoso, el	*(ehl sohs-peh-'choh-soh)*
sweet	dulce	*('dool-seh)*
switch	interruptor, el	*(ehl een-teh-rroop-'tohr)*
syringe	jeringa, la	*(lah heh-'reen-gah)*
system	sistema, el	*(ehl sees-'teh-mah)*
T-shirt	camiseta, la	*(lah kah-mee-'seh-tah)*
table	mesa, la	*(lah 'meh-sah)*
tablecloth	mantel, el	*(ehl mahn-'tehl)*
tailor	sastre, el/la	*(ehl, lah 'sahs-treh)*
talent	talento, el	*(ehl tah-'lehn-toh)*
tall	alto	*(ahl-toh)*
tank	tanque, el	*(ehl 'tahn-keh)*
tape	cinta, la	*(lah 'seen-tah)*
tax	impuesto, el	*(ehl eem-'pwehs-toh)*
tea	té, el	*(ehl teh)*
teacher	maestro, el	*(ehl mah-'ehs-troh)*
team	equipo, el	*(ehl eh-'kee-poh)*
technician	técnico, el/la	*(ehl, lah 'tehk-nee-koh)*
teenager	muchacho, el	*(ehl moo-'chah-choh)*
telephone	teléfono, el	*(ehl teh-'leh-foh-noh)*
temperature	temperatura, la	*(lah tehm-peh-rah-'too-rah)*
ten	diez	*(dee-'ehs)*
tenth	décimo	*('deh-see-moh)*
test	examen, el	*(ehl ehk-'sah-mehn)*
thanks	gracias, las	*(lahs 'grah-see-ahs)*
that	esa (fem.) ese (masc.)	*('eh-sah, 'eh-seh)*
the (fem.)	la	*(lah)*
the (masc.)	el	*(ehl)*
the (fem. pl.)	las	*(lahs)*
the (masc. pl.)	los	*(lohs)*
their	su	*(soo)*
theirs	suyo	*('soo-yoh)*
then	entonces	*(ehn-'tohn-sehs)*
therapy	terapia, la	*(lah teh-'rah-pee-ah)*
there	allí	*(ah-'yee)*
there is, are	hay	*('ah-ee)*
these	estos	*('ehs-tohs)*
they (fem.)	ellas	*('eh-yahs)*
they (masc.)	ellos	*('eh-yohs)*
thick	grueso	*(groo-'eh-soh)*
thin	delgado	*(dehl-'gah-doh)*
third	tercero	*(tehr-'seh-roh)*
thirteen	trece	*('treh-seh)*
thirty	treinta	*('treh-een-tah)*
this	esta (fem.) este (masc.)	*('ehs-tah, 'ehs-teh)*

those	estas (fem.), estos (masc.)	*('ehs-tahs, 'ehs-tohs)*
thread	hilo, el	*(ehl 'ee-loh)*
threat	amenaza, la	*(lah ah-meh-'nah-sah)*
three	tres	*(trehs)*
throat	garganta, la	*(lah gahr-'gahn-tah)*
thunder	trueno, el	*(ehl troo-'eh-noh)*
Thursday	jueves	*(hoo-'eh-vehs)*
ticket	boleto, el	*(ehl boh-'leh-toh)*
tie	corbata, la	*(lah kohr-'bah-tah)*
tight	apretado	*(ah-preh-'tah-doh)*
time	tiempo, el	*(ehl tee-'ehm-poh)*
tire	neumático, el	*(ehl neh-oo-'mah-tee-koh)*
tired	cansado	*(kahn-'sah-doh)*
tithe	diezmo, el	*(ehl dee-'ehs-moh)*
to	a	*(ah)*
today	hoy	*('oh-ee)*
toilet	excusado, el	*(ehl ehks-koo-'sah-doh)*
tomato	tomate, el	*(ehl toh-'mah-teh)*
tomorrow	mañana	*(mahn-'yah-nah)*
ton	tonelada, la	*(lah toh-neh-'lah-dah)*
tonight	esta noche	*('ehs-tah 'noh-cheh)*
tools	herramientas, las	*(lahs eh-rrah-mee-'ehn-tahs)*
toothbrush	cepillo de dientes, el	*(ehl seh-'pee-yoh deh dee-'ehn-tehs)*
toothpaste	pasta de dientes, la	*(lah 'pahs-tah deh dee-'ehn-tehs)*
tow truck	grúa, la	*(lah 'groo-ah)*
toward	hacia	*('ah-see-ah)*
towel	toalla, la	*(lah toh-'ah-yah)*
tower	torre, la	*(lah 'toh-rreh)*
town	pueblo, el	*(ehl 'pweh-bloh)*
toy	juguete, el	*(ehl hoo-'geh-teh)*
traffic light	semáforo, el	*(ehl seh-'mah-foh-roh)*
train	tren, el	*(ehl trehn)*
trainer	entrenador, el	*(ehl ehn-treh-nah-'dohr)*
training	entrenamiento, el	*(ehl ehn-treh-nah-mee-'ehn-toh)*
translator	traductor, el	*(ehl trah-dook-'tohr)*
transportation	transporte, el	*(ehl trahns-'pohr-teh)*
trash	basura, la	*(lah bah-'soo-rah)*
trashcan	bote de basura, el	*(ehl 'boh-teh deh bah-'soo-rah)*
tray	bandeja, la	*(lah bahn-'deh-hah)*
treatment	tratamiento, el	*(ehl trah-tah-mee-'ehn-toh)*
tree	árbol, el	*(ehl 'ahr-bohl)*
trip	viaje, el	*(ehl vee-'ah-heh)*
truck	camión, el	*(ehl kah-mee-'ohn)*
trust	confianza, la	*(lah kohn-fee-'ahn-sah)*
Tuesday	martes	*('mahr-tehs)*
tuna	atún, el	*(ehl ah-'toon)*
tunnel	túnel, el	*(ehl 'too-nehl)*

turkey	pavo, el	*(ehl 'pah-voh)*
turtle	tortuga, la	*(lah tohr-'too-gah)*
tutoring	tutoría, la	*(lah too-toh-'ree-ah)*
TV	televisor, el	*(ehl teh-leh-vee-'sohr)*
twelve	doce	*('doh-seh)*
twenty	veinte	*('veh-een-teh)*
twin	gemelo, el	*(ehl heh-'meh-loh)*
two	dos	*(dohs)*
typist	mecanógrafo, el	*(ehl meh-kah-'noh-grah-foh)*
ugly	feo	*('feh-oh)*
umbrella	sombrilla, la	*(lah sohm-'bree-yah)*
uncle	tío, el	*(ehl 'tee-oh)*
underprivileged	desvalido	*(dehs-vah-'lee-doh)*
underwear	ropa interior, la	*(lah 'roh-pah een-teh-ree-'ohr)*
unemployed	desempleado	*(deh-sehm-pleh-'ah-doh)*
unfortunate	desafortunado	*(deh-sah-fohr-too-'nah-doh)*
uniform	uniforme, el	*(ehl oo-nee-'fohr-meh)*
university	universidad, la	*(lah oo-nee-vehr-see-'dahd)*
up	arriba	*(ah-'rree-bah)*
urgent	urgente	*(oor-'hehn-teh)*
vacuum cleaner	aspiradora, la	*(lah ahs-pee-rah-'doh-rah)*
valley	valle, el	*(ehl 'vah-yeh)*
valuable	valioso	*(vah-lee-'oh-soh)*
value	valor, el	*(ehl vah-'lohr)*
VCR	videocasetera, la	*(lah vee-deh-oh-kah-seh-'teh-rah)*
vegetable	vegetal, el	*(ehl veh-heh-'tahl)*
vest	chaleco, el	*(ehl chah-'leh-koh)*
victim	víctima, la	*(lah 'veek-tee-mah)*
village	villa, la	*(lah 'vee-yah)*
violence	violencia, la	*(lah vee-oh-'lehn-see-ah)*
visitor	visitante, el/la	*(ehl, lah vee-see-'tahn-teh)*
volunteer	voluntario, el	*(ehl voh-loon-'tah-ree-oh)*
wages	sueldo, el	*(ehl 'swehl-doh)*
wagon	vagón, el	*(ehl vah-'gohn)*
waiter	mesero, el	*(ehl meh-'seh-roh)*
wall	pared, la	*(lah pah-'rehd)*
war	guerra, la	*(lah 'geh-rrah)*
warehouse	almacén, el	*(ehl ahl-mah-'sehn)*
warm	tibio	*('tee-bee-oh)*
warning	advertencia, la	*(lah ahd-vehr-'tehn-see-ah)*
washer	lavadora, la	*(lah lah-vah-'doh-rah)*
waste	deperdicios, los	*(lohs dehs-pehr-'dee-see-ohs)*
watch	reloj de pulsera, el	*(ehl reh-'loh deh pool-'seh-rah)*
water	agua, el	*(ehl 'ah-gwah)*
water fountain	el surtidor de agua	*(ehl soor-tee-'dohr deh 'ah-gwah)*
we (fem.)	nosotras	*(noh-'soh-trahs)*
we (masc.)	nosotros	*(noh-'soh-trohs)*

weak	débil (masc. & fem.)	*('deh-beel)*
weakened	debilitado	*(deh-bee-lee-'tah-doh)*
weather	clima, el	*(ehl 'klee-mah)*
wedding	boda, la	*(lah 'boh-dah)*
Wednesday	miércoles	*(mee-'ehr-koh-lehs)*
week	semana, la	*(lah seh-'mah-nah)*
weight	peso, el	*(ehl 'peh-soh)*
welcome	bienvenida, la	*(lah bee-ehn-veh-'nee-dah)*
welfare	bienestar, el	*(ehl bee-eh-nehs-'tahr)*
west	oeste, el	*(ehl oh-'ehs-teh)*
wet	mojado	*(moh-'hah-doh)*
what	qué	*(keh)*
wheel	rueda, la	*(lah 'rweh-dah)*
wheelchair	silla de ruedas, la	*(lah 'see-yah deh 'rweh-dahs)*
when	cuándo	*('kwahn-doh)*
where	dónde	*('dohn-deh)*
which	cuál	*(kwahl)*
white	blanco	*('blahn-koh)*
who	quién	*(kee-'ehn)*
whose	de quién	*(deh kee-'ehn)*
why	por qué	*(pohr keh)*
wide	ancho	*('ahn-choh)*
widow	viuda, la	*(lah vee-'oo-dah)*
widower	viudo, el	*(ehl vee-'oo-doh)*
wife	esposa, la	*(lah ehs-'poh-sah)*
wild	salvaje (masc. & fem.)	*(sahl-'vah-heh)*
wind	viento, el	*(ehl vee-'ehn-toh)*
window	ventana, la	*(lah vehn-'tah-nah)*
windshield	parabrisas, el	*(ehl pah-rah-'bree-sahs)*
wine	vino, el	*(ehl 'vee-noh)*
winter	invierno, el	*(ehl een-vee-'ehr-noh)*
wire	alambre, el	*(ehl ah-'lahm-breh)*
with	con	*(kohn)*
without	sin	*(seen)*
wolf	lobo, el	*(ehl 'loh-boh)*
woman	mujer, la	*(lah 'moo-hehr)*
wood	madera, la	*(lah mah-'deh-rah)*
wool	lana, la	*(lah 'lah-nah)*
word	palabra, la	*(lah pah-'lah-brah)*
work	trabajo, el	*(ehl trah-'bah-hoh)*
worker	trabajador, el	*(ehl trah-bah-hah-'dohr)*
world	mundo, el	*(ehl 'moon-doh)*
worried	preocupado	*(preh-oh-koo-'pah-doh)*
worse	peor	*(peh-'ohr)*
worship	adoración, la	*(lah ah-doh-rah-see-'ohn)*
worthwhile	valioso	*(vah-lee-'oh-soh)*
wrench	llave inglesa, la	*(lah 'yah-veh een-'gleh-sah)*

wrist	muñeca, la	*(lah moon-'yeh-kah)*
year	año, el	*(ehl 'ahn-yoh)*
yellow	amarillo	*(ah-mah-'ree-yoh)*
yes	sí	*(see)*
yesterday	ayer	*(ah-'yehr)*
yet	todavía	*(toh-dah-'vee-ah)*
you (sing.)	usted	*(oos-'tehd)*
you (pl.)	ustedes	*(oos-'teh-dehs)*
yours	suyo	*('soo-yoh)*
zero	cero	*('seh-roh)*
zip code	zona postal, la	*(lah 'soh-nah pohs-'tahl)*
zipper	cierre, el	*(ehl see-'eh-rreh)*
zone	zona, la	*(lah 'soh-nah)*
zoo	zoológico, el	*(ehl soh-oh-'loh-ee-koh)*
zucchini	calabacita verde, la	*(lah kah-lah-bah-'see-tah 'vehr-deh)*

Spanish-English Glossary

Please note that, aside from a few exceptions, only the masculine forms of nouns, adjectives, and pronouns are shown here.

a	to	al revés	inside out	araña, la	spider
a veces	sometimes	alabanza, la	praise	árbol, el	tree
abajo	down	alambre, el	wire	arbusto, el	bush
abeja, la	bee	alarma, la	alarm	archivo, el	file cabinet
abogado, el	lawyer	alcohol, el	alcohol	área, el	area
aborto, el	abortion	alfabeto, el	alphabet	arena, la	sand
abril	April	alfiler, el	pin	argumento, el	argument
abuela, la	grand-mother	alfombra, la	carpet	arma, el	gun
abuelo, el	grand father	alfombrado, el	carpeting	arquitecto, el	architect
		algo	something	arriba	up
aburrido	bored	algodón, el	cotton	arroz, el	rice
abuso, el	abuse	alguien	someone	artículo, el	article
aceite, el	oil	alivio, el	relief	artista, el	artist
acera, la	sidewalk	allí	there	arvejitas, las	peas
actitud, la	attitude	alma, el	soul	ascensor, el	elevator
adelante	forward	almacén, el	warehouse	asiento, el	seat
adentro	inside	almuerzo, el	lunch	asistencia, la	assistance, attendance
adicción, la	addiction	alojamiento, el	lodging		
adicto, el	addict	alrededor	around	asistente, el	assistant
Adiós	Good-bye	alto	tall	asociación, la	association
administrador, el	adminis-trator	amarillo	yellow	asociado, el	associate
		amenaza, la	threat	áspero	rough
adopción, la	adoption	amigo, el	friend	aspiradora, la	vacuum cleaner
adoración, la	worship	amistoso	friendly		
aduana, la	customs	amor, el	love	atún, el	tuna
advertencia, la	warning	anaranjado	orange (color)	autobús escolar, el	school bus
aeropuerto, el	airport			autobús, el	bus
afeitadora, la	shaver	ancho	wide	autor, el	author
afuera	outside	ángel, el	angel	avión, el	plane
afueras, las	outskirts	anillo, el	ring	ayer	yesterday
agencia, la	agency	aniversario, el	anniversary	ayudante, el	helper
agosto	August	año, el	year	azadón, el	hoe
agotado	exhausted	ansioso	anxious	azúcar, el	sugar
agrio	sour	antes	before	azul	blue
agua, el	water	apartamento, el	apartment	baile, el	dance
aguja, la	needle	apenas	just	bajo	shallow, short (in height)
ahora	now	apio, el	celery		
ajo, el	garlic	apoyo, el	support		
		aquí	here	balde, el	bucket

banco, el	bank, bench
bandeja, la	tray
banquete, el	banquet
banquillo, el	stool
bar, el	bar
barato	cheap
báscula, la	scale
bastón, el	cane
basura, la	trash
bata de baño, la	bathrobe
bata, la	robe
batería, la	battery
baúl, el	chest of drawers
bautismo, el	baptism
bebé, el/la	baby
beca, la	scholarship
bello	beautiful
bendición, la	blessing
Biblia, la	Bible
biblioteca, la	library
bicicleta, la	bicycle
bien	fine
bienestar, el	welfare
bienvenida, la	welcome
billetera, la	billfold
bistec, el	steak
blanco	white
blanqueador, el	bleach
blusa, la	blouse
boca, la	mouth
boda, la	wedding
boleto, el	ticket
bolsa, la	purse
bolsillo, el	pocket
bomba, la	bomb
bombero, el	firefighter
bondad, la	kindness
bonito	pretty
borracho	drunk
borrador, el	eraser
bosque, el	forest
botas, las	boots
bote de basura, el	trashcan
botón, el	button
botones, el	bellhop
bragas, las	panties
brazo, el	arm
brillante	bright
bueno	good
Bueno	OK
bufanda, la	scarf
burro, el	donkey
caballo, el	horse
cabaña, la	shed
cabeza, la	head
cadena, la	chain
cadera, la	hip
café	brown
café, el	coffee
cafetería, la	cafeteria
caja, la	box
cajero, el	cashier
cajón, el	drawer
calabaza, la	pumpkin
calabacita verde, la	zucchini
calcetines, los	socks
caldo, el	broth
calefacción, la	heating
calendario, el	calendar
calentador, el	heater
calidad, la	quality
calle, la	street
calmado	calm
calzoncillos, los	shorts
cama, la	bed
cámara, la	camera
cambio, el	change
camilla, la	stretcher
camino, el	path, road
camión, el	truck
camisa, la	shirt
camiseta, la	T-shirt
campamento, el	campground
campesino, el	farmer
campo, el	field
canción, la	song
candado, el	lock
cansado	tired
cántaro, el	pitcher
cantidad, la	amount
cantinero, el	bartender
capataz, el	foreman
capilla, la	chapel
cara, la	face
caracol, el	snail
carbón, el	coal
cárcel, la	jail
caridad, la	charity
carne, la	beef, meat
caro	expensive
carpintero, el	carpenter
carreta, la	cart
carretera, la	highway
carro, el	car
carta, la	letter
cartero, el	mail carrier
cartón, el	cardboard
casa, la	house
casado	married
casco, el	helmet
caso, el	case
catálogo, el	catalogue
catorce	fourteen
causa, la	cause
cebolla, la	onion
celebración, la	celebration
cementerio, el	cemetery
cemento, el	cement
cena, la	dinner
centavo, el	penny
centro, el	center, downtown
cepillo de dientes, el	toothbrush
cepillo, el	brush
cerca, la	fence
cerdo, el	pork
cerebro, el	brain
ceremonia, la	ceremony
cereza, la	cherry
cero	zero
cerradura, la	lock
cerveza, la	beer
césped, el	lawn
chaleco, el	vest

champiñón, el	mushroom
champú, el	shampoo
chaqueta, la	jacket
cheque, el	check
chicle, el	chewing gum
chimenea, la	fireplace, chimney
chistoso	funny
chofer, el	driver
choza, la	hut
ciego	blind
ciego, el	blind person
cielo, el	heaven, sky
cien	one hundred
cierre, el	zipper
cinco	five
cincuenta	fifty
cine, el	movie theater
cinta, la	tape
cirugía, la	surgery
cirujano, el	surgeon
cita, la	appointment
ciudad, la	city
ciudadano, el	citizen
clase, la	class
clavo, el	nail
cliente, el	client, customer
clima, el	weather
clínica de reposo, la	convalescent home
clínica, la	clinic
club, el	club
cobija, la	blanket
cocina, la	kitchen
cocinero, el	cook
coco, el	coconut
código, el	code
codo, el	elbow
colchón, el	mattress
colección de fondos, la	fund raising
colegio, el	school, high school
collar, el	necklace
combinación, la	slip
combustible, el	fuel
comedor, el	dining room
comida, la	food
comidas, las	meals
comité, el	committee
cómo	how
cómodo	comfortable
compañero de cuarto	roommate
compañero, el	acquaintance
compañía, la	company
comportamiento, el	behavior
computadora, la	computer
comunidad, la	community
comunión, la	communion
con	with
condado, el	county
condón, el	condom
conejo, el	rabbit
conferencia, la	conference
confesión, la	confession
confianza, la	trust
conflicto, el	conflict
confundido	confused
congelado	frozen
congelador, el	freezer
congregación, la	congregation
conocimiento, el	knowledge
consejero, el	counselor
consejo, el	counseling
consejos, los	advice
conserje, el	janitor
consultor, el	consultant
contaminación, la	pollution
contenido, el	content
contratista, el	contractor
contrato, el	contract
contribución, la	contribution
contribuyente, el	contributor
contusión, la	bruise
coordinador, el	coordinator
copia, la	copy
corazón, el	heart
corbata, la	tie
cordero, el	lamb
coro, el	choir
correa, la	belt
correo, el	mail
cortado	cut
cortés	polite
cortesía, la	courtesy
cortinas, las	curtains
corto	short (in length)
cosecha, la	crop
cosméticos, los	cosmetics
costo, el	cost
creación, la	creation
crédito, el	credit
creencia, la	belief
crema de maní, la	peanut butter
crema, la	cream
creyente, el	believer
criada, la	maid
criado, el	servant
cruce de peatones, el	crosswalk
cruel	cruel
cruz, la	cross
cuaderno, el	notebook
cuadra, la	city block
cuadro, el	painting
cuál	which
cualquier cosa	anything
cualquiera	anyone
cuándo	when
cuánto	how much
cuántos	how many
cuarenta	forty
cuartel de bomberos, el	fire department
cuarto	fourth
cuarto de baño, el	bathroom

cuarto, el	room	desagüe, el	drain, sewage
cuatro	four	desamparado	homeless
cubiertos, los	silverware	desayuno, el	breakfast
cuchara, la	spoon	desconocido, el	stranger
cuchillo, el	knife	descuento, el	discount
cuello, el	neck	desempleado	unemployed
cuenta, la	bill	desfavorecido	disadvantaged
cuero, el	leather		
cuerpo, el	body	desfile, el	parade
cuidado, el	care	desierto, el	desert
culebra, la	snake	desodorante, el	deodorant
culpa, la	fault	despejado	clear
culpabilidad, la	guilt	despierto	awake
cultivo, el	farming	después	after
cumpleaños, el	birthday	desvalido	underprivileged
cuna, la	crib		
cupones de comida, los	food stamps	desván, el	attic
curso, el	course	detrás	behind
dañado	damaged	deuda, la	debt
daño, el	harm	diablo, el	devil
día, el	day	diccionario, el	dictionary
de la mañana	A.M.	diciembre	December
de la noche	P.M.	diecinueve	nineteen
de quién	whose	dieciocho	eighteen
de	from, of	dieciséis	sixteen
débil	weak	diecisiete	seventeen
debilitado	weakened	dientes, los	teeth
décimo	tenth	diez	ten
dedo, el	finger	diezmo, el	tithe
delantal, el	apron	difícil	difficult
delgado	thin	dinero, el	money
delicioso	delicious	Dios	God
delito, el	crime	dirección, la	address
dentista, el/la	dentist	director, el	principal
dependiente, el	clerk	disciplina, la	discipline
deperdicios, los	waste	discípulo, el	disciple
deportes, los	sports	disfraz, el	costume
depósito, el	storage, deposit	disponible	available
		distancia, la	distance
deprimido	depressed	distrito, el	district
derecha	right (location)	divertido	fun
		divorcio, el	divorce
derecho, el	right (privilege)	doble, el	double
		doce	twelve
desafortunado	unfortunate	docena, la	dozen

doctor, el	doctor
dólar, el	dollar
dolor, el	pain
domingo	Sunday
donación, la	donation
donador, el	donor
dónde	where
dormitorio, el	bedroom
dos	two
droga, la	drug
ducha, la	shower
dueño, el	owner
dulce	sweet, candy
durazno, el	peach
duro	hard
ecología, la	ecology
edad, la	age
edificio, el	building
educación, la	education
educador, el	educator
efectivo, el	cash
ejecutivo, el	executive
ejemplo, el	example
ejercicio, el	exercise
el	the (masc.)
él	he
electrodoméstico, el	appliance
ella	she
ellas	they (fem.)
ellos	they (masc.)
embarazada	pregnant
embarazo, el	pregnancy
emergencia, la	emergency
emocionado	excited
empleado, el	employee
empleo, el	employment
empobrecido	impoverished
empresario, el	employer
en cualquier parte	anywhere
en	at, in, on
encima	above

endoso, el	endorsement	establo, el	stable	felicitaciones, las	congratulations
enero	January	estación de autobús, la	bus station	feliz	happy
enfermedad, la	disease	estación de policía, la	police station	femenino	feminine
enfermera, la	nurse	estación, la	station	feo	ugly
enfermo	sick	estacionamiento, el	parking lot	feria, la	fair
ensalada, la	salad	estado, el	state	ferrocarril, el	railroad
entonces	then	estampilla, la	stamp	fiebre, la	fever
entrada, la	entrance	estas	these (fem.)	fiesta, la	party
entre	between			finanzas, las	finance
entrenador, el	coach, trainer	este, el	east	finca, la	farm
entrenamiento, el	training	este	this (masc.)	firma, la	signature
entrevista, la	interview			flecha, la	arrow
equipaje, el	luggage	estéreo, el	stereo	flor, la	flower
equipo, el	team, equipment	estómago, el	stomach	focos, los	lightbulbs
esa	that (fem.)	estos	these (masc.)	folleto, el	brochure
esas	those (fem. pl.)			fondo, el	bottom
		estrecho	narrow	forma, la	shape
escalera, la	ladder, stairs	estrella, la	star	formulario, el	form
		estudiante, el	student	fósforos, los	matches
escarabajo, el	beetle	estufa, la	stove	fracaso, el	failure
escarcha, la	frost	eternidad, la	eternity	frenos, los	brakes
escenario, el	stage	evangelio, el	gospel	frente, el	front
escoba, la	broom	evento, el	event	fresa, la	strawberry
escritorio, el	desk	evidencia, la	evidence	fresco	cool, fresh
escuela, la	school	examen, el	test	frijoles, los	beans
ese	that (masc.)	excelente	excellent	frontera, la	border
		excusado, el	toilet	fruta, la	fruit
esfuerzo, el	effort	explosivo, el	explosive	fuente, la	fountain
esos	those (masc. pl.)	extintor, el	fire extinguisher	fuente de agua, la	water fountain
espacio, el	space			fuerte	strong
espalda, la	back	extranjero, el	foreigner	fuerza, la	strength
espantado	scared	fábrica, la	factory	función, la	performance
especialista, el	specialist	fácil	easy		
espectáculo, el	show	fax, el	fax	funeral, el	funeral
espejo, el	mirror	factura, la	invoice	furioso	furious
esperanza, la	hope	faja, la	girdle	gabinete, el	cabinet
Espíritu Santo, el	Holy Spirit	falda, la	skirt	galleta salada, la	cracker
esponja, la	sponge	familia, la	family	galleta, la	cookie
esposa, la	wife	famoso	famous	galón, el	gallon
esposo, el	husband	farmacia, la	pharmacy	ganga, la	bargain
esquina, la	corner	fe, la	faith	garaje, el	garage
esta	this (fem.)	febrero	February	garganta, la	throat
esta noche	tonight	fecha, la	date	gasolinera, la	gas station
		felicidad, la	happiness	gato, el	cat
				gemelo, el	twin

gente, la	people	hipoteca, la	mortgage	jabón, el	soap
gerente, el	manager	hogar, el	home	jamón, el	ham
gimnasio, el	gym	Hola	Hi	jardinero, el	gardener
gobernador, el	governor	hombre, el	man	jarra, la	jar
gobierno, el	government	hombro, el	shoulder	jaula, la	cage
		homosexua-	homo-	jefe, el	boss
goma, la	rubber	lidad, la	sexuality	jeringa, la	syringe
gordo	fat	horario, el	schedule	Jesucristo	Jesus
gorra, la	cap	hormiga, la	ant		Christ
gozo, el	joy	horno de		juego, el	game
gracia, la	grace	microonda, el	microwave	jueves	Thursday
gracias, las	thanks	horno, el	oven	jugador, el	player
grado, el	degree	hospital, el	hospital	jugo, el	juice
grande	big	hoy	today	juguete, el	toy
granero, el	barn	hoyo, el	hole	julio	July
granizo, el	hail	huerta, la	orchard	junio	June
gratis	free	huevo, el	egg	junta, la	gathering
grúa, la	tow truck	humildad, la	humility	la	the (fem.)
grueso	thick	humo, el	smoke	ladrillo, el	brick
grupo, el	group	huracán, el	hurricane	lago, el	lake
guante, el	glove	identificación, la	identifica-	lámpara, la	lamp
guapo	handsome		tion	lana, la	wool
guardia, el	guard	iglesia, la	church	langosta, la	lobster
guerra, la	war	impermeable, el	raincoat	lapicero, el	pen
guía, el	guide	importante	important	lápiz, el	pencil
guitarra, la	guitar	impresora, la	printer	las	the
habilidad, la	skill	impuesto, el	tax		(fem.pl.)
hacia	toward	incapacitado	disabled	lastimado	hurt
hambre, el	hunger	incendio, el	fire	lavadora, la	washer
hamburguesa	hamburger	indefenso	helpless	lavamanos, el	sink
harina, la	flour	infierno, el	hell	lavaplatos, el	dishwasher
hay	there is,	información, la	informa-	lección, la	lesson
	are		tion	leche, la	milk
helado	freezing	ingeniero, el	engineer	lechuga, la	lettuce
helado, el	ice cream	ingredientes, los	ingredients	lejos	far
helicóptero, el	helicopter	inmigrante, el	immigrant	lenguaje, el	language
herida, la	injury	insectos, los	bugs,	lentamente	slowly
hermana, la	sister		insects	lentes de sol, los	sunglasses
hermano, el	brother	institución, la	institution	lentes, los	glasses
herramientas, las	tools	instrucciones, las	directions	lento	slow
hielo, el	ice	inteligente	intelligent	letrero, el	billboard
hierro, el	iron	interesante	interesting	ley, la	law
hija, la	daughter	intérprete, el	interpreter	libertad, la	freedom
hijo, el	son	interruptor, el	switch	libra, la	pound
hilo, el	thread	investigación, la	research	librería, la	bookstore
himno, el	hymn	invierno, el	winter	librero, el	bookshelf
		izquierda	left		

libro, el	book
licencia de manejar, la	driver's license
líder, el	leader
liga, la	league
limón	lemon
limonada, la	lemonade
limpio	clean
línea, la	line
linterna, la	flashlight
líquido, el	liquid
liso	smooth
lista, la	list
listo	ready
llamada, la	phone call
llave inglesa, la	wrench
llave, la	key
lluvia, la	rain
lodo, el	mud
los	the (masc.pl.)
lote de carros, el	car lot
luna, la	moon
lunes	Monday
lustrador, el	polish
luz, la	light
maceta, la	pot
madera, la	wood
madre, la	mother
maduro	mature
maestro, el	teacher
maíz, el	corn
mal	bad
maleta, la	suitcase
mañana	tomorrow
manguera, la	hose
mano, la	hand
mantel, el	tablecloth
mantenimiento, el	maintenance
mantequilla, la	butter
manzana, la	apple
mapa, el	map
maquillaje, el	makeup
máquina, la	machine
maquinaria, la	machinery

marca, la	brand
mareado	dizzy
marisco, el	seafood
martes	Tuesday
martillo, el	hammer
marzo	March
más tarde	later
más	more
máscara, la	mask
masculino	male
matrimonio, el	marriage
mayo	May
mayonesa, la	mayonnaise
mayor	older
mecánico, el	mechanic
mecanógrafo, el	typist
medicina, la	medicine
mejor	better
melón, el	cantaloupe
menos	less
mensaje, el	message
mercado, el	market
mercancía, la	merchandise
merienda, la	picnic, snack
mes, el	month
mesa, la	table
mesero, el	waiter
meta, la	goal
metro, el	subway
mi	my
mía	mine (fem.)
mías	mine (fem. pl.)
micrófono, el	microphone
miedo, el	fear
miel, la	honey
miembro, el	member
miércoles	Wednesday
mil	one thousand
milagro, el	miracle
ministerio, el	ministry

minusválido	handicapped
mío	mine (masc.)
míos	mine (masc. pl.)
misericordia, la	mercy
misión, la	mission
misionero, el	missionary
mitad, la	half
mitones, los	mittens
moho, el	mold
mojado	wet
molesto	angry
moneda, la	coin
monja, la	nun
montaña, la	mountain
morado	purple
morena	brunette
mosca, la	fly
mostaza, la	mustard
mostrador, el	counter
motocicleta, la	motorcycle
motor, el	engine
muchacho, el	teenager
mucho	much
muchos	many
muelle, el	pier
muerte, la	death
muerto, el	dead
muestra, la	sample
mujer, la	woman
muletas, las	crutches
multa, la	penalty, fine
mundo, el	world
muñeca, la	doll, wrist
municipio, el	city hall
museo, el	museum
música, la	music
músico, el/la	musician
nacimiento, el	birth
nacionalidad, la	nationality
nada	nothing
nadie	no one
naranja, la	orange (fruit)

Spanish	English
nariz, la	nose
Navidad, la	Christmas
negocio, el	business
negro	black
nervioso	nervous
neumático, el	tire
nido, el	nest
nieta, la	granddaughter
nieto, el	grandson
nieve, la	snow
niña, la	girl
niñero, el	babysitter
niño, el	boy
niveladora, la	bulldozer
norte, el	north
nosotras	we (fem.)
nosotros	we (masc.)
noticias, las	news
noveno	ninth
noventa	ninety
novia, la	girlfriend
noviembre	November
novio, el	boyfriend
nube, la	cloud
nueces, las	nuts
nueve	nine
nuevo	new
número, el	number
nunca	never
obrero, el	laborer
océano, el	ocean
ochenta	eighty
ocho	eight
octavo	eighth
octubre	October
ocupado	busy
odio, el	hate
oeste, el	west
oficial	official
oficina de correos, la	post office
oficina, la	office
ofrenda, la	offering
ojo, el	eye
olla, la	pot
once	eleven
onza, la	ounce
operador, el	operator
opinión, la	opinion
oración, la	prayer, sentence
oreja, la	ear
orfanato, el	orphanage
orientación, la	guidance
oso, el	bear
otoño, el	fall
otra vez	again
paciencia, la	patience
paciente, el	patient
padre, el	father
página, la	page
pago, el	payment
pájaro, el	bird
pala, la	shovel
palabra, la	word
palo, el	stick
pan, el	bread
pandilla, la	gang
panecillo, el	roll
pantalla, la	screen
pantalones, los	pants
pañuelo, el	handkerchief
papa, la	potato
papel, el	paper
paquete, el	package
para	for
parada de autobús, la	bus stop
paramédico, el	paramedic
pared, la	wall
pariente, el	relative
parque, el	park
parquímetro, el	parking meter
parroquia, la	parish
parroquiano	parishioner
pasajero, el	passenger
pasaporte, el	passport
Pascuas, las	Easter
pasillo, el	hallway
pasta de dientes, la	toothpaste
pasta, la	paste
pastel, el	pie
pasto, el	grass
pastor, el	minister, pastor
patio, el	courtyard
pato, el	duck
patrocinador, el	sponsor
patrón, el	boss
pavo, el	turkey
paz, la	peace
peatón, el	pedestrian
pecado, el	sin
pecador, el	sinner
pecho, el	chest
pediatra, el	pediatrician
pegamento, el	glue
peine, el	comb
pelea, la	fight
peligroso	dangerous
pelo, el	hair
pelota, la	ball
penicilina, la	penicillin
peor	worse
pepino, el	cucumber
pequeño	small
pera, la	pear
pérdida, la	loss
perdido	lost
perezoso	lazy
perfume, el	perfume
periódico, el	newspaper
permanente	permanent
permiso, el	permit
pero	but
perro, el	dog
persona, la	person
personalidad, la	personality
pesado	heavy
pesca, la	fishing
pescado, el	fish (caught)
peso, el	weight
pez, el	fish (in water)
picante	spicy

pico, el	peak	presidente, el	president	recuperación, la	recovery
pie, el	foot	primavera, la	spring	recurso, el	resource
piedra, la	rock	primero	first	red, la	net
pijama, el	pajamas	primo, el	cousin	reembolso, el	refund
píldora, la	pill	prisión, la	prison	refresco, el	soft drink
piloto, el	pilot	prisionero, el	prisoner	refrigerador, el	refrigerator
pimienta, la	pepper	privado	private	refugiado, el	refugee
piña, la	pineapple	profundo	deep	refugio, el	shelter
pintor, el	painter	programa, el	program	regalo, el	gift
pintura, la	paint	promedio, el	average	registro, el	record
piscina, la	pool	pronto	soon	regla, la	rule
piso, el	floor	propiedad, la	property	rehabilitación, la	rehabilitation
pizarrón, el	chalkboard	propósito, el	purpose		
planeta, el	planet	próximo	next	relajado	relaxed
plástico, el	plastic	proyecto, el	project	relámpago, el	lightning
plátano, el	banana	psicólogo, el	psychologist	religión, la	religion
plato hondo, el	bowl			religioso	religious
plato, el	plate, dish	público	public (known)	reloj de pulsera, el	watch
playa, la	beach			reloj, el	clock
pleito, el	lawsuit	público, el	public (audience)	reparación, la	repair
plomero, el	plumber			reparto, el	delivery
pobre	poor	pueblo, el	town	repisa, la	shelf
pobreza, la	poverty	puente, el	bridge	repollo, el	cabbage
poco	little	puerco, el	pig	reporte, el	report
pocos	few	puerta, la	door	representante, el	representative
policía, el	police officer	pulgada, la	inch		
		pulmón, el	lung	rescate, el	rescue
polilla, la	moth	qué	what	residente, el	resident
pollo, el	chicken	queso, el	cheese	respeto, el	respect
polvo, el	dust, powder	quién	who	responsable	responsible
		quieto	quiet	respuesta, la	answer
por	for	quince	fifteen	reunión, la	meeting
por alguna parte	somewhere	quinto	fifth	revista, la	magazine
Por favor	Please	quizás	maybe	rico	rich
por ninguna parte	nowhere	rápidamente	quickly	riesgo, el	risk
por qué	why	rápido	fast	río, el	river
por todas partes	everywhere	raro	strange	robo, el	robbery
porcentaje, el	percentage	rastrillo, el	rake	rodilla, la	knee
porque	because	rata, la	rat	rojo	red
portal, el	porch	ratón, el	mouse	ropa interior, la	underwear
portón, el	gate	recaída, la	relapse	ropa, la	clothing
postre, el	dessert	receta, la	prescription	ropero, el	closet
precio, el	price			roto	broken
pregunta, la	question	recibo, el	receipt	rueda, la	wheel
premio, el	prize	reciclaje, el	recycling	sábado	Saturday
preocupado	worried	recreación, la	recreation	sábana, la	sheet
		recto	straight		

sacerdote, el	priest
saco, el	sportscoat
sacrificio, el	sacrifice
sal, la	salt
sala, la	living room
salida, la	exit
salón de clase, el	classroom
salsa, la	sauce
salud, la	health
saludable	healthy
salvación, la	salvation
Salvador, el	Savior
salvaje	wild
sandalias, las	sandals
sangre, la	blood
sanidad, la	sanitation
sartén, la	pan
sastre, el/la	tailor
satélite, el	satellite
secadora, la	dryer
seco	dry
secretario, el	secretary
segundo	second
seguridad, la	safety, security
seguro	safe, sure
seguro, el	insurance
seguro social, el	social security
seis	six
selva, la	jungle
semáforo, el	traffic light
semana, la	week
semilla, la	seed
seminario, el	seminar
señal de parada, la	stop sign
señal, la	sign
Señor, el	Lord
sentimiento, el	feeling
separado	separated
séptimo	seventh
serio	serious
sermón, el	sermon
serrucho, el	saw
servicio, el	restroom, service
servilleta, la	napkin

sesenta	sixty
sesión, la	session
setenta	seventy
setiembre	September
sexto	sixth
sí	yes
SIDA, el	AIDS
siempre	always
siete	seven
silenciador, el	muffler
silla de ruedas, la	wheelchair
silla, la	chair
sillón, el	armchair
simpático	nice
sin	without
sistema, el	system
sobre	over, on top of
sobre, el	envelope
sobresaliente	outstanding
sobreviviente, el	survivor
sobrina, la	niece
sobrino, el	nephew
socio, el	partner
sociólogo, el	sociologist
sofá, el	sofa
sol, el	sun
soldado, el/la	soldier
soledad, la	loneliness
solicitud, la	application
soltero	single
sombrilla, la	umbrella
sonrisa, la	smile
sopa, la	soup
sordo	deaf
sorpresa, la	surprise
sospechoso, el	suspect
sostén, el	brassiere
sótano, el	basement
su	his, her, their
suave	soft
sucio	dirty
sueldo, el	wages
suelto	loose
suerte, la	luck

sufrimiento, el	suffering
sugerencias, las	suggestions
suicidio, el	suicide
sur, el	south
suya	hers, yours (fem.)
suyo	his, yours (masc.)
taladro, el	drill
talento, el	talent
tamaño, el	size
tarde	late
tarea, la	homework, task
tarjeta postal, la	postcard
tarjeta, la	card
tarjetas de saludo, las	greeting cards
taza, la	cup
té, el	tea
techo, el	ceiling
teclado, el	keyboard
técnico, el	technician
techo, el	roof
tela, la	cloth
teléfono, el	telephone
televisor, el	TV
temperatura, la	temperature
temprano	early
tenedor, el	fork
terapia, la	therapy
tercero	third
terremoto, el	earthquake
tía, la	aunt
tibio	warm
tiempo, el	time
tienda, la	store
tierra, la	dirt, earth, soil
tijeras, las	scissors
tina, la	bathtub
tinta, la	ink
tío, el	uncle
tirador, el	knob
toalla, la	towel

tobillo, el	ankle
tocador, el	dresser
tocino, el	bacon
todavía	yet, still
todo	everything
todos	all, everyone
tomate, el	tomato
tonelada, la	ton
tormenta, la	storm
tornillo, el	screw
toronja, la	grapefruit
torre, la	tower
torta, la	cake
tortuga, la	turtle
tos, la	cough
trabajador, el	worker
trabajo, el	job, work
traductor, el	translator
traje de baño, el	bathing suit
transporte, el	transport- tation
trapeador, el	mop
trapo, el	rag
tratamiento, el	treatment
trece	thirteen
treinta	thirty
tren, el	train
tres	three
tribunal, el	court
tripulación, la	crew
triste	sad
tristeza, la	sadness
tubería, la	plumbing
túnel, el	tunnel
tutoría, la	tutoring
un	a (masc.), one
una	a (fem.)
una vez	once
unas	a (fem.pl.)
uniforme, el	uniform
universidad, la	university
uno	one
unos	a (masc.pl.)
urgente	urgent
usted	you (sing.)
ustedes	you (pl.)
uva, la	grape
vaca, la	cow
vagón, el	wagon
valiente	brave
valioso	valuable
valle, el	valley
valor, el	value, courage
vaso, el	glass (drinking)
vecindario, el	neighbor- hood
vecino, el	neighbor
vegetal, el	vegetable
veinte	twenty
vela, la	candle, sail
venado, el	deer
vendedor, el	sales- person
venenoso	poisonous
venta, la	sale
ventana, la	window
ventilador, el	fan
verano, el	summer
verde	green
vestíbulo, el	lobby
vestido, el	dress
viaje, el	trip
víctima, el	victim
vida, la	life
videocasetera, la	VCR
vidrio, el	glass
viejo	old
viento, el	wind
viernes	Friday
villa, la	village
vino, el	wine
violación, la	rape
violencia, la	violence
visitante, el	visitor
viuda, el	widow
viudo, el	widower
víveres, los	supplies
vivienda, la	housing
voluntario, el	volunteer
vuelo, el	flight
y	and
ya	already
yo	I
zanahoria, la	carrot
zancudo, el	mosquito
zapatillas, las	slippers
zapato, el	shoe
zona postal, la	zip code
zona, la	zone
zoológico, el	zoo
zorro, el	fox